Classic Houses of Portland, Oregon
1850–1950

Drawing room, Cicero Hunt Lewis House (1881).

CLASSIC HOUSES

of
Portland, Oregon
1850–1950

William J. Hawkins, III
and
William F. Willingham

Timber Press
Portland, Oregon

Errata

Chapter 4: Correct spelling is Edward J. Jeffery, not Jeffrey. Architects for
the Edward J. Jeffery House are Piper and Burton.

Chapter 10: Correct spelling is Williard J. Hawley, not William P.

Chapter 11: Correct spelling is D. R. Munro, not Munroe.

Chapter 15: Correct construction date for the Frank B. Upshaw House
is 1921, not 1935.

Chapter 20: Correct spelling is George P. Berkey, not Berky.

Library of Congress Cataloging-in-Publication Data

Hawkins, William John.
Classic houses of Portland, Oregon : 1850–1950 / William J. Hawkins and
William F. Willingham.
p.   cm.
Includes bibliographical references and index.
ISBN 0-88192-433-4
1. Architecture, Domestic—Oregon—Portland.
2. Architecture, Modern—19th century—Oregon—Portland.
3. Architecture, Modern—20th century—Oregon—Portland.
I. Willingham, William F. II. Title.
NA7238.P575H38 1999
728'.09795'49—dc21   99-24760
CIP

Published in 1999 by
Timber Press, Inc.
The Haseltine Building
133 S.W. Second Avenue, Suite 450
Portland, Oregon 97204, U.S.A.

Reprinted 2000

Printed in Hong Kong

To Al Hansen,
who (when I was only six)
inspired me with his architecture,
and to Betty Hansen,
who first taught me to draw—
in appreciation
of a lifetime of enjoyment
they have brought me
in residential design.

Contents

Preface

In the last few decades of the twentieth century, the city of Portland has experienced a rising prosperity and a growing population. With the influx of new people, the formerly lush farmlands and valleys surrounding the city have become inundated with an array of new commercial and residential developments. Some are modest in size and affordable to the middle classes, but a considerable number are only for the up-and-coming, the newly wealthy, commanding impressive prices and offering every amenity in size and contrivance.

While the dreams of the newly wealthy are being realized in such developments as "The Streets of Dreams" and "McMansions" of every description, one notable quality is missing that separates these houses from the city's significant social and architectural history. These new, upscale homes, with their marbled kitchens and mirrored Jacuzzis, are not designed by architects, and that fact is quickly revealed. In fact, many contemporary critics argue that even the magazine-inspired houses of the first half of the twentieth century, houses built according to designs featured in popular architectural magazines, have more architectural merit than the non-architecturally designed houses constructed since the 1950s—this despite the technological improvements and the mass production of construction materials that have allowed for the potential to create superior structures. With only a very few exceptions, it is nearly impossible to find a notable architectural talent associated with these modern creations, and the stylistic influences seem foreign and bizarre to the architectural critic. Those who develop and those who build seem no longer to regard quality architecture—the "Mother of the Arts" and the most ancient and visible measure of a civilization—as a necessary element of their plans. Whatever their ambitions, whatever their budgets, whatever their personal dreams or their ideas of utility or of beauty, these designers and builders have not seen the art of architecture as an important consideration, and beautiful houses have not been the end product.

The unfortunate result of this rejection of the centrality of the art of architecture is that this era is not producing substantial quality architecture for its time. Good design, the integrity of plan and elevation, the art of spatial arrangement, the selection of compatible materials, and the execution of fine detail, all the factors that determine beauty have been disregarded in the name of saving costs. Thus, instead of entire streets and neighborhoods of handsomely designed houses, as from all the past eras that have produced exciting residential architecture on an impressive scale, we see a seemingly endless array of expensive houses with strangely considered, ill-proportioned, and uninspired spatial designs—a plethora of dwellings reflecting the modern dream realized. Surely, not a one will ever be recorded by an architectural historian, or restored by appreciative future generations. As a consequence, the houses of past generations have assumed a new importance, for they embody the attention to design and the spirit of quality that is lacking in the present, and as such they deserve special recognition and celebration.

Countless books have been written about the construction of private homes, focusing on man's innate desire not only to surround himself with the comforts and conveniences of life, but also to enhance the environment around him, cultivating the architectural art to provide a truly enriched and lasting visual experience. All past generations have nurtured this art. The Romans had their delightful courtyards; the Italian Renaissance, its exquisite villas; the Chinese, their gardens and courtyards; the English, their country estates—with each civilization leaving a rich record of residential architecture.

During its first one hundred years, the city of Portland similarly left an extraordinary collection of highly refined, architecturally designed homes. The fledgling city of the 1850s was fortunate to have among its first citizens several notable architects, arriving by foot, wagon train, or sailing ship. The record of their work and that of their successors has been continuous and impressive. Portland's architects were blessed in their talents and were fortunate in having an appreciative audience in their clients, people who would never have even considered erecting their private residences without the unique skills that only architects can offer. This outpouring of fine residential architecture in Portland has been duly celebrated since its earliest times in the 1850s. Visitors to the city during the early years remarked on the exceptional quality of the residential architecture that Portland offered. The finest examples were always featured prominently in the promotions for the city. Except for the inevitable demolition of houses located in the original downtown area as the city expanded its business core, the majority of houses designed by the city's foremost architects are still standing.

Some of the best works by the most noted architects working in the city of Portland have been recorded in several written accounts; among the more important of such studies include those written by Richard Marlitt, Ann

The Richardsonian style Julius Loewenberg House, designed by Isaac Hodgson, Jr., in 1891.

The destruction of the Loewenberg House, circa 1960. The demolition of this classic residence was an irreparable loss to the city's architectural legacy.

Brewster Clarke, Michael Shellenbarger, and Jo Stubblebine. However, no single comprehensive work has focused on the broader spectrum of residential architecture, nor on the wide range of talented architects who designed the houses, nor the inspired patrons and clients who supported their art.

This book attempts to bring into focus the complete list of the most talented residential architects of the period from 1850 to 1950, showing specific examples of each one's work and demonstrating how they were influenced and inspired by national and international movements of design. The book is an homage to those great Portland architectural talents who have left an impressive record of stunning structures. And it is also an homage to the original owners of those houses, many of whose names would be lost in time were it not for the welcome fact that they patronized and nurtured a fine art form in general and fine artworks in particular, works that not only were to be enjoyed by the owners during their time in the particular house, but which also have been and continue to be enjoyed by subsequent generations.

This book also seeks to influence the preservation of these architectural treasures for future times. All too often and all too needlessly, these homes are irreversibly altered or even demolished by insensitive owners. Just as this book was being written, one of the finest Bungalow style houses in North Portland was all but ruined by being covered with metal siding; a remarkable house designed by Jamieson K. Parker had its handsome original carved entrance doors removed and demolished, only to be replaced with an ordinary stock door by an unmindful property developer; and one of John Yeon's masterpieces, the nationally acclaimed Lawrence Shaw House, has had its quality essentially eradicated by insensitive "remuddling." When the best examples of the art of architecture are heedlessly destroyed, the civilization of our city suffers. Without the best examples from the past, the measure of our own era will be lost—good design needs its examples in evidence in order to be a force in maintaining architectural quality. If greater appreciation of our best can be nurtured, perhaps the best of our past will survive and inspire a future sense of quality in design, giving dimension and depth to our experience.

Acknowledgments

Numerous friends and associates assisted in the writing of this book. The rare photograph made available to the authors or the important architectural history freely offered and exchanged has been invaluable. Time-consuming research has been extremely helpful. Pleasures particular to that capacity have been known to Judith Rees, whose research resulted in finding the names of original owners and architects of many of the houses. Such revelations have been the highlights in the writing experience.

In the collecting of photographs, Doug Magedanz and Don Wilson were particularly helpful. Their collections have provided many a rare and previously unseen view of the historic houses.

Dan Shallou's re-creation of the houses' plans offers a visual record of all the various styles in house plans during the one-hundred-year span of Portland architecture discussed in the book.

An expansive thank you is extended to the past and present owners of the houses included in this work. Present owners have graciously opened their homes for touring and have offered invaluable information. Past owners and former inhabitants of many of the houses now destroyed have provided insight into the original layouts of those houses.

Finally, a salute to that rare moment when a good client teams up with a good architect. Their mutual product has received the admiration of countless observers of the architectural scene. Portland's finest houses give the city a special character, well worthy of praise, preservation, and inspiration.

Classic Houses of Portland, Oregon: 1850–1950 relies on the accepted stylistic divisions published by the Oregon State Preservation Office. A few terms have been changed, according to the houses shown in the book and the authors' individual interpretation of them.

Introduction

From its inception, the city of Portland, Oregon, has exhibited a notable and impressive architectural character. Despite their isolation from the culture and trends of the East Coast, the city founders of the mid-nineteenth century, whether affluent sea captains or Oregon Trail pioneers, arrived with a true appreciation for architecture and proceeded to construct residences with distinctive architectural style. Portland's very first houses were the miniature "temples" of the then-prevalent, yet waning, fashion of the Greek Revival style, reflecting the popular national interest in the culture and architecture of ancient Greek civilization. The sophisticated Greek Revival style presented a striking contrast to the surrounding wilderness of virgin forest. Although in 1851 Portland had only 805 residents, the new city had already established an architectural tradition, one that considered good architecture a measure of a city's worth.

During the early years of the city's development in the middle of a vast and virgin wilderness, the families of wealth and prominence were the representatives of manners, culture, and taste and style as displayed in their lifestyles and in their homes and gardens. Although perhaps not so rigid as it may have been in the eastern United States, the class system in Portland of the time was a binding social force with strongly established ties and social customs. An interest in the arts and architecture was a shared interest, as the mass population sought to emulate the styles and tastes of the upper classes. The result was a great variety of architectural designs and a rich architectural setting. Portland stayed remarkably abreast of the national trends, and the architects who brought the new styles to the city generally came from the most innovative and prestigious eastern architectural firms. Architecture was often a passion of the wealthy, and this passion was enhanced by close professional and social ties with cities such as San Francisco and others on the East Coast. The intimate scale of Portland further helped to nurture the interest in the arts and the development of the community as a whole.

The early arrival of East Coast architectural trends undoubtedly stemmed from the fact that several architects were among the first settlers in the new city. By 1852, four prominent architects were practicing in the Portland area: Absolom B. Hallock, Lou Day, Harley McDonald, and Elwood M. Burton. Their adherence to the principles of classic architecture established the foundation upon which the city's architectural tastes would evolve. This appreciation of high standards grew and expanded with time, leaving a distinctive heritage in residential architecture in the city over its first hundred years.

The best houses of this tradition can be called "classic" in the purest sense of the term. Classic is defined as that which serves as a model of ex-

Daguerreotype of John M. Drake's home at SW Front and Meade Street, circa 1850.

cellence, is outstanding, and is of lasting historical or artistic significance or worth. The classic house, therefore, has a timeless quality, possessing a recognized and lasting sense of integrity of design, seen as readily today as when it was first constructed. The design reflects not only a well-conceived and purposeful plan, but qualities well beyond that. The houses must exhibit a unified concept, adhering to the principles of proportion, taking into consideration the agreeable nature of adjacent materials, the siting on the property, the general relationship to the landscape or adjacent structures, and the overall quality of construction. A classic house displays style, a quality of design achieved by a talented architect with the necessary skills. The architect adds a pleasing sculptural element to the basic requirements of a residential design; through his or her hands, the plan elements become unified. Building masses are arranged with a consideration for the whole, not just emphasizing the architectural merits of the most visible front facade, but of all elevations. As with any work of art, nothing of the completed work can be removed without reducing the completeness and beauty of the whole. Interior spaces must be equally considered and should reflect the design intentions of the exterior. Rooms relate in scale to one another, regardless of the size or economics of the house, and all details must be consistent with the size and design. The architecture of a classic house reflects "the art of forming dwellings," and its architect has skills and "measures and values the whole."

Of course, not every house of Portland's first century has architectural merit, but many of those that do were the products of contractors or owners who were familiar with the "pattern books," or architectural periodicals, of the times. Pattern books have long been a major influence in establishing a base level of quality construction and architecture. Some that influenced Portland's early architectural development include *The Architecture of Country Houses* by Andrew Jackson Downing (1850) and *Village and Farm Cottages* by Henry W. Cleaveland, William Backus, and Samuel D. Backus (1856). By the 1860s and 1870s, the books of Henry Hudson Holly, such as *Holly's Country Seats* (1860), were influencing the construction of houses in the Italianate and Queen Anne styles. And by the time the Bungalow and Craftsman styles emerged at the beginning of the new century, Gustav Stickley, and particularly his journal, *The Craftsman*, was making a major impression on residential architecture and construction.

After the pattern books went out of vogue, a plethora of architectural magazines emerged, usually offered at modest prices and containing plans and elevations for every type of house. The construction of houses based on the architects' designs that appeared in these magazines added to the quality of the general stock of houses being built at the time.

Portland's classic houses, both large and small, were designed and often constructed by architects of great ability. Of the more than seventy architects whose works are described in this book, most were widely respected in their time, both locally and nationally. The most important of the architects in early residential designs in Portland were Absolom B. Hallock and Elwood M. Burton. Many prominent citizens during the first few decades of the city's emergence and growth had their homes designed by these architects in the then-current styles of the Greek and Gothic Revivals and the Italian Villa style. A second migration of architects brought to the city such impressive talents as Warren H. Williams, of San Francisco, and Justus F. Krumbein, professionally trained from Germany. Henry W. Cleaveland, another successful San Franciscan architect, designed several luxurious homes for the city's leading citizens. The works of these architects resulted in an impressive number of first-rate residential structures and helped to establish Portland as a major architectural center in the West. These later residences reflected various renderings of the Italianate and Queen Anne styles. By the 1870s, many of Portland's affluent citizens began to replace their early homes with larger mansions. These second-generation homes were designed chiefly in the elegant Italianate or Second Empire styles. During that time, etchings of these imposing homes were used as border decorations around bird's-eye views of the city and in other promotional literature touting the appeal and livability of Portland.

As the Italianate and Queen Anne styles waned in the 1890s, several new architects appeared on the scene, contributing their talents to Portland's architectural treasury of houses. Most prominent during this phase was the partnership of William Macy Whidden and Ion Lewis, fresh from work in prestigious eastern firms. They brought with them a working knowledge of the latest architectural styles, and they handled with equal finesse the weighty proportions of the Richardsonian style and the balanced harmonies of the Colonial Revival style. The surviving homes comprise a most significant collection of superior architecture on the West Coast. Working concurrently

with Whidden and Lewis, the architect Isaac Hodgson, Jr., recently arrived from California, designed several fine houses in the Richardsonian style. Emil Schacht, Josef Jacobberger, and Edgar Max Lazarus also established themselves in the Portland architectural scene at the same time, each producing houses of first-rate quality.

Architects produced many fine homes during the early period of the Colonial Revival around the turn of the century. Ellis F. Lawrence began his prolific career during the first decade

Portland, 1865, from a lithograph of the city and its notable architecture.

of the new century, as did architects Morris H. Whitehouse and David C. Lewis. In addition, the venerable Boston firm of Shepley, Rutan and Coolidge was responsible for the design of several important houses in Portland. Whitehouse's career has been little studied and deserves greater attention, particularly his work in partnership with J. Andre Fouilhoux. Portland's inimitable Albert E. Doyle, grand master of the Colonial Revival styles, began his career in the first decade of the 1900s, establishing an unparalleled legacy of superb architectural designs. Surely, his record has been one of the most impressive and valuable contributions to the city's collection of superior residential as well as commercial architecture. Lastly, another architect of great merit, Edward T. Foulkes, designed houses that, although few in number, exhibited excellent taste and impressive scale. The Pittock Mansion, his finest creation in Portland, has become a jewel within Portland's park system.

During the second phase of the Colonial Revival, which began in the 1910s and continued on into the 1950s, other architects, native born or emigrating from other parts of the country, made their mark in Portland's urban landscape. John Virginius Bennes, who had a notable career working in the inventive Prairie style, also designed several Colonial Revival style houses. Jamieson Parker exhibited great taste in his elegant designs in the Colonial Revival style and later during the phase of the Arts and Crafts movement. Roscoe D. Hemenway, another popular residential architect, designed in both the Colonial Revival and Tudor idioms. In today's real-estate market, these architects' names have instant significance and appeal. Even Spokane's famous architect, Kirtland K. Cutter, produced several handsomely designed houses in Portland—his Portland clients undoubtedly knew of his favorable reputation in the region.

When the Tudor and Jacobethan architectural influences began to take form in the city, many of the architects already practicing in Portland were at home in the characteristic features of these new styles. While Ellis Lawrence and Richard Sundeleaf produced the greatest number of houses in these styles, several others continued the tradition, including Charles Ertz, Francis Jacobberger, David Lewis, and Roscoe Hemenway.

Of all the architects practicing in Portland in the early 1920s, Herman Brookman was the most remarkable. His career in residential design skyrocketed after the construction of his design for the country estate of M. Lloyd Frank. Rarely has an architect in Portland spent such energy perfecting each and every detail in creating a masterpiece. Brookman was and always will be remembered as an "architect's architect" for his brilliant talents and the rich legacy of fine houses that he left the city. Equally notable was the brief Portland stay of nationally renowned William Grey Purcell, formerly of Minneapolis. Although rarely recognized locally, Purcell designed houses in Portland that display the talents for which he was acclaimed nationally. These structures demonstrate his ability to adapt his typical Midwest designs to local influences and scale.

William C. Knighton, Josef Jacobberger, and John V. Bennes employed innovative touches in the Craftsman style during the first decades of the twentieth century. In many respects, these men paved the way for the Arts and Crafts architects, who designed the largest number of houses in any one style in Portland. Of the significant architects of this phase, Jamieson Parker, Hollis E. Johnson, Harold W. Doty, A. E. Doyle, and Ernest Tucker stand out. However, the eccentric Wade Hampton Pipes was arguably the most prolific and possibly the most popular. His houses are praised for their tailored English characteristics, their beautiful plans, their spare but effective use of materials, and their superb craftsmanship.

At the beginning of the 1930s, most designs reflected an English orientation, veering into Stripped Traditional or Tudor modes. Herman Brookman excelled in this approach, and he clearly demonstrated a sympathy with a developing contemporary architecture, later called the Northwest style. Before 1950, the aristocratic John Yeon and the Italian Pietro Belluschi were the most prophetic of the new style. They influenced, among others, Walter Gordon and Van Evera Bailey. Both Belluschi and Yeon achieved national stature for their understated, regionally styled houses. They made innovative use of local materials and showed a sympathetic understanding of the demands of the local climate. Richard J. Neutra of Los Angeles, another nationally acclaimed architect, adapted in his designs the International style to the demands of the Northwest climate.

This book salutes Portland's special houses, their architects, and the clients who sought the best in residential design. It also attempts to place the creation of classic homes within the context of Portland's growth and development. By doing so, this study reveals how architectural design not only reflects a city's economic, social, and political life, but also helps to shape that life by its unique expression of those values in a lasting physical form. This book illustrates that, when successful, the alliance of client and architect is a remarkable example of teamwork and cooperation, the product of which results in fine architectural accomplishments for which the positive effects last well beyond the lifetime of those who produce it. This joint contribution to the cultural life of the city deserves praise, continued appreciation, and preservation. In the present climate of apparent mediocrity in residential design, there is real danger of losing one of life's enjoyable amenities—the lasting and renewable pleasures of fine architecture.

"A Few of Portland's Beautiful Homes" and "Portland is Famed for its Homes and Gardens," from *The Pacific Northwest Welcomes the American Legion*, September 1928.

PART I

Classical and Medieval Revivals
1840s–1870s

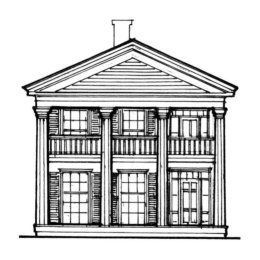

THE GROWTH of the city of Portland began in earnest in the 1850s, and on a much larger scale than its chief rival up river, Oregon City. Portland had several advantages over Oregon City as well as its downstream competitors. Captains of sailing ships discovered that Portland sat at the point where the Willamette River starts to shallow. In addition, boosters for the town of Portland found that its location on the shelf above the riverbank, although thick with virgin timber, offered a much broader expanse for future growth than the site of Oregon City, which was bordered by high cliffs. Finally, towns downstream from Portland realized that Portland's merchants had captured the agricultural produce of the rich adjacent Tualatin Valley by building a road through the hills between the Willamette and Tualatin valleys. The road enabled farmers to send their crops directly to wharfs in Portland more easily than to competing shipping points on the lower Willamette River or the Columbia River. Portland's ascendant position was further assured in 1854, when a United States mail steamer chose the city as its terminus.

The site on which Portland was to be built—an ancient Indian campground—was visited by explorers Meriwether Lewis and William Clark in 1806, without much enthusiasm, and subsequently by trappers from the Hudson's Bay Company from the mid-1820s and on, some of whose cabins dotted the woods. Lucian Etienne built the first farmhouse on the east side of the Willamette in 1826, and William Johnson, an Englishman, built a cabin on the original Portland townsite in 1842. With amazing speed, the perimeter of the land was expanded by the cutting down of huge fir trees, and the surveying and selling of lots began in 1845. Soon a scattering of Greek Revival houses appeared on these lots. The Portland city plan established small 200-by-200-foot blocks with 60-foot-wide public access. Blocks were designated as public squares, "market squares" (Market Street), "district schools," "college" (College Street), "lyceum," and "penitentiary." The city's founders had bold plans, and fortunately, they sought quality designs in their first structures.

Incorporated in 1851 and settled primarily by young, sober Protestant New Englanders and New Yorkers, Portland showed remarkable growth between 1845 and 1870, increasing from a population of 805 in 1851 to nearly 8,300 in 1870. The city's early merchants and traders proved a shrewd and energetic lot. Capitalizing on Portland's strategic location at the confluence of two major rivers and at the head of the richly productive Willamette Valley, they captured the market of the California Gold Rush for lumber and foodstuffs. From this beginning, Portland's rising merchant class took advantage of other economic opportunities to build their fortunes and their city during the 1850s and 1860s: gold rushes in southern and eastern Oregon, Federal military spending to fight the Native American populations, and sustained agricultural production throughout the region.

To market the minerals and produce of the interior, and in turn supply the hinterlands with finished goods, Portland's entrepreneurs developed a transportation network of steamboats and, later, railroads. This activity, best employed by the Oregon Steam Navigation Company, enhanced the fortunes of Portland merchants. Over a thirty-year period, these merchants developed a thriving trade network involving Portland, New York, and San Francisco. Among the notable early merchants were Henry Corbett, Josiah Failing and his sons, Cicero Hunt Lewis, William S. Ladd, and Simeon G. Reed. They were joined by shipping promoters, including Captain John Couch, Captain J. C. Ainsworth, Herman Leonard, John Green, and Robert Thompson, in laying the foundation for Portland's economic future. These men further enriched themselves by investing their profits from mercantile and shipping activities in banking and utilities. This prosperous urban establishment soon had the means to build the very best when it came to their residences, and their far-reaching connections provided the source of cultural influences shaping the style of homes they desired.

In their travels to San Francisco and to eastern cities, Portland's rising merchant elite observed the latest in architectural and furniture styles. They had access to plan books, periodicals, and newspapers that described and promoted the latest fashions in homes and furnishings. Drawing on these sources and hiring the most capable architects and builders, Portland's elite was determined to build residences of which a growing city could be proud. Over time, members of the elite built several homes for themselves, each one reflecting their economic position and the prevailing tastes and styles of the moment.

During the Great Western Migration of 1843 to 1853, the first architects arrived in Portland: Absolom B. Hallock in 1849, Harley McDonald in 1850, Lou Day in about 1850, and Elwood M. Burton in 1852. Initially, each had sought employment in either Oregon City or Milwaukie up river from Portland, but it soon became apparent that Portland had the greater potential for growth. These men had training not only in architectural design and construction, but also in such related fields as surveying or cabinet and furniture making. All these skills proved essential basic services in the growing city. Hallock, the city's first recorded architect, and Burton prospered; Day and McDonald moved elsewhere. (McDonald moved to Forest Grove where he continued to practice, and several of his houses are still standing.) The most visible reminder of Hallock's contribution is Portland's oldest standing commercial building, the Hallock and McMillen Building on Front Avenue and Oak Street, built in 1857. Burton's reminders are the New Market–South Wing and the facade of the New Market Theater (1872), surely one of the city's most venerable landmarks. Both architects enjoyed considerable prestige in the new city. In addition to designing and constructing Portland's first brick commercial building—the Ladd Building (1853)—Hallock designed many fine homes for the newly prosperous merchants. Burton is most clearly remembered for (as Joseph Gaston writes in *Portland: Its History and Builders*) the "large number of the finest residences in the city," and "not only his good competence, but also the priceless heritage of an untarnished name."

CHAPTER 1

Greek Revival

In the vast expanse of the Oregon Territory, jointly occupied by the United States and Great Britain from 1818 to 1846, the British Fort Vancouver was the first European or American outpost prior to the Great Western Migration. It served as the Pacific headquarters of the Hudson's Bay Company, whose domain extended from the Pacific Ocean to the Rocky Mountains and from California to Alaska. Fort Vancouver was located in splendid isolation on the north bank of the Columbia River, just east of the Columbia's confluence with the smaller Willamette River.

The buildings within the fort's stockade revealed the advanced construction skills of the company's employees. The house of the fort's Chief Factor, reconstructed by the National Park Service and now a National Historic Landmark, is the single most remarkable example of early nineteenth-century Euro-American architecture in the Pacific Northwest. Known to virtually every trapper, explorer, trader, missionary, and settler in the area before 1842, the house and its occupant exemplified the high degree of eastern refinement that could be attained even in a rugged frontier setting. The large

Portland, at SW First Avenue looking north from Oak Street, circa 1850.

25

house, built under the auspices of Chief Factor Dr. John McLoughlin in 1838, embodied both early French-Canadian and East Coast architectural and construction traditions. In the house's spacious rooms McLoughlin entertained his guests with gracious hospitality, serving excellent food—brought from the far reaches of the Territory or raised on the company farms—and fine wine on imported china, crystal, and silver. To western adventurers and settlers, Dr. McLoughlin's home at Fort Vancouver was an oasis of civilization after the arduous trip west.

As the decline of British interests in the area became increasingly apparent by the early 1840s, the retired employees of the Hudson's Bay Company, along with newly arriving American settlers, began erecting homes in the Willamette River Valley. Early settlements in the upper valley included Oregon City and Portland, platted in 1842 and 1845, respectively. As early as 1828, John McLoughlin established a land claim on the site where Oregon City was to develop, and in 1845, he built his retirement home there. McLoughlin's associate and chief trader of the Hudson's Bay Company, Francis Ermatinger, also constructed his two-story Greek Revival house in Oregon City in 1845, and Dr. Forbes Barclay, the physician of Fort

Vancouver, built his home in the new city during that period as well. McLoughlin's two-story Federal style house and Barclay's one-and-a-half-story house are similar in that they both have central plans, axially arranged around the entry stair hall, but the veranda columns of the Barclay home reveal considerable Greek Revival detail. Both houses have been handsomely

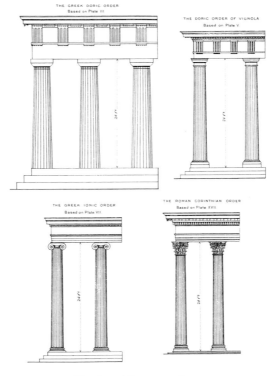

Greek and Roman orders.

restored by the McLoughlin House restoration committees and are listed on the National Register of Historic Places.

Two farmhouses just outside of Oregon City also deserve special mention: the Rose Farm (1847) and the Captain J. C. Ainsworth House (1850). The Rose Farm, site of the swearing-in of the first governor of the Oregon Territory, is a rambling two-story house with a recessed front porch, somewhat in the Federal style. It has the unusual detail of a dropped pendule cornice, in a repetitive jigsaw-cut decorative design, that is possibly a Gothic Revival detail, although the house seems to have no other features of that style. The Ainsworth House, a key house in Oregon's early architectural history, is more straightforwardly Greek Revival, with its classic "temple" front, the floor-to-ceiling windows on the facade, and the side entrance. In every respect, the house reflects the characteristics of the Greek Revival architecture then prevalent on the East Coast.

The city of Portland, lagging somewhat behind Oregon City in the 1840s, did have one distinctive house before 1850: the imported, "knock-down" house of Captain Nathaniel Crosby. It was built similarly to the Barclay House in Oregon City, with a central-entrance plan and even the wide front veranda. The

Crosby House was remodeled as a store around the turn of the century, but its original detailing reflected the Greek Revival style better than either the Ainsworth or Barclay houses, judging from the sophisticated design of the dormers, as shown in photographs taken after the remodeling. As the first frame house in a settlement of crude log cabins, the Crosby House was a fine beginning for Portland's residential development.

The structures designed by Portland's first notable and skilled architects, who had arrived in the city during the early 1850s, had most of the recognizable characteristics of Greek Revival architecture. In plan, most comprised simple rectangles with a kitchen wing in the rear. The facades had either symmetrical central entrances with windows on either side, or side entrances with windows on one side. Some had the classic temple fronts, complete with pediments and free-standing Tuscan-inspired columns. In Portland in 1850, Thomas J. Carter built a large temple-fronted house deep in the woods near Eighteenth Avenue and Jefferson Street. The house featured not one, but two tiers of wrap-around porches and free-standing columns, representing a more true "temple" than the Ainsworth House built that same year in Oregon City.

Other features typical of the Greek Revival included horizontal siding; pilaster trims at the corners of the house structure and a wide water-table trim at the base; double-hung windows with six-over-six (6/6) panes and narrow muntins; entrance doors with a Doric frontis-

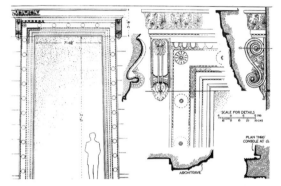

Doorway detail, North Portico, Erechtheion, Athens, circa 420–393 BC, designed by Mnesicles.

The Parthenon, Athens, circa 447–432 BC, designed by Ictinus and Callicrates. From *The Antiquities of Athens* by James Stuart and Nicholas Revett, 1762.

piece (entablature with side pilasters), including paned transoms and sidelights; low-pitched roofs with projecting cornices (ogee trim, ultimately) above wide friezes and architraves encircling the house; and a variety of balustrated porches.

Besides the temple-fronted houses, others in the Greek Revival style had end gables, entrances on the long side, and were generally two or one-and-a-half stories high. Two typical Portland examples were the Captain John B. Price House (c. 1855) and the S. J. McCormick House (c. 1858). The best extant example is the superbly restored James F. Bybee House (1856) on Sauvie Island, now owned by the Oregon Historical Society. Another prominent roof form common to the Greek Revival style was the hipped roof, such as on the one-story Captain John C. Couch House (1850). The Francis Ermatinger House (1845) in Oregon City and the Judge Cyrus Olney House (1854) had flat roofs. The former house was originally sheathed with an interlocking sheet-metal roofing.

Builders of the Greek Revival homes desired a sense of order and simplicity on the exterior, and this was achieved by the typical use of white paint and a contrasting dark green color for the shutters or blinds. The intended effect was further enhanced by the evenly spaced, naturally weathered wood shingles on the roof, and by the red brick chimneys and footings.

Porches, a distinctive adornment to the Greek Revival house, varied with their function and with the size of the house. Some were simple, small projections at the entrance door, whereas larger forms extended across the entire facade of the house. Some houses had porches that were more integral to the overall design of the house, often with the roof of the house extending over the porch or, in some cases, with the porch recessed into the rectangular block of the house. Nearly all forms had added balustrades, such as in the McCormick and Bybee houses. The McCormick House had an additional balustrade on the roof, above the cornice, that reflected the furniture designs of the era. Still other porches boasted lattice infilling around their raised perimeters, good for ventilating the wood structural members below.

To convey a sense of a more ordered territory and of private property, owners surrounded their homes with picket fences. These fences were located adjacent to the public sidewalk, or the property line, and often surrounded entire blocks in residential areas. The fences consisted of vertical rows of turned balusters or square pickets, with posts or piers located at the corners and gates. The posts, which served to sturdy the entire structure, were often decorated with bases, caps, and turned finials or urns. Below the pickets, a wide skirting provided a measure of protection for household pets and children, as well as from unwanted intruders.

The interiors of Portland homes of this era have not been as extensively recorded as the exteriors. The few extant examples of Greek Revival interior spaces reveal a fairly simple yet comfortable ambiance. Restored or reconstructed period rooms can be seen at the Chief Factor's House (1838) at the Hudson's Bay Com-

University of Virginia, Charlottesville, Virginia, 1817–26, designed by Thomas Jefferson. A classic example of Greek Revival influenced architecture in early nineteenth-century America.

pany Fort Vancouver; the Commanding Officers' Quarters (1849) at the United States Fort Vancouver; the Francis Ermatinger (1845), Dr. John McLoughlin (1845), and Dr. Forbes Barclay (1849) houses in Oregon City; and College Hall (1850) of Tualatin Academy (now Pacific University) in McMinnville. The most vivid description that we have of a Greek Revival interior is for the Captain Alexander P. Ankeny House (originally the Judge Cyrus Olney House, until it was purchased by Ankeny in 1858).

The interiors of these houses had several common stylistic features. The trim around the fireplace usually included an entablature, side pilasters, and a projecting mantel that approximated an architectural cornice. Occasionally, wood paneling covered the brick of the chimney on the upper wall of the frontispiece. The trim around windows and doors varied. It most often consisted of either a wraparound trim with an added molding at the perimeter, or a dog-ear detail at the upper corners—the Ainsworth House at Oregon City and the Commanding Officers' Quarters at Fort Vancouver both displayed this latter detail. Interior walls and ceilings were finished with either wide horizontal boards or plaster, and high baseboards were topped with a decorative cap molding. Wallpaper was often added for decorative effect, or possibly to cut drafts in the winter. Few of the houses, if any, had crown moldings at the intersection of the ceiling and walls. Doors varied in the number of panels and in the detailing. One-, four-, or, possibly, six-panel doors represented the norm; the eastern style two-panel doors were uncommon.

The staircases of Greek Revival houses were a special feature, and their design and construction required extensive architectural knowledge. Important elements of the staircases included the turned newel at the foot and the handrail, which curved to a horizontal to meet the newel post. Staircases made of fine hardwoods were finished like the furniture of the time; others, usually made of the softer wood of fir trees, were painted. The railing balusters were typically turned on a lathe, but sometimes they were square or polygonal. Repeated designs and styles suggest that standard patterns were available locally. Another detail that required special attention was the railing at the head

of the staircase. The stairway railing formed a graceful curve at the leveling-off to connect with the railing of the upper landing, which surrounded an open space to the floor below. This graceful device recalled detailing often found in Georgian and Federal designs, and while amazingly simple and obvious, the art of its design has been entirely lost today.

Most interior woodwork in Greek Revival houses was painted, either plain or in imitation of finer-grained woods or even marble. The Commanding Officers' Quarters at the U.S. Fort

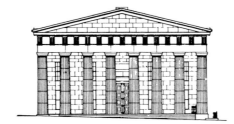

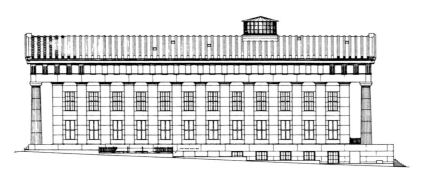

United States Sub-Treasury Building, New York, 1832–42, designed by Ithiel Town and Alexander Jackson Davis, in association with Ross and Grazee.

Vancouver displayed this "false wood" painted effect. Floors were also often painted in a kind of imitation work, as can be seen in the Ainsworth House, where a small patch of the original diagonal floor tiles, alternating in gold and gray colors, is evident.

Typically, the furniture was large and in scale with decidedly Grecian styling. Sofas had roll-over arms and thick squab cushions. Chairs had the lines and curves of ancient Greek models, as in the concave back and legs of the Greek styled klismos chair. Beds either were the sleigh-bed variety, with solid footboards and headboards that roll outward at the top, or they had carved or turned posters at the corners. Secretaries and bureaus were more overtly architectural in design, with ornamental entablatures and side pilasters.

During the first half of the nineteenth century, Americans embraced Classical Greek political and cultural ideas and expressed them in the architecture, sculpture, and even furniture of the time, as well as in government. The Greek Revival style, one of the last clearly multinational styles, had organizational concepts that originated in the Greek art and architecture of the fourth and fifth centuries BC. Newly arrived settlers in the Oregon Territory transplanted these concepts to the wilderness of the West and left a legacy of architectural treasures worthy of note. By the 1870s, the city had transformed its rough wilderness in isolation into a growing metropolis with attractive, classic homes and groomed lawns and gardens.

Wells Fargo Building, Portland, circa 1857. An early Greek Revival building in the growing city.

Greek Revival
CHARACTERISTICS

PLANS: rectangular with a kitchen wing or ell.

ROOFS: pedimented gable ends; return cornice and entablature; full gable with pediment and entablature.

EXTERIOR FINISHES: Tuscan corner boards with a capital and base; horizontal weatherboards, or flush horizontal tongue-and-groove boards.

CHIMNEYS: brick, corbeled.

WINDOWS: double-hung; six-over-six (6/6) panes or more; louvered shutters.

WINDOW TRIM (exterior): corniced casing trim.

ENTRANCE DOORS: one, four, or six panels; transom and sidelights.

VERANDAS/PORCHES: balustrated porches; varied in size.

INTERIOR FINISHES: plastered walls with a continuous plaster cornice and wood baseboards; tongue-and-groove-beaded vertical wainscoting boards in kitchen and dining room.

INTERIOR TRIM: door casings with dog-ear extensions at the top; plain-faced baseboards with top trim.

STAIRS: railings curved at turned newel post at base, and curved at the second floor landing.

FIREPLACE FRONTS: entablatures and side pilasters around a brick border.

PROPERTY SURROUNDS: perimeter picket fences around the property, with varied balusters; support posts at gates and corners.

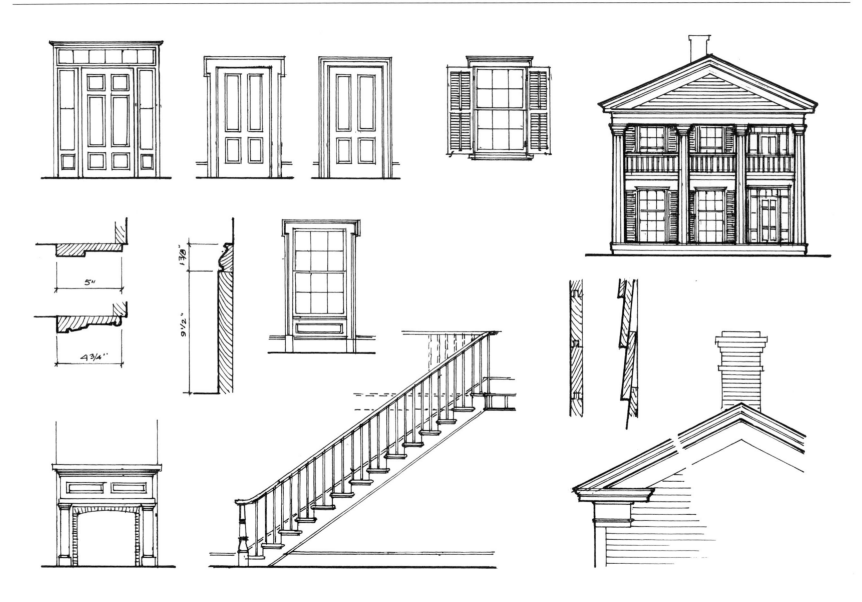

Entrance to the Captain J. C. Ainsworth House.

Greek Revival
HOUSES

1838	Chief Factor's House, Hudson's Bay Company	1850	Thomas J. Carter (attributed to Absolom B. Hallock)
1845	Dr. John McLoughlin	1850	Captain J. C. Ainsworth (attributed to Absolom B. Hallock)
1845	Francis Ermatinger		
1847	Daniel L. Lownsdale	1854	Henry W. Corbett (attributed to Absolom B. Hallock)
1847	Captain Nathaniel Crosby		
1849	Commanding Officers' Quarters, Fort Vancouver	1854	Judge Cyrus Olney
		1855	Dr. Perry Prettyman
1849	Dr. Forbes Barclay	c. 1855	Captain John B. Price
1850	Captain John C. Couch (attributed to Absolom B. Hallock)	1856	James F. Bybee
		c. 1858	S. J. McCormick
1850	Socrates H. Tryon	c. 1859	Dr. James C. Hawthorne

Chief Factor's House
Hudson's Bay Company, Fort Vancouver (1838)

Though the Hudson's Bay Company's outpost at Fort Vancouver was established in 1825, it was not until 1838 that the large Chief Factor's residence was constructed. At eighty feet wide and forty feet deep, the house was surely one of the most impressive structures in the West at the time, certainly north of San Francisco. It embodies several characteristics of early French-Canadian architecture, including the hipped roof and spacious veranda across the entire facade. Few of the then-fashionable American Greek Revival details are in evidence, but the shuttered and paned casement windows reflect East Coast architectural and construction traditions.

Unlike the other buildings within the fort compound, the Chief Factor's residence is elevated five feet above the ground, with a cellar under the main floor. Its exterior appearance has a simply stated grandness,

intended to signify the authority of the Chief Factor within the Hudson's Bay Company as well as to declare the presence of the Company in the Territory. The formality of the house's central-entrance plan is enhanced by the split curved central stairway, leading up on both sides of a reviewing platform. The spacious covered veranda extends along the entire facade, with an iron trellis entwined with grape vines. The central arch of the trellis adds further elegance to the entrance. A white picket fence along the front of the house screened a flower garden, giving a suggestion of the domestic presence within. The fence, perhaps the first in the Oregon Territory, was repeated countless times in nearly all the residential construction that followed in the next several decades.

Constructed in the post-in-the-sill method, with dressed-fir log infilling, the house made for an enormous and sturdy structure. It was, in turn, covered with white-painted weatherboards. The windows are of casement design and, together with the hipped roof and the dark green shutters, contribute to the house's French-Canadian appearance. Other

The Chief Factor's House, Hudson's Bay Company, Fort Vancouver, circa 1860.

The Chief Factor's House, reconstructed.

exterior features include the half-round metal gutters and the single brick chimney, located just to the left of center.

The French-Canadian and eastern American architectural traditions that found expression in the house's overall plan and exterior—the straightforward rectilinear plan with the central entrance and the curved bifurcate stairs—all relate to the symmetrical arrangement of the rooms in the house's interior. The front entry door into the central hall has a transom window above and windows at either side, which illuminate the interior. Off the entrance hall are the ten rooms of the main floor, with a stairway to the large attic above. Directly forward of the central stair hall is the stately dining room, and the living quarters are to the right and left. John McLoughlin's family had the rooms to the west and the family of James Douglas, accountant and later co-Factor of the Hudson's Bay Company, had the rooms to the east. The large mess hall was serviced by a separate kitchen structure, which was connected with the mess hall by a covered passage. Only the gentlemen of the fort and their guests ate their meals here.

The living quarters were designed and constructed to provide both comfort and beauty. Plaster had not yet been introduced into the area, so the walls were covered with finished vertical boards, as was the ceiling. A chair rail encircles each room. A baseboard and ceiling trim extends around the entirety of the rooms; the mess hall has a coved (concave) crown molding. The doors each have six raised panels, divided at the door handle. Fine carpets, imported from England, covered the floors, except in the entrance hall, which has wood flooring.

As was appropriate for a Chief Factor, the interior rooms were furnished with fine English furniture, mostly in the late-Georgian, early Victorian styles prominent in both England and America. Most of the

Mess hall, Chief Factor's House.

Dr. McLoughlin's sitting room, Chief Factor's House.

dining chairs had balloon backs with upholstered, stuffed serpentine-shaped seats. The gentlemen's tufted mahogany armchairs had the classic spoon back and a C-scroll carved frame headed by a flower- and acanthus-carved crest. Much of the McLoughlin furniture, including the dining table, chairs, and desk, moved with the family to their new home in Oregon City in 1845 and can be seen there today.

Dr. John McLoughlin (1845)

The Dr. John McLoughlin House in Oregon City is the second major historical landmark in the Portland metropolitan area associated with the famous "Father of Oregon." After his departure as Chief Factor at Fort Vancouver, having been in charge of the Hudson's Bay Columbia District for twenty-one years, Dr. John McLoughlin moved to his land-grant claim near Willamette Falls at Oregon City. In 1845, he constructed his own home at Fourth and Main streets, when the small town had only a cluster of buildings and a lumber mill, which McLoughlin owned. Lumber from the mill was used to frame the house, and finish materials were shipped from Boston. The house faced the river, as did most of the houses in Oregon City and Portland, being the main approach elevation. The house still faces the river in its present location at 713 Center Street.

In its overall style, the house has the proportions of the late-Federal period, and it is not surprising that the Greek Revival detailing, so prevalent in the East and in the emerging towns of Oregon City and Portland, is missing here. The hipped-roof house has two stories and a root cellar. Though reserved in its ornamentation and detail, the house's imposing appearance is a result of the pleasing arrangement of well-proportioned windows and doors on the facade. The windows are small paned, 16/12 on the main floor and 12/12 on the second floor. The main entrance has a paned transom and sidelights. The present main entrance was the original back door, which connected to a separate kitchen building.

The interior is as reserved as its exterior. Arranged around the central stair hall are a large parlor, a dining room, a reception room, and Dr. McLoughlin's office. Upstairs are three bedrooms and a sitting room. The large second floor halls often served to house the McLoughlins' numerous guests. As with the Chief Factor's House at Fort Vancouver, the walls and ceilings were covered with finished boards, although the walls were wallpapered. The window and door casings are composite pieces of edge-cap and scrolled panel molding, the same as in the 1845 Francis Ermatinger House. The baseboards have the same scrolled cap on top of

Dr. John McLoughlin House.

Parlor, McLoughlin House.

the flush 7.5-inch base. The fireplaces throughout the house are typical for the period: pilasters on either side of the brick surround, connected by an entablature.

Of particular note at the McLoughlin House are the family's original furnishings. They include the hand-carved mahogany four-poster bed, the original dining room table and chairs, John McLoughlin's desk, and a fine Chinese-import cabinet in the parlor.

The house was moved with great effort to its present location in 1909. The McLoughlin House National Historic Site is administered by the McLoughlin Memorial Association, the city, and the National Park Service. It was the eleventh building in the country to become a National Historic Landmark.

Dining room, McLoughlin House.

Bedroom, McLoughlin House.

Francis Ermatinger (1845)

As the oldest standing house in Oregon City and the third oldest in the entire state, the Ermatinger House is one of Oregon's most important historic landmarks. The house's original owner, Francis Ermatinger (1798–1858), had been Chief Trader with the Hudson's Bay Company at Fort Vancouver. When the Company left the region in 1845, Ermatinger moved to Oregon City, where Chief Factor John McLoughlin had retired to that same year.

Francis Ermatinger House.

Architecturally, the Ermatinger House offers the simple, robust characteristics of the Greek Revival style. A prominent entablature surrounds the hipped roof—the roof was originally flat and covered with galvanized tin. A substantial porch, with square boxed columns supporting the roof, crosses the front facade. The windows are the typical 6/6 panes. Window and door casings are composite edge-cap and scrolled panel molding. In plan and elevation, the house has a central entry hall with parlors to the right and left. It was in the left parlor of this house that Francis Pettygrove and Amos Lovejoy tossed the famous coin to determine the name of the new townsite down river from Oregon City—whether it would take the name of Lovejoy's hometown of Boston, Massachusetts, or Pettygrove's hometown of Portland, Maine. Pettygrove won, of course, and from that moment on the city took the name of Portland.

The restoration of the Ermatinger House was undertaken by Ruth McBride Powers in 1988 and 1989, joining the impressive list of her important preservation-restoration projects.

Daniel L. Lownsdale (1847)

The first known temple-fronted house in the city of Portland was that constructed by pioneer tanner Daniel L. Lownsdale. Located to the southwest of the riverfront business district, on the block defined by Fourth and Fifth avenues and Market and Mill streets, the house sat at the edge of the dense virgin forest at the time still inhabited by the local Native Americans.

In typical temple fashion, the Lownsdale House had four support columns, with recessed panels, at the gabled entrance end of the structure. The center two columns were spaced closer together so as to define the central entrance door and also to leave the windows on either side unobstructed. A full-facade balcony with turned balusters extended out to the columns on the second story. One-story gabled wings were built on either side of the building.

In 1859, the house, in poor condition and perhaps never completed by Lownsdale, was purchased by the Sisters of the Holy Names of Jesus and Mary. By 1863, the Sisters had added a two-story chapel and student wings, the latter replacing the original one-story wings. It was used as a day and boarding school while the Sisters established a convent. In 1889, the original house was moved from the property to a new location, and a large brick building was built on the original site to house the growing school for girls, later St. Mary's Academy.

The Lownsdale House just before demolition. Note the missing side wings.

Daniel L. Lownsdale House.

Captain Nathaniel Crosby (1847)

The first architecturally distinctive house built in Portland was that of Captain Nathaniel Crosby, located at the corner of First Avenue and Washington Street. The house was modeled, it has been said, after Crosby's home in Wiscasset, Maine. With its distinctive Greek Revival detailing and interior plasterwork (it was one of only two plastered interiors in the city at the time), the house was considered a "palatial residence." It was actually a knock-down house, constructed with local framing materials but finished with siding, trim, and details imported

Captain Nathaniel Crosby House. Sketch of the original structure before its relocation and subsequent remodeling, but showing the original pedimented roof dormers.

from the East Coast. It cost $15,000 to build at a time when a good carpenter earned about $15.00 a day.

The most distinguishing evidence of the house's early Greek Revival character was found in the three dormers on the original one-and-a-half-story dwelling. The dormers were very sophisticated in design, with pediments above each window and decorative Grecian key work at the upper corners of the window trim. The plan had a central entrance hall with rooms on either side and a kitchen wing in the rear. In about 1859 or 1860, the large front porch was cut off and the house was moved farther west to Fourth Avenue, as were countless other houses when the press of commercial structures forced the residential areas west. By about the turn of the century, the residence was remodeled and converted to a store.

Commanding Officers' Quarters
Fort Vancouver (1849)

Along present-day Officers' Row in Vancouver, Washington, are twenty-one remarkable houses, restored in 1988 to their 1906 appearance. The oldest of these houses is the Commanding Officers' Quarters of the U.S. Fort Vancouver, which was established in 1848 by President James K. Polk with the first United States military sent into the Oregon Territory. The Commanding Officers' Quarters was built in 1849 entirely of unhewn logs, and despite its raw and hefty construction, it was one of the most imposing structures in the Territory. Only the Chief Factor's House of the old Hudson's Bay Company Fort Vancouver, located just below in the decaying fort enclosure, could compete with such a presence.

Although similar to other houses in the area with its central stair hall, this house has a double-tiered veranda completely surrounding it, giving the house a somewhat French air. The hipped roof with dormers on all four sides further suggests the French-Louisiana architectural traditions that were influential in this house's design. The log structure was covered with weatherboards in 1851, along with other major improvements made to the house. In 1860, it was recorded, "the garrison buildings as well as the warehouse at the government warf [sic] . . . were painted a bright yellow," presumably with white trim and green shutters or blinds.

The house has four windows and a door across the entrance facade, with the main door centered on the first floor and a centrally located door above it opening onto the veranda on the second floor. The original entrance door had a transom window and sidelights, but they were replaced by a Colonial Revival style doorway at about the time of the Lewis and Clark Centennial Exposition in 1905. The four main win-

Commanding Officers' Quarters, Fort Vancouver.

Dining room, Commanding Officers' Quarters.

Commanding Officers' Quarters today.

Original painted ceiling medallion, Commanding Officers' Quarters.

dows, once shuttered, have 9/6 window panes on the main floor and 6/6 on the second floor.

The interior of the Quarters was marked by the craftsmanship of the rugged frontier. All the interior walls and ceilings were covered with wide, horizontal, white pine boards. These original boards were uncovered during the restoration of the house in the late 1980s, and the original color was still intact. The original door and window casings, with their dog-ear design, remained untouched, as had some of the fireplace fronts, with side pilasters and an entablature over the fireplace opening. The main entrance stair hall was wallpapered in 1854 in a design imitating large blocks of marble, with a wallpaper border at the ceiling. Fragments of this wallpaper were uncovered during the restoration and remain framed on the second floor landing.

Two fireplaces are located in each the parlor to the right of the entry stair hall and the original dining room to the left. The fireplace trim as well as the window and door casings are marbleized, and the four-panel doors are wood grained. A painted medallion can be seen on the ceiling of the second floor hall, suggesting the more elaborate plaster medallions found in finer homes of the time. In 1853, Kidderminster carpeting (a kind of ingrain carpet) was being imported from England at Fort Vancouver, and perhaps it was used to cover the exposed floorboards of the Commanding Officers' Quarters.

The Commanding Officers' Quarters was replaced in 1887 by a new residence, now known as the Marshall House (see Chapter 6). The original log house became an Officers Club and sometime later was named after General Ulysses S. Grant, who served at Fort Vancouver in the 1850s as quartermaster, although he never actually lived in the house.

Dr. Forbes Barclay (1849)

Similar to the 1847 Crosby House in Portland, the Dr. Forbes Barclay House in Oregon City has a central-hall plan and an extensive four-column porch across the non-gabled entrance side of the house. The extant Barclay House is larger, however, with eight rooms. The entrance doorway is flanked on both sides by the two windows of each of the two front rooms. The windows have 12/12 panes, similar to the second floor windows of the McLoughlin House next door. Because of inflation caused by the California Gold Rush and the demand for lumber and materials from the Oregon Territory, Barclay's house cost $17,000 to build, a large amount of money in 1849. Adding to the cost were the pine finish materials brought around Cape Horn from Maine and the locks, hardware, and doors imported from England. Much of the interior trim and details

Dr. Forbes Barclay House.

remain, and the house has been beautifully preserved, despite being moved several times from its original site on Main Street.

The house was owned by Barclay descendants through the 1920s, still retaining furnishings and heirlooms from the Territorial days. It is presently administered by the McLoughlin Memorial Association, the city, and the National Park Service.

Captain John C. Couch (1850)
Absolom B. Hallock (attributed)

In 1850, Captain John C. Couch constructed a home on his 640-acre land claim, just north of the Portland townsite. The house faced a small lake, called Couch Lake, on its west side, roughly where Union Station is now located at Fourth Avenue and Hoyt Street. Like Captain Nathaniel Crosby, Couch had the finish siding and details shipped from the East Coast, but the structural framing was supplied locally. The house's design is attributed to Absolom Hallock, as he did other work for Captain Couch. The single-story residence was featured on the 1858 promotional lithograph of the city, the only known image of the home. Judging from the lithograph, the house had a symmetrical plan with parlors two-windows wide on either side of the central doorway, which had a transom and sidelights. Notable was the front porch, or piazza, across the entire front of the house and which featured six sets of paired columns, an unusual architectural feature for its time. To the west, or back of the house, was a kitchen wing.

It was in this home that Captain Couch lived with his family for the remainder of his life in Portland. Fortunately, several pieces of furniture are extant from this home and are now arranged in the Couch Bedroom at the Pittock Mansion: a magnificent sleigh bed, an upholstered Rococo

Captain John C. Couch House.

Revival armchair, two portraits, and a sea chest. Another Couch piece remains in a private collection in the city—a black lacquer and gold game table that was undoubtedly acquired by the Captain on one of his sailing trips to China.

Socrates H. Tryon (1850)

On a splendid promontory overlooking a bend in the Willamette River is the only house in the greater Portland metropolitan area that remains on its original 428.57-acre Donation Land Claim. Built in 1850, a year after the Tryon family's arrival in Oregon, the Socrates Tryon House

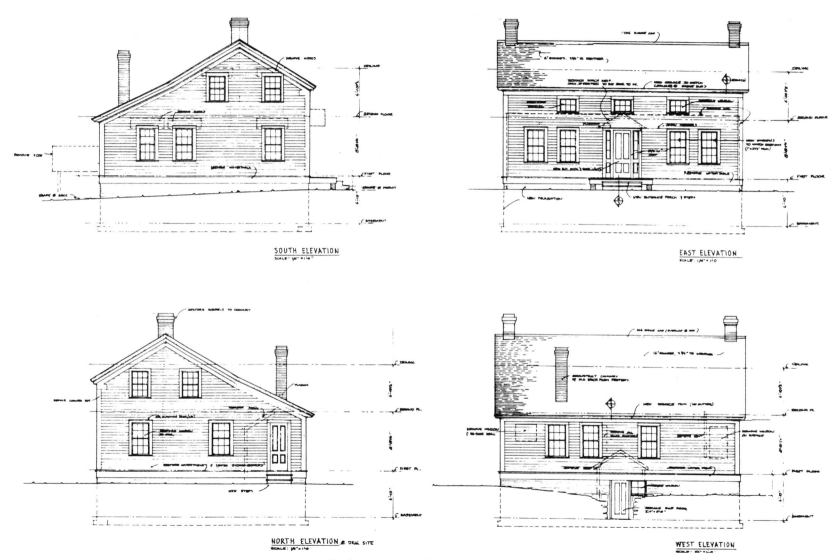

The four elevations of the Tryon House.

Socrates H. Tryon House.

retains today its original rectangular structural form, though the original entrance door on the river side is no longer extant. The current weatherboard siding, windows, and trim are primarily the original materials, as are the stone and brick foundations and chimney. Greek Revival details are greatly simplified in this rural farmhouse. The gable-end cornice returns are simply wrap-around boards, about 8.5 inches wide by 1 inch thick, as are the corner boards. Windows have 6/6 panes with muntins and include much of the original glass. Missing is the weather-table board covering the 10-inch-deep floor joists and sill plate.

Thomas J. Carter (1850–51)
Absolom B. Hallock (attributed)

Surely the grandest house in Portland at the time of its construction was the stately mansion erected by wealthy landowner Thomas J. Carter in 1850–51 on his Donation Land Claim, which encompassed roughly the area between Sixteenth, Canyon, Jefferson, and Spring streets. The house stood on the claim's northeast corner at the head of Eighteenth Avenue (formerly Chapman), on the property now owned by the United Methodist Church. The Carter House was in the temple design of the Greek Revival style, possibly influenced by the Georgia origins of the Carter family. The structure was surrounded on at least three sides by a free-

Thomas J. Carter House.

standing colonnade of boxed columns, which at the entrance side was five bays across. The columns had recessed panels on four sides and detailed capitals and bases.

The house's design is attributed to Absolom B. Hallock, Portland's principal architect at the time and the designer of the commercial Carter House three years later on Front Street. The residence was inhabited by the Carter family until 1874 and was torn down sometime near the end of the century.

Captain J. C. Ainsworth (1850–51)
Absolom B. Hallock (attributed)

The only remaining temple-fronted Greek Revival house in the Portland metropolitan area is the Captain J. C. Ainsworth House, constructed in 1850 to 1851 at Mount Pleasant, just east of Oregon City. A full pediment at the attic story surmounts four octagonal, wood, two-story columns of the portico, all set into the rectilinear mass. Large pilasters on the house mirror the end columns; all have articulated capitals and no bases. The portico has a free-standing balcony, not attached to the columns as were the balconies in the Carter and Lownsdale houses in Portland. Distinctive tall, double-hung windows extend down to the floor at the entrance elevation and have 6/9 panes. To the right is the entrance door with transom and sidelights. Only the windows of the entry elevation have shutters. On the north-facing side elevation, the windows have been rearranged from their original configuration and are now paired at the front parlor. A new bay window was also added to the dining room and the bedroom above.

The plan is typical for a side-entrance scheme. The parlor opens to the left from the stair hall, with the dining room to the rear. The kitchen extends to the back of the house, behind the dining room. Original to the house are the dog-eared casing trims and the fine staircase. The staircase has a fine mahogany newel post and handrail, which curves at the bottom in transition to the newel and at the top of the flight, where it curves around into the upper-hall stair rail.

Captain J. C. Ainsworth and Jane White, Ainsworth's second wife and daughter of pioneer Judge S. White of Oregon City, built the house at Mount Pleasant and lived there until business interests moved them to more prosperous Portland. They constructed a new house in 1862, and the architect for that house was Absolom B. Hallock, who had been in Oregon City in 1849 and might have designed their Mount Pleasant home as well before he too moved to Portland by 1852.

Captain J. C. Ainsworth House.

The Ainsworth House was first restored by Ruth McBride Powers in 1965. It underwent another restoration, completed in the early 1990s by Claire and Tom Met, which should ensure its survival for many years to come, although the once-spacious property has been considerably reduced by neighboring residential developments. Its present address is 19130 Lot Whitcomb Drive.

Henry W. Corbett House.

Henry W. Corbett (1854)
Absolom B. Hallock (attributed)

Though similar in plan to the Ainsworth House at Mount Pleasant, the house built by Henry W. Corbett in 1854 had an entirely different appearance. Instead of the temple front found in the Ainsworth House of 1850–51, Corbett's had instead a single-story porch and a central hipped roof. In both houses, the main entrance door was on the right, and two tall windows faced the porch from the parlor on the left. In typical Greek Revival style, the cornice and entablature below the roof were strongly emphasized. Large pilasters with Doric capitals adorned each corner of the Corbett House. A large two-story wing extended to the rear, and the side entrance probably led to the kitchen. A prominent picket fence surrounded the property, with substantial posts at the corners and entrance gates; each post had a rounded finial. This mode of enclosure of the property was nearly universal in early Portland, giving a sense of private enclosure and security from the street. The house was located at Fifth and Sixth avenues and Yamhill and Taylor streets.

The Corbett House may have been designed by Absolom B. Hallock, Portland's only resident architect from 1851 to 1854. Henry W. Corbett commissioned Hallock to design a brick building for him in 1853.

Judge Cyrus Olney (1854)

Constructed on the block where the New Market Theater is presently located at Second Avenue and Ankeny Street, the Judge Cyrus Olney House of 1854 combines stylistic qualities of both the Greek Revival style and the emerging Italian Villa style. Gone are the heavier boxed columns and pedimented facade; in their stead are thinner porch columns, defining the Italian piazza influence. Likewise, the proportions of the elevation are taller and more elegant, and the cornice at the flat tinned roof extends out farther than is usually seen in the Greek Revival style. The

well of water, decorative shrubbery, and cherry, apple, pear, and plum trees. The interior was finished in the latest fashion, including rosewood and mahogany furniture, much of it covered in green plush, forty-five yards of velvet carpet, fine rugs, and a piano.

The house was featured on the 1858 promotional lithograph of the city, showing the towering virgin fir trees in the distance.

Dr. Perry Prettyman (1855)

The farmhouse built by Dr. Perry Prettyman in 1855 was located at what is now SE Hawthorne Boulevard and Fifty-fifth Avenue. Both home and outbuilding had the well-detailed eave of the Greek Revival style, with cornice returns at the gable ends. On the west, or entrance, side were

Judge Cyrus Olney House.

plan, however, is typical of the side-entrance form, with the adjacent-parlor arrangement found throughout Greek Revival plans. Despite its apparent narrow width, defined by the entrance hall and a single room, wings to the rear made it a much larger house.

After the house was purchased by Captain Alexander P. Ankeny in 1858, an account of it read (Thomas Emmens, *Ankeny's New Market Theater*, unpublished, Portland, 1976):

The house faced First, and had eleven rooms, all hand finished, a wood shed, stables in the rear on Second, an outhouse, a good

Dr. Perry Prettyman House.

seven evenly spaced windows at the second floor and five at the main floor with two entrance doors, indicating that this was a large house. The house was covered by weatherboards and had corner boards and a water table. Sometime in the 1860s, a fashionable Italian Villa style porch was added to the entrance facade, with narrow posts and scroll brackets at the intersection of the posts and the beam above.

The naming of Hawthorne Boulevard was credited by Prettyman descendants to the rows of hawthorn trees planted along the boulevard by Dr. Prettyman. (Others credit the name to the pioneer physician Dr. James C. Hawthorne, whose home and sanitarium was located near the same street.)

Captain John B. Price (c. 1855)

The quality of Portland's residential architecture during its first decade is well revealed by the 1890s photograph showing two houses constructed on the southwest corner of Second Avenue and Jefferson Street. The house on the left was built by Captain John B. Price in about 1855. For what would be relatively modest houses—only one room deep from the entrance facade—they exhibit all the qualities of design and craftsmanship that gave Portland the appearance of a New England village. The two major types of roof design are shown: the return cornice and entablature on the Price House to the left, and the full-pedimented gable ends on the house to the extreme right in the photo. Both houses have louvered shutters on the windows and 6/6 window panes. The house on the right clearly has a three-color paint scheme: white trim, a darker body color, and most likely a dark black-green shutter color. Jefferson Street was still not paved by the turn of the century, remaining a dirt road with only the wood boards for sidewalks.

Captain John B. Price House.

James F. Bybee (1856)

One of the most outstanding houses of the Oregon Territory still standing in the Portland metropolitan area is the James F. Bybee House constructed in 1856 on Sauvie Island. Beautifully restored by the Oregon Historical Society in 1966, it exemplifies the substantial architecture of the Greek Revival style. It sits on its raised site above the island's farmlands, as a Greek temple would have sat in the landscape, making full use of the geometric volumes—simple but beautifully proportioned elevations and very much a piece of sculpture. The house has the pedimented ends, with full cornice and entablature, that define the style. The centrally planned stair hall has parlors on either side, with bedrooms above and a kitchen wing to the back of the house, adjacent to the dining room.

James F. Bybee House.

Dining room, Bybee House.

South parlor, Bybee House.

Bedroom, Bybee House.

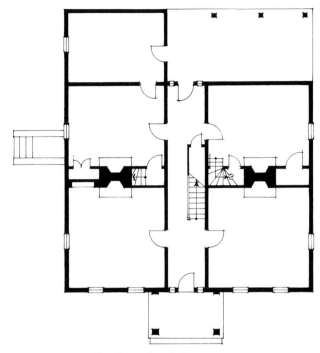

First floor plan, Bybee House.

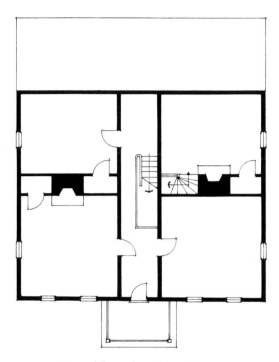

Second floor plan, Bybee House.

The interior detailing of the Bybee House is especially fine. In the south parlor, the window casing is far more sophisticated than is usually seen in a rural farmhouse. The window casing is made of built-up pieces, classic in nature, with the same dog-ear extensions at the top corners as are found in the Commanding Officers' Quarters at Fort Vancouver and the Ainsworth House at Mount Pleasant; similar to the former structure, detailed panels fit in below the windows and the casing trim. The original plaster walls and ceiling and a fine plaster cornice remain on the interior, as does the central ceiling medallion, which provided a decorative transition for a hanging lamp fixture.

Other details of note are the central-hall stair—with turned newel post and balusters, painted in this case—and the fireplace fronts. The parlor fireplace has fluted pilasters with a paneled entablature and cornice (mantel) above; the back room fireplace fronts are less sophisticated. The dining room has a vertical board wainscoting and a built-in cupboard beside the fireplace and the outside wall. The living room also has a built-in cupboard. A small winding staircase leading up from the living room provides the only access to an upstairs bedroom, which perhaps was intended to house farm help without imposing on the other bedrooms upstairs.

S. J. McCormick (c. 1858)

Similar in plan to the Bybee House on Sauvie Island, the S. J. McCormick House was built on the northwest corner of First Avenue and Columbia Street. As with the Bybee House, it had five windows across the facade

S. J. McCormick House.

and a central entrance doorway. But unlike the Bybee House, the Mc-Cormick House had a wide entrance porch, three bays across, and three doorways. One door opened to the central stair hall, and the two others entered into the front parlors on either side of the stair hall. Other differences are apparent from the 1858 lithograph of the house. It had chimneys at the pedimented gable ends of the house, instead of between each of the front parlors and the rooms behind them, as in the Bybee House. The siding was made of flush horizontal wood boards, meant to imitate stuccoed masonry. Most unusually, a solid decorative balustrade was built above the cornice along the front end of the roof, with embellished carvings on the top much like a bed headboard of the period. Finally, the pilasters at the corners of the house are much heavier than is usual for the style, with well-defined capitals, and the porch railings have crossed members, much in the Classical tradition.

Dr. James C. Hawthorne (c. 1859)

Dr. James C. Hawthorne constructed his first home in Portland shortly after his 1859 arrival in the city. The Greek Revival style house was located between Eleventh and Twelfth avenues on Hawthorne Boulevard, then on a large tract of land later subdivided by his widow and two daughters as Hawthorne Park. In the 1850s and 1860s, the acreage was mostly rural, but the house captured much of the temple-fronted theme of Greek Revival architecture, with a pedimented gable-end portico and second floor balcony. Actually, the house was almost identical to the 1847 Lownsdale House, with a side wing perpendicular to the central rectangular mass of the house. It had typical 6/6 window panes, shuttered windows, lap siding with corner boards, boxed columns, and a dentil course below the cornice. On the side wing, the gable end had return

Dr. James C. Hawthorne House.

cornices and a two-window bay, presumably looking west toward the city. In later years, a larger two-story addition was added to the back. The house remained standing until it was replaced by a much grander Italianate style home sometime before Dr. Hawthorne's untimely death in 1881.

CHAPTER 2

Gothic Revival

Although the Greek Revival style dominated the residential architecture of Portland in the 1850s, it had competition from the charming Gothic Revival style. Just as the Greek style paid homage to the origins of western civilization and the roots of democracy, the Gothic Revival style also had its historical allusions—the mystery and romance of the Middle Ages. The Gothic Revival style represented a break from what some felt was a too rigid confinement within the Classical mode. Moreover, the Classical ideal was thought inappropriate or unsuited to rural landscapes because of its rigid geometrical composition. The Gothic style, on the other hand, with its limitless possibilities of asymmetry and decorative potential, appealed to those rejecting Classicism in architecture. The Gothic clearly spoke to those embracing the values of untamed nature.

The beginnings of the break from Classical tradition can be traced in England to Sir Horace Walpole's remodeling of his country house, Strawberry Hill, which began construction in the 1750s, in the medieval style. From this start, the Gothic Revival style slowly spread, achieving considerable influence in both domestic

Portland, 1858, as shown in the Kuchel and Dresel lithograph of the city and its architecture.

and commercial building architecture during the early years of the nineteenth century. The first American to employ the style was Alexander Jackson Davis. He popularized the Gothic style in Glen Ellen, a country house he de-signed for Robert Gilmor near Baltimore in 1832. Davis's 1837 plan book, entitled *Rural Residences*, displayed not only house plans, but also attractive gardens that complemented the homes and gave them an organic feel. Andrew

53

Jackson Downing, Davis's friend and an architectural critic and writer, expanded on Davis's work, producing his own enormously influential pattern books: *Cottage Architecture* (1842) and *The Architecture of Country Houses* (1850). Downing's promotional efforts succeeded in spreading the Gothic style across America in the 1850s. Certainly, his pattern books, or the ideas they represented, were highly portable and probably arrived in Oregon with the earliest eastern settlers.

The stylistic characteristics of the Gothic Revival had all the energy and thrust of their inspirational models—the thirteenth- and fourteenth-century Gothic cathedrals of Europe. The most notable identifying feature was the steeply pitched roof (with a slope often greater than 45 degrees off the horizontal), combined with equally steep cross gables adorned with decorative bargeboards at the edge of their extension from the roof. The cross gables were often in the plane of the sides of the structure. This gable commonly featured the medieval lancet window. Almost as typical as the roof and window treatments was the main floor piazza or veranda, with its thin support columns—these columns, completely different in size and appearance from their Greek Revival counterparts, were often composite or made up of reeded members with cut-out designs between.

Other features further emphasized the medieval origins of the design. The vertical presentation often was heightened by the use of board-and-batten siding. Windows became narrower and taller, with two-over-two panes, although in Portland six-over-six panes were

Fonthill Abbey, Wiltshire, England, 1749, built for Sir Horace Walpole, designed by Richard Bentley.

Lyndhurst, Tarrytown, New York, 1832–42 and 1864–67, designed by Alexander Jackson Davis.

still in vogue. The Gothic style windows also had muntins that crossed at the top in a tracery pattern. Tudor diagonal panes could sometimes be found in combination with diagonally peaked windows. Even transoms and sidelights at the entrance doors used the diagonal panes. When the designs showed direct influence from the plates of Downing's *The Architecture of Country Houses*, pairs of windows projected out into a shallow bay, out sufficiently far enough to warrant support brackets and a separate shed roof. The use of full, one-story bay windows came into prominence, extending the interior floor out into its window perimeter. The bay often had side windows diagonally sloped, with a pair of windows on the outermost plane. Other elements that enhanced the houses' verticality involved the addition of a balustrade at the roof and the use of paneling on the wall below the windows to make them stand out from the facade.

The drip mold was used extensively at the top of windows. This feature, taken from medieval and Tudor stone architecture, served the purpose of throwing rain water cascading down the outside wall away from the head of the window. Sometimes a similar detail was used from the head of the Gothic windows, ending at about the level of the radius of the arch. When arches were too complicated to construct, or when the dictates of a large gable influenced the design, the same drip cap dropped off a central window and extended out over two small side windows. This detail often appeared on flush-sided houses, which enhanced the masonry effect.

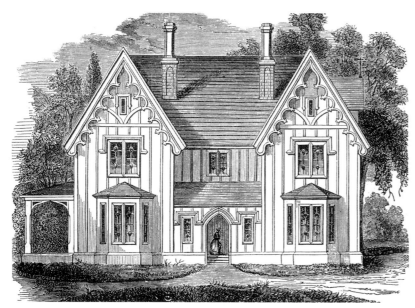

"Plain Timber Cottage Villa," from *The Architecture of Country Houses* by Andrew Jackson Downing, 1850.

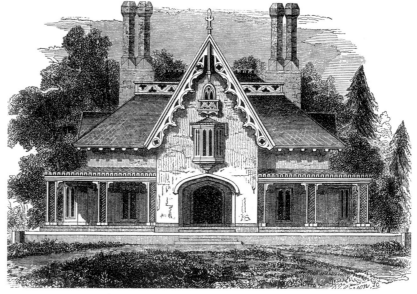

"Rural Gothic Villa," from *The Architecture of Country Houses* by Andrew Jackson Downing, 1850.

Finally, paint colors played an important role in the expression of the Gothic Revival style. Just as the great Gothic stone cathedrals conveyed a sense of permanence, so, it was felt,

FIG. 68.—A PARSONAGE.

FIG. 69.—CELLAR PLAN.

FIG. 70.—FIRST FLOOR.

FIG. 71.—SECOND FLOOR.

A Gothic Revival style design, showing floor plans, from *Woodward's Architecture and Rural Arts* by George E. Woodward, 1868.

should the more humble Gothic wooden cottage. Gone were the white-colored houses, which Downing declared "unsuitable and in bad taste." The new colors were those of nature: soft grays, browns, and muted brown-greens. The acceptable colors melded the Gothic residence with its bucolic surroundings, as poetically as the Gothic spire and church mediated between heaven and earth.

Although no Gothic Revival houses are extant in Portland, we can gain some impressions from the period illustrations and from those examples still remaining outside of the city. The Shaver House (1852) was a gray tone, emphasized by the lighter trim color. The brownish tones of the Fort Dalles Surgeon's House (1857) are an excellent example of the soft muted colors considered appropriate and fashionable on the Gothic Revival structures. The 1874 Trinity Episcopal Church Parish House in Portland represents yet another example; its coloring appears so stone-like that the structure is barely visible in photographs. Researchers uncovered much evidence for this aesthetic during the 1970s restoration of the 1882 Calvary Presbyterian Church in Portland. A dark olive-gray-brown was determined to be the original color. Tastes have changed so radically since the late nineteenth century, however, that when the re-

storers sought donors to underwrite the church's rehabilitation, including repainting, potential donors were hesitant to give money for a color they felt too dark. The church is now painted a much lighter version of the stone aesthetic.

The first houses in Portland to use elements of the Gothic Revival are known through the Kuchel and Dresel lithograph of the city, published in 1858. The lithograph displayed in the borders surrounding the general view of the city sketches of the significant dwellings and buildings of the young city. These included the T. J. Holmes, W. C. Hull, and H. C. Hoyt houses. In effect, these cottages wed the basic Greek Revival rectangular shape with roofs, porches, and trim details of the Gothic Revival. Absolom B. Hallock designed the Holmes residence, showing his mastery of both revival styles. Likewise, architect E. M. Burton was credited with designing the Gothic-inspired Trinity Episcopal Church of 1854—with its arched door and windows, vertical board-and-batten siding, and decorated bargeboard—as well as the Gothic Revival, two-story Vigilance Hook and Ladder Fire House of 1857, with its arched openings and a rose window in its upper facade. The Hull and Holmes houses showed typical roof arrangements: the former has a front gable with pendule decorations at the bargeboard, drip molds over the upper and lower floor windows, columned porch posts, and Tudor-arched detailing supporting the porch roof; the latter's roof ridge was perpendicular to the front, offering a central entrance and porch, with a facade gable and Gothic window with diagonal panes above the porch. Both houses managed to accommodate second floor windows under the low side roofs, and small windows appeared just under the eaves only a few feet above the second floor line. Since the low-pitched Greek Revival roof did not afford this possibility, the Gothic Revival style must have seemed an advantage to the modest-budgeted owner of the 1850s.

The aforementioned George W. Shaver House had the same facade gable as the Holmes House, but with curvilinear ornaments at the bargeboard. Its other decorative features seem more Greek Revival, as in the pediment at the top of the side windows and in the entrance door treatment. The porch columns are thin, however, showing a Gothic rather than Greek influence. The Shaver House thus supports the observation that, in practice, many of the early houses exhibited both Greek and Gothic Revival design features. During the 1860s and 1870s, a more refined version of the Gothic Revival style emerged.

The most prominent Portland residence in

Fort Dalles Surgeon's House, The Dalles, Oregon, 1857.

Trinity Episcopal Church, Portland, 1854, designed by E. M. Burton.

the Gothic Revival style after 1860 was the Parish House (1874) for Trinity Episcopal Church. Architect Warren H. Williams's design complemented the board-and-batten covering of the 1870s church behind it, designed by Albert H. Jordan, and the original Trinity Church to the north, designed by E. M. Burton in 1854. With a streetscape featuring mature trees and orderly picket fences, the churches and the Parish House presented a sophisticated ensemble of which early Portland could be proud.

Vigilance Hook and Ladder Fire House, Portland, circa 1857, designed by E. M. Burton.

Gothic Revival
CHARACTERISTICS

PLANS: rectangular for cottages; asymmetrical for larger houses.

ROOFS: steeply pitched, with facade dormers.

EXTERIOR FINISHES: plain and narrow corner boards; water table over joists at foundation; horizontal weatherboards, or flush horizontal tongue-and-groove boards.

CHIMNEYS: brick, corbeled.

WINDOWS: double-hung at most openings; featured lancet windows in the facade dormer; diagonal panes sometimes in lancet windows.

WINDOW TRIM (exterior): eared dripmoldings.

ENTRANCE DOORS: include transom and sidelights.

VERANDAS/PORCHES: entrance porches with thinner, often composite, columns; Tudor arches; decorative cut-out top railings.

INTERIOR FINISHES: plastered walls with a continuous plaster cornice and wood baseboards; tongue-and-groove-beaded vertical wainscoting boards in kitchen and dining room.

INTERIOR TRIM: door casings plain, with applied moldings.

STAIRS: straight run; stair railings curved at newel post and at second floor landing.

FIREPLACE FRONTS: side pilasters and low-arched top piece.

PROPERTY SURROUNDS: perimeter picket fences, sometimes with wrought-iron pickets; support posts at gates and corners.

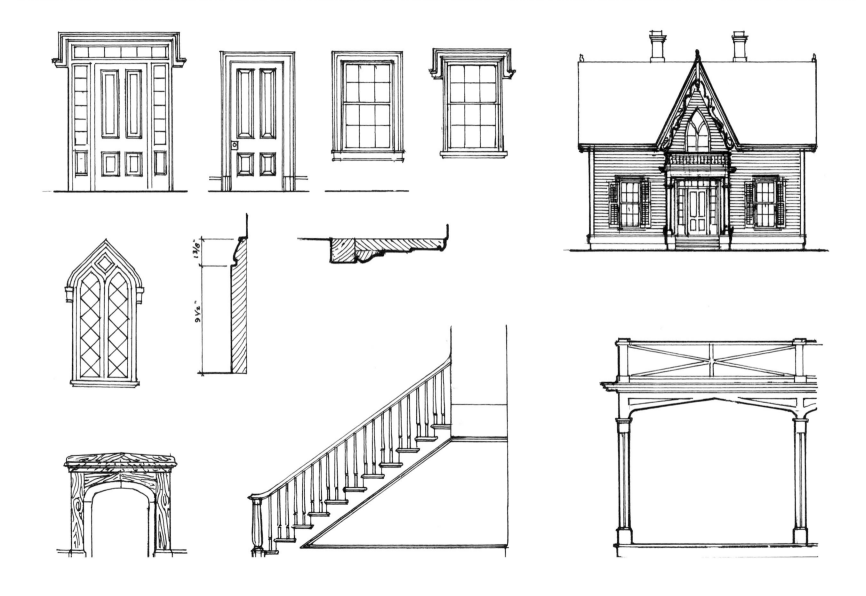

Entrance to the Francis Xavier Pacquet House.

Gothic Revival
HOUSES

1852	George W. Shaver
c. 1852	James W. Chase
1852	Francis Xavier Pacquet
1852	General Stephen Coffin (Absolom B. Hallock)
1856	Hiram Straight
1858	T. J. Holmes (Absolom B. Hallock)
c. 1858	W. C. Hull (attributed to Absolom B. Hallock)
1858	H. C. Hoyt (attributed to E. M. Burton)
c. 1859	Painter Residence
c. 1865	Harvey A. Hogue
1874	Parish House, Trinity Episcopal Church (Warren H. Williams)

George W. Shaver (1852)

The basic cottage in early Portland often utilized Gothic design elements, not only for their charm, but for certain practical features of the design. If the simple cottage had a second floor, and if it had very low walls because of the roof slope, it was called a floor-and-a-half design. This left little headroom at the short-wall side, but it could be rectified by adding a facade dormer. In the dormer could be placed a window, gaining not only useful space but additional light. The George W. Shaver House, constructed in 1852, made full use of this detail, probably adding light for the second floor hall, as well as adding access through the lancet window to the small porch over the central doorway below. With the addition of jigsaw gingerbread-cut to the bargeboard, the Shavers achieved a picturesque residence in the latest fashion.

James W. Chase (c. 1852)

The Oregon City home of James W. Chase, originally located at Seventh Avenue and Water Street, had a plan similar to that of the Shaver House. It was slightly larger, with a kitchen wing on one side. It had the same steep-roofed (very steep here) facade dormer with lancet-design casement windows, and the entablature trim under the cornice continued

George W. Shaver House.

James W. Chase House.

up the sides of the gable. The other windows had pedimented cornice trims in the Greek Revival style. Most of the original windows in the house had six-over-six (6/6) panes. The bay window to the left of the center entrance was added later (1880s), with full 1/1 panes. The entrance porch had turned balusters, and the porch columns were bracketed. Corbeled brick chimneys at the gabled sides of the house suggest that there were parlor fireplaces to the right and a kitchen and dining room to the left.

Francis Xavier Pacquet (1852)

Shipbuilder Francis Pacquet built his fine home in Canemah, just east of the Willamette Falls at Oregon City, after crossing the plains with his family in 1852. Built high on a bank at 902 S McLoughlin Boulevard (at Pacquet Street), its design was inspired by the architect Andrew Jackson Downing's pattern books of the 1840s and 1850s. The porch columns with delicate paired members are a Downing feature, as is the window above the porch. A large pair of casement windows in the middle is flanked by shorter windows on either side. The eared drip-molding follows the dropped side windows, although the drip mold is treated in a more usual manner at the main floor. An original Gothic style entrance door, perhaps the only one of its kind surviving, is presently removed from the house. The 6/6 double-hung windows at the sides of the house have low wood pediments over them. The only other remnants of Greek Revival detailing are the eave returns, abstracted in this case to mimic the horizontal boards carried around from the sides of the house. Although the house is small and modest, it adds great character to the town of Canemah.

Francis Xavier Pacquet House.

General Stephen Coffin (1852)
Absolom B. Hallock

An elaborate example of a Gothic Revival house was the Portland residence of pioneer Stephen Coffin. Coffin had settled first in Oregon City in 1847 and then moved to Portland. His was one of the first houses recorded in the city by Portland's acknowledged first architect, Absolom B. Hallock. In his well-kept journals Hallock wrote, "Leased from Stephen Coffin for six months from October Fourth in exchange for small house." The house was designed in the picturesque Gothic style,

General Stephen Coffin House.

with steep roofs, lancet windows, a balcony, a bay window (probably added in the 1870s), porches, and an extensively landscaped garden. Across the front walkway was an ivy-covered archway, perhaps framing the view of Mount Hood from the bay window in the parlor, looking directly east.

In about 1864, Richard B. Knapp purchased the property and made various improvements. It is Knapp, in top hat, who sits proudly in the family buggy in the photograph. Knapp prospered in Portland and later was to build the famous Queen Anne style Knapp House in 1882.

Hiram Straight (1856)

The restored Hiram Straight House of 1856 in Oregon City expresses many features of both the Gothic and Greek Revival styles. The plan is asymmetrical, with intersecting rectangles. In the wing to the left, one roof wide, is the main entrance hall, accessed by a covered porch. The parlor, in the central portion of the house, which is two rooms deep, has its own porch on the entrance side. While the roof is steeply pitched in Gothic fashion, the windows of 9/9 panes are more typical of the Greek Revival designs. The house was well built, to this day having a good stone foundation. Original interior details remain in the well-designed

Hiram Straight House.

stair to the second floor, with an excellent turned newel post and balusters. The restored exterior colors of the house, white with green trim, represent the original scheme.

T. J. Holmes (1858)
Absolom B. Hallock

Another cottage designed by architect Absolom B. Hallock was the T. J. Holmes House. It was similar to the 1852 Shaver House in plan and features, but in addition it had low windows under the eaves. These win-

T. J. Holmes House.

dows gave added light to the upstairs bedrooms even though they were just off the floor. The facade dormer lancet window, however, gave considerable light to the second floor hall. The lancet window had diagonal panes, imitating leaded Tudor designs, and its window arch was trimmed with an imitation-stone eared drip-molding, as were the 6/6 double-hung windows of the main floor. To add to the impression of a stone dwelling, the siding was made out of horizontal tongue-and-groove flush siding, the same as was seen in the McCormick House of the same year.

The house was illustrated in the 1858 Kuchel and Dresel lithograph, which also showed the Hallock and McMillen Building of 1857, Portland's oldest standing commercial structure. T. J. Holmes served as Mayor of Portland in 1866 and 1867.

W. C. Hull (c. 1858)
Absolom B. Hallock (attributed)

The W. C. Hull House of circa 1858 is a good example of the gable-fronted house. Only about sixteen feet wide, including a small parlor and the stair hall, it was a small cottage indeed. In such a small house, the low-eaved roof made for a less convenient plan upstairs, as the stair would come up to the second floor and confront a head-height problem. The facade of the house was quite attractive, however, with its Gothic and Tudor detailing. Bargeboards at the gable ends were decorated with considerable cut-out designs, and the windows were headed with eared drip-moldings at both the first and second floors. As in the Coffin House, the porches had the low Tudor arches so often used in Gothic Revival houses. With so many details similar to those found in the houses of Absolom B. Hallock, this house's design is attributed to him.

W. C. Hull House.

H. C. Hoyt (1858)
E. M. Burton (attributed)

The H. C. Hoyt House, originally located on the northwest corner of Broadway and Alder Street, exemplifies a departure from the current Greek and Gothic Revivals. It heralds, instead, the beginnings of the Italian Villa style in Portland. The plan was asymmetrical (a T shape and side addition), with a side entrance under a covered porch to the right. A polygonal bay, perhaps the first in the city, emphasized the parlor room, with the rounded tall bedroom window above it. The house had a definite vertical element in its design, especially with the elongated windows of the main and second floors. It is possible that this house was designed by architect E. M. Burton, whose own home between Stark and Washington streets on Fourth Avenue had similar design features and vertical emphasis.

H. C. Hoyt House.

Painter (c. 1859)

The small town of Canemah near Oregon City still retains several architectural jewels from the 1850s and 1860s. The Painter House, built around 1859, featured in its prime a highly decorated gingerbread bargeboard and eave. A fine central entrance porch, accessed by a steep flight of stairs, had trimmed columns and a fine pierced balustrade rail above. More typical of the Greek Revival style were the windows and doors. The 6/6 double-hung windows had low pediments over them, and the main entrance door had a transom and sidelights.

Despite the fact that the house has been drastically altered over the years, it could be a primary landmark in the Canemah Historic District if restored to its original appearance.

Harvey A. Hogue (c. 1865)

Stylistically, the Hogue House of circa 1865 combines Gothic Revival designs with those of the Italian Villa. The last remaining vestige of the Gothic Revival style is the steeply pitched facade gable with lancet window, much like that on the T. J. Holmes House of 1858. However, all the proportions have been heightened in the Hogue House. The rooms have higher ceilings, and with them taller windows with 4/4 panes. Even the loggia, in the Italian Villa style, has more vertical than horizontal proportions. In addition, the house offers an early example of a polygonal bay window, which projects from the first floor parlor on the north side of the house. In plan, the house repeats what was standard for a smaller

Painter House.

Harvey A. Hogue House.

home: a central entrance and stair hall, rooms to either side, each with fireplaces adjacent to the hall, and a small kitchen wing in the rear.

Parish House
Trinity Episcopal Church (1874)
Warren H. Williams

The most outstanding Gothic Revival house in Portland was that constructed by the Episcopal Church on a site immediately east of the Church building at the northwest corner of Fifth Avenue and Oak Street and to the immediate south of the original Trinity Episcopal Church of 1854, which is attributed to Absolom B. Hallock. The new Parish House

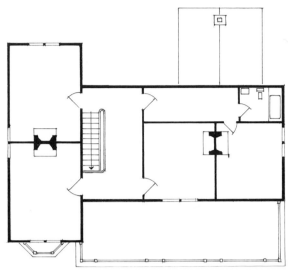

Second floor plan, Parish House.

Parish House, Trinity Episcopal Church.

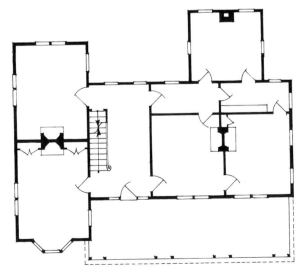

First floor plan, Parish House.

was the home of Reverend Alexander A. Morrison and his family, and it was designed by architect Warren H. Williams, who had arrived from San Francisco after the disastrous fires of 1872 and 1873. Williams was then in practice with E. M. Burton, who was well established at the time.

The Parish House was a much larger dwelling than any others in the city constructed with Gothic Revival detailing. As a neighbor to the Gothic Trinity Episcopal Church—designed by A. H. Jordan in 1872 and completed in 1873—the combination presented a most handsome architectural composition in the city. Williams used the same basic Gothic idioms of steeply pitched roofs, gabled dormers, and decorated bargeboards, in addition to the more domestically scaled entrance porch and the polygonal parlor bay. Chimneys were in the Andrew Jackson Downing mold, medieval in their basic forms.

In plan, the house was basically T shaped, with the addition of a kitchen wing. The two gables dominated the entrance facade. Entrance was gained from Fifth Avenue, under the welcoming porch at the intersection of the two major wings. The elaborate entrance porch featured paired columns with Tudor arches between, all constructed with thin wood members. The parlors, or reception rooms, were to the left, and the family living room and dining room to the right, with the kitchen wing adjacent to the dining room. The house was one-and-a-half stories, due to the low eaves.

PART II

Renaissance and Baroque Revivals
1860s–1880s

IN THE 1870s and 1880s, Portland experienced a period of remarkable growth. The metropolitan population increased from just shy of 8,300 to over 59,000 in the twenty-year period from 1870 to 1890. With the arrival of the transcontinental railroad in 1883 and the creation of an improved ship channel for ever-larger ocean-going vessels, Portland established itself as the commercial and trading center of the Pacific Northwest. At the time that the Army Corps of Engineers opened an office in Portland in 1871, numerous river bars, rocks, and other obstructions proved serious obstacles to the development of Portland's ocean-bound trade. By 1875, however, the Army Engineers had established a 17-foot-deep safe water channel, which supported almost 185,000 tons of traffic, chiefly carrying wheat and lumber. In the 1890s, the Corps increased the ship channel's depth to 23 feet, and total tonnage averaged over 1.4 million tons during that decade. The continued improvement of navigation on the Columbia and Willamette rivers in the late nineteenth century allowed for vast quantities of wheat and other agricultural products to pour into Portland from the hinterlands for trans-shipment overseas.

The steadily expanding foreign trade combined with banking and commercial activity, designed to supply the interior of the region, made Portland a rich little city. As buildings of brick, stone, and cast-iron fronts replaced wooden-frame structures, the business district of Portland took on an atmosphere of bustling sophistication. Fires in 1872 and 1873 hastened the process of transformation. The city's prosperous merchant elite also reflected this growing sophistication in their residences. Just as the expanding business district took on the look of Florentine palaces, the homes of the newly rich took life in the shape of evermore elaborate examples of the Italian Villa style. Neighborhoods with elm-lined streets and substantial houses with spacious yards began to grace the city. It was during this era that the term "city of homes" came into vogue, and the town's most fashionable residential district, known as Nob Hill, emerged. The district centered on NW Nineteenth Avenue, sporting villas, chateaus and castles, and examples of the new Queen Anne style, reflecting, in the words of Harvey Scott, editor of *The Oregonian*, a place of "substantial comfort and tasteful display."

By the late 1880s, Portland underwent a major economic boom. The founding of ten banks and two insurance companies in the city between 1885 and 1891 reflected this commercial renaissance, as did the awarding of twenty-four separate street-railway franchises, the organization of two electrical utilities, and the establishment of the Port of Portland in 1891. In 1889 alone, investors and homeowners poured over $54 million into residential and commercial construction. The bridging of the Willamette River in 1887 laid the foundation for urban growth on the east side of the river. The following year, a second bridge spanning the Willamette was built, and by 1889, electric trolleys were crossing the river. Soon, public transit lines served all parts of the expanding city and encouraged the growth of newer subdivisions on the city's margins. Portland's boom, however, came to a crashing halt with the Depression of 1893. This sharp economic contraction stalled the city's growth until renewed activity, stirred in part by the Klondike Gold Strike of 1898, occurred at the turn of the century.

While Portland thrived economically during the last quarter of the nineteenth century, it also became more cosmopolitan. As early as 1890, foreign-born people accounted for 37 percent of the city's population. A steady influx of Asian and ethnic European immigrants added diversity to the heavily Protestant New England and midwestern cast of the Rose City. Chinese and Japanese immigrants, Jews, Italians, African-Americans, and Scandinavians constituted the chief elements of this ethnic mix. They created the foundations for a modern urban center, with diverse lifestyles and cultures.

CHAPTER 3

Italian Villa

As one historian has noted, residential Portland was to undergo another transformation during the decade of the 1860s.

> The classical cottages, those shanty temples of the wilderness, gradually gave way to more impressive structures—the towered, gabled Gothic and four-square, bay-windowed "mansions" of the Italian Villa style. Elm-lined streets and somber, substantial houses set in spacious gardens—proper Portland was beginning to create its domestic habitat.

As interest waned in the Greek and Gothic Revivals, a new freedom developed in American residential architecture, one phase of which was the Italian Villa style. The new freedoms had actually begun simultaneously in the Gothic style, which had introduced asymmetrical, if not Romanic, plans. The functions of the rooms were more clearly delineated in the picturesque arrangements, but their practical relationships were actually of paramount concern. As houses broke away from the rectangular form of the Greek Revival, major rooms could have light and air available on three sides,

Portland, circa 1870s.

71

and their arrangements with interior stairs of-fered endless variety. The national trends were, of course, developed long before their influences reached Portland. Great wealth had hardly begun to affect Portland house designs in the early 1860s. Houses remained relatively simple, if not rectilinear, in plan until the passing of the Civil War. The evolution of style passed easily from the first phase of the new movement toward Renaissance and Baroque modes, the Italian Villa style through to the Second Empire and Italianate styles, beginning in 1860 and lasting just over twenty years.

The interest in Italian architecture, particularly the asymmetrical country villas of the Italian countryside, began as early as the 1830s. Several books widely read by American architects began to influence their designs. John Claudius Loudon (1773–1843) was editor for three influential journals in England: *The Gardener's Magazine*, *The Magazine of Natural History*, and *The Architectural Magazine*, published during the 1820s and 1830s. His most influential work was the book entitled *An Encyclopaedia of Cottage, Farm, and Villa Architecture* (London, 1833). In the book, cottages and villas were separately defined. Villas were more than utilitarian, as a cottage might be; they implied "the gratifications resulting from the display of wealth and taste." Hence villas, though they might not be large, were specially considered, and undoubtedly would have "the taste and judgement of others involved," especially the assistance of a trained practitioner or architect.

The first villas to appear in the United States were on the eastern seaboard. Richard Upjohn

A "Villa in the Italian Style," from *The Architecture of Country Houses* by Andrew Jackson Downing, 1850.

Italian Villa design, from *An Encyclopaedia of Cottage, Farm, and Villa Architecture* by J. C. Loudon, 1842.

designed an Italian style villa in Newport, Rhode Island, for Edward King in 1845 that displayed many of the early characteristics. The house had square corner towers of various heights, suggesting the Italian farmhouses and villas constructed on the ruins of ancient towered fortifications. The towers on the King House were separated by the arched openings of recessed and added loggias. Roofs were hipped over the towers and gabled on the projecting wings, all with widely extended bracketed eaves. Arched windows were featured, some with pedimented hoods and often grouped. Small cantilevered balconies were often constructed under the windows, and in some cases they were covered.

Another early example of an Italian Villa style house appeared in Andrew Jackson Downing's *The Architecture of Country Houses* (1850). A single Tuscan tower, or campanile, is balanced in an asymmetrical arrangement against two perpendicular side wings. The villa also included arched openings, loggias, or verandas attached to the house and a combination of low-hipped roofs and gable ends with bracketed and extended eaves. Downing was also suggesting Gothic and Norman style villas, some of which had turreted towers and steeper pitches, but all had asymmetrical plans and elevations. Alexander Jackson Davis often was the architect of these country villas, and his romantic illustrations were also instrumental in the promotion of the Italian Villa style. The Downing publications continued after his death in 1852, throughout the early settlement period in Oregon and well through the Civil War. It is undoubtedly these books that influenced the first Portland houses with Italian Villa characteristics.

Portland Italian Villa style houses were modest in the beginning. One of the first houses to show definite signs of the style was the James B. Stephens House (c. 1864). The house's most notable feature was its roof-top belvedere, clearly reminiscent of the Italian-influenced

Another Italian Villa from J. C. Loudon's *An Encyclopaedia of Cottage, Farm, and Villa Architecture*, 1842.

originals. (As examples, the Villa Lante, designed by Giulio Romano in 1518–20 in Bagnaia, and the Villa Lenbach, designed by Gabriel von Seidl in 1887 in Munich, show the long span of interest in the cupola.) The plan of the Stephens House, however, continued the central-entrance scheme favored in the Greek Revival style house. The more expansive and costly Captain J. C. Ainsworth House of 1862, on the other hand, had an asymmetrical plan, an arched front loggia, the paired windows advocated by Davis, and a cupola at the low-pitched roof. This general concept continued in a number of smaller houses. Typically, they had flat or low-pitched roofs, with or without cupolas, and wide eaves supported by paired brackets.

The other roof form of the Italian Villa style was the gable-ended house. In 1864, the first house in Portland with this roof form was constructed for Dr. J. A. Chapman. The Chapman House also had widely extended eaves supported by paired brackets, giving a cap-like appearance to the roof. Besides the new roof style, the Chapman House also introduced one of the first single-story polygonal bay windows in the city. A number of smaller houses were constructed with these characteristics, though only

An Italian Villa style design, from *Holly's Country Seats* by Henry Hudson Holly, 1860.

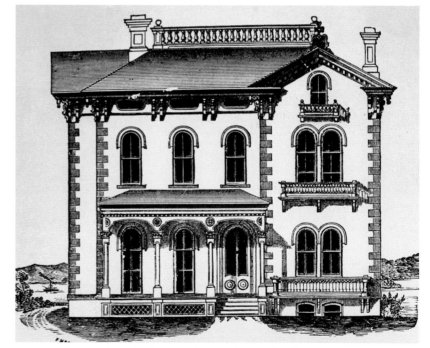

"Design of a Suburban Residence," from Bicknell and Comstock's *Specimen Book of One-Hundred Architectural Designs*, 1880.

a handful remain. Most were beautifully detailed and are a pleasure to observe even today. In them we see that windows had become longer and more elegant, and they usually were hooded or had small projecting cornices. The wood siding often imitated stone to some extent, adding quoins at the corners to suggest their Italian masonry precedents. Another elegant touch was the paired entrance doors, often with glass that gave needed light to the entrance halls, although transom windows continued with the change in styles. The Italian Villa style in turn developed into the much more flamboyant Second Empire style, which did maintain some of the features of the earlier movement.

Villa Lante, Bagnaia, Italy, 1518–20, designed by architect Giulio Romano.

Italian Villa
CHARACTERISTICS

PLANS: asymmetrical or symmetrical in L or T shapes.

ROOFS: low-pitched hipped, gabled, or flat; wide over-hanging eaves with paired brackets.

EXTERIOR FINISHES: flush horizontal tongue-and-groove siding; wide rusticated boards; lap or drop siding; plain, paneled, or quoined corner trim.

CHIMNEYS: brick; corbeled caps; interior locations.

WINDOWS: tall, double-hung; four-over-four (4/4) or one-over-one (1/1) panes; top window often with segmental, round arches; paired in major rooms, or groups of four at single-story polygonal bays; stacked in series for conservatories.

WINDOW TRIM (exterior): corniced, with plain side-casings; weather blinds or shutters.

ENTRANCE DOORS: single or double doors, with transom and/or sidelights.

Verandas/porches: two-column porches, or three- to four-column verandas.

INTERIOR FINISHES: plaster walls; coved plaster cornice.

INTERIOR TRIM: molded wrap-around wood casings on doors and windows; plain base-boards with cap molding.

STAIRS: primarily straight run, with curved bends; turned newels and balusters.

FIREPLACE FRONTS: marble surrounds and mantels.

PROPERTY SURROUNDS: perimeter picket fences, with boxed and finialed support posts at gates and corners.

Entrance to the Governor George L. Curry House.

Italian Villa
HOUSES

c. 1862	Josiah Failing	c. 1865	William J. Van Schuyver
1862	Captain J. C. Ainsworth (Absolom B. Hallock)	c. 1865	Governor George L. Curry
		1865	J. Duthie
c. 1864	James B. Stephens	1866	John Sheffield
c. 1864	Frank Dekum	c. 1870	Ben Holladay (attributed to Albert H. Jordan)
1864	Dr. J. A. Chapman (attributed to William W. Piper and E. M. Burton)		
c. 1865	James F. Failing	1873	William Wadhams (E. M. Burton)
		c. 1875	Captain Charles Holman

Josiah Failing (c. 1862)

Josiah Failing located his new home at the edge of town, between Fourth and Fifth avenues on the south side of Yamhill Street, and faced the house to the north. To the extreme left in the background of the photograph is the Second Empire style Henry Failing House, constructed and photographed approximately ten years after the Josiah Failing House was built. The Josiah Failing House, though modest, was well designed in the new Italian Villa style, with tidy 2/2 panes in the windows—available in the city for the first time in the early 1860s—and a box-columned single-bay entrance porch. The house was shorn of extraneous detail, having plain corner-board trim, dentils only at the entablature under the projecting cornice, and a flat roof. Smaller houses retained the rectilinear plan of the earlier Greek Revival style, this one with a typical side entrance to the left and parlor to the right, similar to (though in reverse) the Henry W. Corbett House (1854), which was located on the block immediately west of this house. In both houses, a parlor fireplace chimney was located at the side of the house, and a two-story kitchen wing was behind the main volume of the home.

Josiah Failing House.

Captain J. C. Ainsworth (1862)
Absolom B. Hallock

When the Ainsworths moved from their Mount Pleasant home (1850) outside Oregon City to Portland in 1862, they moved into an Italian Villa style home located on Third Avenue between Pine and Ash streets. Designed by architect Absolom B. Hallock, the house was asymmetrical in plan, and it boasted what was possibly the first tall, round-topped, paired windows in the city. The round-arch theme was carried out to the bracketed three-bay entrance porch and the rounded windows of the fashionable belvedere on the flat roof.

Sometime in the 1870s, after Captain Ainsworth had remarried for a third time, large additions were made to the house, including an extensive four-story wing to the right of the original structure and a third floor atop the mansard roof. In this house were born an additional six children to the Ainsworths, and they lived in the house until the Captain retired to Oakland, California, in 1880. The large house was used by the Arlington Club for some years, moved to Fourth and Pine in 1891, and eventually was demolished. The original property now houses the Embassy Suites Hotel in the old Multnomah Hotel building.

Captain J. C. Ainsworth House, from an 1865 Portland Panorama.

James B. Stephens House.

James B. Stephens (c. 1864)

The second-oldest extant house in Portland (after the Socrates Tryon House of 1850) is the James B. Stephens House, constructed around 1864 on the east bank of the Willamette River near present-day Stephens Street. Moved to the northwest corner of SE Twelfth Avenue and Stephens after the turn of the century, it still retains many of its original Italian Villa style features: the extended cornice with paired brackets, paneled corner boards, corniced window trim, and a typical entrance-door frame with transom and sidelights. When originally constructed, it featured a prominent belvedere, centered on the low-hipped shingle roof. Two brick chimneys, now gone, were centered between the front and back rooms on each side of the central stair hall. Missing today is the original entrance porch and the 6/6 double-hung windows, now altered to 1/1. Classically styled turned balusters were used at the front porch, its roof balcony, and around the viewing platform of the belvedere. The inside retains some original features, such as original doors and trim, baseboards and plaster cornices, newell post, and turned railing balusters.

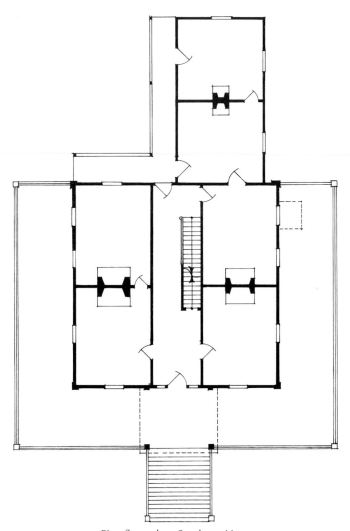

First floor plan, Stephens House.

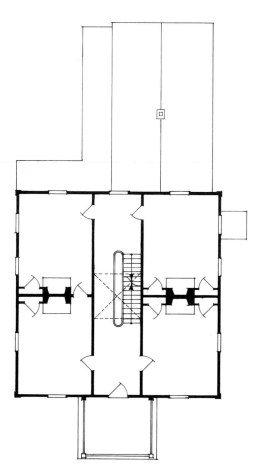

Second floor plan, Stephens House.

Frank Dekum (c. 1864)

By the mid-1860s, Portland houses had become considerably larger and more extensively embellished. In about 1864, when most homes were designed with T-shaped plans, Frank Dekum constructed a three-story house well outside the city, on the block defined by Thirteenth and Fourteenth avenues and Morrison and Yamhill streets. In plan and style, the Dekum House was very similar to the 1862 Ainsworth House, except for the small, square third floor windows, partially concealed within the paired brackets of the extended cornice. The exterior wall surfaces were more detailed than those of the Ainsworth House, with staggered quoins

Frank Dekum House.

at the house's corners and horizontal rustication created by leaving a reveal at the top of each horizontal siding board. These reveals, an elegant detail, all lined up with the joint lines of the quoins, as they would have been in masonry construction. Other details included the three-bay entrance porch, the segmental-arched windows, each with its own cornice above, and a conservatory (or what could be termed a sun room today) located on the south side of the house. The featured room would be found on numerous fine homes in the following decades.

Dr. J. A. Chapman (1864)
William W. Piper and E. M. Burton (attributed)

Located at the southwest corner of Front and Market streets, the Chapman House presented, when constructed in 1864, one of the grander houses in the city. Prominent in the design were the Italian Villa features of a widely extended roof supported by paired wooden brackets, the three-bayed entrance porch, quoined corners (with even sides), and rusticated horizontal siding. The most striking feature of the house was its gable ends, formed by the moderately pitched roof rising from several feet above the attic side walls. Because each wing was relatively narrow, say only the width of a single room, and the ceilings tall, the house had the appearance of a much larger structure. In addition, the windows were tall and narrow, with Gothic-inspired tops and cornices, all design devices to further enhance the size of the structure.

In actual size, the plan was similar to that of the Dekum House. Typically, the T-shaped plan had a front room (probably the doctor's office in this case) and hall at the facade gable, with the hall extending through the front and side wings and providing access to the parlor, sitting room, and dining room and kitchen in the rear wing. The entrance hall and sit-

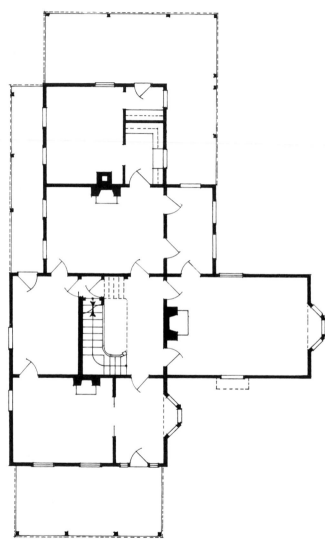

First floor plan, Chapman House.

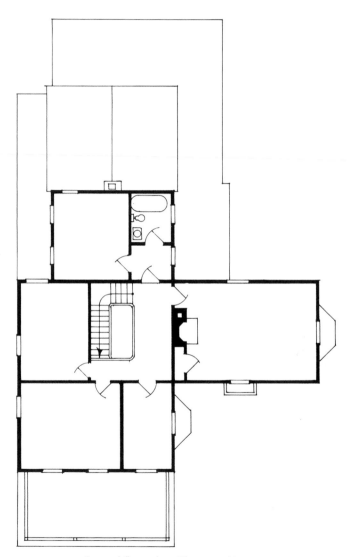

Second floor plan, Chapman House.

Dr. J. A. Chapman House.

James F. Failing (c. 1865)

The James Failing House of circa 1865, originally located at the southwest corner of Eleventh Avenue and Main Street, was typical in plan and appearance for houses with the symmetrical central-hall design. For practical as well as economic construction, it was the favored plan and was used countless times for homes, though now nearly completely vanished by the expanding city. The Failing House was particularly well designed, though not lavish in detail. The entrance portico was supported by groupings of three columns at each outside corner, with seg-

ting room had polygonal bays projecting on the north side of the house. Small balconies, in the tradition of the Downing country villa, extended from second floor windows, their railings matching the front veranda roof balustrade.

The house's location was directly in the path of the expanding commercial core of the city, necessitating its move to another property and its eventual demolition in the 1940s when Front Avenue was improved.

James F. Failing House.

Entrance hall, Failing House.

mental arch cut-outs between them. The portico roof was decorated with intertwining circles, the same design as in the balustrades over the one-story polygonal bays. Surfaces were simply treated: flush horizontal tongue-and-groove siding with plain corner boards. The roof cornice had evenly spaced brackets above the paneled entablature and dentils, capping the flat-roofed composition. Unusual were the front windows, grouped in pairs, much like those in the Ainsworth House. Such grouping admitted considerably more light to interior rooms, but offered some confusion in how to arrange the shutters between the two windows.

Parlor, Failing House.

One-over-one window panes were used in both commercial and residential buildings at the time, when the client could afford the larger sized panes.

Rare photographs of the interior of the Failing House reveal the typical characteristics of the 1860s Italian Villa style home. The entrance had magnificent paired doors with elaborate marquetry decorations. These were possibly the interior vestibule doors, which would not receive the heavy weather. The entry hall had a circular stair, a fine newel post, not turned in this case, and a frescoed ceiling. Large paintings lined the curved wall of the stair, with a recessed niche at the curve of the stair for sculpture. Floors were carpeted, with the patterned border cleverly running up the treads and raisers of the stair. The hall was lit by a rectangular pendent ceiling light, gas lit. The parlor, decorated for a family wedding in the photograph, was more elaborate. Its cornice, one of the largest to date, had a handsome acroterion design stencil immediately below the plasterwork. Stencils decorated the ceiling plaster, and a highly patterned carpet covered the floor. As was appropriate for an Italian Villa style parlor, the matching set of furniture was in the Rococo Revival style, with walnut or rosewood frames and tufted damask upholstery. Well-to-do owners bought considerable artwork to further embellish the interiors, such as marble statuary on pedestals, large-scaled paintings, both on the walls and on stands, and numerous objets on every horizontal surface.

William J. Van Schuyver (c. 1865)

A photographic portrait in front of the family home became a traditional way to record a special moment in time. Not unusually, the son's favorite horse was tethered to the curb trees, and his siblings posed on the

William J. Van Schuyver.

porch steps and on the lawn, behind the protective confines of the handsome picket fence, which was adorned with handsome posts topped with finials. It pictured an age, reflecting the dignity of the Italian Villa city of Portland, with rows and rows of attractive, well-constructed and detailed houses.

The William J. Van Schuyver House was located at the intersection of Twelfth Avenue and Washington Street, on the northwest corner. Its date of construction is estimated as 1865, the year Van Schuyver married. The house had a T-shaped plan, with entrance hall and front parlor in the facade wing. The drawing room, facing south, had a polygonal bay window. The Italian Villa features included the tall, 1/1-paned, shuttered windows, the vine-covered entrance porch, and the bracketed roof cornice.

Governor George L. Curry (c. 1865)

When George Curry, the former Territorial Governor, moved from Oregon City to Portland, he constructed a small, but rather elegant, Italian Villa style home on the outskirts of the city, still partially defined by pastures with rail fences. The house's single rectangular volume, which remained through the 1870s, had a flat roof defined by a double-bracketed cornice and paneled entablature. The fine single-bay entrance porch or portico had details similar to, but smaller than, those of the James Failing House. Its boxed columns and bracketed cornice were photographed by Minor White in the 1930s, when they still appeared in pristine condition. Handsomely detailed were the 4/4 segmental-arched windows, one on each side of the entrance portico. The double entrance doors,

with transom, opened to a central-hall plan, with parlors on either side and kitchen and dining room in the back. Later additions to the house enlarged the plan. In 1954, when the Stadium Freeway was constructed, the house was moved by Mr. and Mrs. James A. Powers to its present location on SW Cheltenham Court, thoroughly restored and renovated.

J. Duthie (1865)

Another example of the smaller Italian Villa style house is the extant Duthie House, located on its original site at 1728 SE Belmont Street. The width of the house is the combination of a single room and an entrance stair hall beside it, the hall giving access to the dining room and kitchen in the rear. The street facade, facing north, has a front gable with a sim-

Governor George L. Curry House.

J. Duthie House.

ple bracketed cornice. There are three tall, corniced windows, evenly spaced, with 4/4 panes, and shuttered. The lower floor has a three-bay entrance loggia, with an entrance door on the east side. Boxed columns with cut-out wood brackets, very similar to those on the Curry House, support the loggia roof. What makes this house special is the drop siding that covers the house, with staggered quoins at the corners. Quoins, imitating stonework, were much more expensive than simple corner boards, requiring a finish carpenter and much fitting, but the decorative effect was great, adding considerably to the quality of appearance.

John Sheffield (1866)

The Italian Villa style spread rapidly within and without Portland. By 1866, when John Sheffield constructed his farmhouse at what is now the southwest corner of SE Forty-third Avenue and Washington Street, major stock details of the style were available from local suppliers to enhance the appearance of any house. The tall windows, with 4/4 panes, were standard, as were the cornice brackets for the extended roof and the stock entrance doors with transom lights. These few features, along with the by-now standard drop siding, could give a house, even a modest one, an elegant appearance and a distinctive air. The Sheffield House had much of the character of the considerably larger Chapman House of 1864, due to the similar nature of the architectural details and the T-shaped plan. Today the house is one of the very few remaining in the city displaying Italian Villa characteristics and is among the oldest extant residences in all of metropolitan Portland. It has been carefully restored by its present owners, Donald and Patricia McAllister, which should give it a new lease on life well into the twenty-first century.

John Sheffield House.

Ben Holladay (c. 1870)
Albert H. Jordan (attributed)

Ben Holladay, at the height of his railroad building fame and before his ultimate disgrace, lived in this unusually designed Italian Villa house. It bears little resemblance to other houses constructed in Portland during the 1860s and 1870s, and it may have been designed by Albert H. Jordan while he worked in Portland. The house had many similarities with a variant of Italian Villa style houses along the eastern seaboard from Maine to New Orleans, notably the unusually wide extension of the roof

Ben Holladay House.

William Wadhams (1873)
E. M. Burton

The architectural work of E. M. Burton records only a few houses, although his biography states that he designed "a large number of the finest residences in the city." The William Wadhams House of 1873 was one of those houses. In many ways it represents the hundreds of middle-class homes constructed in the 1870s, having the excellent design qualities that gave Portland its well-heralded architectural reputation. The Italian Villa characteristics of the house included the T-shaped plan, the paired-bracketed cornice, the tall, segmental-arched windows with shutters, and the sitting room's rectangular bay windows. The house sat

cornice and the boxed, almost Moorish, front loggia columns. The capitals of the columns had curved solid brackets, and the loggia roof railing had pierced decorations, also Moorish in character, seemingly cut from a single board nearly two feet wide. However, the house had the more usual T design, and the tall, shuttered, 4/4 windows had segmental-arched tops, above which were horizontal cornices. The siding was flush tongue-and-groove boards, framed by wide-paneled corner boards. Similarly, the picket fence surrounding the property had paneled posts with finials.

William Wadhams House.

high on the property after the public street improvements carved the street to a lower and more practical level. The bank was supported by a stone wall with a decorative cast-iron railing. Street trees were planted in the strip between the curb and the sidewalk.

Captain Charles Holman (c. 1875)

The last house designed in the Italian Villa style in Portland was the Captain Charles Holman House, constructed in about 1875 on the southwest corner of Twelfth Avenue and Salmon Street, where the First Unitarian Church is now located. Similar in plan to the James F. Failing

House, but wider across its facade, it also had paired windows. The paired center windows had rounded tops, topped by a horizontal cornice. All windows were 1/1. To maintain the vertical emphasis of the Italian Villa style, a central bay, running the full width of the entrance hall, projected out from the main facade. On the north facade was a full two-story polygonal bay, providing welcome light for the parlor on the first floor and the bedroom above. The three-bay entrance porch, at the same height as the belt cornice of the polygonal bay, had brackets to match the bay and had turned balusters at the porch and roof levels. The boxed columns had small brackets.

The interior photograph, possibly taken in the late 1880s, shows the

Captain Charles Holman House.

Interior, Holman House.

north parlor, with the bay windows on the right. The parlor is the full depth of the house, with a round-arched marble fireplace on the end wall. Other architectural finishes are subdued compared to those of the grander houses. The walls are plain, with a decorative band of wallpaper just below the plaster cornice. Wallpaper is also used on the ceiling as a perimeter decoration, and the floors are covered with an elaborately patterned Wilton carpet. The most elaborate decorative piece, however, is the gilt overmantel mirror, with fanciful cresting and side columns.

These were often installed as an integral part of the fireplace, along with the mantel, but many have been saved and now adorn other Portland homes. The furnishings shown in the room are not grand: a bent-wood rocker, an Eastlake-design rocking chair and table, and an upright piano. Large prints in simple black frames decorate the walls, and the number of objects are restrained to only a few on each horizontal surface. This was a typically furnished interior, not overly elaborate, but comfortable

CHAPTER 4

Second Empire

In 1851, Charles Louis Napoleon, son of Louis Bonaparte, King of Holland, re-established the empire established and lost by his uncle Napoleon Bonaparte, and he took the imperial title Napoleon III. Upon his marriage to Eugénie Marie de Montijo, Countess de Teba, fashionable tastes in Europe as well as the United States closely followed the life and times of the Emperor and Empress. During the early period of their reign, there was a rekindling of interest in the major monuments of France. The Chateau de Versailles was restored as a national shrine, as were numerous Romanesque and Gothic monuments. Leading the crusade for restoration was the writer Prosper Merimee and two young architects, J. Lassus and Eugène Viollet-le-Duc. A pivotal rebuilding of the Paris Hotel de Ville (1837–49) was followed closely and with considerable admiration. The major additions to the building by architects E. H. Godde and J. B. Lesueur were in the early Renaissance style, sympathetic with the original building, and had impressive mansard roofs. (The roofs are distinguished by two sets of rafters, with the lower roof slope more inclined than the upper slope.) The distinguishing roof

Portland, at Sixth Avenue and Yamhill Street, circa 1878.

shape, named after its inventor, seventeenth-century architect François Mansart (1598–1666), was to become immensely popular in the many significant restoration and construction projects in Paris at the time. One major undertaking was the additions to the Palais du Louvre (1850–57), completed by architect Visconti. Huge wings were added to the Palais at the north and south ends of the Place Louis-Napoléon, an idea conceived of by Napoleon III to connect the Louvre with the Palais des Tuileries. (Unfortunately, the ancient Tuileries Palace was destroyed by a Communist uprising in 1871, leading to construction of the Nouveau Louvre.) The projects included corner pavilions, such as the Pavillons Richelieu and Turgot. Their handsome designs set the stage for broad acceptance of the Second Empire style, as it became popularly known. Additional refaced pavilions and wings by H. M. Lefuel during the 1870s, as well as other extensive improvements, made the Palais du Louvre one of the most admired buildings in Europe and the world over.

The admiration for the Second Empire style led to its export. All over Europe and America, it became the accepted standard style for public and bureaucratic buildings. In England, the Foreign Office (1860–75) was constructed in designs remarkably similar to the Louvre projects. Following the construction of the famous Paris Opéra (1861–74) by architect Charles Garnier, the Burgtheater was constructed in Vienna

Pavillon Richelieu, the Louvre, Paris, 1850–57, designed by Visconti.

Hotel de Ville extension, Paris, 1837–49, designed by E. H. Godde and J. B. Lesueur. Etching from circa 1840.

between 1874 and 1888, and it was nearly as illustrious as its predecessor; both were designed in the Second Empire style. Of the numerous government buildings in the United States, two of the finest were designed by Alfred B. Mullett: the State, War and Navy Building (Executive Office Building) constructed in 1871 in Washington, D.C., and the Old Post Office in St. Louis, Missouri. In Philadelphia, the City Hall designed by John McArthur sported a huge tower in the style, and it was the largest building in the United States at the time it was constructed in 1874–81. The Second Empire style had been accepted at the highest levels, and it was to be closely followed by its pre-eminence in residential architecture.

In residential design, several distinctions between the new style and its predecessor, the Italian Villa style, are evident. One major difference is the accent on more vertical proportions. Most Second Empire houses were considerably taller than those of the Italian Villa style. With higher ceilings, the windows themselves tended to be wider and taller. Cornices extended from the

wide eaves, which were supported by single or paired brackets. Italian Villa houses, especially in the East, generally had towers that were fairly stout and were always roofed with low-pitched hipped roofs. The towers of the Second Empire style were much more pronounced, with their tall, steeply pitched mansard roofs. Cast-iron cresting was an additional feature, contributing much to the decorative effect. In fact, in comparison with the more modest Italian Villa houses in Portland, the new houses in the Second Empire style were considerably

State, War and Navy Building, Washington, D.C., 1871, designed by Alfred B. Mullett, Arthur Gilman consultant.

more impressive. After the construction of the first mansard-roofed house in Portland, all the finest homes were built with this feature. Clothing, furniture, and architecture avidly followed the French fashions, led by Emperor Napoleon III and his Empress Eugénie.

The first mansard-roofed house in Portland was constructed in 1868, concurrent with the peak of the style in Europe, in the home of brick manufacturer E. J. Jeffrey. E. M. Burton, to whom the design is attributed, may have had access to plan books showing houses with mansard roofs. Such a book was *Holly's Country Seats* by the architect Henry Hudson Holly, printed in 1860. In Burton's design, the mansard is similar to that illustrated in Holly's book, as are the pedimented dormer windows and the arched loggia and polygonal bay, although in Burton's design incorporated into a two-story house. The style was adaptive, and the details could well be incorporated into one-story designs. Additional houses with mansard roofs and further Second Empire characteristics were presented in Bicknell and Comstock's *Specimen Book of*

Charles Crocker Mansion, San Francisco, 1877.

One-Hundred Architectural Designs of 1880, including both one- and two-story versions.

The first of Portland's grand mansions was constructed in 1869 for William S. Ladd in the Italian Villa style, but it was subsequently enlarged to incorporate a concave mansard roof at the new third floor and a fashionable tower. The most proper design in the style was by German-born Justus Krumbein. His mansion for Jacob Kamm (1871) is handsomely propor- tioned, clearly imitating stone construction in wood. It has no tower, but the mansard roof is a distinct attribute, probably the closest in design to those in France. The Kamm House was followed by a series of elegant mansions, usually with concave mansard roofs, cresting, and ultimately with two-story polygonal bays. One such design was the Simeon Reed mansion of 1873, designed by noted San Franciscan architect Henry W. Cleaveland, himself the author of early house-design books. Inventive dormers were incorporated in the design, where three windows fill the end of the gable. Such innovations were cleverly added to the proper Second Empire designs, invoking both European culture and Queen Anne style invention. Cleaveland's second house in the city was for Henry Failing. Here, the style was entirely appropriate for the plan, which incorporated large two-story polygonal bays, numerous covered verandas, and a porte-cochere. The detailing was especially handsome in the Failing House, using much of the new vocabulary being developed in the Italianate style. Splendid turned balustrades adorned the veranda roofs, and iron railings of Rococo design decorated the third floor balcony. Dormers were spirited with finials, and the window detailing above the French style arched windows displayed rich carvings.

Other mansions in the style developed unique features. The A. H. Johnson House (1873) had a belvedere added to its mansard roof, adopting a theme from the previous Italian Villa style. The belvedere roof was convex and supported a concave-like adornment above it. These viewing belvederes were a delightful aspect of early residences, for if one made the effort to climb the stairs to what was in effect the fourth floor, the panorama was well worth it. The distant mountains of the Cascade Range were always a spectacular treat when the clear skies made the snow-covered slopes glisten in the distance.

The last of the great houses constructed in the Second Empire style was completely different from the others. The Henry W. Corbett mansion borrowed the giant pediment designs from the older buildings of the Louvre, such as the courtyard of the Vieux Louvre or the old gallery facing the Seine, designed by Du Cerceau. These designs were equally a part of the Second Empire style, where inspiration from Renaissance models, with considerable leeway in their adaptation to contemporary use, were completely acceptable. Henry Corbett as well as his neighbor Henry Failing traveled considerably, and they used ideas from their travels in the construction of their mansions. Returning from the "grand tour," they filled their homes with treasures, covering their walls with stencils and frescoes in the highest style and fashion.

The Corbett mansion of 1874 was the last residence constructed in Portland with definite Second Empire stylings. Napoleon III and Eugénie were deposed in 1870 and fled to England the following year, bringing an end to the Second Empire. In the U.S., President Ulysses S. Grant, who was closely associated with the style through architect Alfred Mullett, was bogged down in scandal. In addition, the eastern U.S. experienced a considerable recession in 1873, and though not felt dramatically in Portland, the cumulative effect, both political and eco-

A Second Empire style design, from *Holly's Country Seats* by Henry Hudson Holly, 1860.

"French Cottage," from Bicknell and Comstock's *Specimen Book of One-Hundred Architectural Designs*, 1880.

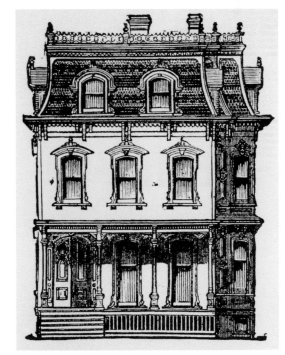

"Suburban House Design," from Bicknell and Comstock's *Specimen Book of One-Hundred Architectural Designs*, 1880.

nomic, brought a quick demise to the French-inspired style. By the beginning of the 1880s, when the economy had recovered, the next series of mansions were constructed in the Italianate style, returning to the low-pitched roofs.

Another Second Empire design from Bicknell and Comstock's *Specimen Book of One-Hundred Architectural Designs*, 1880.

Second Empire
CHARACTERISTICS

PLANS: asymmetrical in L or T shapes.

ROOFS: mansard style, curved or steep sloped; dormer windows in mansard.

EXTERIOR FINISHES: flush or wide rusticated boards; wide decorated corner boards or quoins (staggered or even); few, if any, trim boards at second floor.

CHIMNEYS: stuccoed brick; corniced tops; interior locations.

WINDOWS: tall, double-hung; one-over-one (1/1) panes; top sash with round or segmental arch. Paired at feature windows; groups of three or four in polygonal bays; stacked in conservatories.

WINDOW TRIM (exterior): plain, corniced, or highly decorated; window blinds.

ENTRANCE DOORS: paired, with transom above; small vestibules with paired inner doors.

VERANDAS/PORCHES: two or three bayed, kept to front, side, or rear of house; turned roof balustrades.

INTERIOR FINISHES: plaster walls and ceilings; coved plaster cornice.

INTERIOR TRIM: molded wrap-around wood door and window casings; plain baseboards with cap molding.

STAIRS: primarily straight run, with curved bends; turned newel and balusters.

FIREPLACE FRONTS: marble surrounds and mantel.

PROPERTY SURROUNDS: picket fences with square or turned posts at corners and gates; cast-iron fencing over stone walls.

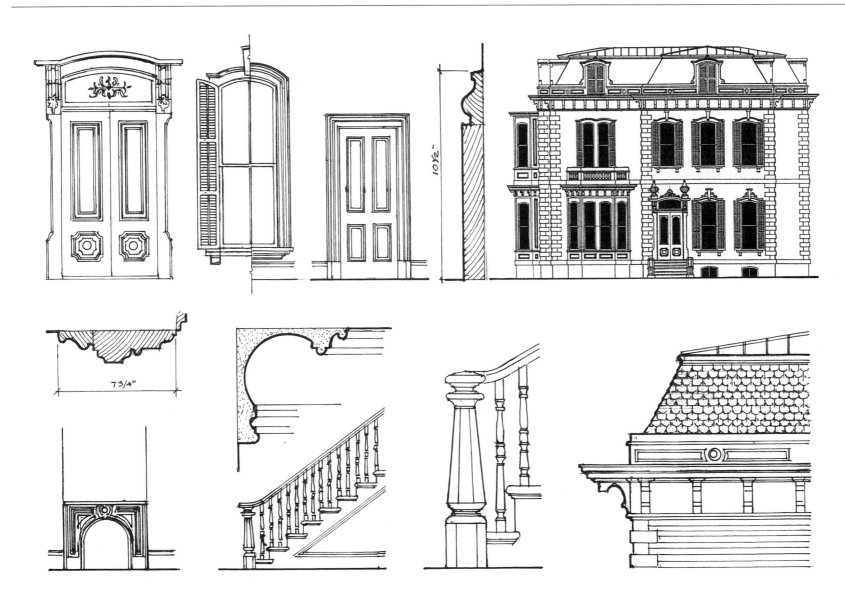

73/4"

10½"

Entrance to the Jacob Kamm House.

Second Empire
HOUSES

1868	E. J. Jeffrey (attributed to E. M. Burton)	1873	Henry W. Failing (Henry W. Cleaveland)
1869	William S. Ladd (E. M. Burton)	1873	A. H. Johnson (attributed to William W. Piper)
1871	Jacob Kamm (Justus F. Krumbein)		
1873	Simeon G. Reed (Henry W. Cleaveland)	1874	Henry W. Corbett (Warren H. Williams)

E. J. Jeffrey (1868)
E. M. Burton (attributed)

E. J. Jeffrey, a prosperous brick manufacturer, built his own home in brick, the first residence in the city constructed in solid masonry, and the first to incorporate the Second Empire design feature of a mansard roof. The architecture of the house is attributed to E. M. Burton, who used the new mansard designs both on the St. Charles Hotel (1869) and later on the Masonic Hall (1871). In fact, the handsome dormers in the Jeffrey House, both single and double, are identical to those in the Masonic Hall. Likewise, the curved outward slope of the mansard and the bracketed cornice are similar in scale and detail.

E. J. Jeffrey House.

The house was located in the fashionable northwest area of the city, on B Street (later Burnside) at Twentieth Avenue. Entrance to the T-shaped plan was off B Street, through a covered porch, and a parlor was located to the right (or east) of the entrance. The parlor had an ample polygonal bay, with four arched and shuttered windows. The shutters uniquely pivoted out awning-style at the top half of the double-hung, single-pane windows, with regular side-hinged shutters at the lower half. A small veranda was on the east side of the parlor, facing the city.

William S. Ladd (1869)
E. M. Burton

The quick ascent from the more modest Italian Villa designs to the Second Empire style is seen in the William S. Ladd House designed by E. M. Burton. In fact, the house was an Italian Villa house, without the mansard, in its first phase of construction. Soon thereafter the house was enlarged for the growing Ladd family. The mansard was added to gain additional space, and the tower was added over the front entrance. Other additions were made some years later by architect William P. Lewis, which included enlarging the windows in the parlor polygonal bay, opening the top floor of the tower to a mountain-viewing belvedere, and removing the decorative cast-iron cresting and window shutters. As was stated in *The Oregonian* on 27 March 1927,

> As the house now stands it has thirty rooms. The staircase is wide, the rooms spacious; windows reach floor to ceiling and doors are ample. Decorative woods, richly carved and inlaid, line wainscoting and mantels everywhere. Rosewood, maple and mahogany predominate. These art panels came from the east, brought in ships' holds around the Horn.

The rooms were especially handsome, elegantly proportioned and furnished. In the music room, the woodwork was inlaid with "olive and rosewoods in an elaborate manner." These works of great craftsmanship were moved by Helen Ladd Corbett (William Ladd's daughter), when the mansion was demolished in 1927, to her new home in Riverwood. On the two-block property once owned by the Ladds, the *Oregonian* Building now stands where the mansion was located, but the original carriage house on the block to the west remains, now converted to offices.

Parlor, Ladd House.

William S. Ladd House.

Jacob Kamm (1871)
Justus F. Krumbein

Portland's singular remaining great mansion from the decade of the 1870s and from the stylistic type of Second Empire design is that constructed by Jacob Kamm and designed by the great architect Justus Krumbein. It survives because of its 1951 move from its original thirteen-acre site, which Lincoln High School now occupies, to its present location on SW Twentieth Avenue between Jefferson and Market streets.

Justus Krumbein, newly arrived from Germany in 1871, designed the house with a decidedly European taste. It has few of the architectural extravagances that adorned other houses of the same generic style and size in Portland, depending more on excellent proportions and the care-

Jacob Kamm House, on its original site.

Interior, Kamm House.

ful juxtaposition of architectural mass and features. It was currently fashionable with the one-and two-story Italianate polygonal bays and its elongated windows, while it presented a more accurate attempt at simulating a French stone mansion, with flush horizontal siding and quoins imitating stuccoed stone walls with exposed dressed-stone trim. The mansard part of the roof has scalloped shingles to suggest slate, and the upper roof is finished with raised-rib galvanized sheet-metal.

The gracious interior, largely intact, has a large central stair hall, with rooms to either side and the kitchen in a rear wing. Being far from the river, the house faced north, with the parlor and sitting rooms facing east; most houses at the time were built to face east, toward the center of town and toward the Willamette. The curved stairway to the second floor is typical of the finer houses, and it employs the recessed niches at the curved corners along the stair wall. Upstairs, the bedrooms have been altered, now containing, in what was originally the master bedroom, the entrance-hall paneling from the extraordinary Knapp mansion of 1882. The parlor and sitting room still have their original ceiling and wall frescoes and stencils, the only extant 1870s example of a once-predominant method of interior decoration. The wall stencils are located just below the original plaster ceiling cornice and above the high wood baseboard. Also extant are the original suites of parlor and dining room furniture, which can be seen in the collections of the Old Church at Eleventh Avenue and Clay Street.

Simeon G. Reed (1873)
Henry W. Cleaveland

The 1870s produced, in quick succession, some truly remarkable mansions, most having as their chief adornment the French-inspired mansard roof. The great house constructed by Simeon G. Reed, and designed by noted San Franciscan architect Henry W. Cleaveland, had all the prominent features of the Second Empire style. Cleaveland designed a house with more elaborate detailing than that on the more conservative Kamm mansion, but the Reed House displayed a similar two-story polygonal bay and corner quoins. The siding was not flush, however, but emphasized continuous horizontal joints between each siding board, giving a more woody appearance while adding surface richness. The windows were tall, like those of the Kamm House, with segmental arches and topped with wood cornices. A concave curve was added to the mansard, and the dormer above the polygonal bay had three windows under a pediment, a decidedly inventive feature. Likewise, the wood balustrade of the mansard matched in size and detail the similar railing above the Italian Villa–inspired entrance porch, which had narrow columns and brackets. To add further ornament and decorative-

Simeon G. Reed House.

Parlor, Reed House.

ness, a fine cast-iron fountain was sited on the front lawn, and a decorative cast-iron railing atop a stone wall surrounded the property.

Not to be outdone, the interiors of the house were beautifully embellished and furnished. The photograph of the parlor is one of the earliest of any of the great houses, showing excellent style and taste. In addition to the usual ceiling frescoes, the plasterwork included not only a fine cornice, but additional ornaments defined the areas of fresco work. Hanging from an elaborate plaster medallion was an elaborate crystal gas-lit chandelier. Equally enormous in size were the paintings, typically purchased by the wealthy to complete the rooms, often with pre-Raphaelite themes. In addition, the parlor had an enormous square grand piano, and above the fireplace was a huge overmantel mirror, which became a requirement for any finished room in the next two decades. Another popular piece was the *étagère*, in Rococo style, displaying prized porcelain collections. Chairs were in the Louis XVI styling. In the dining room beyond can be seen one of the highly carved buffet pieces, with a high backpiece adorned with carvings, mirrors, and shelves for display.

Henry W. Failing (1873)
Henry W. Cleaveland

The Henry Failing House was clearly one of the great houses of the 1870s. It embodied the full range of Second Empire decorative effects, sitting grandly on its full city block, defined by Fifth and Sixth avenues and Salmon and Taylor streets. The mansion faced east (still relating to approach from the eastern business district and the Willamette River), with an east-facing entrance porch and a full veranda on the south elevation, which protected the sitting room, drawing room, and dining room from the summer sun. A large porte-cochere was located on the north side of the house. Both the east main entrance and the porte-cochere entrance opened into the central hall. Henry Cleaveland stated in his letters to Henry Failing, "The plan more than meets my expectations. I think it is the most convenient house I have ever designed." The plan was as practical as it was grand. The major rooms, very large for the city at that time, were splendidly appointed, but not extravagant. Accordingly, Cleaveland stated, "I shall try to keep the finish of the house plain and neat rather than overload it with ornament."

Compared with the very elaborate mansions to follow, the Failing House interiors were not overloaded. In many respects, they were sim-

Henry W. Failing House.

Entrance hall, Failing House.

ilar to the Kamm House interiors. Though bolder in scale, the stair railing, newel, and curved walls resembled those in the Kamm House, and the wall stencils at the cornice and at the baseboard were all but identical. Plaster cornices were multicolored, and the ceiling frescoes, not completed until 1882, were probably of designs similar to those in the extant Italianate Morris Marks House, completed in that year. Doors were four panel, with wide casings embellished with trim, and all painted a light cream color, same as in the Kamm House. Arched pediments were built over most first floor door casings, except above the sliding doors into and between the major first floor rooms. The huge double sliding doors were new to Portland, and they may have been used for the first time in this house. Other features were the imported fireplaces fronts,

Library, Failing House.

brought from San Francisco, and the large decorative overmantels. In the drawing room, the more traditional tall framed mirrors were attached to the mantel, while in the library Cleaveland employed new variants of design, which he claimed were "quite different from anything in Portland and may please from their oddity if not from their beauty."

This remarkable house was lived in by the Failing family until 1922, when it was razed to make way for the Power and Light Building. Some of the original furnishings can be found in the Pittock Mansion, notably a library bookshelf and the master bedroom suite, originally purchased by the Failings at the 1876 Philadelphia Centennial Exhibition during one of their extensive travels.

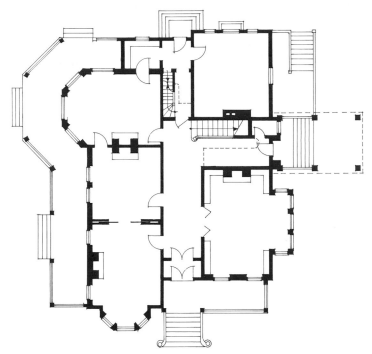

First floor plan, Failing House.

Dining room, Failing House.

A. H. Johnson (1873)
William W. Piper (attributed)

For years the photograph of the estate of A. H. Johnson has intrigued the student of Portland architectural history. The house, water tower, and stable form a compelling composition, situated in what was then countryside well outside the city. It was located at the edge of a still-existing stand of giant virgin firs between what became King Avenue

A. H. Johnson House.

The Johnson estate, showing water tower and stable.

Parlor, Johnson House.

and Vista Avenue (Ford Street) at approximately the western terminus of Yamhill Street. All memories of the handsome house are now gone; only the remaining giant sequoia planted in the gardens nearly a century ago gives any reminder of the once-prominent mansion.

The architecture of the house is attributed to William W. Piper, architect of the 1873 Deady Hall at the University of Oregon, Eugene, and of the 1872 Portland Central School addition (once located between Sixth Avenue and Broadway at Morrison and Yamhill streets on the site currently occupied by Pioneer Courthouse Square), and co-architect with E. M. Burton on the 1872 Marion County Courthouse in Salem. All the buildings had mansard roofs to some degree, and all had towers at the symmetrical front facade. The Johnson House mansard was concave in shape, and the roof of the tower, or belvedere, was obtuse. With the trim and shutters painted in contrasting colors, it must have been clearly visible from the city, more than twenty blocks away.

Although symmetrical in appearance, the entrance was actually to the left of the central tower protrusion. To the right of the entrance hall was the spacious parlor, with French doors leading to a small covered porch on the east facade, and a polygonal bay on the north facade. The walls and ceiling of the parlor room were covered with patterned wallpaper. This may have been a less expensive treatment than the frescoed and stenciled walls of the more expensive mansions—but with the patterned carpet, the effect was rich indeed. The room was finished with the marble fireplace front, family portraits on the wall, and the varied mixture of furniture styles fashionable from the 1870s through the 1890s.

Henry W. Corbett (1874)
Warren H. Williams

After occupying their Greek Revival style home for twenty years, the Corbett family decided to replace it with a Second Empire style mansion. The new house was placed slightly south of their first house, closer to Yamhill Street, but a carriage entrance off Fifth Avenue maintained the primary entrance facing east and the city. The three-story mansion was designed by Warren H. Williams, the San Franciscan architect who had moved permanently to Portland in 1872 after the disastrous fires that swept Portland's business district. Williams's design for the Corbett

House reflected the general plan that Henry W. Corbett sketched after his extensive European travels, incorporating French fashions first introduced to the United States in the 1850s.

The plan was T shaped, having a side entrance to allow the spacious parlor and master bedroom above to enjoy views to the east. The east, or primary, facade was distinguished by its arched gable at the third floor and the exedra-shaped porch off the parlor. For the first time in Portland, full Classical details were luxuriously used, primarily through the Corinthian style columns and balustrades of the porches. Combined with their elegant appearance were Italianate details more typical of the time: tall arched windows, paired brackets supporting the cornice, and

Henry W. Corbett House.

rusticated siding, imitating stonework. The cartouche decorations, within rectangular panels at the second floor, were particularly handsome.

The interiors of the Corbett House were quite amazing when considering the fact that Portland's first house of any consequence, the imported Crosby House, had been constructed only twenty-seven years before. Senator Corbett preferred to entertain on a high scale and so appointed the house to receive friends and visitors to the city with every amenity, and to remind them perhaps that, though the virgin firs had yet to be cleared only blocks to the west, Portland was on the map and could be counted among the beautiful and civilized cities of the country.

Entrance to the home was off the north carriage drive, up a long flight of stairs, directly into an enormous hall with a spacious curved stairway to the second floor and giving access to the south parlor, the east draw-

Parlor, Corbett House.

Side facade, Corbett House.

Drawing Room, Corbett House.

ing room, and the west dining room, with the kitchen wing behind it. The walls of all the formal rooms were stenciled and the ceilings were frescoed. The Senator brought the Italian fresco artist Signor Moretti specially to Portland to decorate the family home. To complete the rooms, the floors were covered with Wilton carpets, often with Oriental rugs over them. The Corbett painting, sculpture, and memorabilia collection filled almost every vertical and horizontal surface. In the parlor, the mantel alone displayed two candelabras, a center clock and two side artworks under glass domes, and miscellaneous porcelains, all under a large gilt-framed landscape painting. The furniture was of eclectic fash-

ion, with highly inventive forms: some pieces in the Classical Revival styles, some Renaissance and Rococo Revival, and others lacking definition. Both the parlor and the drawing room had comfortable upholstered armchairs, all sporting antimacassars at the headrests and armrests. The huge, glass globed chandeliers were gas lit, with the crystal-and-prism hanging fixtures reserved for the parlor. The dining room furniture was matched in design and included high-back chairs with turned front legs and upholstered seats and backs. The sideboard, with a mirrored centerpiece flanked by display shelves on either side, was imposing in scale and very similar, if not identical, to Henry Failing's

Dining room, Corbett House.

Master bedroom, Corbett House.

dining room set in the house on the block immediately to the south. Quite baronial, the master bedroom featured an enormous Renaissance Revival bed angled from the corner. It was also a private sitting room, with upholstered armchairs, a tufted chaise longue, and various vanity and work tables. Walls and ceilings were finished on a par with those of the lower floor, with no expense spared in finish and appointments.

By 1936, the second Mrs. Corbett moved to a new home in Dunthorpe, as the house had become surrounded by tall buildings (the YMCA, the Public Service Building, and the Pacific Building). An *Oregonian* article by Stewart Holbrook in 1936 stated:

> It seems too bad to at least one Portlander that the wreckers must pull it apart and level it to make room for, possibly, some modernistic and streamlined monstrosity fashioned by the same school of art that considers bent cast-iron pipe a suitable medium for swell furniture.

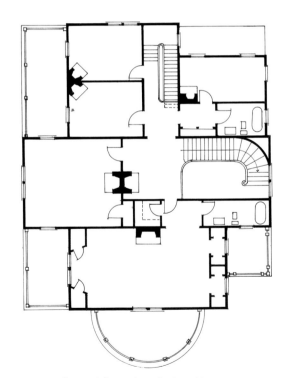

First floor plan, Corbett House.

Second floor plan, Corbett House.

CHAPTER 5

Italianate

It is nearly impossible today to envision Portland as it was in the early 1880s, a city full of Italianate style architecture. Block after block of Italianate houses, large and small, on tree-lined streets, as well as the bustling commercial center, made Portland one of the more celebrated cities of the West, remarkably distinguished for being only three decades old. That brief moment of time was the last in which the city could boast of having an architectural cohesiveness, when the buildings were primarily in a common style, when each was of a compatible scale to the others, and when commercial buildings were never more than four stories in height. Beginning at the city waterfront, on the banks of the Willamette River, the commercial blocks were filled with Italianate cast-iron "palaces." Only four blocks to the west, the residential areas took over, thinning out before reaching the western hills. Most of the commercial and residential structures were designed with details from the Italian Renaissance. To their common skyline were added the further adornments of Gothic spires of its churches and the domes and towers of its public and private buildings. The more magnificent houses were

The South Park Blocks, Portland, circa 1882.

well within walking distance or a short carriage or trolley ride, scattered among the blocks immediately south of the Pioneer Court House (Fifth Avenue and Morrison Street), along the South Park Blocks, and in the expanding areas around NW Eighteenth Street, where the descendants of Captain Couch built lavish estates on properties of the old Couch Addition

(Couch's original land grant) in northwest Portland. That the city had such an attractive environment was the product of its prosperous citizens, many well educated and established in the East before their arrival in the West. Their tastes for fine architecture showed in their patronage of the enormously talented architects who had migrated to Portland. Each new building or residence added its presence to the face of the city, and together they created an architectural environment that could be enjoyed by all. All this is gone now—the slower pace, the appreciation for the architecture, and the handsome houses comprising the city of the early 1880s. Only a few scattered houses remain, subsequently moved or shorn of their original environments, uncomfortable beside later apartment houses or parking lots.

The Italianate style in residential design was partially the result of the valiant style war being waged in England and America between the forces that promoted the Gothic style and those favoring the Classical designs. Gothic country villas, or Italian villas with Romanesque features, as championed by Andrew Jackson Downing, slowly gave way to the Second Empire style, and after Napoleon III's fall from grace and the scandals of the Grant presidency brought that style in disfavor, the Italianate style emerged. Despite coming from England and not Italy, the

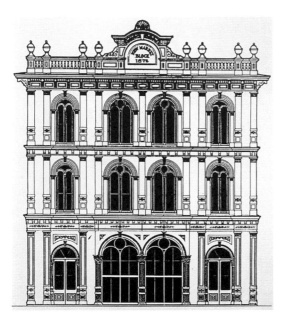

New Market Theater, Portland, 1872, designed by Piper and Burton.

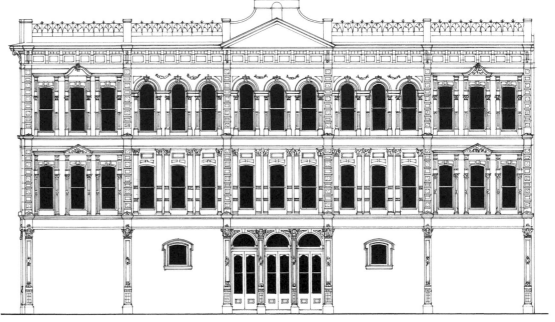

Smith and Watson Building, Portland, 1883, design attributed to Warren H. Williams.

style's acceptance was appropriately timed to reflect on the new unity of the Italian peninsula, now one independent country rather than a series of smaller states governed separately or by other nations. Garibaldi, the Italian national hero, was instrumental in the unification of the country, which was followed by the first king of a unified Italy, Victor Emmanuel, in 1878. American tourists flocked to the ancient cultural grounds, viewing the grand palazzos in every city center. These palazzos were a major inspiration for much of the Classical Revival in England and the United States. Their splendors were illustrated and accessible in tourist souvenirs, in the thousands of reproduced architectural plates brought back to Portland and other cities to adorn private homes. Giambattista Piranesi's etchings of the Palazzo della Consulta (1723–34) and of Villa Albani (1760) are still available to tourists today as they were in the 1870s and 1880s. Bound volumes of architectural photographs were also increasingly available to architects. In them the classics of the Italian Renaissance were featured, such as the Villa

Giulia for Pope Julius III (1550–55) designed by Vignola and Bartolomeo Ammanati in collaboration with Michelangelo and Vasari. All these palazzos had common features: rectangular blocks accented by a strong cornice, individual windows with hoods or cornices, a base story, and prominent entrances. The entrances most typically were flush with the facade, centered, and featured arched portals or columned entrance loggias. It was this concept that originally was incorporated into the Italianate

Palazzo della Consulta, Rome, 1723–34, built by Ferdinando Fuga.
Etching by Giambattista Piranesi.

houses in Portland, though with considerable mingling of Italian Villa design features.

The most remarkable of the Italianate houses were the four constructed along the South Park Blocks, on either side of Montgomery Drive: the Whalley, Fechheimer, and twin matching Jacobs mansions. Fortunately, the houses of the Jacobs brothers were recorded by photographer Minor White for the Portland Art Museum before their demolition in the 1940s. They were recorded because they were true works of art, both for their magnificent exterior designs and for the lavish artwork that covered their interiors. No such magnificent interiors of the Italianate era remain today. Only the Morris Marks houses of 1880 and 1882 can give us a suggestion of the lost mansions today. The second Marks House, on SW Harrison Street, still has traces of the original ceiling fresco work, the only Italianate style remnants of the lost art form.

The typical Italianate house in Portland added considerable sculptural enrichment to the basic rectangular block of its Italian palazzo inspiration. Bay windows were a primary addition, either one story, as in the Judge John Whalley House (1879), or two story, as in its magnificent neighbor, the M. W. Fechheimer House (c. 1880). The two-story rectangular bays had pedimented roofs, and their windows were contained between Corinthian style pilasters. A favorite of the earlier Gothic Revival style, the bays evolved quickly into the two-story versions, with polygonal sides, and in the transformation dramatically changed the proportions of the houses, making them considerably more vertical than their Renaissance predecessors. The entrance porch was a further additional feature. Whether centered or asymmetrically placed to the side, entrance porches were brought forward to create an impressive portico. To one degree or another the porticos remained a feature of the style, later being incorporated into wrap-around verandas when influences from the Queen Anne style began to make their presence felt.

Other details continued some adherence to Italian Renaissance inspiration. In the early homes, the corners of the houses had wood quoins applied to simulate in wood their stone origins. On the simpler houses these were replaced with simple corner boards, combined with horizontal trim at the floor line and a water table. Above, the modillions, which added cornice support in the Italian originals, were slowly replaced with larger brackets, also of scroll design. Roof balustrades surrounded the low-pitched or flat roofs and had turned balusters or were plain, much as they had been in Italy. Cast-iron cresting was added to the upper flat part of the roof, however, as in the Ralph and Isaac Jacobs mansions (1880), providing a very rich effect. Other details of Italian origin were found in the windows. The ear-

Villa Albani, Italy, 1760. Etching by Giambattista Piranesi.

Villa Giulia, Rome, 1550–55, designed by Vignola and Bartolomeo Ammanati, in collaboration with Michelangelo and Vasari.

lier houses had window cornices supported by scroll brackets, or broken pediments as in the Captain George Flanders mansion (1882). Window details on the third floor of the Palazzo Farnese, designed by Michelangelo in the mid-sixteenth century, and those on the Flanders House bear comparison, as both have pediments and non-flat headers to the upper window sash. On the polygonal bays of Portland's Italianate houses, all the details combined into a cohesive whole. Windows were no longer separately detailed frames, but were made integral with the roof and belt cornices, the paired columns between them, and the paneling below the sills. Italianate houses made some distinction between floors, usually with belt cornices or an entablature or, most simply, a horizontal trim board.

The magnificent Italianate houses were among the finest architectural creations ever seen in the city. Hundreds of houses were constructed in the style, sufficiently so as to create the impression of an entire city constructed in

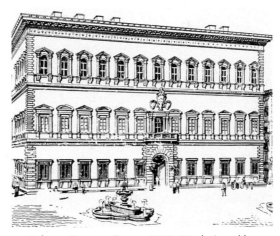

Palazzo Farnese, Rome, 1515–89, designed by Antonio da Sangallo and Michelangelo.

the Italianate mode. Styles were evolving so quickly in the early 1880s, however, that the influences of the Queen Anne style, with its far more fanciful roofs and elaborate towers, soon overtook the more conservative Italianate. New fortunes had been made, and the new clients had a taste for the unusual. There was an admiration for more inventive and original forms, and, of course, a more compelling need for opulent display. Yet the Italianate houses remained in the city for many years, solidly enhancing the city's reputation as a premier architectural center in the country. Portland's pioneer families remained in the houses well into their later years, when the quickly growing city had completely engulfed them. Sadly, their era had ended, and with it came the demise of their handsome houses.

Italianate
CHARACTERISTICS

PLANS: symmetrical and asymmetrical in rectangular, T and L shapes.

ROOFS: low-pitched hipped, to flat top, sometimes surrounded by cresting; hipped roof over two-story polygonal bays; flat veranda roofs. Shingled or galvanized sheet metal covering.

EXTERIOR FINISHES: flush siding, drop siding, or wide curved horizontal boards; simple corner boards, quoins, paneled corner boards, or mitered flush siding; simple board trim at second floor line.

CHIMNEYS: stuccoed brick, with decorative cap; interior locations.

WINDOWS: tall, double-hung; one-over-one (1/1) panes; top sash with rounded or segmental arch. Paired at feature windows; groups of three or four in polygonal bays; banked windows at tower.

WINDOW TRIM (exterior): bracketed pediments; pilaster casings; unified belt cornice at second floor in polygonal bays. Window blinds moved to interior.

ENTRANCE DOORS: paired, with transom above; small vestibules with paired inner doors.

VERANDAS/PORCHES: single-bay entrance porches; two- or three-bay verandas; wrap-around veranda.

INTERIOR FINISHES: plaster walls and ceilings; coved plaster cornice; paneled wainscoting; pressed wallpaper wainscot and dado. Stenciled and frescoed walls and ceiling.

INTERIOR TRIM: pedimented and corniced doors and windows in main rooms, molded; wrap-around molded trim in other rooms.

STAIRS: curved stairs, circular stairs; square decorated newels, turned balusters.

FIREPLACE FRONTS: cast-iron and marble fronts with overmantel mirrors.

PROPERTY SURROUNDS: picket fences with square or turned posts at corners and gates; stone walls, with or without cast-iron fencing.

Entrance to the second Morris Marks House.

Italianate
HOUSES

1879	Judge John W. Whalley (attributed to Albert H. Jordan)		1882	Morris Marks, II (Warren H. Williams)
c. 1880	M. W. Fechheimer (attributed to Albert H. Jordan)		c. 1881	Richard Milwain (Richard Milwain)
1880	Ralph and Isaac Jacobs (Warren H. Williams)		1882	George V. James (Justus F. Krumbein)
c. 1880	Justus F. Krumbein (Justus F. Krumbein)		1882	Captain George Flanders (Justus F. Krumbein)
1880	Morris Marks, I (attributed to Warren H. Williams)		1882	Charles P. Bacon (Warren H. Williams)

Judge John W. Whalley (1879)
Albert H. Jordan (attributed)

In the late 1870s and early 1880s, four remarkable houses were built in a row on the west side of the South Park Blocks. The first two of these shared the common park frontage between Harrison and Montgomery streets: the Judge John W. Whalley House and the M. W. Fechheimer House; the other two were the twin mansions of the brothers Ralph and Isaac Jacobs, one block to the north. The first constructed was the Judge Whalley House on the northwest corner of Harrison and Park. Distinctly

different from other Portland houses of the time, the design is attributed to architect Albert H. Jordan. Jordan designed a nearly identical house in Detroit, the Chandler House of 1858, suggesting that he repeated the design when he moved his practice to Portland. Essentially, the architecture of the house followed design sources from the Italian Renaissance, or the Italian palazzo. Notable in the Whalley home was the balustraded parapet above the roof cornice, the balustraded single-story rectangular bays, and the entrance loggia, centered above a wide, sweeping flight of stairs. Adding surface elegance were the rusticated first floor siding and flush second floor siding, which simulated masonry construction in wood.

Judge John W. Whalley House.

M. W. Fechheimer (c. 1880)
Albert H. Jordan (attributed)

Similar in plan to the Whalley House, the M. W. Fechheimer House of circa 1880, located to the immediate north, was much richer in detail. The rectangular bays in this house were two stories high, each with a pediment, and had Corinthian style pilasters beside each window. The grandly balustraded main entrance stairway, up nearly a full floor from the sidewalk, led to a spacious entrance portico supported by three Corinthian columns on each side. The house was clearly meant to complement the Whalley House in general scale and appearance, having similar horizontal rustication at the first floor and flush horizontal siding at the second. Handsome paneled pilasters visually supported the wide entablature and extended cornice, which was adorned with modillions and capped by a balustraded parapet. Equally impressive in design was the north elevation, with its exedra porch and bifurcated stair in the Baroque tradition—possibly the most impressive stair ever crafted in Portland. The two houses, along with their neighbors to the north, the Jacobs mansions, brought to Portland the highest design standards in the Italianate style, and had they survived they would remain among the finest architectural achievements ever built on the Pacific Coast.

M. W. Fechheimer House.

Entrance hall, Fechheimer House.

Dining room, Fechheimer House.

Parlor room, Fechheimer House.

Library, Fechheimer House.

Drawing room, Fechheimer House.

Ralph and Isaac Jacobs (1880)
Warren H. Williams

The twin houses built in 1880 for the brothers Ralph and Isaac Jacobs on the block to the north of the Whalley and Fechheimer houses brought a glorious moment to Portland's residential architecture. The four two-block-long, park-fronting houses were uniform in size, scale, and general arrangement. All had central-hall plans, rich entrance porticos, and bays to each side. Of the four houses, only the Jacobs mansions have the architect recorded, Warren H. Williams, then at the peak of his illustrious career. The designs for the mansions, Williams's version of the popular Italianate style, were so influential that hundreds of homes in Portland were constructed during the 1880s with similar layouts, proportions, and detailing.

The two mansions were identical but reversed in plan. The Isaac Jacobs House was located to the north, and the Ralph Jacobs House to the south. Each had handsome entrance stairs and porticos as well as polygonal side porches enhanced by grouped Corinthian columns and segmental arches, much like the Fechheimer House. The double polygonal bays, two stories high, were the distinguishing feature of the houses, with segmental-arched windows at the first floor and round-arched windows at the second. Windows were framed by engaged Corinthian columns, with a bracketed belt cornice separating the upper from the lower windows. A bracketed Italian Villa cornice capped the houses just below their low-pitched hipped roofs, which rose to a cast-iron crested top, concealing the round skylights over the circular interior staircase. The facades were treated similarly to those of the Fechheimer and Whalley houses, with rusticated first floor walls and flush siding at the second floor. Over the main entrance porticos were Venetian style pedimented

Ralph and Isaac Jacobs Houses.

Ralph Jacobs House.

Isaac Jacobs House.

windows—two arched windows framed within a larger arch and with a rounded medallion in the tympanum. Other details were exceptional in their design, such as the portico balustrade with its finialed posts and decorative cast-iron railing.

The interiors of the Jacobs houses are forever memorialized by the handsome series of photographs taken by Minor White before the demolition of the houses in 1942. Most notable in the identical houses were the entrance halls, which were divided into two contiguous spaces by a massive Palladian arch. The first space gave access to the parlor and drawing room on either side, and the second contained the magnificent two-story circular staircase, which rose toward the domed skylight. The

Side entrance, Isaac Jacobs House.

Entrance hall, Jacobs Houses.

Ceiling fresco, front entrance hall, Jacobs Houses.

Domed skylight and ceiling frescoes over the stairway, Jacobs Houses.

Oriental parlor, Jacobs Houses.

Drawing room, Jacobs Houses.

Bedroom, Jacobs Houses.

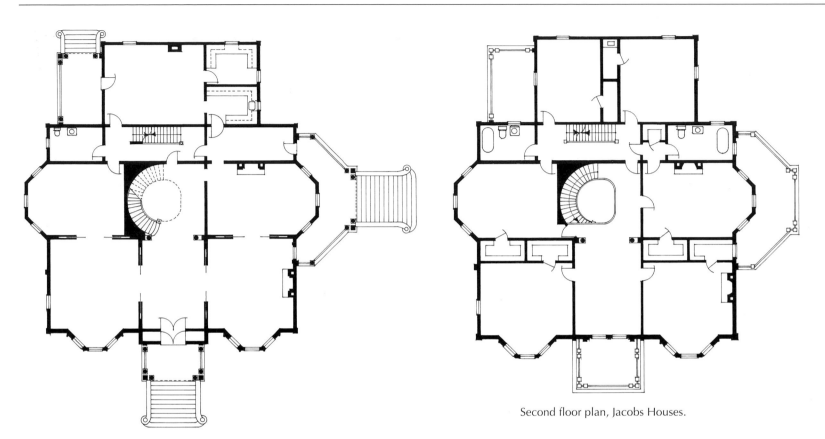

First floor plan, Jacobs Houses.

Second floor plan, Jacobs Houses.

inner surface of the dome, beneath the skylight, was divided into trapezoidal panels and filled with frescoed muses depicting the various arts.

The other main rooms followed suit. The "Oriental" parlor featured ebony and gold woodwork, with enormous overmantel mirrors reflecting the gas-lit chandeliers. Some of the rooms had embossed wainscoting or dado, made to look like carved Spanish leather. All rooms had extensively frescoed ceilings with geometric designs and lunettes of frescoed allegorical scenes. The tall windows had fold-away shutters and corniced valances for draperies to pull in winter. More carvings and details were to be found in the fireplace fronts: side columns, medallions, brackets, and sculptured panels, and imported tiles surrounding the fire-box openings and on the hearths. Every feature, like the stair newel, was decorated with exotic woods and marquetry panels or carved relief heads in round medallions. Such lavish display of artistry, which required that the architect command a small army of artists and craftsman, had never before been seen in Portland. This renaissance of the arts was to come and go, however, demolished before any perspective could be gained to realize that this was a symphony that would never be heard again.

Justus F. Krumbein House.

Justus F. Krumbein (c. 1880)
Justus F. Krumbein

Justus Krumbein, the second exceptional architect in Portland of the 1870s and 1880s after Williams, provided plans that displayed his mastery of design. The proportions employed were first rate, as shown in this single-bay, medium-sized Italianate house. Typically, the single-bay, asymmetrical plan had an off-center entrance hall, with the parlor adjacent to one side. The entry hall, in addition to housing the main stair to the second floor, gave access to the family sitting room and the dining room. A small guest closet and lavatory was located under the curved stair. The kitchen, in a wing to the rear of the house, had a separate pantry for food storage and a china closet, where the dishes were washed and stored. A second stair provided separate access to the second floor and attic for live-in help, as well as access to the basement.

The second floor had four chambers for the family, some with separate lavatories and clothes closets, and a servant's bedroom above the kitchen wing. One bath served the floor, with a tin or copper-lined tub, a corner marble-topped lavatory (washbowl), and a "water closet" (w.c.). The rear hall also had a linen closet, a convenience not employed in earlier decades.

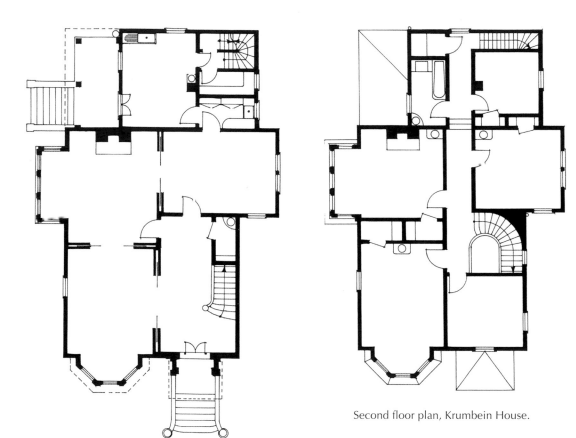

First floor plan, Krumbein House.

Second floor plan, Krumbein House.

Morris Marks, I (1880)
Warren H. Williams (attributed)

Of the hundreds of well-designed houses in the Italianate style in Portland, only a handful remain today, and two of the best of these were constructed by Morris Marks. The first house, a single-bay Italianate built in

Morris Marks House, I.

1880, sits on its original site at 1134 SW Twelfth Avenue. The design is attributed to Warren Williams, who also designed the splendid Temple Beth Israel (1888), once sited diagonally across Twelfth Avenue, and the second Morris Marks House, a double-bay Italianate built in 1882. The facade of the L-shaped house is exceptionally well composed, balancing the single two-story polygonal bay with the portico and entrance doors. The details include staggered quoins at the house's corners, drop siding, and segmental-arched windows. At the bay, the arch details cleverly combine with the pilasters separating the windows, giving a highly articulate form and unity to the entire composition. Other fine details are found in the Corinthian portico columns, missing their capitals, and the bracketed cornice, which integrates well with the polygonal bay. The house is deserving of every effort made to preserve it as an exceptional work of architecture.

Morris Marks, II (1882)
Warren H. Williams

The most exceptional double-bayed Italianate house remaining in Portland is the second Morris Marks House, built in 1882. In 1910, it was moved to its present location at 1501 SW Harrison Street from its original location at the southwest corner of Eleventh Avenue and Clay Street. The architect Warren H. Williams created a simple but beautifully balanced house, impressing one with its innate dignity and stately presence. The Corinthian columned portico, with its broken-arch pediment, beckons the visitor ceremoniously to enter. On either side, the two-story polygonal bays show excellent proportion and attention to detail. The rounded first floor windows and the segmental second floor windows have unique sculptured keystones, although the greatest enrichment is

Morris Marks House, II.

Richard Milwain (c. 1881)
Richard Milwain

Little is known of the architect Richard Milwain, who designed his own home constructed on the southwest corner of Seventh Avenue and Washington Street in about 1881. He did use in his design many of the idioms being developed by Justus Krumbein, for whom he served as a draftsman from 1883 to 1885. Though similar in plan to the Krumbein Italianate design, Milwain's house employed wider polygonal bays, including two windows instead of one at the outer wall, which provided for a very well-lit room. Windows on both floors had segmental arches, with wood keystones in the trim. A full-bracketed cornice and low-sloped hipped roof completed the composition.

Richard Milwain House.

reserved for the balustraded portico, with its handsome finials and Classical carved head in the entablature. No less fine are the interiors, which include a fine curved stair at the end of the entrance hall and remnants of the once-remarkable ceiling frescoes. A recent owner, Des Connall, made extensive improvements, restoring exterior detail and the missing west cornice.

The Milwain House typified the middle-income Italianate houses in Portland of the 1880s. The house was practical in nature and attractive in appearance, yet fitted in so well with the other houses of the era. Portland had become Italianate, and proud of it. With the picket fences, the orderly planting of street trees, and the luxurious growth in gardens, afforded by the climate and soil, the new city was indeed impressive to city visitors, whose compliments are well recorded.

George V. James (1882)
Justus F. Krumbein

Justus Krumbein designed this Italianate house for George V. James in 1882. Originally located on the block surrounded by Eighteenth and Nineteenth avenues and Irving and Johnson streets, it was a larger house, with parlors on both sides of the entrance hall. Instead of creating a double-bayed Italianate, Krumbein chose to balance the single polygonal bay on the front facade with a wide veranda and a recessed area off the left-hand, or south, parlor. This parlor was further extended by a large polygonal bay facing south. The fireplace chimneys are contained within the main volume of the house. They served the two parlors, indicating the greater refinements of the house. On the exterior, the lower floor windows were rounded and the second floor windows had segmental arches. The trim around the windows was unusual, an exaggeration of the dog ears found in Greek Revival houses. Also unusual were the small pendules that hang from the porch roof brackets and the impressive exterior stair newels, which serve more like large urns, or finials. In all, such qualities added to the noble character of these Italianates, appearing like small villas atop their mounded properties.

George V. James House.

Captain George Flanders (1882)
Justus F. Krumbein

Located on the double block between Nineteenth and Twentieth avenues and Flanders and Glisan streets, the George Flanders House was one of the largest, most impressive houses constructed in Portland during the early 1880s. Expanding on Italianate forms, architect Justus F. Krumbein added an engaged polygonal corner tower with a steeply pitched geometric roof, a very extensive wrap-around veranda, and numerous polygonal bays. With several bays in the veranda, one pedimented at the entrance and one rounded at the tower, the wrap-around was possibly the first of its kind in Portland. Krumbein used a variety of architectural motifs, from the paired Corinthian columns of the veranda to the geometric, almost Eastlake patterns of the porch railing and roof balustrade. His windows were very unorthodox, having flat and angled tops at the main floor and almost Tudor arches at the second. The latter had cornices that complemented the arches. A profusion of windows seemingly covered a good half of the facades, which mostly faced east and south, admitting great quantities of light, even with the veranda.

Charles P. Bacon (1882)
Warren H. Williams

The Charles P. Bacon House designed by Warren H. Williams was very similar to the Krumbein-designed house for George James of the same year. Essentially, the house was a wide single-bay Italianate on the entrance facade, with a second bay facing in a perpendicular direction to the left. The second polygonal bay contained the parlor fireplace, the chimney hidden discretely behind the outside wall but seen emerging from the low-hipped roof. During this period, only the chimney tops were exposed and celebrated, not the entire masonry structure.

Captain George Flanders House.

Charles P. Bacon House.

The Bacon House had other similarities to Krumbein's James House: the same dog-ear trim at the windows, an identical bracketed cornice, and similar porch detailing. The Bacon House sported the newly fashionable cast-iron roof cresting. It also had a carriage drive, which approached the entrance stairway. Only those houses with more expansive property could enjoy this amenity, as the owners had to stable their horses on the property or elsewhere. The gracious carriage entrance was used only with the largest houses, where it became a major feature of house and grounds.

PART III

Eclectic Styles of Mixed Origins
1880s–1890s

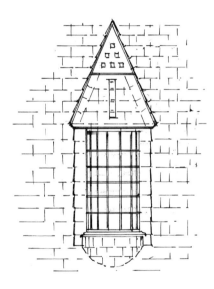

CHAPTER 6   Queen Anne

Portland, circa 1888, with the Knapp House prominent in the foreground.

During the early 1880s, a new and different style was introduced into residential architecture: the Queen Ann Style. In a matter of only a few years, it had replaced in popularity the restrained and elegant Italianate style. The new style became popular in almost every city and town in Oregon as well as across the country, as witnessed by the construction of great numbers of Queen Anne style houses. For slightly more than ten years, the style held sway, with influences affecting it from a variety of sources, including Flemish, chalet, German, French, Chinese, and medieval elements. The combination made it one of the most inventive and, ironically, most American styles in residential architectural history.

The term "Queen Anne" is a curious misnomer. The style was named and popularized by a group of nineteenth-century English architects, led by Richard Norman Shaw (1831–1912), who actually designed more with medieval house models, and not the late Renaissance architecture of which Queen Anne was a part. The namesake Queen reigned from only

1702 to 1714, the last monarch of the Stuart Period (1625–1714) and just preceding the late Renaissance period of the four King Georges (1714–1830). Nothing in the vocabulary of the late Renaissance can account for the popularly accepted term. Nevertheless, the designs of the English architects in the 1860s and 1870s, especially the houses designed by Shaw, led to the development of the style. Shaw's Leyswood (1868), in Withyham, Sussex, and his Hopedene (1873), in Surrey, sketches of which appeared in the journal *Building News* in 1871 and 1874, respectively, paved the way for the British Exhibit in the enormously popular 1876 Centennial International Exhibition in Philadelphia. Several houses of the distinctive Tudor design were constructed for the British executive commissioner and delegates at the Exhibition (see Chapter 11). They were widely acclaimed and were published that same year in the influential magazine *American Builder*. Considering the staid Italianate then in favor, with its controlled but elegant taste, the residences seemed to offer a fascinating exuberant alternative. The asymmetrical plans of the houses had great practical reasoning behind them. Without the restrictive symmetries of the Italianate, they could accommodate the variety of individual needs of the homeowner. Besides,

the houses had an abundance of charming features, like the rich profusion of multiple gables, soaring medieval chimneys, delightful leaded casement windows, and romantic half-timbering. Or, if medieval influences didn't suit, Chinese or Japanese touches were possible. The 1876 Centennial displayed whole complexes of Oriental architecture. The interiors were especially attractive to viewers. Spaces flowed one into the other, separated by sliding Shogi screens and open above with spindled grilles. These influences, as well as those from other

Old House, Brunswick, England, circa
fifteenth century.

parts of the globe, all became sources for further architectural enrichments.

House plans had already undergone considerable changes from the formal Greek Revival architecture of the 1840s and 1850s, evolving through the symmetrical, as well as asymmetrical, Italian Villa style of the 1860s and the Italianate style of the 1870s and 1880s. While Portland was experiencing the richness of the Second Empire and Italianate styles, in the East architects were exploring new directions. One of the most avant-garde architects was Henry Hobson Richardson (1838–1886) of Boston, Massachusetts. His designs for the F. W. Andrews House (1872) and the William Watts Sherman House (1874), both in Newport, Rhode Island, had already set the stage for a dramatic change in fashion. Offering multiple towers with finials and leaded windows, the Andrews House appeared like a shingled medieval castle, but with an elaborate wrap-around porch. The Sherman House, constructed during Richardson's partnership with Charles D. Gambrill, is considered the first real Queen Anne style house in the country. It was a tour de force of intersecting gabled forms, banks of leaded windows, half-timbering, and huge brick Tudor chimneys. *American Architect and Building News*, one of America's first architectural magazines, featured the houses with handsome steel-plate etchings, romantically drawn. T. G. Appleton's house of 1875–76 in Newport, Rhode Island, designed by Richard Morris Hunt (1827–1895), had the appearance of a medieval German house, complete with vine-covered porch posts and viewing balconies under the jerkinhead roof.

Adding to the thrust of the new fashion were the style books, such as Henry Hudson Holly's *Modern Dwellings* and Bicknell and Comstock's *Specimen Book of One-Hundred Architectural Designs*, which were subscribed to from coast to coast during the period. Eugene C. Gardner's *Illustrated Homes* (1875) featured plans, elevations, and arrangements and considered the entire house, particularly its appropriateness to the individual owner; a certain type of house was appropriate for the well-to-do, another for the newly married, and another for "old maids." An earnest home builder could have an array of possibilities in front of him in only the time it took to have the mail delivered. In not much greater time, he could order prebuilt decorations—such as the gingerbread and spindlework details seen on countless Queen Anne style homes—all made accessible by the newly connected rail lines now reaching every major city of the country.

The first of the Queen Anne style houses in Portland simply placed a variety of Queen Anne style roofs over otherwise Italianate plans and elevations. The Senator Joseph N. Dolph House (1881) added fantastic gable decorations, somewhat reminiscent of Bernese middle-land farmhouses, or perhaps reflecting the roof of the Appleton House in Rhode Island, which appeared in the first issue of *American Architect and Building News* in 1876. Brackets

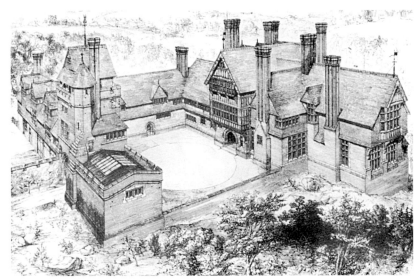

Leyswood, Sussex, England, 1868, designed by Richard Norman Shaw. Printed in *Building News*, 1871.

Hopedene, Surrey, England, 1873, designed by Richard Norman Shaw. Printed in *Building News*, 1874.

supported these decorative features in the same manner as on a Swiss chalet. Swiss influences appeared also in the roofs of the Cicero Hunt Lewis House (1881) and the home that architect Justus F. Krumbein designed for himself in 1884. In other houses, the gable ends were treated quite the opposite. In the George H. Williams House (1881), the gables resembled the masonry gables of Holland or the English-Dutch architecture introduced to England by William of Orange. Both the Dolph and Williams houses, despite their gable treatment, had asymmetrical Italianate plans and, for the most part, Italianate window treatment. Polygonal bays were still highly favored, and cast-iron ridge cresting was equally at home on Queen Anne style homes as it had been on Italianate style homes.

House designs in the 1880s, especially those with Queen Anne characteristics, concentrated on good planning. For the smaller well-designed home, the entrance hall was ample, and usually the stair to the second floor was immediately accessible. Off the hall was the parlor for the guests, where the best furniture was displayed. Depending on the circumstance, it had

William Watts Sherman House, Newport, Rhode Island, 1874, designed by Gambrill and Richardson.

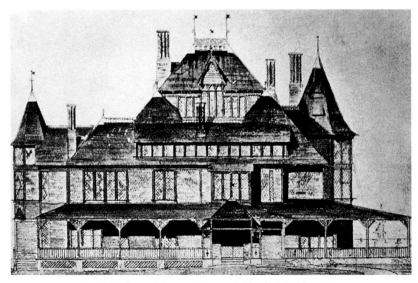

F. W. Andrews House, Newport, Rhode Island, 1872, designed by H. H. Richardson.

T. G. Appleton House, Newport, Rhode Island, 1875–76, designed by Richard Morris Hunt. Printed in *American Architect and Building News*, 1876.

House at Medford, Massachusetts, 1877, designed by Peabody and Stearns. Printed in *American Architect and Building News*, 1877.

"A Modern Villa Residence," from Bicknell and Comstock's *Specimen Book of One-Hundred Architectural Designs*, 1880.

a fireplace and inevitably a polygonal bay. Usually through large sliding doors from the parlor was the sitting room, sometimes called the library, where the family spent its time. The sitting room too had a fireplace and a large bay window. Adjacent to it was the dining room, served through the china pantry from the kitchen. Since families used their dining rooms, the china was readily available for setting the table. The kitchen was spacious, but had limited counter space, relying partly on tables. There was hot water for the sink, a food pantry near the back porch, and a wood stove. A back stair was often provided, particularly if the family could afford servants, which accessed the upper floors and the basement. In the basement was the wood-burning gravity furnace, the wood cellar, the laundry, possibly a wine cellar, and access to the outside. A w.c. was also provided for the servants in the cellar. Another w.c. was located on the main floor and a third for the second floor bedrooms or chambers. A single bathroom served the entire family, as bathing was not as frequent as it is today. Tubs, usually copper lined, were filled with hot water by having the piping pass through the furnace or wood stove. Simple hot-water heaters were constantly being improved upon, but they lacked the quantities of

hot water that were available by the 1890s. The larger mansions, of course, could afford more elaborate devices and were more amply served in most conveniences.

It was in the Knapp House of 1882, Portland's most extravagant of the period, where the essential Queen Anne elements were found and the full romance inherent in the style revealed. Here were the gabled projections, the wide decorated bargeboards made fashionable by Shaw and others, the diagonally placed bay, an amazing porte-cochere, and the city's most fantastic wrap-around porch. The details of the porch have no precedent in architectural history. The house also had one of the more beloved architectural features—a three-story tower, complete with conical roof and finial. Every surface was artfully adorned, carefully proportioned, and superbly sculpted. Likewise in the interior; the entry hall was a wonder of the West Coast, with gorgeous woodwork decorating a fabulous space. This was baronial architecture in a city hardly a few decades old, mature in its concept and sure in its execution. Its architect, as yet unknown, had a full grasp of his talents and a client willing to fully invest in the realization of a brilliant dream.

The Queen Anne style was the perfect vehicle for displaying the new-found wealth of

Portland's successful citizens. There was great pride in these houses. To the owners, the houses offered the visible assurance of their new position in Portland society, a badge of their success. To the public, another beautiful city ornament was given for their enjoyment. Even the promotional maps proudly displayed the wonders of these private residences in the borders of the carefully drawn perspectives of the handsome city. In quality of design and the artistry of craftsmanship, these houses could be held up anywhere proudly in comparison. Portland had arrived. Its business center was full of Italianate commercial palaces, its residential areas filled with a variety of remarkable homes, and all in a setting of snow-covered peaks and tree-covered hills. Portland had much to offer and was justly proud. In retrospect, we can only wonder how the residents of a city could reach such rare design heights, individually and collectively, and then allow the masterpieces of their most ingenious talents to totally disappear over time.

Queen Anne
CHARACTERISTICS

PLANS: asymmetrical, with extensions, diagonally placed corner bays, polygonal bays, and towers.

ROOFS: moderately and steeply hipped roofs with gabled extensions; cresting at ridges and upper flat areas; hipped, shed, or flat roofs over bays and verandas; steep conical or pyramidal roofs over towers. Introduction of jerkinhead at gabled extensions. Shingled roofs.

EXTERIOR FINISHES: flush, drop siding, shingles, or lap siding; vertical or diagonal boards or paneling at feature strips in entablature, second floor line, and water table.

CHIMNEYS: brick with corbeled or decorated top, ribbed sides; terra-cotta insets; single or double terra-cotta flue extensions; interior and exterior locations.

WINDOWS: tall, double-hung; one-over-one (1/1) panes; segmental or rectilinear tops. Paired or tripled at feature windows; groups of three to five in polygonal or conservatory bays. Some picture windows with stained-glass transom lights. Half-rounds or Palladian windows.

WINDOW TRIM (exterior): some bracketed cornices, most tied to vertical and horizontal trim lines.

ENTRANCE DOORS: paired or single, with transom above; vestibules with inner paired doors. Some sidelights found on Queen Anne houses with Colonial Revival influence.

VERANDAS/PORCHES: front, side, or wraparound verandas; detailed spindlework and ventilators.

INTERIOR FINISHES: plaster walls and ceilings; coved plaster cornices; paneled wainscoting; pressed wallpaper wainscoting and dado; wallpapered walls and ceilings.

INTERIOR TRIM: molded casings with head and foot blocks; multiple trimmed baseboards.

STAIRS: multiple landings; turned and Eastlake-design newels and railings; lights atop newels.

FIREPLACE FRONTS: cast-iron and marble fronts, with wood trim and overmantels.

PROPERTY SURROUNDS: picket fences with square or turned posts at corners and gates; stone perimeter walls and gate posts.

Entrance-stair newel of the Richard B. Knapp House.

Queen Anne
HOUSES

1881	Senator Joseph N. Dolph (Henry W. Cleaveland)	c. 1885	Blaise and Antoine Labbe (Warren H. Williams)
1881	George H. Williams (Joseph Sherwin)	1885	George H. Weidler (Warren H. Williams)
1881	Cicero Hunt Lewis		
1882	Richard B. Knapp (attributed to Justus F. Krumbein)	1886	Commanding Officer's Quarters, Fort Vancouver (William F. McCaw)
1884	Justus F. Krumbein (Justus F. Krumbein)	c. 1888	William E. Brainard
		1890	Frederick Bickel
c. 1885	Martha S. Thorton (William F. McCaw)	1890	George H. Durham
		1890	Johan Poulsen
1885	Rodney Glisan (attributed to Justus F. Krumbein)		

Senator Joseph N. Dolph (1881)
Henry W. Cleaveland

Once known as the finest mansion in the city, the enormous Joseph Dolph House introduced, in a grand manner, the Queen Anne style to Portland. The house's prominent gables, extending from its hipped roof, added exuberant visual pleasures as a cap to an otherwise Italianate polygonal-bayed house. In addition to the gables, with their wide, curved bargeboards, there was a four-story corner tower, two floors of which were fully exposed. It too had small, gabled facade dormers, in keeping with their larger counterparts, and a finialed, steeply hipped roof. On the north side of the house was a porte-cochere, by now *de rigueur* for the larger mansions. The house was designed by Henry W. Cleaveland, who continued to design homes for wealthy Portland families despite the growing number of prominent and exceptionally talented local architects.

The Dolph House sat on the rising block bounded by Jefferson and Columbia streets and Fifth and Sixth avenues, with the front entrance facing east, as were the major rooms. Main entrances of most houses were still located at the most accessible place for approach on foot from

Senator Joseph N. Dolph House.

The Dolph House in its prime.

the river and the city center. With the entrance located on the north side of the front elevation, under the tower, the major east-facing rooms could fully enjoy the considerable view of the eastern mountains, still undiminished by taller buildings.

The interior plan resembled that of the Second Empire Henry W. Corbett mansion of 1874 designed by Warren Williams. Its main entrance hall, entered from the house's northeast corner, was located just west of the major rooms. The library was located to the immediate left of the hall, and it had a large rectangular bay much like the one in the Henry Failing House of 1873, a Second Empire home also designed by Cleave-

The "Napoleon" drawing room, Dolph House.

The Dolph House shortly before demolition.

Master bedroom, Dolph House.

land. At the south end of the hall was the "Napoleon" drawing room, famous for its glittering social activity. Ample verandas protected these rooms from summer exposure. At the north end of the hall, opposite the entrance doors, was access from the porte-cochere. It was through these grandiose entrances that President Ulysses S. Grant and General William T. Sherman must have passed as guests of U.S. Senator Joseph

Dolph, then at the peak of his success. The Senator remained in the house until his death in 1897, after which his brother Cyrus A. Dolph came to occupy it. Years later, when the descendants had moved elsewhere, the house became The Casa Rosa rooming house. On 25 July 1926, *The Oregonian* stated the house was "marked for demolition to make way for progress."

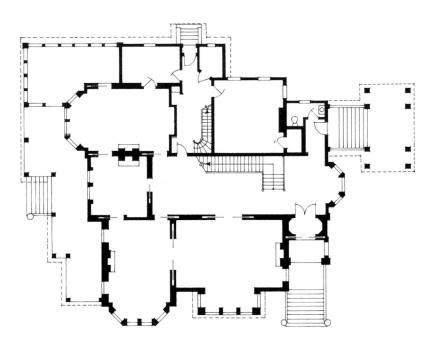

First floor plan, Dolph House.

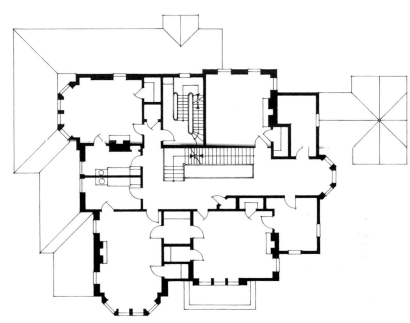

Second floor plan, Dolph House.

George H. Williams (1881)
Joseph Sherwin

The period of the 1880s and early 1890s saw incredible invention and experimentation. One large house that evades easy stylistic categorization was the mansion designed by architect Joseph Sherwin for former U.S. Senator and Attorney General, and later Portland Mayor, George H. Williams. Instead of the predominant gable with bracketed bargeboard, the architect chose for inspiration the masonry gable of medieval ancestry. Accordingly, all the details simulated their masonry counterparts. Other details were more of the Italianate style. The house had polygonal bays on every elevation and an extensive wrap-around porch. Cast-iron railings surmounted the porch, and a similar detail was used as roof cresting. Finials were found on the three-story east-facing tower, above the principal entrance, and on the tops of the masonry-like gables and facade dormers. A very high porte-cochere was entered on the south elevation, with a wide stair ascending to the main floor level. The spacious home was replaced on its site at Eighteenth Avenue and Couch Street by the Tudor Arms Apartments in 1915.

Cicero Hunt Lewis (1881)

Another roof variant used during the last decades of the nineteenth century was what might be called the Swiss-chalet style, as on the Cicero

George H. Williams House.

Cicero Hunt Lewis House.

Drawing room, Lewis House.

Hunt Lewis House of 1881. It is distinguished by an extensively projected low-pitched roof, supported by brackets, and decorative outer rafters with cross-ties. There were no bargeboards at the roof edge, which made the roof a cap-like top to an otherwise Italianate house, complete with two-story polygonal bays and spacious wrap-around verandas. Its facade treatment was similar to that of the Dolph House: horizontal drop siding at the first and second floors and vertical siding at the third floor, where third floor windows combined to make an entablature. Most distinctive was the fourth level open belvedere, commanding excellent views of the western hills, mountains, and central city from its location

between Nineteenth and Twentieth avenues and Glisan and Hoyt streets.

The drawing room of the Lewis home was one of the most handsome and gracious in the city. In an age proud of its eclecticism, the spacious room had considerable unity and luxurious appointments: the parquet floor, Oriental rugs, embossed wainscoting, marble fireplace with Eastlake style overmantel mirror, gas-lit chandeliers, and tufted Egyptian style furniture.

Richard B. Knapp (1882)
Justus F. Krumbein (attributed)

Still celebrated, long after its demise, as the premier Victorian construction in Portland, the Richard Knapp House of 1882 exemplified the incredible burst of architectural energy that came upon the city in the 1880s. The house had it all: a conical-roofed engaged tower, a steeply hipped central roof with gabled extensions, wide-projecting bargeboards, an angled corner bay, a porte-cochere, exposed chimneys with ribbed sides and corbeled tops, a wrap-around veranda with turned columns and balustrade railings, and a profusion of stained glass, all offering the spectacle of a fantastic, miniature-scaled castle.

The balance of elements was what made this house first rate. Its architect, as yet unknown but likely Justus Krumbein, exercised masterful control over the asymmetrical composition. Each facade weighed a projecting gable against a bay or tower, such that wherever the eye viewed the house, the elements were sculpturally in balance. For the first time in Portland, the nearly three-story brick chimneys were a prominent feature. No longer recessed behind an exterior wall, as they were in Italianate houses, the Knapp House chimneys were fully exposed, with brick, stone trim, and most remarkably, with windows above the mantels on both

Richard B. Knapp House.

the first and second floors. Inset in the brick-work were terra-cotta ornaments and the date of construction, 1882.

Other exceptional detailing was found in the cast-iron cresting, paneled bargeboards, cor-niced windows, and the fantastic wrap-around veranda. It combined Classical elements, in the pediments, and Eastlake elements, in the turned and paired columns, with spindlework at the entablature. Railings were inventive, having circular-pierced square panels, balusters, and geometric sculptures at the three-column clus-ters at the entrance porch. Surface finish mate-rials were drop siding at the main floor, flush horizontal siding at the second, and scalloped shingles within the gables and belt cornices of the tower. All surfaces were framed within sim-ple corner boards. The enrichment of surfaces extended to the roof, where regular horizontal shingle courses were embellished with bands of scalloped shingles.

The Knapp House interiors brought new dimensions to Portland in the theater of archi-tectural space. While the house enjoyed the practical nature of a central-hall scheme, new geometries came into play. The drawing room, for one, had an angled corner bay, balanced by the door to the entrance hall, which was itself balanced in the hall. A similar door on the other

Knapp House chimney, showing construction date inset.

Main entrance doors, Knapp House.

Entrance hall, facing east, Knapp House.

Entrance hall, Knapp House.

Main interior stairway, Knapp House.

Dining room, Knapp House.

Library, Knapp House.   Bedroom, Knapp House.

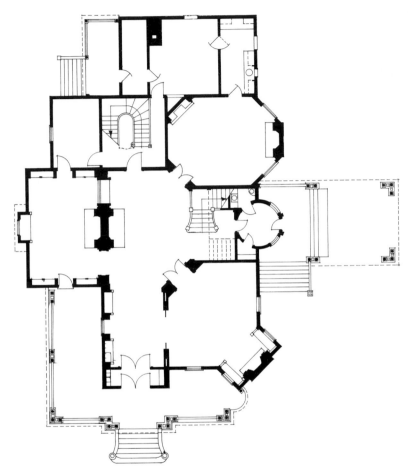

First floor plan, Knapp House.

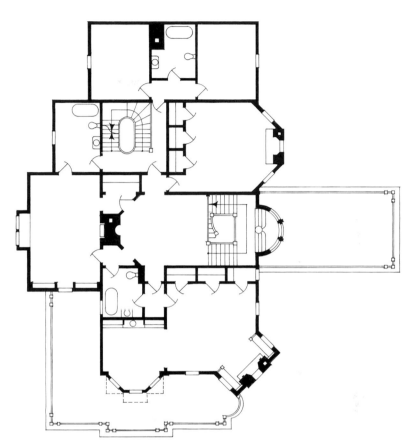

Second floor plan, Knapp House.

side of the stair gave access diagonally into the dining room, reflected again by the adjacent angled corners of the dining room, where a huge built-in buffet was placed, complete with over mirror, coved and recessed top, open shelves, and silver drawers below. The various reflecting angles formed the opus maximum—the baronial entrance hall with the main entrance on the east facade, facing the city, and the side carriage entrance, typically, on the north facade. The hall had coffered and beamed ceilings, full floor-to-ceiling wall paneling, elaborate door and window casings, built-in coat storage, and recessed seating niches. The elaborate sense of detailing extended to built-in lavatories and cabinets in the main bedrooms, bookshelves and corner niches in the library and parlor, and the extraordinary coffered third floor ballroom, with gilded wallpapers in the coffer panels. The exceptional glasswork at the front entry and in the tower were without peer in Portland. The interiors were fully recorded by photographer Minor White in the 1940s, when the Lindley family occupied the house. When the house was demolished in the 1950s, all salvageable parts were sold at auction, like pieces of a fine sculpture, and scattered across the city.

The house was situated on the block surrounded by Seventeenth and Eighteenth avenues and Davis and Everett streets. Only the beautifully wrought stone perimeter walls remain to remind us of what was and never could be again—the Northwest's pre-eminent Queen Anne style house, a truly irreplaceable masterpiece.

Justus F. Krumbein (1884)
Justus F. Krumbein

In 1884, the architect Justus Krumbein had his own home constructed on Sixteenth Avenue off Everett Street in the fashionable northwest area of Portland. Though appearing to be a modestly sized story-and-a-half house, it actually contained nine rooms, six on the main floor and three chambers on the second. Its design was from the Swiss-chalet school of the Queen Anne style, noted for the extended rafters and truss-like ties supporting its jerkinhead gable. The jerkinhead design was used here possibly for the first time in Portland. Remaining Italianate features were the one-story polygonal bays and the popular "conservatory" rectangu-

Justus F. Krumbein House.

lar bay off the dining room. The asymmetrical plan was masterfully ful-filled in the elevations, revealing a careful balance of sculptural forms, ap-propriate to their uses. Finishes included drop siding, a horizontal band of vertical siding at the second floor, and scalloped shingles at the gables and just under the roof. The house had every amenity, including a wine cellar, kitchen wood-hoist, gravity wood-burning furnace, and first floor study, possibly used by the architect for architectural work at home.

Martha S. Thorton (c. 1885)
William F. McCaw

A full set of working drawings has survived for a house designed by once-prominent architect William F. McCaw. The house was built for Martha Thorton on Irving Street midway between NW Twentieth and Twenty-first avenues in about 1885. The style was Queen Anne applied to a typical central-hall, double-bayed Italianate plan. Practical within the house's basic square, the parlor and library flanked the entrance stair hall, with the dining room behind the library and kitchen behind the

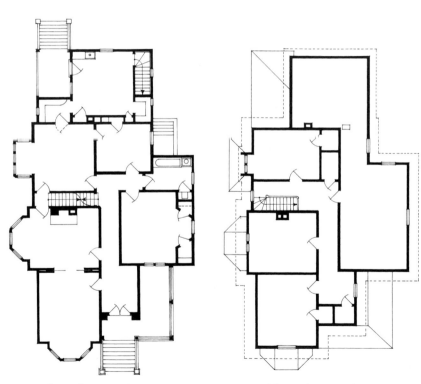

First floor plan, Krumbein House.   Second floor plan, Krumbein House.

Martha S. Thorton House.

parlor. The china pantry connected the kitchen and dining room, and a separate food pantry and back stair were off the kitchen. A servants' w.c. was accessible off the service porch. Five chambers and one bathroom were located on the second floor, with back stairs connecting to the attic.

The exterior elevations showed a careful balance between vertical and horizontal elements, adapted to the Queen Anne style. The first floor was separated from the second by an exterior band, similar to a belt cornice. Panels above and below the windows unified the design. The five-window bays had gabled tops, complete with bargeboards and scalloped shingle siding.

Rodney Glisan (1885)
Justus F. Krumbein (attributed)

When Rodney Glisan married Captain John Couch's daughter Elizabeth, they were given one of the 200-by-400-foot blocks allotted to the Couch children. The Glisan House was located between Nineteenth and Twen-

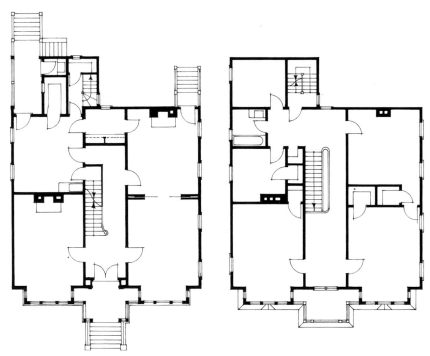

First floor plan, Thorton House.   Second floor plan, Thorton House.

Rodney Glisan House.

tieth avenues and Irving and Johnson streets, near the southeast corner of the big block. It was a large Queen Anne style house, bearing some similarities to the Knapp House of 1882. Although it had similar barge-boards and porch details, the Glisan House lacked the overall composi-tional unity of the Knapp House, with unresolved balance and confu-sions in its planning and elevations. The gabled third floor extension over a polygonal bay, however, was an idea that would come to be widely used in hundreds of Queen Anne style houses, if not entirely with success here.

Blaise and Antoine Labbe (c. 1885)
Warren H. Williams

Many of the blocks of Portland Heights had large homes constructed on them in the 1880s. They were accessible by carriage via Montgomery Drive, before the Vista (previously Ford Street) Bridge and Vista Avenue were constructed after the turn of the century. Two of these large homes were erected by the Labbe brothers, Blaise and Antoine, successful mer-chants in meat processing. The double mansions, located between Lau-rel and Myrtle streets on Nineteenth Avenue, were designed by architect Warren Williams. Though different, both houses featured extended ga-bles and prominent view-directed, three-story corner towers. Unusual were the large picture windows with transom lights above, a common feature of houses designed later in the 1890s. The houses were demol-ished by the 1910s and replaced with smaller Colonial Revival style homes.

Blaise and Antoine Labbe Houses.

George H. Weidler (1885)
Warren H. Williams

Another of the very large houses designed by architect Warren Williams with Queen Anne attributes was the impressive mansion for George H. Weidler built in 1885, sharing a large 200-by-400-foot block on Nine-teenth Avenue between Kearney and Lovejoy streets. Its exceptional height, and stature beyond its floor area, was achieved by having the

George H. Weidler House.

Commanding Officer's Quarters
Fort Vancouver (1886)
William F. McCaw

One of the few Queen Anne style houses remaining in the Portland metropolitan area, and open to the public, is the Commanding Officer's Quarters at Fort Vancouver, now known as the Marshall House on Officers Row, Vancouver. The house is relatively straightforward, befitting its military function. Plans for the central-hall scheme were drawn by Portland architect William F. McCaw. It incorporates the popular engaged tower, combining with it a viewing belvedere accessible off the

Commanding Officer's Quarters, Fort Vancouver.

main floor nearly a full floor above grade, adding to it very tall first and second stories, then a steeply pitched roof over half-story-high attic walls, and a full four-story tower over the entrance. Italianate features included the one- and two-story polygonal bays and the paired windows with short shed roofs, as were used in the Gothic Revival style. Likewise, the facade dormers were a new variant of an old idea, also used in the Gothic Revival period.

attic floor, and a considerable wrap-around veranda with pedimented extensions at the exterior entrance stair and the diagonal of the tower. Arched brackets, turned columns, and spindlework add to the classic Queen Anne details. McCaw employed an exterior paneling treatment around the siding similar to what he used in the Thorton House (c. 1885). In its original paint scheme, the house had dark trim with light siding. The present color scheme reflects more the Colonial Revival scheme found on the row after the last houses were constructed. The interiors feature a large parlor, with a fine fireplace surround, and an impressive entrance hall, with a handsome two-landing stairway.

Parlor, Commanding Officer's Quarters.

Commanding Officer's Quarters (Marshall House) today.

William E. Brainard (c. 1888)

Remarkably intact, except for the missing tower roof, cresting, and window shutters, the William E. Brainard House of circa 1888 at 722 SE Fiftyfourth Avenue is a handsome, if not typical, example of the Queen Anne style. It features a diagonally placed rectangular bay, extended to become an engaged three-story tower, and two polygonal bays, one with a hipped roof on the entrance facade and the other with a jerkinhead gable extended out over the bay. A unique porch with an oval opening is located under the jerkinhead. Verandas are situated at both the primary entrance and the side entrance, and they are designed with turned posts, balusters, and spindlework. A long flight of stairs, with a railing matching that of the veranda, provides access to the city-facing entrance doors.

    The house achieves its architectural unity by the careful tying together of its paneling system. Paneling is used at the entablature, the horizontal belt course, and the banding under the windows, the latter in line with the porch rail. Windows were not isolated but always a part of an overall geometric pattern. As such, the Brainard House remains a fine example among the extant Queen Anne style houses in Portland.

Frederick Bickel (1890)

Similar to the Brainard House was the home Frederick Bickel constructed in the King's Hill area of Portland between Vista and St. Clair avenues on Park Place. With a typical Italianate double-bay plan, the house combined a variety of design elements. Porch columns, corner boards, and bay pilasters had Corinthian capitals, while the hipped roof sported paired, onion-domed dormers. The gable-like roofs over the

William E. Brainard House.

Frederick Bickel House.

bays were pure invention, with no architectural precedents. New directions were heralded with a return to lap siding, this time framed by the water table, paneled belt course, entablature, and corner pilasters. Likewise, stained-glass transoms were found over the first floor windows, as in the Brainard House, but with Classically carved panels above them. Most handsome was the long entrance stair, with staggered side railings, facing the city.

Until the early 1970s, the house, still occupied by Bickel descendants, remained an island of ordered architecture and landscaping. Upon the death of Bickel's daughter, the house was sold and demolished. It was replaced, except for the street trees, by the Park Plaza Apartments.

George H. Durham (1890)

The home of George Hannibal Durham located at 2138 SW Salmon Street was perhaps the first house in Portland to combine Queen Anne and Colonial Revival details. The 1890 house has a typical Queen Anne style asymmetrical plan, with an L-shaped entrance hall, fronting on Salmon Street and with a side entrance on King Avenue. The gabled extensions off of the hipped roof and the fine gabled diagonal bay all have deep bargeboards. Likewise, a Queen Anne style corbeled brick chimney is fully exposed on the west elevation. Colonial Revival details are displayed primarily in the wrap-around north porch and west portico, the casing details of the entrance doors, and the lap siding with mitered corners. While the railings and Ionic column capitals remain intact on the west porch, they have been replaced with simpler details on the north porch.

The interiors are among the finest remaining in the city. Superb Corinthian style fluted columns and pilasters, with elaborate modil-

George H. Durham House.

lioned cornices and entablatures, adorn the entrance hall. Equally fine detailing is found in the stairway and in the living and dining room fireplace fronts.

Johan Poulsen (1890)

Queen Anne style houses were being constructed well into the 1890s, but with increasing evidence of Colonial Revival detailing. One of the finest extant examples in the city is the 1890 Johan Poulsen House located at 3040 SE McLoughlin Boulevard. Its hipped central roof has gabled extensions and a fine round corner tower, corbeled out from the first floor. The tower bears similarities with the one on the 1886 Commanding Officer's Quarters at Fort Vancouver; the spire finial, in fact, is identical. The primary viewing orientation from the tower belvedere

Johan Poulsen House.

and main rooms is northwest toward the city center, which is clearly visible from this Willamette bluff location. Another distinctive feature is the oriel window of the interior stair, placed over a polygonal bay between the corner tower and the north gable. The west gable, curiously, cantilevers out without a polygonal bay below it. In this gable is a Palladian window, a feature of both the Colonial Revival and Queen Anne styles. Exterior finishes include shingles and drop siding. The veranda, with boxed columns and railings, was added in about 1915.

CHAPTER 7

Eastlake

Although relatively few houses were constructed in Portland with Eastlake characteristics, the Eastlake style nonetheless produced some of the most remarkable houses ever constructed in the city and is, therefore, worthy of special attention. In dealing with the Queen Anne and Eastlake styles, it is difficult to draw any precise lines between them. Their plans were all but identical, practical in arrangement and designed for their particular sites. It was the exterior appearances, and especially the applied ornament, that stretched the Queen Anne style's assertiveness into the extraordinary of the Eastlake. However they are defined, the Eastlake houses in Portland, as elsewhere in the country, made some of the most dramatic and extreme statements in the history of American architecture. Yet the influences in their designs were so varied, and from such obscure sources, that it is unusually difficult to describe them. We do know that Charles Locke Eastlake, whose name is ascribed to the style, disassociated himself from the "Eastlake style" as it developed and was known in this country. Eastlake was a British furniture designer and author of *Hints on Household Taste in Furniture, Uphol-*

Portland, overlooking the King's Hill District, circa 1891.

167

stery and Other Details, a publication of 1872, with numerous reprintings, that profoundly influenced American interior design. He promoted interiors, as well as architecture in general, that would shed the excesses of the elaborate Italianate and Second Empire styles. He preached for simple, straightforward architecture and furniture, without the curved lines, the lavish carvings, and the endless bric-a-brac. Charles Eastlake is attributed with designing one house in the United States, the Sottile House (1895) in Charleston, South Carolina, and it provides some insight into the architecture he espoused. The other houses designed in the United States and labeled Eastlake, however, seemed to him "extravagant and bizarre." It is to those designs in Portland that we address this introduction.

The Eastlake style in Portland began much later than it did on the East Coast. By the early

Horseshoe arch, Islamic Empire, circa 480.

Sottile House, Charleston, South Carolina, 1895, design attributed to Charles Eastlake.

Chateau de Chenonceaux, France, 1515–23.

1880s, elements of fanciful and exotic detail began to appear on local residences. The extraordinary porch on the Knapp residence of 1882 had imaginative turnings but seemed to hold on to Classical proportions, substituting spindlework for an architrave. In 1884, in the design for the home of John Bridges, Justus Krumbein edged the porch detail considerably further into the fantastic. While some smattering of a gable is present above the porch opening, it appears supported by an incongruous turned-wood tension member. Columns, and particularly the small horseshoe-arched openings between the columns, are unlike any designs previously seen. Was it in imitation of a Moorish, or horseshoe, arch used throughout the Islamic Empire during the eighth century, or simply imagination gone rampant? Such novelty extends to the front gable, where a combination of theretofore unimaginable arrangements is offered over a polygonal bay. Arched ornaments span the central window, adjacent to brackets supporting the gable corners. But the gable is almost hidden by turned knob decorations, the spire at the ridge, shingles, dentil-like rows, and egg-and-dart detailing at the verge. To complete the originality of the porch and gable, the conical roof of the diagonally placed corner bay sits atop the bay somewhat like a dunce cap. De-

spite this novelty of forms, the front elevation is remarkably cohesive and surprisingly attractive. Such a distinctive departure inspired others to be bolder and display more detail.

Eastlake elaborations were further explored on the William W. Spaulding House (c. 1884). The entire sculpture of the house was fanciful,

adding gabled extensions, recessed openings, spindlework, or wall decorations wherever possible. It would seem that the houses of the period attempted to conjure up images of a complete French castle, such as the sixteenth-century Chateau de Chenonceaux, all on a 50-by-100-foot lot. The French examples had tow-

Tower, Chateau de Pierrefonds, France, fourteenth and fifteenth centuries; restored by Eugène Viollet-le-Duc, 1858–95.

Sixteenth-century house, Le Mans, France.

ered forms and remarkable roofs, all piled high with finialed spires, dormers, and chimneys. Perhaps this was the extreme statement that a man's home is his castle, whether it be merely balloon-frame construction, or even modest in size and in number of rooms.

Other houses showed comparatively more restraint. The Levi White House (1886) by architect Krumbein also had elements of a French chateau, mostly in its corner tower. Classical detailing can be seen, and there is some historical precedent, but this all is combined with Krumbein's remarkable Germanic gables. Krumbein added a recessed and projecting porch under the gable at the third floor. It was the romantic viewing spot of the eastern mountains, high above the other houses and trees, that invited one to climb the long staircases to the third floor to partake of the view. Eastlake architecture added experiences by design, places where the owner and friends could relate to the broader countryside, somewhat like the belvedere on Italian Villa or Italianate houses of the previous decades.

The extreme statement of the Eastlake style in Portland was the remarkable C. M. Forbes House of circa 1887 on Vista Avenue and Park Place. Here, imaginative decorations were given full play. Dominated by massive steeply pitched gables, a multitude of dormers, finials, a high corner tower, and vast quantities of spindlework, the house combined, it would seem, every style and influence in one. The

Siena Cathedral, Italy, 1245–1380.

Mark Hopkins Mansion, San Francisco, circa 1882.

Queen Anne style was presented in the plan and the multiple cross gables. The bargeboards were much more intricately pierced or decorated, however, in almost Gothic forms. Rounded corners at the eaves hovered out over the second floor corner porches, each decorated with further detail. Surprisingly, the gabled entrance of the wrap-around porch had elements of medieval Gothic Italian cathedrals, suggesting the portals of the cathedral of Siena (1245–1380) in Italy, which have similar pointed arches within steep gables. The Gothic quatrefoil parlor window in the Forbes House was totally unique, especially in its combination with a pointed arch. But it must have been a magnificent frame for the city view, with the outer windows filled with luxuriant stained glass. Similar windows lined the stairwell within the tower and were found in the paired entrance doors. While individual elements could be argued in the realm of taste, the entire composition was a remarkable tour de force, unquestionably an exciting and challenging piece of architecture.

Though the Forbes House dominated its surroundings, its neighborhood was dotted with other elaborate houses, each vying for the most turrets, towers, and belvederes. Nearby was the Spaulding House (c. 1884), with similar towers; the Bickel House (1890), immediately east, Queen Anne style with onion-dome dormers; the A. H. Johnson House (1873) with its fourth floor belvedere; the Henry Green mansion (c. 1883), with an array of French towers; the massive, Richardsonian style Loewenberg mansion (1891) just behind it with a huge tower; and St. Helen's Hall Episcopal Girl's School (1888–89), with viewing cupola diagonally across the street. What a splendid combination of fantastic forms crowning King's Hill, the effect of which can only be imagined from the photograph from the early 1890s. Despite its exuberances and decorative displays, the entire era of the Eastlake style came to an abrupt halt in the 1890s, when the restraint and massiveness of the Richardsonian and Shingle styles became fashionable and eventually superseded it. Though they were designed, built, and enjoyed with great enthusiasm, all of these remarkable Eastlake houses have long disappeared, lost to the indifference that has plagued highly imaginative and irreplaceable architectural treasures in our midst.

Eastlake
CHARACTERISTICS

PLANS: asymmetrical, with extensions, diagonal corner towers, and polygonal bays.

ROOFS: moderately and steeply pitched hipped; steep conical towers with large finials; ridge cresting or decorative ridge flashing. Shingled in decorative designs.

EXTERIOR FINISHES: drop siding or shingled with decorative patterns; vertical or diagonal patterns or paneling at feature strips in entablature, second floor line, or water table.

CHIMNEYS: stuccoed brick; ribbed sides; terra-cotta insets; single or double terra-cotta flue extensions; interior and exterior locations.

WINDOWS: tall, double-hung; one-over-one (1/1) panes. Paired or tripled at feature windows; three to five stacked in polygonal bays or conservatory extensions. Picture windows in keystone design, or with stained-glass transom lights.

WINDOW TRIM (exterior): inventive pediments, bracketed, most tied to vertical and horizontal trim.

ENTRANCE DOORS: paired or single, with transom lights.

VERANDAS/PORCHES: front, side, or wraparound; fanciful spindlework and railings; diagonal latticework ventilators at porch foundations.

INTERIOR FINISHES: plaster walls and ceilings; coved plaster cornices; paneled wood wainscoting or pressed wallpaper, and dado; wallpapered walls and ceilings.

INTERIOR TRIM: molded casings, with head and foot blocks; multiple trimmed baseboards.

STAIRS: multiple landings; geometrical, nonclassical newels with turned balusters, or square balusters infilled with cut-out patterned designs; decorative gas lights on newels.

FIREPLACE FRONTS: cast-iron and marble surrounds, with wood trim; shelved and mirrored overmantel.

PROPERTY SURROUNDS: stone walls replace picket fences.

Entrance porch of the John B. Bridges House.

Eastlake
HOUSES

1884   John B. Bridges (attributed to Justus F. Krumbein)
c. 1884 William W. Spaulding
1886   Levi White (Justus F. Krumbein)
c. 1887 C. M. Forbes
1890   John Palmer
1890   Bernard L. Stone
1892   Hon. William S. Mason

John B. Bridges (1884)
Justus F. Krumbein (attributed)

Though missing some of the original decorative trim, the John B. Bridges House remains on its original site at 1423 SW Columbia Street. The design is attributed to Justus Krumbein, as his name appears on the back of a period photograph. Although a smaller home, with no second floor, the house exhibits a great deal of stylistic bravado. A diagonal bay is stretched to become a miniature tower, complete with conical roof. Beside it is a low-sloped gable over a polygonal bay, unified by arched brackets and trimmed with decorative egg-and-dart molding. More

Parlor, Bridges House.

John B. Bridges House.

spectacular was the entrance porch detail, which has since been removed. Its miniature gable was supported by a cantilevered entablature, further extended with ties and roof brackets, clearly following artistic whim rather than structural clarity. The remainder of the house, covered with drop siding, is more conventional, having only a conservatory bay in the dining room (which Krumbein used in his own home). The parlor with the gilt overmantel mirror remained in the house late into the 1950s, when it too succumbed to neglect and vandalism. Restored, the house could again become an excellent example of the eclectic Eastlake style.

William W. Spaulding (c. 1884)

Once located on the northeast corner of Park Place and St. Clair Avenue, the William Spaulding House of circa 1884 commenced a series of spectacular houses in Portland, notable in their extraordinary invention and decorative exuberances. The design concept and plan were relatively comprehensible: gables extended on each facade from a central, steeply pitched hipped roof; a corner tower, commonly found on the more lavish homes, was placed to balance two opposing gables; in turn, a wraparound porch tied the two gables together, presenting a unified sculpture. The extremes of this house were its profusion of decorative ornaments. The porch columns, railings, and spindlework were extravagant with invention. The gabled elevations grabbed most of the attention; pedimented keyhole-shaped windows, open porches, and triangulated pediment extensions to the gables, all enriched by elaborate detail, combined to create a fanciful castle of eclectic origins. These tastes briefly flourished even after the more sober Colonial Revival styles entered the scene, as can be seen in the house in the background to the left in the photograph.

William W. Spaulding House.

Levi White (1886)
Justus F. Krumbein

From plans designed by architect Justus Krumbein, Levi White constructed one of the last of the huge mansions in northwest Portland. The house, in fact, was remarkably similar in plan to another Krumbein house, the Italianate Captain George Flanders House of 1882. The tower of the White House had an identical geometric roof and finials but was an additional story in height. The wrap-around veranda was similar, as were the main entrance steps and pedimented portico. Differences were evident in the gabled and extended bay above the entrance and the flatter polygonal bay to the right, which was topped with a facade dormer. The White House was celebrated in *The Oregonian* (1 January 1887), which stated,

> One of the largest, handsomest and most costly residences erected in Portland for several years is that belonging to Mr. Levi White

Levi White House.

on Twentieth Street. This elegant house occupies a prominent location, and in respect to architectural detail bears a most favorable comparison with any private residence in the city. It is an ornament of which the city should be proud.

This famous house was too large to remain in private hands, and it later became the North Pacific Sanitarium. Its grounds were described as "beautifully adorned by more than a hundred varieties of ornamental tress and shrubs, gathered at great expense and care from every continent of the globe." When the house was demolished, it was replaced by what is now the Couch School.

C. M. Forbes (c. 1887)

The quintessential Eastlake design house in Portland was the stupendous C. M. Forbes mansion of circa 1887, located at the northwest corner of Vista Avenue and Park Place. Though not as large as the Levi White mansion, the Forbes House managed to convey a gesture of ultimate decoration; every element, every surface, received maximum attention. The house used a typical asymmetrical plan, extended gable system, and corner tower, but it added considerably more. The gables had an extremely steep pitch, ending with rounded shoulders; the pierced and laced bargeboards were fanciful beyond belief; the windows were of extraordinary shape, with quatrefoils entwined with lancets; the wraparound veranda not only had spindles, but stalactite pendants and imaginatively adorned railings as well; and the tower, nearly hidden in its lacy surroundings, had a fine conical roof, facade dormers, and almost Tibetan-inspired finials. Gabled balconies project from every facade, providing what must have been magnificent viewing of the city and mountains beyond. This house came into being near the end of one of the most decorative periods in American architecture, marking a supreme confidence in inventive craftsmanship and ingenuity. Styles would shift drastically toward simplicity in the subsequent years, but it was great fun getting there.

C. M. Forbes House.

Forbes House.

John Palmer (1890)

Of all the large decorative Eastlake houses constructed in Portland, only the John Palmer House at 4314 North Mississippi Avenue remains standing. Its asymmetrical plan is reflected in the roof gables—two on the west facade and one on the south—each one different: the one to the left on the west facade houses a curved-wall third floor porch; the right one on the west facade is the pedimented roof for a second floor porch over the entrance doors; and the one on the south facade over a polygonal bay contains the attic windows. Extensive jigsaw work decorates the gable pediments. Additional porches on the second floor, with spindlework and horseshoe brackets, are built over the large wraparound veranda, later remodeled with Colonial Revival columns and stonework terraces. The main portion of the house is covered with drop siding, simple corner boards, and a paneled frieze, with scalloped shingles at the balcony rails. Fine stained-glass windows are used in the entrance doors and featured transom windows. The current owners, Mary and Richard Sauter, have completely restored the house with handsomely furnished period interiors, now using it as the John Palmer House Bed and Breakfast.

John Palmer House.

Bernard L. Stone (1890)

The well-known jeweler Bernard Stone constructed his residence in 1890 on SW Tenth Avenue between Taylor and Salmon streets, where the Medical Arts Building is now located. The house had unusual gables extended out over polygonal bays, each decorated with bracketed curved bargeboards or frets and spindlework. The main entrance porch featured a large horseshoe arch, with turned posts, pedimented roof, and clustered corner columns. Similar details were found in the open porch on the second floor. A fine broken-arch pediment surmounted the polygonal bay window of the front parlor, displaying a dropped round medallion, and the central hipped roof sported many finials of fanciful design. Dormers, added later, further complicated the roof structure while providing additional attic light. The interiors apparently matched the exteriors. According to Louise Aaron in "This Was Portland" (*Oregon Journal*, 1956), "people still talk about the intricately carved newel posts, balusters and handrail of the great staircase. That carving was the work of the late William J. Standley, first supervisor of mechanical training in Portland Public Schools."

Bernard L. Stone House.

Hon. William S. Mason (1892)

Surely the same imaginative hand that designed both the Spaulding and Forbes houses must have designed the William Mason House on Irving Street between Twentieth and Twenty-first avenues. The pedimented keyhole-shaped window of the Spaulding House is found here, as are elements of the unusual curved shingled walls of the second floor. Details of the spindled porch are relatively restrained, with Romanesque-like column capitals. The porch rail with an open space below the balusters is used in all three houses. Of all the unusual details, the arched gable, or facade dormer, is probably the most amazing, with dentiled bargeboard, horizontal spindlework across the top, and support columns over cantilevered brackets. Other window openings, such as the segmental-arched window below the gable, were symmetrically arranged, but often contrasting with oddly placed round medallions. Surfaces were drop siding at the main floor and highly textured shingle patterns at the second. The bracketed frieze, belt cornice, and decorative ribbed band above the water table tied together the various design elements.

Hon. William S. Mason House.

CHAPTER 8

Shingle/Richardsonian

A truly great period of American architectural creativity developed in the 1880s and 1890s, when emerged a style generally referred to as the Richardsonian style. In commercial buildings, it responded to the need for new designs following the invention and perfecting of the elevator, which had been patented by Elisha Graves Otis in 1853. Taller commercial structures were then possible, as well as a new aesthetic to accommodate them. The great names in the development of commercial buildings are legend to students of architecture. Great strides were accomplished by William Le Baron Jenney (1832–1907) in Chicago, followed by Henry Hobson Richardson (1838–1886) and Louis H. Sullivan (1856–1924). The Romanesque Revival, an offshoot of the Gothic Revival style, was initiated by Richardson. His celebrated Trinity Church (1873–77) in Boston adapted the design of the Salamanca Old Cathedral in Spain, a massive Romanesque style stone structure with impressive arches. The construction of Trinity Church was followed by McKim, Mead and White's designs for the Newport Casino (1879–81) in Rhode Island, which employed similar massive forms ac-

Portland, overlooking the King's Hill District, circa 1892.

181

cented by large, steeply pitched triangular gables, rounded turrets, and facade dormers. The Casino's facade combined rusticated stone at the first floor and a tight skin of shingles at the upper floors. With the era's concentration on sculptural form, any superfluous decorative elements were eliminated, achieving a similar design aesthetic with structures sheathed in shingles (Shingle style) as those constructed of heavy masonry (Richardsonian style).

In the early 1880s, a multitude of houses were designed by ingenious architectural talents in the United States, the most important of which included Richardson, the firm of Peabody and Stearns, and the firm of McKim, Mead and White. One of the first residential structures to emphasize the arch, rounded forms, and rusticated stonework that defined the period was the Ames Gate Lodge in North Easton, Massachusetts, designed by H. H. Richardson in about 1880. The building, with plan, appeared in the 1885 edition of *American Architect and Building News*, deeply influencing architects around the country. One small new feature also appeared on it: the eyebrow dormer,

which provided attic light without sacrificing the pure sculpture of the building. This feature appeared later on countless houses throughout the country and on a number of Portland houses in the style. The same eyebrow appeared in a later Richardson design, the Crane Library (1880–83) in Quincy, Massachusetts, along with the massive entry arch and Romanesque tower and window fenestration. Another impressive arch, designed in shingles, was for the G. N. Black residence in Manchester-by-the-Sea, Massachusetts, called Kragsyde (1882), by the firm of Peabody and Stearns. Its design also emphasized the sculptural volume, all shingled at the upper floors and sitting

Trinity Church, Boston, Massachusetts, 1873–77, designed by H. H. Richardson.

Newport Casino, Newport, Rhode Island, 1879–81, designed by McKim, Mead and White.

Ames Gate Lodge, North Easton, Massachusetts, 1880–81, designed by
H. H. Richardson.

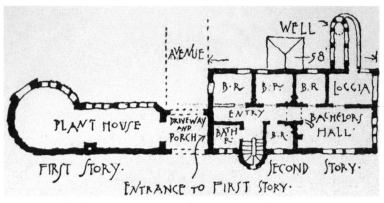

Plan for the Ames Gate Lodge by H. H. Richardson. Printed in
American Architect and Building News, 1885.

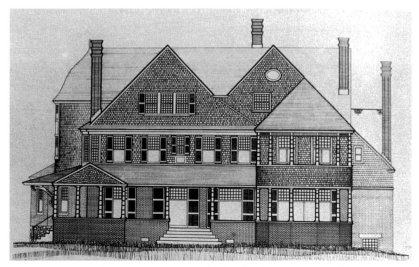

Isaac Bell House, Newport, Rhode Island, 1882, designed by
McKim, Mead and White.

M. F. Stoughton House, Cambridge, Massachusetts, 1883, designed
by H. H. Richardson.

above a base of rough stone. Despite its complexity and angled wings, the tight skin of the house unified the composition.

A somewhat similar house, and equally influential, was that of Isaac Bell in Newport, Rhode Island, designed by McKim, Mead and White in 1882. Its massive triangular pediment had three rounded attic windows, in series, which suggested in shingles the same three windows used in the pediment of Richardson's

Lionberger House, Chicago, Illinois, 1886, designed by H. H. Richardson.

Crane Library. The Bell House had a rounded engaged tower projecting from the main volume of the house, and a two-story piazza had thin columns supporting its tiered balconies and conical roof. An even more important house, also widely published, was the severely tailored M. F. Stoughton House (1883) designed by H. H. Richardson in Cambridge, Massachusetts. The area of the windows in the facade was reduced in proportion to the area of the shingled siding, later a trademark of the Richardsonian style. The Stoughton House offered an overall massiveness, including an engaged tower with conical roof, openings carved into its structures, and most unusual, virtually no historical reference to its design, other than its slightly Romanesque forms.

Severity of basic structure was continued farther north in the houses designed by John Calvin Stevens. In his James Hopkins Smith House (1885) in Falmouth Foreside, near Portland, Maine, the shingled roof, gambrel-roofed gables, and pedimented dormers meld into one architectural whole. The sculptured mass is entwined by a rustic-stone first floor elevation, complete with the massive arch that was the signature feature of both the Shingle and Richardsonian styles.

Several of the houses designed by H. H.

Richardson in Chicago were repeated in various forms around the country. The Lionberger, Franklin MacVeagh, and John J. Glessner houses (all dating from 1885 to 1887) emphasized an engaged turret, rounded arches, transomed windows, and ashlar-bond stonework. This aesthetic influenced on the West Coast Dunsmuir Castle in Victoria, British Columbia, designed by Portland architect Warren H. Williams in 1889. It took inspiration from Trinity Church, Boston, as well as from the Chicago houses of Richardson, and even from the Eastlake style, the exuberances of which it did not entirely shed. It was the Julius Loewenberg House of 1891, Portland's truly outstanding masterpiece in the style, that captured all the great design features of Richardson's impressive Chicago houses. These features were known to Portland architects through architectural publications. Influential magazines such as *American Architect and Building News*, *American Builder*, *Architecture and Building*, and *Inland Architect and Builder* brought the best of the Chicago and New England houses to Portland through the 1880s and 1890s, fully illustrated and with plans. Of particularly appealing artistry were the sketches by Eldon Deane that appeared in the issues of *American Architect and Building News* during the 1880s.

More important to Portland was the arrival of two notable architects with direct experience in the most famous eastern firms. William Macy Whidden had worked for McKim, Mead and White, and Ion Lewis had worked for Peabody and Stearns, when they formed their famous and productive partnership in Portland in 1889. Their most important house in the Richardsonian style, the Mackenzie residence of 1892, survives in the city, albeit with extensive additions. Its design in stone and slate shingles is exceptional and matches its extraordinary interior. The larger and more remarkable Loewenberg mansion did not survive, a loss to the city's history as irreparable as the loss of McKim, Mead and White's Portland Hotel.

Portland's Shingle style houses also were influenced by the major national design trends. When the Queen Anne style still predominated, shingles were used to cover only the upper stories or more modest triangular attic gables. This trend continued on through the Eastlake style, well into the 1890s. The transition began in 1888 with the shingle-covered James C. Van Rensselaer House. Simple geometric forms dominated the design, with shingles covering the roof and two stories of exterior walls. Engaged towers shorn of all dec- oration replaced the wildly exuberant Eastlake towers of previous designs. The Howard Stratton House (c. 1894) and the Quinn House (c. 1890) offer designs tending toward other styles, the Queen Anne and the Colonial Revival, respectively.

John J. Glessner House, Chicago, Illinois, 1886, designed by H. H. Richardson.

Dunsmuir Castle, Victoria, British Columbia, 1889, designed by Warren H. Williams.

The Friedlander House, designed by Edgar M. Lazarus, and the H. C. Campbell House, which is attributed to Whidden and Lewis, fully brought the Shingle style to Portland. Certainly, elements of McKim, Mead and White's Newport Casino can be found in the Campbell House, particularly in the polygonal tower with its bell-shaped roof. More exaggerated shingle forms are evident in the gambrel-roofed Frederick V. Holman House of 1890 and the Isaac Hodgson, Jr., House of 1891. The high fashion of the Shingle style came to Portland with all the vigor and vitality of its eastern counterparts, evolving slowly until after the turn of the century, when the stylistic features seemed to meld into the Arts and Crafts style.

Shingle/Richardsonian
CHARACTERISTICS

PLANS: asymmetrical with extensions; polygonal bays; round or polygonal engaged towers; rounded three-story bay window projecting above cornice. Generously proportioned medieval-style hall or living hall.

ROOFS: moderately or steeply pitched, with triangular flush gable ends; recessed or shed-roofed porches; steep conical towers or turrets, sometimes with belvederes; facade dormers; eyebrow dormers. Slate or shingled.

EXTERIOR FINISHES: ashlar-bond stone (larger houses), or shingles (smaller houses); battered stone or shingled base. Sometimes stone at the first floor, shingles at the second floor.

CHIMNEYS: stone or brick at interior locations, or featured on exterior; decorative iron ties to the roof.

WINDOWS: double-hung; one-over-one (1/1) panes, or diagonally paned upper sash; arched openings; large picture windows with transom. Stone houses had windows with transoms and heavy lintels between.

WINDOW TRIM (exterior): minimal in both wood and stone houses.

ENTRANCE DOORS: heavily paneled oak, with upper windows protected by decorative iron grille; leaded transom and sidelights.

VERANDAS/PORCHES: recessed entrance porch with large rounded arches, or shingled piers.

INTERIOR FINISHES: quarter-sawn oak paneling at walls and ceilings; heavily carved feature elements; transom spindlework. Plaster walls and ceilings in shingle-covered houses.

INTERIOR TRIM: elements blend together, no one element taking precedence over the others.

STAIRS: elaborate bifurcated stairs; large stair windows; inglenooks under landings; elaborately carved newels and balustrade.

FIREPLACE FRONTS: Renaissance or Tudor details, extensive carvings.

PROPERTY SURROUNDS: ashlar-bond stone walls to support banks, or berming with lawn.

Entrance to the Dr. Kenneth A. J. Mackenzie House.

Shingle/Richardsonian
HOUSES

c. 1888	James C. Van Rensselaer	1892	Henry J. Hefty (Henry J. Hefty)
c. 1890	Quinn Residence	1892	Henry J. Corbett (Whidden and Lewis)
c. 1890	Friedlander Residence (Edgar M. Lazarus)	1893	William Honeyman (Whidden and Lewis)
c. 1890	H. C. Campbell (attributed to Whidden and Lewis)	1893	Theodore B. Wilcox (Whidden and Lewis)
1890	Frederick V. Holman (Edgar M. Lazarus)	c. 1894	Howard Stratton
1891	Isaac Hodgson, Jr. (Isaac Hodgson, Jr.)	c. 1895	Henry Noble
1891	Julius Loewenberg (Isaac Hodgson, Jr.)	1896	Hardy C. Wortman
1892	Dr. Kenneth A. J. Mackenzie (Whidden and Lewis)	1902	Emil Schacht (Emil Schacht)
1892	George F. Heusner (Edgar M. Lazarus)	1908	R. B. Lamson (Josef Jacobberger)

James C. Van Rensselaer (c. 1888)

The transition between styles is often inadequately recorded. Fashion does not abruptly change into convenient time periods beginning and ending on certain days. Between the ornate, if not extravagant, Queen Anne and Eastlake styles and the more subdued Shingle and Richardsonian styles, a number of houses were constructed showing influences of both. The James C. Van Rensselaer House, once located on SW King Avenue at Park Place, was one of the first houses to strip away the extraordinary detail such as that displayed in the Eastlake C. M. Forbes mansion, its nearby neighbor to the west on Park. The Van Rensselaer House was simply clad with shingles at its second floor and gables, without the confines of corner-board trim or sculpted patterns. Large triangular gables were likewise unadorned, and the eaves had no projection, clearly reflecting the new design trends from the East. The only decorative elements were the turned porch posts, and possibly the unassuming half-timbering at the large front gable, or the modest broken pediment over the second floor side windows. Shingles were left to weather, and the trim was dark, another innovation of the Shingle style.

James C. Van Rensselaer House.

Quinn (c. 1890)

Other houses continued the mix of styles. Furthering the development of the large, Shingle style front gable, the Quinn House of circa 1890 adapted the additional influence of the Colonial Revival style. Shutters adorn its windows, and the porch features simple Roman Doric columns. The modillioned and extended cornice is also a design characteristic of the emerging Colonial Revival. Yet the Shingle style is clearly represented by the shingle siding without corner boards. Unassigned to any particular style are the rounded bays under the attic gables. No designs of this nature were found in the Portland Queen Anne style houses, but they could be associated with late-nineteenth-century English residential architecture, or perhaps with the Colonial Revival. The Howard Stratton House, built about four years later, is another example of this eclectic mix of styles during the 1890s.

Quinn House.

Friedlander House.

Friedlander (c. 1890)
Edgar M. Lazarus

The first in a series of Portland houses to clearly exhibit the influences of such eastern architects as Henry H. Richardson was a house designed by Portland architect Edgar M. Lazarus, still standing at 2233 NW Flanders Street. Though not large, the Friedlander House manages to capture the major Shingle style features: shingle siding with oval designs in diagonal patterns; a round corner tower with conical roof; hipped central roof with gable extensions; and diagonally pedimented dormers. Simplicity

is the rule, with no corner boards, little or no window casing, patterned shingles in place of trim for the gable wall and roof, and instead of an added front porch or veranda, the entrance was recessed into the main volume of the house (now altered from the original). In fact, almost all detail that would distract from the purity of the forms was discarded. This alternate style was not only a refreshing change from the excesses of the Eastlake style, but it could be called an architectural revolution, still using the fondly appreciated corner tower, but clothing it in the more modest garments of shingles and without accessories.

H. C. Campbell (c. 1890)
Whidden and Lewis (attributed)

One of the finest of the 1890s Shingle style houses in Portland was constructed for H. C. Campbell on the northwest corner of SW Vista Avenue and Carter Lane. Basically, the house was side gabled, with a large wraparound veranda and a polygonal tower with bell-shaped roof. A roof dormer, with a cantilevered balcony, projected at the third floor. All surfaces were shingled, except the stuccoed gables. Even the balcony piers and the porch supports were shingled, simulating their masonry counterparts. Balcony railings between the shingled piers had simple square balusters. Windows, equally simple, had little casing trim, twelve-over-one (12/1) panes at the attic, and were transomed at the first and second floors. Only the handsome ashlar-bond stone wall, which surrounded the property, remains to this day, the house being replaced by a home designed by Albert E. Doyle for Allen Meier, and later by a 1950s Meier home designed by Walter Gordon in the Northwest style. The Campbell House's architect is unrecorded, but the design is attributed to Whidden and Lewis, whose 1892 Mackenzie House bears strong resemblance.

Frederick V. Holman (1890)
Edgar M. Lazarus

The gambrel roof came to Portland, Oregon, via Portland, Maine. Printed in numerous architectural publications, the work of architect John Calvin Stevens in Maine in the 1880s featured the Shingle style and

H. C. Campbell House.

Frederick V. Holman House.

Side elevation, Holman House.

Parlor, Holman House.

the gambrel roof. Portland, Oregon, architect Edgar Lazarus took up the gambrel roof with great gusto in his 1890 Shingle style design for Frederick Holman. Extant at 1500 SW Taylor Street, the highly modified house still shows evidence of its once-exuberant forms and architectural detail. The gambrel-roofed gables dominate all elevations, combining both single and double-entwined gambrels. The gambrels are steep, even exaggerated, containing both the second and third floors. Other features of eastern influence are the front-elevation Palladian window and the shingle-covered arched entrance porch. Originally, the house was detailed with shingle courses following the curve of the porch arch and with a roof railing of shingled piers and square, closely spaced

balusters. These remarkable features have been removed and the house covered with other sidings. If restored, however, the house could once again be an excellent example of the Shingle style.

Isaac Hodgson, Jr. (1891)
Isaac Hodgson, Jr.

Another architect in Portland, and one who dealt with the new influences from the East, was Isaac Hodgson, Jr. He constructed his own home on the park-like triangle formed by SW Elizabeth and Hawthorne streets in 1891. The large Shingle style home was remarkably daring for its time, introducing cantilevered gambrel-style gables and porches. Large picture windows, some diagonally placed at corners, captured the impressive view from the property; other windows had 4/2 panes. The shingled dormers, with cantilevered pediments, were prominent on the gambrel roof. As in other houses of the period, the footings and chimney were masonry, in this case rubble stone. Oval and half-round ventilators at the peak of the gable were Colonial Revival in nature, as were the painted shingles and green shutters. Later improvements to the house were made by the subsequent owner, John C. Ainsworth, who

was a prominent banker and son of Captain J. C. Ainsworth. Ainsworth lived in the house for most of its existence and hired landscape architect Thomas Hawkes to design a Classical balustraded entrance turnaround and stairs to Elizabeth Street below. These remain, although the Hodgson House was demolished and replaced by a Roscoe Hemenway designed house in the 1950s.

Julius Loewenberg (1891)
Isaac Hodgson, Jr.

The pre-eminent Richardsonian design to be constructed in Portland in the 1890s, and the city's largest house to that date, was the thirty-two room mansion constructed by Julius Loewenberg, wealthy capitalist and President of the Merchants' National Bank. The house, named Cedar Hill, was located on a 200-by-200-foot lot situated at the top of SW Park Place, adjacent to Washington Park. Specially brought to Portland to design and supervise construction, architect Isaac Hodgson, Jr., had a first-rate talent for designing structures in the new Richardsonian style. Hodgson created a masterpiece, truly without peer on the West Coast and possibly among the finest examples of this style of architecture in the country. The house's massive forms, carefully sculpted to take advantage of the location and views, sat majestically on its site. A circular drive gave access to the porte-cochere and the arched stone entrance porch, with their Romanesque columns. The two entrances provided a gracious and impressive entry into the two-story balconied entrance hall, noted for its oak paneling. Off the entrance hall was a delightful glass conservatory filled with exotic plants.

The best of the Richardsonian designs were applied to the exterior. Particularly impressive were the three-story tower, with belvedere, pro-

Isaac Hodgson, Jr., House.

Julius Loewenberg House.

jecting from the central hipped roof, and the projecting stone gables, the most memorable of which topped the arched porte-cochere. At the corner of the main house volume was a corner turret, complete with narrow windows and polygonal roof. Large facade dormers projected from the roof, making the third floor fully usable. The windows were exceptionally designed, each having the typical transom lights with stone lintels between, sometimes one above the other. Stonework extended over the entire structure, smooth-cut in feature areas, but mostly stacked rows of large and small horizontal courses of rough-finished stone. The smooth-cut frieze, a unifying design feature, extended even into the tower's stone railing, where it was pierced with openings. The entrance terrace bore solid railings, unified into the conservatory stonework. The house roof, in contrast but complementary to the handsome stonework, was covered with smooth red-slate shingles, possibly the only use of this material in the city.

The financial panic and crash of 1893 did not bode well for Loewenberg's fortune. As part owner of the Merchants' National Bank, he was forced to cover bank-runs with his personal funds. In considerably reduced circumstance, Loewenberg remained in the mansion until his death in 1899. His widow then sold the house in 1903 to Frederick Ledbetter, wealthy son-in-law of Henry Pittock. The house remained in the Ledbetter family until 1951, when it was given by Ledbetter's widow to the Oregon Historical Society. It was later owned by the Commerce Investment Company, who by 1960 had demolished the famed structure. An architectural treasure vanished without a trace, to be replaced by an undistinguished apartment house.

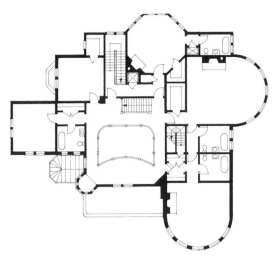

Second floor plan, Loewenberg House.

Entrance hall, Loewenberg House.

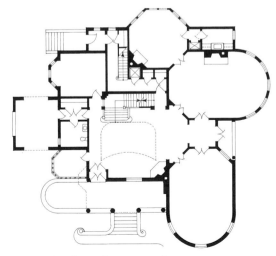

First floor plan, Loewenberg House.

Dr. Kenneth A. J. Mackenzie House.

Dr. Kenneth A. J. Mackenzie (1892)
Whidden and Lewis

Though considerably smaller than the Loewenberg mansion, the Dr. Kenneth A. J. Mackenzie House at 615 NW Twentieth Avenue can be ranked among the city's best works of architecture, and a superb example of the Richardsonian style. Particularly appealing is the dynamic sculpture of the intersecting cone-roofed tower and the large side-gabled central volume of the house. With unparalleled flair, the architects Whidden and Lewis united design forms of Henry H. Richardson with the triangular gabled dormers influenced by English architect Richard Nor-

Entrance hall, Mackenzie House.

man Shaw. The massive stonework, laid in broken range bond, combines handsomely with the blue-gray slate shingles covering the roof and gable. Wood modillions support the roof eaves on both the tower and main roof. A typical Richardsonian feature is the stone arched entrance porch, recessed into the main house structure. An arched window recess, outlined with radiating shingles and featuring a huge cast-iron stag's head, lies above the stone bay of the dining room on the Hoyt Street elevation. The recessed windows of the facade have leaded transoms at the main floor, a variety of pane work in the tower, and 1/1 panes elsewhere. Seen for the first time in Portland, a notable eyebrow dormer

Main stairway and fireplace inglenook, Mackenzie House.

Main stairway, Mackenzie House.

Dining room fireplace, Mackenzie House.

Library, Mackenzie House.

Original dining room buffet, Mackenzie House.

is seemingly carved out and lifted up from the roof shingles just above the entry porch. A pair of small dormers on the Hoyt Street elevation echo the large front-elevation dormer, with their curved and paned window glass and unique triangular gables. Balancing the composition are the massive stone chimneys at each end of the house, one serving the library and dining room and the other the main parlor. Keeping with the simplicity of the structure, the chimneys have clean-cut tops, without the corbeling favored by the Queen Anne and Eastlake designs.

The house's interiors remain among the finest of the period. The oak paneling of the entrance hall and dining room is exceptional. With coffered and beamed ceilings, fireplace inglenooks under the stair landing and in the library, and columned hall divisions with spindlework, the interior spaces reveal the richness of interior design work that is possible when quality construction and first-rate finish work is carried throughout the house. Particularly noteworthy are the support figures of the intricately carved dining room fireplace mantel, which match in design similar support figures on the massive buffet.

After Dr. Mackenzie's death in 1920, the house remained in family ownership until 1936. Eventually, it was purchased by the Episcopal Laymen's Mission Society, later becoming the William Temple House. An extensive addition was sensitively added to the back of the house, while the main structure and impressive interior rooms have been beautifully restored, some with original furnishings. Only the former parlors have been significantly altered, and they now serve as a chapel.

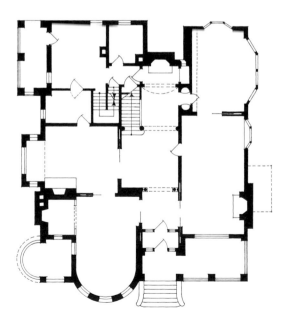

First floor plan, Mackenzie House.

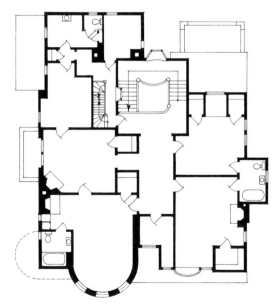

Second floor plan, Mackenzie House.

George F. Heusner (1892)
Edgar M. Lazarus

Architect Edgar M. Lazarus achieved one of his most notable successes in the large Shingle style George Heusner House located at 233 NW Twentieth Avenue. Constructed in 1892 on its quarter-block frontage, the house has a steeply pitched gable extending from its hipped central volume, balanced with an engaged corner tower topped with a bell-shaped roof. An extensive wrap-around veranda faces the street. The veranda piers and railing, the house's foundation, and three massive chimneys are all constructed out of ashlar-patterned sandstone. Stone

George F. Heusner House.

piers also support the corner veranda extension, diagonally planned somewhat like an attached gazebo. To give the shingled house a slightly medieval air, the window top sashes at the second floor have diagonal mullions, while the bottom sashes have a single pane. Lazarus experimented with a variety of new window treatments, such as the eyebrow dormer near the top of the roof and a partially recessed dormer with a hipped roof. Most of the Lazarus houses had widely projecting eaves, supported by modillions, and graceful concave curves at the eave extension.

Henry J. Hefty (1892)
Henry J. Hefty

Swiss-born architect Henry J. Hefty designed a home for himself in 1892, with design forms similar to those used in plans for a massive new Portland City Hall, which was never constructed because of exorbitant costs. Like the City Hall scheme, and his Grand Central Hotel of a few years earlier, Hefty's house had an engaged corner tower and was constructed of ashlar-bond stone. The second floor had a stuccoed finish, using the stone as window and cornice dressing. Details of the dressed-stone porch and belvedere columns were in the Ionic style, unusual for a Richardsonian styled structure. More typical features of the period were the 1/1 window panes, the central hip of the roof, the arched stone window, and the hipped-roof dormer. The fine drawing of the house, a lost art form today, was featured in the 1892 *Oregon Souvenir* booklet promoting a new residential district in the city. It is possible, though, that the house was never constructed by the architect. Both the loss of the City Hall project and the business recession of 1893 undoubtedly caused Hefty considerable duress.

Henry J. Hefty House.

Henry J. Corbett (1892)
Whidden and Lewis

With influences from the resort work of McKim, Mead and White of New York, the Henry J. Corbett House on SW Madison Street and Park exemplified the varying designs brought to Portland by architects Whidden and Lewis. In the Corbett House of 1892 can be seen elements of the grand "cottages" of Newport, Rhode Island, summer homes for wealthy New Yorkers. The shingled gables, turned veranda posts, and latticed round openings were prominent elements of the Newport homes. This house, however, had ashlar-bond stonework at the first floor and extending to the veranda balustrade posts, which tied it to the Richardsonian influences out of Chicago. Because of the stonework, main floor windows were deeply recessed and double-hung with 1/1 panes, smaller on the top than the bottom, and the upper floor windows had 20/1 panes. Sitting on an expansive lot, with mature plantings, the house expressed a rural quality, despite its being increasingly surrounded by commercial buildings. By 1924, the Corbett House was one of the few remaining private residences on the South Park Blocks, when it was replaced by the Masonic Temple.

Henry J. Corbett House.

William Honeyman (1893)
Whidden and Lewis

The permanent qualities of the Richardsonian style appealed to wealthy homeowners. Houses constructed of tenino sandstone and roofed with slate could last without extensive maintenance for hundreds of years. William Honeyman had Whidden and Lewis design for him an impressive mansion on King Avenue in the King's Hill District, where the King Tower Apartments are presently located. The 1893 house had the usual corner tower—with flared conical roof and topped with a copper finial—

William Honeyman House.

and the transomed windows found in the Richardsonian style. The veranda across the King Avenue facade had stone railings and support piers and a thin, flat roof. Dormers, adorned with the same finials as the corner tower, proliferated across the central hipped roof, from which arose massive chimneys, all in somewhat medieval designs. The house was praised for its handsome bifurcated central-hall staircase and great windows over the entrance doors. As was the case with many drawing rooms, the one in the Honeyman House had white painted paneling, and it was considered French in character. Such rooms contained the more formal gilt-covered French furniture with needlepoint tapestry upholstery.

Theodore B. Wilcox (1893)
Whidden and Lewis

Of the great houses that once covered King's Hill, the Theodore B. Wilcox House is one of the few remaining and one of the finest. In the early 1890s, architects Whidden and Lewis were providing first-rate designs for their clients in both the Richardsonian and the new Colonial Revival styles. The Wilcox House at 931 SW King Avenue was designed partially in the former—primarily in the sandstone construction of the first floor—but with elements of the Shingle style at the second floor and Tudor style details in the dormers of the third floor. The first floor windows have the typical stone detail of transom lights, supported with dressed-stone lintels, whereas the exceptional carvings around the entrance portal are much more Classically inspired. The unusual double dormers on the hipped roof have decorated gable ends. The decorative designs on these gables display Tudor motifs made popular by the English architect Richard Norman Shaw in the 1860s and 1870s, not popular in the United States until the 1876 Philadelphia Centennial and the British commissioner and delegates' residences constructed there. By the 1890s, the influence of such Tudor details had reached Portland, remaining a design influence for the next forty years.

The interiors are the crowning glory of the Wilcox House. Of particular merit is the luxuriously rich entrance hall, completely paneled in quarter-sawn golden oak and featuring a bifurcated stair, on axis with the main parlor. The designs have elements of Tudor influence as well as Classical Roman. Ceiling-panel work is Tudor, yet the column capitals and ceiling cornice have egg-and-dart detailing. Most handsome is the stair railing, with Tudor-influenced urns on the newels and a woven-metal mesh in the railing openings. The original wallpaper is still in

Theodore B. Wilcox House.

Entrance portal, Wilcox House.

Entrance hall, Wilcox House.

Main interior stairway, Wilcox House.

Dining room, Wilcox House.

place, imitating richly tooled Spanish leather. Equally fine is the dining room, paneled in Honduran mahogany and with an embossed plaster ceiling and inlaid wood floor. An impressive marble fireplace with carvings, paneling, and columns decorates the end wall, and a buffet is recessed into the side wall. Handsome original light fixtures complete the room. Still in prime condition, these charming rooms rank among the finest in the city, irreplaceable in the quality of their design and craftsmanship of construction.

Howard Stratton (c. 1894)

Although constructed in 1894, the Howard Stratton House still incorporates considerable Queen Anne style detail. Extant at 2182 SW Yamhill Street, the house displays the large triangular front gable of the new

Howard Stratton House.

Shingle style, but it maintains the flourish of a decorative wrap-around porch. Further Queen Anne enrichments are found in its pedimented opening at the front door, the arched spindlework at the second floor balcony, and the semicircular city-viewing loggia. In addition, the large front gable, supported by large brackets, is further articulated with a recessed polygonal bay at the attic, and it features ventilators and block designs on the gable shingles.

Henry Noble (c. 1895)

The gambrel roof was often used by architects during the 1890s. Its use held several advantages: a second, and possibly third, story could be accommodated within its framework; it provided an attractive sculptural form; and it made historical allusions to the country's Dutch residential architecture of the Colonial period. In the Henry Noble House at 2370 NW Flanders Street, that allusion to our Colonial past was added to with the Palladian window in the gable end of the house. Newer architectural influences are seen in the use of ashlar-bond stonework for the massive chimney, foundations, and terrace work. Other prominent design features include the shed-roofed dormers and the one- and two-story cantilevered bays. Windows are casement or double-hung with 12/1 panes. A large picture window, with a transom at the top, looks toward the eastern mountains. Inside, the rooms are well finished, with a spacious entrance hall and stair, a parlor with an inglenook at the fireplace, and an attractive use of bay windows. It has been well maintained, although its original shingle siding was covered over years ago.

Henry Noble House.

Hardy C. Wortman (1896)

Massive and substantial, the Hardy C. Wortman House at 1111 SW Vista Avenue still commands its impressive site on King's Hill. It once was one of several mansions that came to surround the block on which the turreted brick-and-stone St. Helen's Hall was constructed in 1888–89, where the Vista St. Clair Apartments are now located. The Wortman property was larger then, with huge trees and lawns planted where condominiums are now located on the north side of the house.

The Wortman House is of a special brand of innovative architecture, defying easy categorization. Its asymmetrical plan is reflected in the attractively sculpted roof forms, huge steep gables, boldly cantilevered second floors, and large arched windows and porch details. The house is unified by the scalloped shingle siding, without corner boards, at the second floor and the ashlar-bond stonework of the first floor. Its recessed entry, under the sweeping roof with eyebrow dormer, ties the structure to design influences of both the Shingle and Richardsonian styles.

Emil Schacht (1902)
Emil Schacht

The prominent architect Emil Schacht designed his own home, constructed in 1902 at 733 SW Vista Avenue, on a small triangular lot at the base of King's Hill. The house, once described as one of Portland's most beautiful residences, shows Schacht's imaginative talents in the developing Shingle style. Most striking in the design is the use of steep trian-

Hardy C. Wortman House.

Emil Schacht House.

gular gables at each of the four sides of the almost square plan, which meet at the corners of the house. At the upper part of each gable, the attic cantilevers out, supported by modillions, much as in the Wortman House. Colonial details are included in the design, as seen in the Palladian-like second floor window with swan's-neck pediment and the elliptical north attic window with radiating wood keystones. Windows are double-hung, with multiple panes in the upper sash. The full-facade, shed-roofed entrance porch immediately above the sidewalk was the primary welcoming space, and it was supported by tapered paired columns on shingled bases. The house has been well maintained, and it is intact except for the enclosure of the character-defining entry porch.

R. B. Lamson (1908)
Josef Jacobberger

Josef Jacobberger designed the architecturally significant R. B. Lamson House in 1908, combining the Shingle style with the new-to-Portland Arts and Crafts style. He carried on the tradition of the Shingle style, covering the roof, walls, porch foundation, and roof support piers entirely with shingles, mitered at the corners and with little or no trim. The steep triangular gables, without trim at the roof-gable intersection, are an element of both styles and here predate the work of Wade Hampton Pipes in the Arts and Crafts style by several years. Other elements of both styles include the recessed porch under the second floor gables on the entrance facade, and the paned windows, both casement and double-hung. In this case, the window treatment is typical of the earlier pe-

riod in Portland, as only the upper sash has panes (8/1). The small attic dormer has angled sides, most unusual for the time but sympathetic to the angled bay windows of the first floor. Located at 1611 NW Thirty-second Avenue on Willamette Heights, the Lamson House remains in excellent condition and a demonstrative example of the great talents of Josef Jacobberger.

R. B. Lamson House.

PART IV

The Early Colonial Revival Period
1880s–1920s

IN THE first decade of the new century, Portland underwent its greatest period of growth. Between 1900 and 1910, the city's population exploded from 90,426 to 207,214. The economy of the city also expanded, fueled by lumber, shipping, wholesale distributing, construction, and finance activity. The Lewis and Clark Centennial Exposition of 1905 both reflected Portland's renewed self-confidence stemming from this economic boom and itself sparked further growth. This extravaganza of international mechanical, agricultural, and cultural exhibits and displays drew nearly five times the population of the entire state. Many of these visitors were from other parts of the country; liking what they saw in Portland, many decided to stay on permanently.

During this period, public and private building boomed. The value of new building permits jumped by 400 percent. Wells Fargo Bank built the city's first "skyscraper" in 1907, and by the peak of the boom in 1920, Portland had ninety-five buildings of six stories and sixteen buildings of ten or more stories. The new office buildings, department stores, and public buildings—built of light brick and glazed terracotta in the style of the Classical and Renaissance revivals—considerably brightened the look of the downtown business core. Promi-

nent architects, such as A. E. Doyle and Whidden and Lewis, left behind the cast-iron, dark red brick, and heavy stone of the Victorian era and readily employed the new look for such structures as the county courthouse, the Benson and Imperial hotels, the Meier and Frank and Lipman and Wolfe department stores, and the United States National Bank.

Handsome new residential districts flourished on both sides of the Willamette River. On the east side, established districts such as Ladd's Addition, Holladay's Addition, and Irvington filled up, and new ones such as Laurelhurst and Eastmoreland were laid out. Much of the land for these latter developments had once been part of William S. Ladd's real-estate holdings, known as Hazelfern and Crystal Springs farms. Laurelhurst's Olmsted-influenced park, its curving street plans, and the restrictions on commercial development indicated that the neighborhood was designed for families of businessmen and professionals. Similarly promoted by its developers, Eastmoreland grew in close relationship to the adjacent Reed College campus and the Eastmoreland Golf Club, and thus attracted an upper-middle-class clientele. On the west side of the Willamette, residential expansion occurred on hill sites. Portland Heights and four new housing areas in the west hills

blossomed: Arlington Heights, King's Hill, Westover Terraces, and Willamette Heights. As in commercial building, residential architectural styles changed. Victorian styles gave way to the newer Colonial Revival, Bungalow, and Arts and Crafts modes. Portland architects quickly adapted the popular styles to the Portland setting.

Population growth and residential expansion demanded heavy public expenditure to upgrade the infrastructure. Improvements to the water system, streets, and sewers cost $29 million between 1905 and 1914. The city's streetcar lines expanded to serve new neighborhoods and in turn helped to insure the success of those neighborhoods. To meet the increasing transportation needs, Portland and Multnomah County replaced outmoded Willamette River bridges prior to the First World War, and a new one—the Broadway Bridge—was built in 1913. In 1925, the county completed the Sellwood Bridge and added the Burnside and Ross Island bridges the following year.

Many of the east-side neighborhoods served by the streetcar lines began to take on a decidedly ethnic cast. Italian and Irish immigrants congregated in the inner southeast, while Scandinavians and African-Americans lived in Albina. Eastern European Jewish immigrants settled in inner south Portland. Working-class neighborhoods, as well as middle- and upper-class ones, were filled with homeowners rather than renters. In 1906, 46 percent of all homes were owner-occupied, compared to an average of 32 percent in other large cities across the nation. It was also during this time, however, that investors built the first apartment houses. By 1910, several apartment buildings had appeared in northwest Portland. Still, apartment living remained the exception, as the single-family dwelling and ample land space contin-ued to be hallmarks of the city's residential lifestyle.

From a cultural perspective, the first two decades of the twentieth century have been called Portland's golden age. In addition to a well-established library and a growing art museum, the city's institutions of higher education emerged during this period with the founding of Reed College. Architect Albert E. Doyle proposed a master plan of grand proportions for the fledgling college, patterned after an Oxford University college campus. The city also boasted an opera house and eight theaters. Every neighborhood had its city park, the product of Portland's first attempt to plan a comprehensive park system. An outgrowth of the City Beautiful movement then sweeping the nation's cities, Portland's park plan was drawn up by John Olmsted of the prominent national landscape architecture firm of the Olmsted Brothers of Brookline, Massachusetts.

Promoters of the City Beautiful movement sought to improve urban life through proper planning that emphasized order, beauty, and efficiency. Expanding on the concepts embodied in the Olmsted park plan, Portland's business and professional leaders formed the Civic Improvement League in 1911 and hired Edward Bennett, a nationally known planner, to

Portland, overlooking Laurelhurst, circa 1930.

produce a comprehensive plan for the city's betterment. Bennett designed a plan to accommodate a population of 2 million. The plan redesigned streets, refocused business expansion to the north and west, proposed a civic center containing cultural recreational elements, expanded the park system, and redirected the use of the Willamette River waterfront by pushing commercial activities downstream and freeing the central waterfront for public use. In spite of wide public approval for Bennett's plan, it was never fully implemented. An economic recession in 1914 and political turmoil in city hall blocked action in the short term, and when resources later became available, the shift from the streetcar to the automobile made Bennett's plan obsolete.

During the 1920s, Portland experienced a new round of growth. Between 1921 and 1925, money spent on building permits jumped from $17 million to $38 million, while builders put up an average of 3,400 new houses each year. A six-year building spree added 400 new apartment buildings by the end of 1926. Planners struggled to win adoption of housing standards and zoning codes in the face of land speculation and haphazard growth. A dramatic change to the heart of the city took place when officials removed the under-utilized warehouses and decaying downtown wharves along the waterfront and built a seawall to protect the downtown business district from flooding.

The 1920s also marked the advent of the automobile age in Portland. In 1916, Multnomah County had fewer than 10,000 motor vehicles. By 1929, the county had registered over 90,000 vehicles—one car for every four residents, compared to the national average of one car for every five people. The automobile accelerated the dispersal of population and the congestion of commuting as people abandoned public transportation. New shopping patterns emerged. Older residential areas suffered declining property values as Portlanders used their newfound mobility to move to new houses on the edge of the city. Traffic problems and suburbanization dominated city planning concerns until the eve of the Second World War.

The Great Depression of the 1930s left its mark on Portland, as it did on the entire nation. Portland's population stagnated at 300,000 throughout the decade, and new construction all but ceased. Portland experienced its share of unemployment, bankruptcies, and labor strife. Substandard housing grew as old low-income neighborhoods decayed from overcrowding and lack of maintenance. The new housing that was built came as infill in existing neighborhoods.

For those who managed to get by or even get ahead during this period, the increased use of electricity in homes affected lifestyles by introducing many new creature-comforts and time-saving appliances for everyday living. The completion of the Bonneville Dam, 42 miles up the Columbia River from Portland, ushered in an era of cheap electricity for both homes and industry. Portland had hardly begun to take advantage of the economic potential offered by cheap, abundant electrical power when the advent of World War II brought new economic life to the city.

CHAPTER 9

Colonial Revival—First Phase

Without question, one of the greatest architectural treasure-troves in Portland is the impressive collection of houses designed in the Colonial Revival style. The style was introduced to Portland at the earliest stage of its popularity on the East Coast and lasted through two main phases, for a period of over sixty years. Architect William M. Whidden introduced the style to the city. Whidden came to Portland to oversee construction of the Portland Hotel (1883–88), designed by the famous New York architectural firm of McKim, Mead and White. The New York firm had begun designing Colonial Revival houses in New England in the early 1880s, and it was those houses that strongly influenced Whidden when he designed the first Colonial Revival house in Portland in 1888. With the firm of Whidden and Lewis, Whidden and his partner, Ion Lewis, created a long series of first-rate houses in the Colonial Revival style.

The Colonial Revival style can trace its beginnings to the Centennial International Exhibition in Philadelphia in 1876. America's interest in its Colonial past was celebrated at the

Portland, overlooking Portland Heights, circa 1910.

Exhibition, with reconstruction of historic interiors showing the life and times of the founding fathers. The exhibits had a strong appeal both to the public and to architects, particularly with the comfortable, low-ceilinged interiors and the respectable details of Georgian and Federal dwellings. Architects, then practicing and promoting the fashionable Queen Anne style, found it particularly intriguing to add Colonial detail to their rambling, irregularly planned, and asymmetrical dwellings. Modest details appeared at first. One of the first houses to have considerable Colonial detail was Shingleside in Swampscott, Massachusetts, designed

in 1880 by Arthur Little (1852–1925). The asymmetries of the house's plan were confined within a rectangular roof. Colonial shutters were added to the side-gabled structure, and considerable Colonial detailing was incorporated throughout the interior. The house, as it appeared in *Building News* in April 1882, added Colonial furnishings to a Colonial detailed stair, all arranged with the inglenooks, bay windows, and balconies so enjoyed by architects designing Queen Anne and Shingle style homes. By 1883, McKim, Mead and White developed their house for the Misses Appleton of Lenox, Massachusetts, with a profusion of

Interiors, Shingleside, 1880, designed by Arthur Little. Printed in *Building News*, 1882.

Shingleside, Swampscott, Massachusetts, 1880, designed by Arthur Little. Printed in *Building News*, 1882.

Interiors, Shingleside, 1880, designed by Arthur Little. Printed in *Building News*, 1882.

Colonial detail. In plan, the house has several angled wings, but under a simple yet angled hipped roof, complete with Colonial cornices, swags, oval and arched openings, shuttered windows, and a pedimented entry porch. The house, therefore, enjoyed both worlds: the practical, unregimented plans of the Queen Anne style and the respectability offered by the proper Colonial details.

Another early house to combine a Queen Anne plan with Colonial details is the George D. Howe House in Manchester-by-the-Sea,

Massachusetts, designed in about 1886 by Arthur Little. Despite the shuttered windows, pedimented dormers, and symmetrical chimneys, the house retained an angled Queen Anne style plan and the highly favored wraparound porch. In a truly dramatic gesture of confidence in the possibilities of the Colonial style, McKim, Mead and White put aside their preferences for picturesque asymmetry and designed in 1885–86 a large Colonial Revival style house for H. A. C. Taylor in Newport, Rhode Island, without the familiar rambling

George D. Howe House, Manchester-by-the-Sea, Massachusetts, circa 1886, designed by Arthur Little.

The Appleton House, Lenox, Massachusetts, 1883–84, designed by McKim, Mead and White.

H. A. C. Taylor House, Newport, Rhode Island, 1885–86, designed by McKim, Mead and White.

plan. Instead, the firm designed a largely symmetrical house, with a perpendicular side wing for the kitchen, pantries, and servants' quarters. The formal rooms were arranged around a spacious central hall within the central mass of the house in Colonial style, with parlor and study to one side and dining room and library to the other. Symmetrical columned porches flanked one entrance to the hall, under the stair landing, and the other entrance, at the main entrance doors, was celebrated with an exedra-shaped porch. Massive chimneys, symmetrically arranged, projected from the hipped roof, and a balustraded widow's walk surmounted the roof. With an abundance of Palladian windows, the house was by no means an exact copy of a true Colonial-era house, but it indeed captured the dignity and balanced equilibrium inherent in the style. A variety of Portland homes a decade later were profoundly influenced by this design.

The first of the numerous Colonial Revival houses in Portland borrowed much from the McKim,

Mead and White houses on the East Coast. The early houses were designed with axial, central-hall plans, their facades reflecting their formal arrangements. They had hipped roofs, sometimes a widow's walk, symmetrically placed brick chimneys, and a profusion of shuttered windows. Usually a columned porch designated the central entrance, complete with Clas-

House at 34 Chestnut Street, Salem, Massachusetts, 1824.

sical balustrade and Ionic column supports, almost identical to the porches found in the Taylor House in Newport. The facades varied in the early houses: some had rounded bays and others had full-facade porches. It was in the Zera Snow House of 1891 that Whidden and Lewis experimented grandly with shingled forms, more influenced by the lavish Shingle style summer homes on the Maine coast or in Newport. A variety of these massive houses with similar rounded bays, rooms, and piazzas appeared in the late 1880s in such architectural magazines as *Architecture and Building* and *American Architect and Building News.* The Snow House displayed a quality design sense, fully the equal of the houses designed in similar fashion on the East Coast.

Portland architects employed every version of the Colonial Revival in houses constructed during the early phase of the style. Some employed axial and formal designs, while others took considerable architectural liberties. The three-storied Judge Wallace McCamant (1899) and William E. Mac-

Kenzie (1902) residences have the formalities of the great houses constructed on the eastern seaboard during the 1820s, whereas the Nahum King House of circa 1904 is almost Baroque in its use of multiple columned porches intertwining with massive two-story porticos. The massive porticos have their precedents in the southern states, particularly the antebellum plantation houses. The David T. Honeyman House of 1907 designed by David C. Lewis has a full-facade columned porch, two stories high and crowned by turned balustrades. Abbott Mills had a Georgian style mansion designed by the famous Boston firm of Shepley, Rutan and Coolidge, fashioned after a mid-eighteenth-century house in Pennsylvania. In detail and execution, it offers first-rate quality.

After the first decade of the century, other houses tended toward more conservative interpretations of the style. They always had balustraded side additions or porches, and often minor wings toward the back of the house. Most of the houses had side-gabled roofs, fully detailed with wrap-around cornices. Georgian style dormers predominated on the roofs, sometimes combined by shed roofs to create more third-story headroom. Many of the houses incorporated asymmetrical windows, or bays, balanced in the facade design, but harking back to the Queen Anne approach there were impressive stair-landing windows, where they never would have been found in Colonial times. All the bolder, imaginative forms of the first phase of the Colonial Revival style slowly evolved into more authentically detailed houses of the second phase, beginning about 1916, although the two phases intermingled for several years.

Colonial Revival—First Phase
CHARACTERISTICS

PLANS: symmetrical and asymmetrical; prominent entrance or side porches; curved bays.

ROOFS: central hipped, side gable, or gambrel; pedimented dormers in solid balustrade, or roof dormers, sometimes combined; return cornice at gable ends; widow's walk. Shingled.

EXTERIOR FINISHES: lap siding or shingles; mitered or with pilasters at corners; modillions or dentils at the cornice.

CHIMNEYS: brick or stone, with plain end; bisects roof cornice; exterior locations.

WINDOWS: wide versions of Colonial double-hung windows; symmetrically located; ten-over-one (10/1) or eight-over-one (8/1) panes. Sometimes double windows at main floor, with shared cornice; Palladian windows in feature locations. Lunette or semicircular attic windows.

WINDOW TRIM (exterior): prominent wide casing, often with high cornice; trim integrated with cornice at second floor; late-Georgian dormers; arched-head sash with pointed-arch panes in upper sash. Working louvered shutters.

ENTRANCE DOORS: single, six-panel, with sidelights. Often with elliptical fanlights.

VERANDAS/PORCHES: entrance porches, often pedimented, with clustered columns; side porches with deck on second floor. Combinations of two-story porticos with one-story verandas, or full two-story verandas with balustrade above.

INTERIOR FINISHES: plaster walls and ceilings; plaster cornices; paneled wainscoting. Entrance halls often had Tudor woodwork; living rooms had Federal or Georgian detail; dining rooms had high wainscoting and beamed ceilings. Floor often inlaid with rare woods.

INTERIOR TRIM: molded casings and baseboards.

STAIRS: straight run, or reverse run with landings over vestibules or coat rooms. Georgian or Federal style railings, with hardwood handrail curved at bottom and painted balusters.

FIREPLACE FRONTS: marble surround, flanked by Classical pilasters and surmounted by entablature; overmantel with side pilasters; broken pediment over paneled frame.

PROPERTY SURROUNDS: bermed lawn; no fences, unless small-scale open-mesh iron fence.

Entrance to house on SW Vista Avenue,
designed by George Foote Durham.

Colonial Revival—First Phase
HOUSES

1888	Lucien W. Wallace (William Whidden)
1889	Charles B. Bellinger (Whidden and Lewis)
1890	Theodore B. Trevitt (Whidden and Lewis)
1890	Winslow B. Ayer (Whidden and Lewis)
1891	Zera Snow (Whidden and Lewis)
1899	Judge Wallace McCamant (Whidden and Lewis)
1902	William E. MacKenzie (attributed to Whidden and Lewis)
1903	Isom White (Whidden and Lewis)
c. 1904	Nahum A. King (Whidden and Lewis)
c. 1905	Dr. Henry Coe (attributed to Whidden and Lewis)
1907	David T. Honeyman (David C. Lewis)
1908	Philip Buehner (Whidden and Lewis)
1908	Abbott Mills (Shepley, Rutan and Coolidge)
1908	Max H. Hauser (attributed to Morris H. Whitehouse)
1910	James E. Wheeler (McNaughton, Raymond and Lawrence)
1910	George H. Watson (attributed to George F. Durham)
1912	Mayor H. Russell Albee (Albert E. Doyle)
1913	Dr. Ami Nichols (Edward T. Foulkes)
1914	J. W. Creath (attributed to George F. Durham)
1914	Riverview Cemetery Caretaker's House (Ellis F. Lawrence)
c. 1914	James G. Gault (Harrison Corbett)
1915	Samuel Rosenblatt (Edward T. Root)
1915	Osmond B. Stubbs (Whitehouse and Fouilhoux)
1916	Harold T. Prince
1918	Dr. Lawrence Selling (Josef Jacobberger)
1921	Iva L. McFarlan (Josef Jacobberger)

Lucien W. Wallace (1888)
William Whidden

Concurrent with the excesses of the Eastlake style, and possibly in revolt from it, the Lucien W. Wallace House exemplified the new simplicity and restraint of the Colonial Revival style. When William Whidden came to Portland to complete work on the Portland Hotel, and apparently before he joined Ion Lewis in partnership, he immediately was commissioned to design the Wallace House, located at 2381 NW Flanders Street. The house incorporated the dignity of Colonial architecture with new innovations: a polygonal conservatory on the southwest corner of the house and the ashlar-bond stonework of the porch founda-

Lucien W. Wallace House.

tion walls. Unlike Colonial precedents, the windows had mixed-sized multiple panes on the second floor. The unusually handsome facade had symmetrically placed pedimented dormers and corbeled chimneys and, at the top of the hipped roof, a widow's walk with balustrade.

The house still stands, though considerably altered. With the removal of the widow's walk and conservatory, plus additions to the porch, much of the design quality was lost in the process.

Charles B. Bellinger (1889)
Whidden and Lewis

Similar in concept to the Wallace House of the previous year, the Charles B. Bellinger House helped establish the Colonial Revival style in Portland. The house was located in Holladay's Addition on NE Holladay Street between Grand and Sixth avenues, where once were located a number of significant and handsome homes, now replaced by the Lloyd Center development. The Bellinger House was symmetrically designed around its Ionic columned entrance porch, with hipped roof, dormers, chimneys, and single-story side additions. Windows were paired on both floors of the main facade, with high cornices uniting them. The roof balustrade over the entrance porch carried through the design of the three columns below with three posts at the corners, and the design repeated in the roof balustrade of the side additions as well. Similar to the Wallace home, the Bellinger residence had a three-toned paint scheme: white trim, medium-toned siding, and dark sashes, shutters, and entrance doors. The Bellinger and Wallace houses, designs of Ion Lewis and William Whidden, helped establish Portland as one of the first and most significant centers for the Colonial Revival style in the United States.

Charles B. Bellinger House.

Theodore B. Trevitt (1890)
Whidden and Lewis

Whidden and Lewis added considerable variety to their interpretations of the Colonial Revival style. In the 1890 Theodore B. Trevitt House, still standing at 2347 NW Flanders Street, the architects introduced paired polygonal bays and a full-facade veranda with paired posts and latticework. The bays are much flatter to the house facade than their Italianate predecessors, and without the perpendicular emphasis of the plane of

the facade. The windows had the Colonial Revival proportions, with 6/1 panes, and were shuttered, even though the shutters overlapped one another in their open position. The central hipped roof extends out over the polygonal bays farther than it does at the side elevations. A wide entablature with dentil course runs at the roof eave and across the top of the second floor windows and lap siding. On the roof are shingled, pedimented dormers, and on the west elevation a large facade dormer houses the chimney and two oval dormer windows with wood keystones. The house was painted a single color of soft cream-gray, with only the window sash, front door, and shutters painted dark.

Theodore B. Trevitt House.

Winslow B. Ayer (1890)
Whidden and Lewis

In an era when a gentleman was known by the architecture he constructed, Winslow B. Ayer was first class. Whidden and Lewis designed for him an eminently fine home, remarkable in its proportion and dignity. Still located at 1808 NW Johnson Street, the 1890 house repeated the floor plan of the central-entrance Trevitt House, but the bays on this house are rounded, including the lap siding, cornice, window trim, and the 1/1 glass window panes. Even the entrance porch was semicircular, with fine Roman Doric columns and a simple, low balustrade. The detail work is exceptional, particularly the dentils and modillions of the cornice and the molded window casings with cornices, especially high at the first

Winslow B. Ayer House.

floor. A brick terrace extends across the entrance facade, including brick stairs and balustrade. Grecian acroteria adorn the paired entrance piers, possibly original to the house. The five-panel entrance door, typical of Whidden and Lewis houses, has cut-crystal leaded sidelights. Though the house has lost many of its neighbors and now stands nearly isolated, it is an extraordinary example of Colonial Revival architecture in the city.

Zera Snow (1891)
Whidden and Lewis

In plan and elevation, the Zera Snow House, originally located on the northeast corner of Twentieth Avenue and Johnson Street, was one of the more remarkable Whidden and Lewis designs. With great imagination and architectural ingenuity, they created a house that combined symmetrical elements with very asymmetrical ones. An organizing symmetry was achieved in the side-gabled roof anchored by two impressive brick chimneys on either side of the centrally located main entrance and large second floor windows. At the attic level, double gabled dormers were set between the chimneys, with paired windows centered in each gable. Balancing these symmetrical elements were the main floor covered piazza and the angled library bay, which shared a continuous balustrade above. Other decorative additions were found in the rounded bay of the drawing room, the kitchen wing, and the angled bay of the oval dining room. The materials selected for the house tended to both unify and enhance its sculpture. For the exterior finish, shingles were used at the second floor, and small-scaled bricks at the first floor. The bricks extended to the lower balustrade of the covered piazza, which wrapped around the house, and out to the brick terrace of the back garden. To further connect all the diverse features, a wide entablature, painted white, surrounded the entire house. Shingles were natural, trim white, and shutters probably a traditional dark green.

The plan had many diverse interior spaces. From a small vestibule, visitors entered the Great Hall, a living space that contained a large fireplace, the main staircase, and entrances to the dining room and drawing room. Accessed under the main stair landing, the library had its own fireplace, and there was a private first floor toilet, a luxury in those days. The main hall also provided access to the rear hall, the servants' stair, the kitchen, pantry, and china closets. Five bedrooms, four of which had

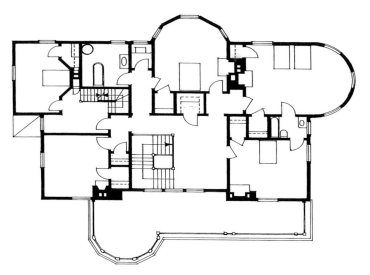

Second floor plan, Snow House.

Zera Snow House.

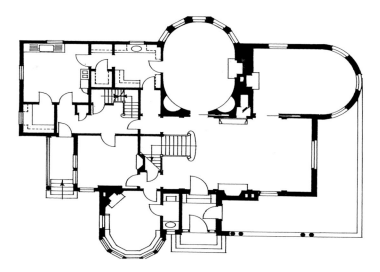

First floor plan, Snow House.

fireplaces, and two bàthrooms were located upstairs. All the rooms of the house were conveniently planned, commodious in size, and finished with fine wood paneling, marble fireplaces, and other refinements of Colonial Revival design.

Judge Wallace McCamant (1899)
Whidden and Lewis

Significant Whidden and Lewis houses were constructed through the turn of the century, and they tended to contribute an air of great architectural character to Portland. Two particularly elegant city houses were

Judge Wallace McCamant House.

constructed in the King's Hill Historic District, nearly across from each other on King Avenue. They were the Judge Wallace McCamant (1899) and William E. MacKenzie (1902) houses. The McCamant House is sited at 1046 SW King Avenue, on the axis of Main Street. Its imposing and dignified facade, three windows across, is typically symmetrical, with a central door and entrance porch. The porch is supported by paired Ionic columns, with a box-piered balustrade above. The windows are unusually small paned, double-hung 15/15, with high cornices and window shutters. The three-story facade tucks the third floor under the modillioned extended roof cornice, without an entablature. Wide pilaster corner boards frame the lap siding. Given a handsome new coat of paint, which probably approximates its original appearance, the house shows why it is not surprising that Portland once had the reputation of being the "Boston of the West."

William E. MacKenzie (1902)
Whidden and Lewis (attributed)

Similar to the McCamant House with its central entrance, the William E. MacKenzie House at 1131 SW King Avenue further elaborates its handsome three-window facade. Most distinctive is the same extended cornice, with modillions and dentil course between. An entablature is suggested at the third floor, however, defined by a prominent horizontal band. The corners of the house have staggered quoins, each aligned with two rows of beveled siding, and the double-hung windows are more typical of the predominating fashion than those of the McCamant House in that they have 6/1 panes. All windows had operable shutters, including the small third floor casement windows, but the original shutters have been replaced by stock shutters bolted to the house. A porch

William E. MacKenzie House.

Isom White (1903)
Whidden and Lewis

In one masterful house after the other, Whidden and Lewis continued to develop and evolve their extraordinary talents in the Colonial Revival style through the first decade of the 1900s. Their house for Isom White, still standing at 311 NW Twentieth Avenue, was among the finest, if not the most expensive per square foot. Fine detailing can be seen in the handsomely proportioned street facades on Everett Street and on Twentieth Avenue, as well as in the handsome interior. Basically, the house is designed around a hipped-roof central mass with side extensions, noted for

Isom White House.

similar to that on the McCamant House, with paired Tuscan columns, covers the entry, and a balustrade very similar to the McCamant House's, though now removed, originally ran along the porch roof. Because of the deep roadway cut, the house sits high up on its berm, a typical treatment for houses at the turn of the century. Stone or brick walls were used only if necessary. This generally left the grounds in lawn and plantings, without the addition of extended architectural features, which could conflict with the house's tailored architecture.

their arched porches and semicircular bay. Corinthian pilasters, two stories high, frame the entrance facade. The typical front-facade porch is flanked by Roman Doric and square columns at each side. The balustrade, with turned balusters, matches the balustrades on the two side extensions and on the sweeping brick terrace across the front of the house, now the roof over a new under-terrace garage, accessed from street level. Windows are paired in the major rooms, the large living room to the left and the dining room to the right. The third floor is contained behind an enclosed balustrade, with three pedimented dormers symmetrically arranged.

Nahum A. King (c. 1904)
Whidden and Lewis

Nahum A. King, son of pioneer Donation Land Claim owner Amos N. King and developer of the King's Hill Addition, had a fine home constructed on the northwest corner of Salmon Street and Twentieth Avenue. It was one of the more Baroque designs of the Colonial Revival period, and one of the more intriguing houses by the firm of Whidden and Lewis. On the basically rectilinear, central-hall plan, the architects attached a magnificent two-story portico, which uniquely combined with a wrap-around porch that culminated in a porte-cochere entrance on Salmon Street. Above the main entrance portal, the second floor porch balustrade cantilevered out in a semicircle. No expense was spared in the detailing, from the modillioned cornice and Ionic columns to the turned balustrades at the roof, upper porches, and main floor terraces. The substantial brick foundations, with arched foundation windows, extended to the bifurcated entrance steps. Impressive lanterns stood at the mid-level landing. Colonial detailing was used in the Palladian windows and in the pedimented dormers rising out of the blind balustrade.

Nahum A. King House.

Dr. Henry Coe (c. 1905)
Whidden and Lewis (attributed)

The idea of a two-story portico intersected by a one-story, full-facade roofed porch was taken up by several architects, and numerous examples are found throughout the city. One not recorded in the records of Whidden and Lewis, but decidedly influenced by their work, was the Dr. Henry Coe House, originally located at 2509 NW Lovejoy Street. The house had the same Ionic columned portico and half-round cantilevered balcony as the Nahum King House. Yet, it borrowed from other previous and contemporary fashions. The polygonal corner bay was a carry-over from the Queen Anne designs of the previous decade. Influence of the Richardsonian style was found in the ashlar-bond stonework of the foundation, chimneys, and bifurcated entrance steps. Reflecting the Craftsman style was the fully paneled dining room, which had a Crafts-man glass-fronted recessed buffet and a Tiffany style chandelier. Fur-nished with handsome tooled-leather chairs and a claw-foot table in the Renaissance style and a Classical Revival style carpet, and combined with the deeply stained and highly polished woodwork, the room must have been innately attractive.

Dr. Henry Coe House.

Dining room, Coe House.

David T. Honeyman (1907)
David C. Lewis

When constructed in 1907, the David T. Honeyman House commanded one of the finest sites in the city. Its location at 1728 SW Prospect Drive, at the crest of the first ridge of Portland Heights, then nearly bare of trees and other houses, afforded sweeping panoramic views east to the city and the mountains. The front facade acknowledges this outlook with its handsome two-story covered porch. Supported by six enormous fluted Corinthian columns, its entablature aligns with the roof cornice, much like the design of the Buehner House's (1908) porte-cochere. On either

David T. Honeyman House.

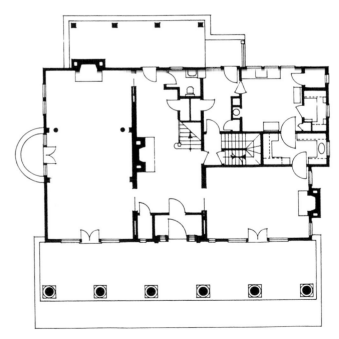

First floor plan, Honeyman House.

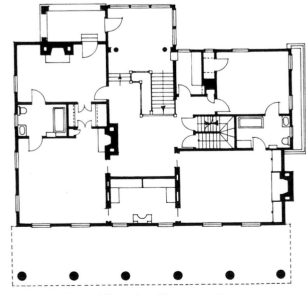

Second floor plan, Honeyman House.

side of a central door, with sidelights, the major windows of the living and dining rooms have unusual terrace doors centered between large double-hung windows. Second floor windows align above these windows. The smaller windows on the second floor are to a dressing room above, and the two small windows on the first level are located in a closet to the left of the entry vestibule and, unusually, in the dining room to the right. Designed by architect David C. Lewis, it is one of his finest houses. The interiors are well detailed, and the rooms, if not numerous, are very spacious and conveniently arranged.

Philip Buehner (1908)
Whidden and Lewis

One of the last of the fine houses designed by the illustrious firm of Whidden and Lewis is the Philip Buehner House, still standing at the east end of Hawthorne Boulevard at Fifty-fifth Avenue. Previously, the site had held the 1855 Greek Revival home of Dr. Perry Prettyman. The Prettyman House was still standing, though badly dilapidated, when Philip Buehner bought the property. As the Prettyman home had before it, the huge mansion Buehner constructed in 1908 has long been a landmark, notable from Hawthorne Boulevard by its imposing two-story porte-cochere. Its paired and fluted Corinthian columns are finely detailed, and they support the modillioned, widely extended cornice. This part of the large house projects forward, with symmetrically placed paired windows on either side of the porte-cochere. Corinthian corner pilasters match the columns. The main entrance door, with sidelights, has a scrolled broken pediment, and it enters the house under the landing of the main stair. At the stair landing above the entrance door is a large window with stained leaded glass. On the south side, French doors

Philip Buehner House.

on either side of the main fireplace in the living room provide access to a trellis-covered terrace.

Abbott Mills (1908)
Shepley, Rutan and Coolidge

The Abbott Mills House at 733 NW Twentieth Avenue is a special part of Portland's affiliation with old and proper Boston. Abbott Mills, President of the First National Bank, had as a close friend from his Harvard University years Jefferson Coolidge, later of the Boston architectural firm of Shepley, Rutan and Coolidge. The architect's design for Mills's

Portland home was influenced by Mrs. Mills's particular interest in a 1750 Georgian style house in Germantown, Pennsylvania. Located on the Twentieth Avenue side of the property, the Mills House replaced an earlier Whidden and Lewis designed Colonial Revival house at the back of the property, which was demolished when the new Mills residence was completed in 1908.

The slate-roofed, two-and-a-half-story brick house has a symmetrical front elevation, with an imposing and elaborate extension of the central entrance hall. Its door and fanlight transom are below a cantilevered, half-round balustraded roof supported by engaged Corinthian columns. The extension includes paired two-story Corinthian pilasters and a modillioned pediment over its entablature. Within the pediment is a shield-and-swag design. Two main windows with 8/8 and 12/12 panes at the second and first floors, respectively, are positioned on each side of the extension. The lower floor windows have entablatures and cornices. Small, narrow windows are fitted between the symmetrically placed second floor windows to accommodate bathrooms. The side elevations are reminiscent of Colonial Pennsylvania architecture, with a horizontal parapet between two chimneys and steep-sloping front and back roofs. The rear wing, along Johnson Street, has a similar parapeted gable-end wall, itself with a brick chimney at the ridge. The wing forms a barrier for the rear garden, which is further enclosed by high brick walls. En-

Abbott Mills House.

Main interior stairway and entrance hall, Mills House.

trance from the house to the garden is from the entrance stair hall, through a glass door with transom and sidelights. A Roman Doric columned portico with balustrade covers the back entrance. The house is exceptional in every detail, including its fine interior woodwork. Its

main stair, with a landing over the entrance door, is especially handsome. Fine crown molds, fireplace mantels, and paneling make this one of the finest residential structures ever constructed in the city.

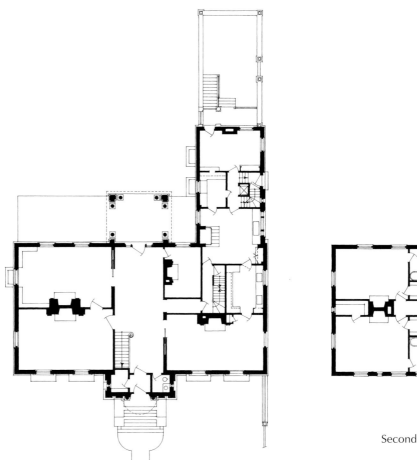

First floor plan, Mills House.

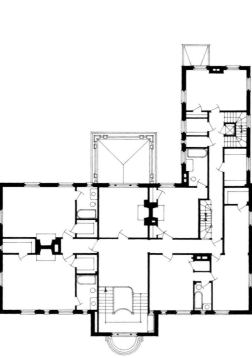

Second floor plan, Mills House.

Max H. Hauser (1908)
Morris H. Whitehouse (attributed)

Of all the diverse directions in which the Colonial Revival style went, the most typical became the symmetrically planned, side-gabled house, complete with a balconied central-entrance portico, three pedimented dormers on the roof, and symmetrically placed first and second floor windows. More often than not, the windows had 6/1 panes, and the first floor windows were often paired or grouped, featuring a picture window. One of the first houses in the city to present these particular features was the Max H. Hauser House, still standing at 1975 SW Mont-

gomery Drive. Yet, despite its prototypical facade, the house added some unusual features. On the west elevation, a side gable telescopes from another gable, with a similar modillioned cornice, and incorporates a polygonal bay. At the front elevation portico and at the side porch, triglyphs enhance the entablature, a feature used in the residential architecture of Morris Whitehouse, to whom this house's design is attributed. The house has had some alterations. Curiously, the current shutters are not original, and the small window on the left over the balcony (originally a multi-paned casement window) has been altered to match the others in size.

James E. Wheeler (1910)
McNaughton, Raymond and Lawrence

The firm of McNaughton, Raymond and Lawrence, with Ellis Lawrence as chief residential designer, was well established when Lawrence designed this handsome Colonial Revival house for James E. Wheeler in 1910. Extant at 2417 SW Sixteenth Avenue, the house replaced a large Queen Anne style house on its half-block property. Taking precedent from the Hauser House's design, Wheeler's home added an authentic replica of a Georgian style Colonial entrance portico, with Roman Doric columns and return-corniced gable. The roof dormers have a similar treatment with their arched windows. To somewhat simplify the facade, only single windows are on each side of the entrance portico, instead of pairs. The windows above the portico were also brought closer together to bring the symmetrical facade into better balance. These windows, seen in most Colonial Revival homes, are where the bathrooms are located, between the two bedrooms on either side. A fine porch, with new stock columns and balustrade that replaced the original Roman Doric

Max H. Hauser House.

James E. Wheeler House.

was similar to that of the 1850 Greek Revival house of Captain J. C. Ainsworth at Mount Pleasant outside of Oregon City. In plan, the Watson House follows the side-entrance scheme, with a parlor to the side and the dining room behind. It is, however, a more sophisticated version of Classical architecture, with finely detailed triglyphs at the entablature and a turned balustrade at the entrance terrace and balcony railings. The windows, with their 8/1 panes, have dog-ear trim, a detail also found in the Ainsworth House. What gives the house its somewhat southern mansion air, besides the Greek Revival facade, are the arched fanlight over the entrance door, the half-round light in the attic, and the French doors leading onto the front terrace. The architecture of the house is attributed to George Foote Durham, based on the similarity of details with his other houses.

columns that had matched those of the entrance portico, is on the east side of the living room, and it once afforded a fine city view before trees and houses were to obscure it.

George H. Watson (1910)
George F. Durham (attributed)

Located at 4036 North Overlook Terrace, the George H. Watson House of 1910 commanded a fine view toward the city and the western hills. Facing the view is the almost Greek Revival pedimented gable front, which has four fluted Roman Doric columns and a second floor balcony. Its facade

George H. Watson House.

Mayor H. Russell Albee (1912)
Albert E. Doyle

During his remarkable twenty-year career, Albert E. Doyle designed numerous houses in the Colonial Revival style. His fine design for Portland mayor H. Russell Albee is situated on a superb site overlooking Laurelhurst Park. The spacious house, located at 3360 SE Ankeny Street, has a symmetrically planned entrance elevation with side wings, featuring a pedimented entrance portico, paired double-hung windows, and prominent triglyphs in the entablature. The entablature and the widely extended cornice emphasize the horizontal elements of the design, typical of the Colonial Revival style first phase. It is the parkside elevation that reveals Doyle's artistic talents. Multiple elements combine

H. Russell Albee House.

Rear parkside elevation, Albee House.

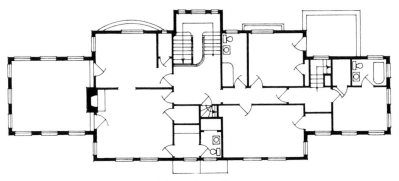

Second floor plan, Albee House.

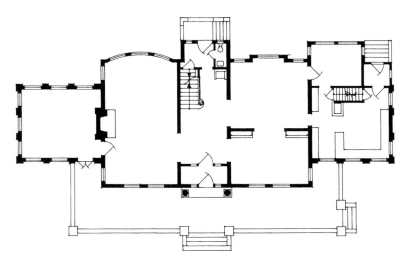

First floor plan, Albee House.

around the extended stair tower, notably the Palladian window at the stair landing. To the right of the tower is the rounded end of the living room, forming a large bay, and to the left is the rectangular bay of the dining room. Above the recessed buffet of the dining room is a high leaded window in the bay, with windows on either side. With turned balustrades above the bays, and the prominent cornice, it is one of Doyle's most imposing and inventive designs.

Dr. Ami Nichols (1913)
Edward T. Foulkes

The house designed by the firm of Foulkes and Hogue in 1913 for Dr. Ami Nichols is a prime example of Colonial Revival architecture in Portland. Well maintained at 1961 SW Vista Avenue, the Nichols House is an

Dr. Ami Nichols House.

anchor for the other excellent Colonial Revival houses in its immediate neighborhood. In most aspects, the plan and facade are symmetrical. There is a hipped central roof and a kitchen wing to the rear. A large portico with balcony faces east toward the city, and it is supported by four Ionic columns, a design repeated in the corner pilasters. The house's fine cornice is supported by modillions, and the entablature is dignified by egg-and-dart molding, all accomplished with unparalleled craftsmanship. The details extend to the recessed entrance porch and balcony above. At the entrance level, concave niches with a shell motif at the top align on either side of the entrance door. The main floor windows are unusual, with 1/1 panes and a transom light above. Quality of detailing is also found in the interior, where the Ionic column theme is repeated in the large entrance hall. Further Colonial Revival characteristics are seen in the main stair, the built-in dining room buffet, and the fireplaces.

J. W. Creath (1914)
George F. Durham (attributed)

The handsome Colonial Revival house at 1526 NE Thompson Street is likely the work of little-known architect George Foote Durham. The house built for J. W. Creath bears comparison with the work of Whidden and Lewis, Josef Jacobberger, and Edward Foulkes. Its hipped roof, for instance, has the same dormer design—three windows with a facade gable in the center—as is used in Foulkes's Dr. Ami Nichols House (1913) and in Jacobberger's Iva L. McFarlan House (1921). Likewise, the windows of the second floor have the same horizontal emphasis in the sashes as is found in the works of the other architects. The lower floor

casement windows and the pedimented entrance with sidelights seem to be uniquely Durham's invention. Other details are much the essence of the Colonial Revival style: paneled wide corner boards, modillioned cornice, lap siding, operable louvered shutters, and prominent water table. Durham's two small windows over the entrance is found in many houses of the era. They usually signify bath or dressing rooms over the entrance hall, but they inevitably are well composed and balanced within the overall facade design.

J. W. Creath House.

Riverview Cemetery Caretaker's House (1914)
Ellis F. Lawrence

In 1914, the Riverview Cemetery replaced its earlier Victorian caretaker's house with one suitably fashionable in the Colonial Revival style. The house, designed by Ellis F. Lawrence, still guards the lower entrance to the cemetery at 8421 SW Macadam Avenue. It is one of the very few houses of this period constructed in brick. Ellis used the wide Colonial Revival window sashes, but he added panes in both the upper and lower sash, making 8/8 panes. Shutters, for the first time, do not have operable louvers, but instead have fixed panels, the upper one of which has a cres-

Riverview Cemetery Caretaker's House.

cent-moon design. In an individual style, Lawrence designed the entry door with sidelights and a half-round, shell-design pediment supported by scroll brackets. The house has a hipped roof, leading up to a flat area surrounded by a balustrade. Two terraces, one on each side of the house, also have balustrades of similar design. The modillioned cornice stands out in the reserved design. Finally, as with many of the central-hall plans, the bathroom is located above the entrance doors, where its window could be shorter to allow greater emphasis to the point of entry.

James G. Gault (c. 1914)
Harrison Corbett

Colonial Revival designs used a variety of elevation treatments. One device, going back to Colonial days, was the large facade dormer. In the James G. Gault House located at 1150 SW Kings Court, the dormer is centered over the columned entrance portico, with multiple windows centered at the second floor. The full effect of the facade favors the horizontal elements, typical of the first phase of the Colonial Revival. Windows have wide 1/1 panes, without mullions, and strong horizontal cornices. The design of the house was by Harrison Corbett.

Though the house was constructed by Gault, its association with architect John Yeon is particularly noteworthy. Yeon's widowed mother purchased the house in 1936, and soon after Yeon designed a handsome and highly original garden for the terraced slopes at the side of the home. It incorporated curved brick walls with grillework, a reflecting pond, and expansive lawns.

James G. Gault House.

Samuel Rosenblatt House.

Samuel Rosenblatt (1915)
Edward T. Root

Another brick-constructed house of great merit is the Samuel Rosenblatt home at 2359 SW Park Place. Colonial Revival quality is found in the fine proportions and detailing of the symmetrical front elevation as well as in the more permanent materials of brick walls and slate roof. The house has a typical side-gabled plan, featuring a recessed central entrance. The entrance design utilizes an arched pediment above an architrave, supported by free-standing Roman Doric columns flanked by boxed pilasters. Inside the recess, the door has sidelights and transoms. At both gable ends of the house are columned, balustraded porches, similar in detail to the entrance design. The east-end gable has a smaller telescoping gable, still unusual at this time. Lunette windows are located at the upper part of each gable. Typically, the house has three pedimented dormers on the slate roof, a well-defined modillioned cornice with wrap-around ends, and paired shuttered windows, with 6/1 panes, on each side of the entrance at both the first and second stories.

Osmond B. Stubbs (1915)
Whitehouse and Fouilhoux

The three-story home at 1824 SE Twenty-third Avenue was built by Osmond Stubbs on property inherited from his wife's family and named Six Oaks from Territorial days—five of the oaks remain in front of the house. Architects Whitehouse and Fouilhoux designed the house in the

Osmond B. Stubbs House.

and Fouilhoux innovation is the dormer design, which has a pair of dormers connected by a shed roof, allowing for more headroom within the hipped roof.

Harold T. Prince (1916)

One of the most inventive houses in the Colonial Revival style is the Harold T. Prince House located at 2815 NE Alameda Drive. Built by the Oregon Home Builders, its architect is unknown. It is an excellent example of asymmetrical architecture, both in plan and its elevations. Basically, the house consists of a central mass with a hipped roof and two side wings, which have prominent gable ends. At the left wing, the main

Colonial Revival style, strictly symmetrical on its front facade. The house has a central entrance, emphasized by the fine brick entrance stairs and the Roman Doric columned entrance porch. Missing from the design are the porch roof's original balustrade (the posts of which aligned with the columns below), the original operable window shutters, the balustraded widow's walk, and the trellises that extended from the French doors off the two side projections. On the back, or east, facade, additional wrap-around trellised porches face the lovely garden. A large Palladian window is above the landing of the main stair, the hallway of which runs from the front to the back of the house. A Whitehouse

Harold T. Prince House.

entrance is framed by a columned porch with Roman Doric columns and balustrade. Balancing the entrance is a one-story polygonal bay, also balustraded, placed on the front of the central mass. Pedimented dormers with round-top windows and cornice returns are located on the slate-covered roof. Windows are typically 6/1 and double-hung, with operable shutters that feature crescent moons in their upper panels. French doors with sidelights open onto the first floor terrace. A notable feature of the brick house is the strong accents: white keystones, horizontal stones in the gable-end exposed chimney, and the wide modillioned cornice with returns at the gable ends. More refined, and less bold, are the Federal style interior details.

Dr. Lawrence Selling (1918)
Josef Jacobberger

Necessity being the mother of invention, Josef Jacobberger made some adaptations to Colonial architecture for Portland's rainy winters by his inventive treatment of the entrance portico and doorway. On the 1918 house designed for Dr. Lawrence Selling at 2228 SW Twenty-first Avenue, the open pediment over the columned entrance is further protective by its extension supported by scroll brackets. The pediment frames a lovely entrance door, itself unusual in that its fanlight transom is enclosed within a half-ellipse the width of the door and sidelights. Windows are fully paned in this house, 8/8 and 10/15, with operable louvered shutters. The house has a symmetrical front facade and, as with most houses of this period, asymmetrical features on the gabled side elevations and the back wings. On the right side gable is an interesting treatment of a cantilevered polygonal bay; its roof is actually the wide cornice return. Also, in the gable ends at the third floor, quarter-round windows open

Dr. Lawrence Selling House.

on either side of the exposed brick chimney. The house is in excellent condition, with changes only at the entrance stairs and a new garage built into the hill.

Iva L. McFarlan (1921)
Josef Jacobberger

Architect Josef Jacobberger, one of Portland's most impressive talents, designed in several styles. Besides the many Bungalow, Arts and Crafts, and Craftsman houses to his name, Jacobberger was equally talented with his version of the Colonial Revival style. The house at 2215 NE

Iva L. McFarlan House.

Twenty-fifth Avenue well attests to his diverse abilities. Though it has a typical central-hall scheme and side-gabled roof, the house also displays some of Jacobberger's inventive design features. Most notable is the exedra-shaped entrance porch, now missing its upper balustrade. Combined with the trellised extensions on either side of the house, it recalls the Whidden and Lewis designs of the previous decades. The covered trellis area off the living room is now enclosed as a summer room, and the one to the right helps to screen the entrance to the garage. Garages, a new design challenge to the architect, at first were simply added somewhere on the property; then, gradually, they were located near the kitchen entrance, and finally became integrated with the house. Another innovation of the McFarlan House is Jacobberger's version of the dormer window, where the central dormer combines a Palladian window with a gabled roof.

PART V

Historic Period Styles
1900s–1930s

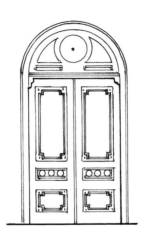

CHAPTER 10

Colonial Revival—Second Phase

Beginning at the turn of the century, a tremendous interest in a vast array of revival styles in the United States flowered with as much diversity as would be suggested by the terms Tudor, Mediterranean, and Colonial. In its second phase, the Colonial Revival style joined this national revival movement, reflecting the great popularity of Classical designs both in this country and in England. There indeed was pride in the achievements of the now more mature democracy, and "colonial" often implied a certain nostalgic adherence to the values that supported that democracy. Realizing that many of our most historic monuments or homes of our founding fathers were falling into ruin, preservationists undertook a serious effort to restore them before they disappeared entirely. Such was the impetus for the twentieth-century restoration of Colonial Williamsburg and Sturbridge Village, huge undertakings requiring substantial sponsorship. Whole cities began a renewal with tourism, such as Charleston's historic district, Boston's Beacon Hill, or the early Philadelphia buildings associated with the founding of the republic.

Colonial Revival houses on Portland Heights.

As early as 1876, the Centennial year, it was noted in *American Architect and Building News* that Colonial architecture, "with all its faults of formality and meagerness, was, on the whole, decidedly superior in style and good breeding, if we may say so, to most that has followed it." In a later issue, the magazine added some clarification to this statement:

> It was a style whose ancestry was good, and whose breeding had always been careful. . . . Work done in this way always retained the mark of its good descent. It might be monotonous and uninteresting, but never lost the character of good breeding and refinement which its progenitors impressed upon it.

At the time this was written, American architects were deeply involved with the Queen Anne style, and they loved the picturesque variety that it offered and the forms that evolved from a practical approach to house design. Yet, the "good breeding" suggested by the Colonial period captivated the public and their architects, and "old families" as well as the newly arrived sought the ready acceptability they believed the style offered. The term Colonial was sometimes vague, referring either to the Georgian architecture before the Revolution or to

the Federal style that followed thereafter. These were mixed together indiscriminately in the popular mind.

The first house in Portland to fit the style of the second phase of the Colonial Revival had decidedly good breeding associated with it. The banker Abbott Mills hired the eminent Boston firm of Shepley, Rutan and Coolidge to

Entrance porch of the James Semple House, Williamsburg, Virginia, eighteenth century.

design a home for his son Lewis in 1916. At first appearance, the house was an exact copy of any number of eighteenth-century houses found throughout New England, which, in turn, bore strong similarities to the English models, as can be seen in the illustration of an eighteenth-century wood house in Close, Salisbury. Such typical smaller English houses utilized wood construction, hipped central roofs, pedimented dormers, symmetrically placed double-hung windows, and a pedimented porch cover. Smaller details, such as the design of the cornice with consul brackets, went directly from England to the Colonies, and were copied quite exactly in the Lewis H. Mills House of 1916 in Portland. Georgian style dormers, double-hung

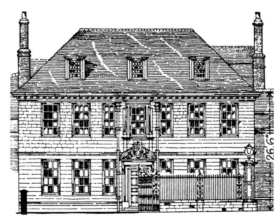

House in Close, Salisbury, England, eighteenth century.

windows with 6/6 panes, and a broken pediment around the fanlight over the entry door marked this house as the most authentic in Colonial design to be constructed in the city to that date. The broken pediment of the entry seems to have been copied directly from examples such as that seen on the porch of the Bristol House in New Haven, Connecticut. The second-phase Colonial Revival house was so authentic in detail that none of the Queen Anne attributes could be found here: no curved bays, nor wrap-around verandas, certainly no engaged towers or rambling plans. The details were so beautifully crafted in the Mills House that when the owners moved out of the neighborhood, they took the pedimented entry, the stairs, and the fireplace woodwork with them to another Colonial Revival home designed especially to house these features. Such was the reverence for the historically correct detail.

The eighteenth- and early nineteenth-century architects who provided the models of Classical form for the Colonial Revival style became famous all over again when studied, copied, and emulated by the twentieth-century architects. Who has not heard of Thomas Jefferson's plans for the University of Virginia (1817–26) or Monticello (1768–1809), or of the White House (1792) designed by James Hoban. William Thornton designed our national Capi-

Bristol House entrance porch,
New Haven, Connecticut.

Typical New England Colonial Revival house, Greenfield Hill, Connecticut.

tol Building (1793) in Washington, D.C., based on the Palladian plans of English country mansions. Charles Bulfinch designed the Federal style State House in Boston (1795). These were the great names, those who also designed the residences that others avidly studied, and whose inspiration and designs greatly influenced the second phase of the Colonial Revival period in Portland. Though on a considerably smaller scale, the temple-fronted porticos of the J. C. Braly House (1926) or the William P. Hawley House (1927) certainly were influenced by the porticoed southern antebellum mansions, as the William Haseltine (1935) and Dr. John P. Cleland (1936) houses were influenced by the great New England Colonial houses, such as the Craigie House (1759) of Cambridge, Massachusetts, with its pedimented extension at the central entrance.

Parallels between designs on the West Coast and those of the East can easily be drawn. A famous house designed by Stanford White in 1901 for Alfred A. Pope in Farmington, Connecticut, would seem the direct inspiration for a house designed several decades later in Portland. The Dr. D. C. Burkes House of circa 1928 designed by Roscoe Hemenway has a two-story portico almost identical to that of the Pope House, much in the spirit of George Washington's Mount Vernon home. The Burkes House exhibits the same rambling plan as the Pope House, where formal elements are mixed with those seemingly informal. The result is a compellingly attractive house, especially for those who wish to construct large homes having the "respectability" of Colonial designs, but also

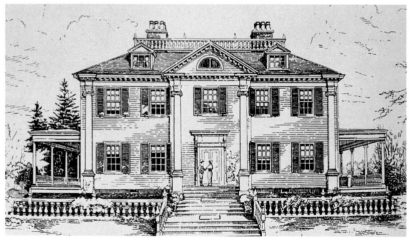

Craigie House, Cambridge, Massachusetts, 1759.

Alfred A. Pope House, Farmington, Connecticut, 1901, designed by Stanford White.

shun the monumental aspects of great pillared mansions.

Most Portland architects were capable of a fine Colonial Revival design when called upon to do so. The firm of Whitehouse and Fouilhoux designed the Raymond Wilcox residence of 1916 with much of the formalities of the Mills House of that same year. Jamieson K. Parker was a noted practitioner of the style; his handsome Milton Markewitz House (1924) and especially the Edward D. Kingsley House (1926) are milestones of elegant design in the Colonial Revival style. Later, Roscoe Hemenway enjoyed a reputation for years as THE architect of respectable Portland homes because of the great number of houses he designed in the style, and their sometimes profusion of elegant details. This wonderful era of the Colonial Revival lasted from 1888 until eclipsed in the 1950s, when the Northwest style came to dominate housing design.

Colonial Revival—Second Phase
CHARACTERISTICS

PLANS: symmetrical and asymmetrical; prominent entrance porticos.

ROOFS: central hipped, or side gabled; telescoping gable wings; pedimented dormers, sometimes combined; pedimented gable ends, or with return cornices at gable end. Shingled.

EXTERIOR FINISHES: beveled lap siding, or shingles; mitered siding, pilasters, or staggered quoins at corners; modillions or dentils at the cornice.

CHIMNEYS: constructed of brick; interior locations within exterior facade, usually at gable ends. When exposed, often featured with a window placed at second floor in center of chimney.

WINDOWS: traditional proportions of Colonial and Federal style windows, symmetrically located. Six-over-six (6/6) upper panes, six-over-nine (6/9) lower panes; Palladian feature windows; half-ellipse, semicircular, or circular gable-end attic windows.

WINDOW TRIM (exterior): detailed casings, often with cornices at first floor windows; working louvered shutters; late-Georgian dormers with full or broken pediments and rounded window openings.

ENTRANCE DOORS: six panels, with sidelights and semicircular or half-ellipse leaded transom windows.

VERANDAS/PORCHES: pedimented entrance porticos, with free-standing columns or pilasters; occasional two-story entrance or garden porticos, or covered balustraded verandas.

INTERIOR FINISHES: plaster walls and ceilings; paneled or wainscoting halls; paneled living rooms or libraries. Dark stained oak floors.

INTERIOR TRIM: molded casing trim, often with pedimented cornices; elaborate crown molds and baseboards.

STAIRS: straight run, or reverse run with landings over vestibules or entrances; Colonial style railings with hardwood rails, painted and turned balusters; curved at the bottom.

FIREPLACE FRONTS: marble surround, flanked by Classical pilasters and surmounted by entablature; overmantel paneling and side pilasters.

PROPERTY SURROUNDS: return of picket fences, with gates and finialed posts.

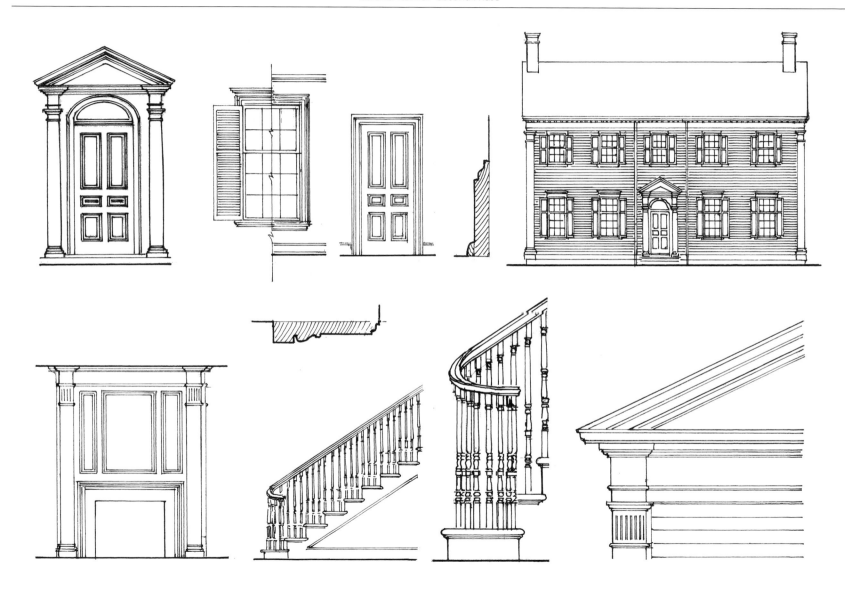

Entrance to the Lewis H. Mills House.

Colonial Revival—Second Phase
HOUSES

1916	Lewis H. Mills (Shepley, Rutan and Coolidge)	1927	William P. Hawley (Ellis F. Lawrence)
1916	Raymond Wilcox (Whitehouse and Fouilhoux)	1927	William T. Waerner (George M. Post)
1917	Leslie M. Scott (John Virginius Bennes)	c. 1928	Dr. D. C. Burkes (Roscoe D. Hemenway)
1919	Theodore B. Wilcox (Kirtland K. Cutter)	1935	William Haseltine (Jamieson K. Parker)
1924	Milton Markewitz (Jamieson K. Parker)	1936	Dr. John P. Cleland (J. Irving Lawson)
1925	Paul C. Carey (Harold W. Doty)	c. 1940	Donald McGraw (Jamieson K. Parker)
1926	J. C. Braly (Lee Thomas)	1940	Ernest Haycox (Glenn Stanton and Associates)
1926	Edward D. Kingsley (Jamieson K. Parker)		

Lewis H. Mills (1916)
Shepley, Rutan and Coolidge

When Abbott Mills's son Lewis married a relative of Boston architect Jefferson Coolidge, the firm of Shepley, Rutan and Coolidge gave the young couple plans for their Portland residence as a wedding present. The property, located at 2039 NW Irving Street, was on the same block as the Abbott Mills home of 1908 and shared the back gardens. The Federal architectural design influences used in the house made it one of the first

Lewis H. Mills House.

houses of the second phase of the Colonial Revival style. The narrower and taller window proportions, with their 6/6 (upper floor) and 9/6 (lower floor) panes, were to be predominant characteristics for the remainder of the Colonial Revival period. The most elegant feature of the house was its broken-pedimented central doorway, now removed. The eight-panel door had a louvered fan design over it and partially fluted side columns. The entablature and cornice extended over the sidelights on both sides. Other refined details were in the modillioned cornice, the corner rustication, the rounded dormer windows—the pediments of which matched in design that of the entrance portico—and the balustraded widow's walk, also now removed. An underhouse garage, with driveway, now further imposes on this house's exceptional facade.

Raymond Wilcox (1916)
Whitehouse and Fouilhoux

The second phase of the Colonial Revival style spread quickly to other developing residential areas of the city. Most prominent architects rendered their own interpretation of the classic forms and designs. Whitehouse and Fouilhoux, known for their elegantly designed private-club buildings, designed a home for Raymond Wilcox, still standing but with an overly detailed side addition, at 2111 SW Twenty-first Avenue on Portland Heights. The house was constructed the same year as the eastern-influenced home of Lewis H. Mills, and it bears much resemblance. The entrance porch and gabled roof dormers are nearly identical to those on the Mills House. Bowing to still-prevalent local custom, the first and second floor windows have 6/1 panes. The house's original operable window shutters have been replaced by new ones that are not operable,

Raymond Wilcox House.

Leslie M. Scott (1917)
John Virginius Bennes

Architect John Virginius Bennes, better known for his designs of Prairie style homes, is credited with having designed at least one Colonial Revival house. It was for Leslie Scott, and it is located at 2116 NE Sixteenth Avenue. In true Bennes fashion, the house has the most unusual characteristic of four large pilasters located on either side of the entrance porch and the stair-landing Palladian window above it. To enhance their presence, gabled dormers center on the pairs of pilasters, and the front of the house extends slightly forward to tie them together in design. The house has a large symmetrical central mass, and the gabled side exten-

and they tend to lessen the design's quality. The cornice is finely detailed, with scroll modillions, similar to that on the Whitehouse and Fouilhoux designed Osmond Stubbs House of 1915. The handsome original telescoping gables of the north elevation are now covered by somewhat Baroque additions. Nonetheless, this is a timeless Colonial, the symmetrical plan and elevation of which helped set the standard for Colonial designs for the next four decades.

Leslie M. Scott House.

sions center on the larger gable. The side extensions have the same cornice height, which conceals the gutter within the cornice design. The windows have 1/1 panes. A featured Palladian window, centered over the entrance portico, and dormer windows on the roof have pointed-arch panes in the round tops. All lower floor windows have cornices, whereas the second floor windows are directly connected with the entablature. Added to the house are new, nonoperable shutters and hoods over the basement windows.

Theodore B. Wilcox (1919)
Kirtland K. Cutter

When Theodore Wilcox and family moved from their 1893 Shingle/Richardsonian home on King's Hill, they moved to Glenwood Farm, a lavish country estate located west of the city. No expense was spared. Wilcox hired Kirtland Cutter, a notable Spokane architect, to design the house, and L. M. Thielsen to design the lavish gardens. With Georgian and Federal details, the house was shingled and had white trim and dark green shutters. The shingles were left to weather, and they were an essential part of the character of the house, until painted by later owners. In its heyday, the house was a center of Portland social life. Enormous rooms for entertaining ran the full width of the house and opened onto the terraced and walled back gardens. The large mass of the house hinges on a gabled porte-cochere entrance. To the left is the living room wing, the fireplace of which provides the focus or center point for the formal gardens to the rear of the house. To the right is the dining room, kitchen, and garage wing of the house, brought forward from the living room wing. Pedimented dormers, shingled on their sides, are recessed into the roof and have balustraded balconies. On the front elevation, an

elliptically arched arcade provides protection from the sun for the windows and French doors of the living room.

Federal details are employed with great style throughout the house. The elliptically arched entrance has elegant fluted side columns and fine leaded fanlights and sidelights. Inside, the wainscoted entry hall houses the wide staircase, the cut-out balustrade of which winds to the second floor. Intricate cornice work is displayed throughout the house, with

Theodore B. Wilcox House and estate.

Front elevation, Wilcox House.

Rear elevation and formal gardens, Wilcox House.

Main entrance, Wilcox House.

Main interior stairway, Wilcox House.

Entrance door interior, Wilcox House.

some of the finest detail work to be found. The living room fireplace, on the garden-side wall, is enormous, also with Federal detailing. Though huge by today's standards, the house functioned well—of course, staffed fully to keep it running smoothly.

The house became the Columbia Preparatory School after the Wilcox family sold the property, and eventually it was divided into multiple residential units, which carefully attempted to preserve the architectural integrity of the original house. Today, it remains one of Portland's finest examples of Colonial Revival architecture.

Second floor plan, Wilcox House.

First floor plan, Wilcox House.

Milton Markewitz (1924)

Jamieson K. Parker

In the same year that he designed the First Unitarian Church, Jamieson Parker, of the firm of Johnson, Parker and Wallwork, was commissioned by Milton Markewitz as architect for his home at 2165 SW Main Street. Most of the houses designed by Parker were in the Colonial Revival style, and the Markewitz House is one of the most successful. The plan and entrance facade, with a glassed-in balustraded side porch, are symmetrical under a central hipped roof supporting three pedimented dormers. Symmetrical fireplaces are located at the outside walls of the living and dining rooms. Though hidden for years behind majestic rho-

Milton Markewitz House.

dodendrons, the half-ellipse, with fan motif, of the entrance portico is especially handsome. Paired round and boxed Roman Doric columns support the portico roof. Fine detailing is found in the staggered quoins at the house corners and in the modillioned cornice under the eave. The windows are typically 6/6, with smaller six-pane casement windows above the entrance portico and at the dormer windows. Unfortunately, the fine interiors have been altered considerably for offices.

Paul C. Carey (1925)
Harold W. Doty

Though small, the Paul Carey House at 2572 SW Arden Road reveals considerable architectural merit. Designed by architect Harold Doty in 1925, the house was included in the 1932 "List of the Finest Architectural Work in Portland" compiled by the local chapter of the American Institute of Architects. Doty shared an office with renowned architect Wade Hampton Pipes during the 1920s and 1930s, though his work stands well on its own merits. The Carey House is arranged in townhouse fashion: two bedrooms and a bath on the second floor; living/dining room and kitchen on the main floor; and a finished daylight basement opening to a hillside garden. A single-car garage, its gable perpendicular to the main roof gable, is attached to the main volume of the house. The straightforward house is dominated by its massive central brick chimney, with windows and recessed entry carefully balanced on the front elevation. The back, or garden, elevation has two attractive Colonial style polygonal bay windows, cantilevered from the house wall, and gabled dormer windows. Original materials included unglazed ceramic tile on the kitchen floor, wrought-iron hardware, and polished wood floors.

Paul C. Carey House.

J. C. Braly (1926)
Lee Thomas

Though little known, architect Lee Thomas practiced in Portland for nearly forty years. During construction of the J. C. Braly House at 2846 NW Fairfax Terrace in 1926, he worked at his firm called Thomas and Mercier, the latter partner being an engineer. The firm produced a well-designed and detailed residence for Mr. Braly, dominated by its two-story pedimented entrance portico. The side-gabled central mass projects both on the front facade, with the portico, and on the rear view side, with a central gabled extension. A spacious central hall, entered under the stair landing, opens on axis to the city view off of a polygonal sun room. All rooms are symmetrical off the central hall, with the living and dining rooms on the view side of the house. In its detailing, both exterior and interior, the house is especially fine. The exterior is influenced by Federal designs, as in its finely carved pilaster capitals, the box-modillioned cornice, and the lively brickwork with corner quoins. Inside, the central stair, with curved balustrade at the second floor, dominates the large hall. A large Palladian window at the stair landing looks out through the entrance portico.

Edward D. Kingsley (1926)
Jamieson K. Parker

When looking to architectural precedent for inspiration, architect Jamieson K. Parker chose with impeccable taste. His design for Edward D. Kingsley at 2132 SW Montgomery Drive is as fine as any in our Colonial past in its siting, construction, proportions, and detailing. The side-gabled house has one telescoping wing consisting of the kitchen and servants' quarters, with pediments obscuring the gable-end chimney. Completely symmetrical elevations are found on both the street and garden sides of the central mass. An open pediment supported by free-

J. C. Braly House.

Edward D. Kingsley House.

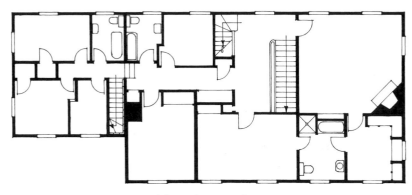

Second floor plan, Kingsley House.

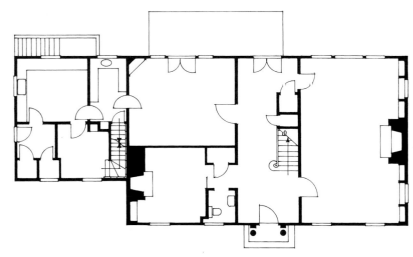

First floor plan, Kingsley House.

standing Roman Doric columns frames the entrance door, which also displays a half-ellipse transom. Dentil work is used in the cornice. The house has massive corner pilasters, in Federal design, and a box-modillioned cornice. Pedimented dormers are found on the back elevation, the center one combining two dormers in a three-window arrangement. The house sits close to the sidewalk on its quarter-block property, and it is surrounded by a handsome finialed picket fence in the Federal style.

The interiors are focused around the wainscoted central hall that runs through the house, with entry to the garden in the back. A paneled living room runs the depth of the house. Sidelighted French doors open from the living room out to the large garden, as does a matching pair in the dining room. The fireplace paneling and pilasters of the living room repeat the Federal details seen on the exterior. To the left of the central hall is a library with fireplace and the dining room, through which access is gained to the kitchen wing. Original Chinese style wallpaper and arched display cabinets are features of the garden-oriented room.

William P. Hawley (1927)
Ellis F. Lawrence

Using more "correct" Colonial details, architect Ellis F. Lawrence designed for William Hawley one of his most handsome houses. Located at 2033 SW Jackson Street, the large home has especially fine detailing on both the exterior and interior. The pedimented two-story entrance portico, with paired Corinthian columns, has elaborate cartouche and swag decorations in its tympanum, similar to such decorations on the widely publicized Governor's Palace at Colonial Williamsburg in Virginia. Other Colonial detailing is found in the arched and scalloped cornice

William P. Hawley House.

work, the paneled corner pilasters, and the entrance doorway with side-lights and the Palladian window above it. Symmetrically placed on the side-gabled roof, unusual recessed dormers have rounded panes in the top sash and return cornices. The large central mass has telescoping gabled side wings, with paired pilasters at the extension corners and round windows in the gables.

Inside, the large staircase has its landing over the entrance door. The turned balusters and newels are finely designed and crafted, as are the details of the paneled rooms and fireplace mantels.

William T. Waerner (1927)
George M. Post

Federal-period design influences were used by several architects during the second phase of the Colonial Revival. Architect George M. Post employed such influences in his house design for William Waerner at 4206 NE Alameda Drive. The delicate detailing of the Federal period is found in the exedra-style entrance portico, with its slender Roman Doric columns. The half-ellipse theme is repeated in the transom light over the paneled and sidelighted entrance door. Above, a Palladian window with arched upper panes is framed within paneling to the box-modillioned cornice. Architect Post used his own version of dormer design. On the hipped central roof, he employed French-style arched-roof dormers

William T. Waerner House.

with 4/8 double-hung window sashes. Other windows are 6/6, which were being used quite regularly by the late 1920s. Hinged shutters, painted dark green against the brick construction, have louvered top panels and fixed bottom panels. The symmetrically planned house is well maintained, and it enjoys a neighborhood of many well-designed homes, sharing fine western views of the city and excellent quality.

Dr. D. C. Burkes (c. 1928)
Roscoe D. Hemenway

The Colonial Revival style was readily adapted to asymmetrical plans and sculptural balance. McKim, Mead and White, the prestigious New York architectural firm, had developed asymmetrical Colonial Revival designs many years earlier, and these were highly influential to architects all over the country. The large home designed by Roscoe Hemenway for Dr. D. C. Burkes at 1315 NW Cumberland Road was influenced by the designs of the eastern architectural firm, and it exemplifies the possibilities for flexibility in the style. In plan, the house is organized around a gabled central mass that has various side wings and extensions. In the brick gabled front extension, a pedimented and recessed entrance portal, with arched opening, includes a fanlight above the door.

Dr. D. C. Burkes House.

Garden elevations, Burkes House.

Beveled lap siding covers the central mass and side wing and is painted a historically influenced light ochre color, in contrast to the white trim and dark green shutters. The surprise of the house is the two-story balustraded porch—in the fashion of George Washington's Mount Vernon home—located at the back of the house. The covered porch has paired boxed columns, the simple details of which are repeated on the house pilasters.

William Haseltine (1935)
Jamieson K. Parker

Architect Jamieson Parker designed a reserved Colonial Revival house for William Haseltine at 3231 NE U. S. Grant Place in 1935, just as the Depression was beginning to subside. The design of the house closely followed Colonial precedents, mainly in the slightly extended and pedimented central portion. Parker used wide Roman Doric pilasters to frame the extension as well as at the house's corners. Within the tympanum is a half-ellipse fanlight. The New England style recessed doorway has a flat cornice and fluted pilasters, a most elemental Colonial style doorway. The cornices are also found over the main floor 6/9 windows, which are wider and longer than those of the second floor (6/6). Both levels have hinged shutters, but not with operable louvers. A large chimney is seen to the left, centered on the living room side of the house. To the right of the central hall is the dining room, with kitchen behind it, and a maid's bedroom and a study in a back wing. For convenience and economy of space, the central-hall plan, with all rooms radiating off of the hall, cannot be excelled; Parker's version is a prime example.

William Haseltine House.

Dr. John P. Cleland (1936)
J. Irving Lawson

Toronto architect J. Irving Lawson, of the firm of Marani, Lawson and Morris, designed a handsome residence for his Oregon City relatives, Dr. and Mrs. John P. Cleland. Located at 14343 South Clackamas River Road, the rambling house has a formal entrance within a side-gabled central volume. The two side wings are also gabled. One wing is a single story tall and the other is a story-and-a-half in height. The central portion has flush tongue-in-groove siding with staggered quoins at the cor-

Dr. John P. Cleland House.

ners. Beveled lap siding covers the remainder of the house, and the siding on the garage wing is within elliptically arched false arcades. Other fine details include the box-modillioned cornice and the curved pediment and plain side pilasters of the main entry. In this house, the main stair runs parallel to the front elevation, thus allowing ample frontage for main rooms on the view, or river, side, quite different from typical plans centered on the stair hall. In siting, basic plan, and detailing, the Cleland House is an example of the gracious environments to be found in Colonial style homes, and it reminds us that architects across the continent well-knew the Colonial vocabulary.

Donald McGraw (c. 1940)
Jamieson K. Parker

Jamieson Parker designed a gracious Colonial Revival style home for Donald McGraw in Dunthorpe, utilizing the unique features of the site to full advantage. The house is situated at 01845 SW Military Lane, a location full of magnificent original Douglas fir trees. Approached in classic angled fashion, the drive culminates at the circular turnaround in front of the entrance. In contrast with this contained entrance space, the major rooms of the house are oriented toward the rear view of the distant Cascade Range mountains. Parker, with his inevitable sense of style and classic good taste, gave the house a fine sense of scale, despite its large size. The two-story structures have well-detailed pedimented gables at the sides, shuttered double-hung windows, and a pedimented recessed entry, all with recognizably accurate Colonial Revival second

Donald McGraw House.

phase details. The attention to quality continues in the interior rooms, with fine paneling, period moldings, and fine fireplace and stair details. It remains today a handsome Portland home, beautifully maintained by descendants of the original owners.

Ernest Haycox (1940)
Glenn Stanton and Associates

Among the finest of the Colonial Revival homes in Portland is the large house constructed for noted writer of western tales, Ernest Haycox. Located at 4700 SW Humphrey Boulevard, on the lower slopes of Greenhills, it is one of the few residential designs produced by the successful firm Glenn Stanton and Associates. An attractive and spacious approach

Ernest Haycox House.

highlight the house's beautiful site. The front elevation has a projected gable centered on the entrance with a Palladian window above. Symmetrically placed windows and end chimneys balance the composition. The garden side of the house has a two-story columned porch, reminiscent of Mount Vernon. Particularly noteworthy is the home's handsome oval entrance hall, with a curved open stair to the second floor, and its exceptional library. The library has a sixteen-foot-high ceiling and a wrap-around balcony with a Chippendale-Chinese style balcony railing. Bookshelves line the walls of both floors of the library. A Federal style fireplace is centered on the long wall and a polygonal bay window faces the garden. It is possibly one of the most handsome private rooms in the city.

Theodore B. Wilcox (1950)
Roscoe D. Hemenway

The life and times of the wealthy changed drastically by the Second World War. With taxes and the high cost of maintenance, the larger homes were sold, and the families moved to smaller dwellings. Such was the case with Theodore B. Wilcox, who sold his 1919 Glenwood Farm country estate and moved to Portland Heights. The new house, designed by architect Roscoe Hemenway, is located at 2728 SW Greenway Avenue. It carries on the Colonial Revival tradition of the former house and bears some similar features. A gabled front entrance facade, with its recessed and columned entry, and the prominent chimney window likely were favorite features of Mr. Wilcox. The house consists of a large central mass with gabled ends, off of which is a perpendicular kitchen, family room, and garage wing. Through the garage wing, an open drive connects to SW Talbot Road. Most impressive is the pedimented and recessed portico on the garden side. On axis with the main entrance door, French doors open out from the entrance hall to the rear garden. Both the front and back elevations are symmetrical, with centered entrances, and both have rounded dormer windows on either side of the central gables. The house is covered with beveled lap siding framed by staggered quoins at the corners and a modillioned cornice along the top.

As in Glenwood Farm, the interior detailing is first rate. An extensive crown molding runs throughout the first floor. Elegant paired and paneled doors enter into the living and dining rooms at either side of the entrance hall, each with elaborately pedimented cornices. The winding stair has paneled wainscoting, and its railing has turned and twisted

Garden elevation, Wilcox House.

Theodore B. Wilcox House.

Entrance hall and stairway, Wilcox House.

Dining room door and wallpaper, Wilcox House.

balusters. Broken pediments are used in the casing trim over the dining room doors, and the walls are covered with beautifully copied period wallpaper. The house is a tribute not only to the architectural patronage of the Wilcox family, but also to the talents of its architect, Roscoe Hemenway. He carried on the Colonial Revival tradition in Portland long after fashionable tastes had moved to regional Northwest contemporary styles. The house is considered by many to be Hemenway's finest work.

CHAPTER 11

Tudor

The duration of the Tudor style in Portland left a wide collection of houses bearing its characteristics. The Tudor style began at the turn of the century and lasted well into the Depression years of the 1930s. Although exhibiting other stylistic influences, such as from the Craftsman and Arts and Crafts styles, even Norman architecture, the houses grouped into this category have at least some elements of the Tudor style in common. The development of the style has a long history, beginning in the Tudor Period (1485–1603) in medieval England, resurfacing in England in the 1860s, and coming to the United States shortly thereafter.

The original source influences of the Tudor style in Portland are the Tudor houses constructed in England during the first half of the sixteenth century, erected during the reign of Henry VIII (1509–1547) after his suppression of the monasteries in 1532. The suppression of monastic wealth and lands provided the newly created nobility and trading families with the means to build their estates. Most of the manor houses constructed during this time followed ancient patterns and were still built around quadrangular courts. The increase in the num-

The William Gadsby House, on NW Twenty-fifth Avenue.

ber of rooms reflected a new emphasis on comfortable living accommodations. Studies, summer and winter parlors, private dining rooms, and even separate bedrooms were now accommodated, although bedrooms, still in tandem, were often part of a continuous corridor, or "thoroughfare," through which one must pass to get to other rooms of the house. The larger houses had many bedrooms, of course, and additional rooms such as kitchen offices, pastry rooms, laundry, and linen rooms, all not found previously in English homes. The English homes that were comparable in size to American homes were not those of the feudal lords, but those of their retainers attached to the monastic communities. These were the countless smaller houses clustered under the protective walls of the great castles and monasteries, displaying the features of what we consider Tudor architecture.

The architectural characteristics of the Tudor style have remained fairly constant since the fifteenth century. The most readily recognizable characteristic is the half-timbering, where the post-and-beam construction is revealed on the exterior of the house and is infilled with nogging of stuccoed brick or stone. Even the bracing is revealed, often elaborated into designs and giving a highly decorative effect. Second floors often cantilevered out over the narrow

streets of old England, providing additional floor space on the crowded lots. In England, the style of houses with the half-timbering is referred to as "black and white," the timbers being painted dark or black for protection and the infilling painted white. Whole towns were constructed in this method, and those that remain today are charming historic attractions. The second defining characteristic of the Tudor style is the decorated and fanciful bargeboards. Those found in the fifteenth-century Ockwells Manor House in Berkshire, England, for example, are especially attractive, and such historic designs also greatly influenced design in the Gothic Revival period of the 1840s and 1850s. Other bargeboards, such as that on Leycester's Hospital (1571) in Warwick, were simpler, but

they had highly carved surfaces. These bargeboards influenced the Queen Anne style houses in Portland during the 1880s and 1890s as well as many of the Tudor style houses after the turn of the century. A third characteristic is the abundant use of windows. England is known for its dark winters, and more interior light was desirable during those long winter months. This became possible with the increasing availability of glass and leaded windows. New windows were banked in series, often creating huge two-story expanses of glazing. Wide polygonal bays were introduced, often under the protective shelter of the cantilevered second floor. Of course, of the many characteristics typical to this architectural style, the Tudor arch was a particularly prominent feature. It

Ockwells Manor House, Berkshire, England, fifteenth century.

Leycester's Hospital, Warwick, England, 1571.

Leycester's Hospital courtyard.

appeared in and around doorways, open loggias, and throughout interior detailing.

The medieval revival styles flourished in England during the 1860s and 1870s and directly influenced American architectural trends. Richard Norman Shaw, one of England's most talented and original architects, employed the style considerably in his early projects. Several of these appeared regularly in American architectural magazines of the period. His Hopedene, constructed in Surrey in 1873, was featured in *Building News* in 1874, complete with a handsome perspective and plan (see Chapter 6). Shaw designed another house, at Sunninghill, England, in 1879 that appeared in *American Architect and Building News* in 1880. Both of these houses employed such typical Tudor elements as the half-timbering, the continuous banks of leaded windows, mostly with transoms, the tall brick chimneys with expressed individual flues, and the steeply pitched roofs with decorated bargeboards. The houses had a profound effect on American designs. As early as 1874, the Boston architect Henry Hobson Richardson designed the

William Watts Sherman House in Newport, Rhode Island, showing Shaw's influence in the United States in a highly original interpretation (see Chapter 6).

Nothing had as great an influence, however, as the display of domestic architecture at the Centennial International Exhibition in Philadelphia in 1876. Houses designed by Thomas Harris for the British executive commissioner and delegates' residences and staff offices were viewed by countless patrons of the Exhibition. Both *Building News* and *American Builder* mag-

azines featured the houses in sketches and plans. Such designs were promptly assimilated in the Queen Anne and Eastlake styles. The Queen Anne style houses used the simpler bargeboards, while the Eastlake style houses employed those highly elaborate. Half-timbering was by this time false, being added to frame construction rather than post and beam.

The earliest Portland houses in the Tudor style reflected dual influences. They adhered to Craftsman floor plans while exhibiting elevation details in the Tudor style. Decorated bargeboards, cantilevered second floors, and extensive half-timbering were found in most of the early designs. The William Gadsby House (1908) designed by Emil Schacht was one of the finest examples from this early period. An interesting example from the 1920s is the Cameron Squires House designed by Ellis Lawrence in 1920. With the passage of time, architects and builders incorporated elements of the Tudor style in other historic period designs, such as the Arts and Crafts· style, where, although the bargeboards were removed entirely— the verge of the roof and walls sim-

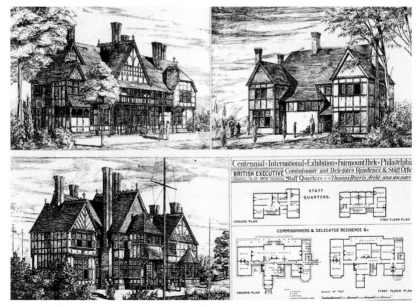

British executive commissioner and delegates' residences and staff office, Centennial International Exhibition, Philadelphia, 1876, designed by Thomas Harris.

ply detailed without overhangs or decoration—Tudor banked windows with leaded glass did continue, as did some elements of half-timbering or carved lintels. A particularly notable design from the latter period of the Tudor influence is the Thomas J. Autzen House of 1927, showing a handsome combination of half-timbering with Arts and Crafts designs. A final example of Tudor style elements used in combination with other styles is the four-centered Tudor arch incorporated into the entry portal of the Roy Gangware House of 1932.

Tudor
CHARACTERISTICS

PLANS: asymmetrical, with entrance hall centrally located; prominent entrance porticos.

ROOFS: steeply pitched central hipped, or side gabled; telescoping gables (or catslide), gabled dormers, multi-gabled facade; little or moderate eave extension, with wide, often decorated or fretted bargeboards. Wood shingled.

EXTERIOR FINISHES: half-timbering, combined with brick, stone, stucco, or beveled lap siding. Clinker brick introduced.

CHIMNEYS: massive chimney stacks with multiple flues; exterior or interior locations.

WINDOWS: primarily multiple-paned casements, often in groups; sometimes with diagonal wood or leaded mullions. Some bay windows or oriels.

WINDOW TRIM (exterior): trim integral with half-timbering. Trim boards adzed, or rough sawed, to exterior.

ENTRANCE DOORS: portico-covered, recessed entry with decorative carved beams; four-centered Tudor arch used on or around entrance doors. Oak doors with fake pegs.

VERANDAS/PORCHES: gabled entrance porches with brick steps; telescoping entrance porches; open side porches under extension of main roof or attached shed roof.

INTERIOR FINISHES: beamed ceilings, combined with ornamental plaster; oak paneling with linen fold. Polished, stained oak floors. Craftsman or Arts and Crafts interiors intermingled with Tudor or Colonial details.

INTERIOR TRIM: molded casing trim and baseboards, often oak and stained dark.

STAIRS: oak tread and risers; substantial newels with finials and turned balusters. Paneled stair hall.

FIREPLACE FRONTS: stone or cement surrounds, with Tudor arch; ceiling-high paneled overmantels. Openings sized smaller than original Tudor designs.

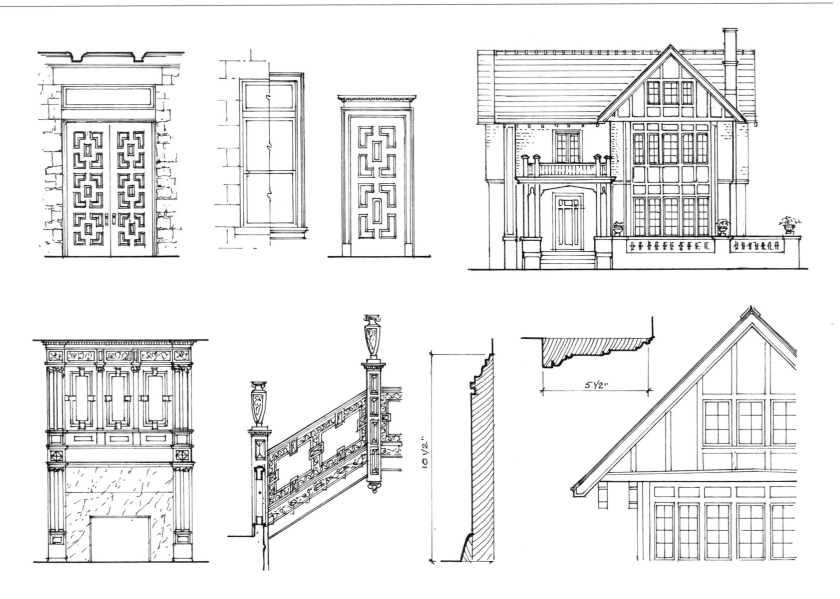

Entrance to the D. R. Munroe House.

Tudor
HOUSES

1900   Frank E. Hart (Whidden and Lewis)

1908   William Gadsby (Emil Schacht)

1908   Blaine R. Smith (Ellis F. Lawrence)

1911   Rev. Charles Scadding (David C. Lewis)

1911   Henry Miller (Ellis F. Lawrence)

1913   D. R. Munroe (Francis Jacobberger)

1920   Cameron Squires (Ellis F. Lawrence)

1923   Stanley C. E. Smith (Ellis F. Lawrence)

1924   M. Lloyd Frank (Herman Brookman)

1925   Dr. Zimmerman (Carl L. Linde)

1927   Thomas J. Autzen (Kirtland K. Cutter)

1930   Carl C. Jantzen (Charles Ertz)

1931   J. L. Easson (attributed to Ellis F. Lawrence)

1932   Roy Hunt (attributed to Richard Sundeleaf)

1932   Roy Gangware (Roscoe D. Hemenway)

1933   Dr. James J. Rosenberg (Henry Herzog)

1934   Paul F. Murphy (Richard Sundeleaf)

1936   Dean B. Webster (Richard Sundeleaf)

1936   Wesley P. Steinmetz (attributed to Charles Ertz)

Frank E. Hart (1900)
Whidden and Lewis

The development of Carter's Addition on Portland Heights evolved slowly when it was accessible only by carriage on evenly graded Montgomery Drive. With the advent of the automobile, new construction on the western hills commenced at a much greater pace. On the table of land between Carter Lane and Spring Street, one of the first large residences in the emerging Tudor style was the house for Frank E. Hart designed by Whidden and Lewis and located at 1942 SW Montgomery Drive. The house carried the distinctive Tudor style features in its steep gabled roof and dormers, with wide bargeboards, and the half-timber-

Frank E. Hart House.

ing effect of its stuccoed second floor exterior, which combined with vertical and horizontal decorative boards. Of note are the intersecting double gable ends, a feature developed by English architects prior to the turn of the century. The decorative bracing of the false timbering in the partial quatrefoil design, the cantilevered joists at the third floor, and the multi-column entry porch were design features decidedly derived from English seventeenth-century Tudor sources.

William Gadsby (1908)
Emil Schacht

Architect Emil Schacht, whose career in Portland spanned over forty years, was in mid-career when he designed the home for William Gadsby in 1908, still standing at 1205 NW Twenty-fifth Avenue at Northrup Street. Schacht was a particularly gifted designer, and as the fashions changed with the years, he was adept at designing within the evolving popular styles. For this Tudor style home, Schacht employed much of the style's vocabulary, but he adapted them for the practical central-hall, two-story plan that worked so well for narrow city lots. Brick with stone dressing is the exterior finish material of the first floor, with half-timbering at the second floor and the third floor gable ends. The wide decorated bargeboards and the cantilevered attic floor over the second floor bay are within the Tudor tradition. Leaded glass is used in the bay and transom windows. Inside, with the parlor to the right and the dining room to the left of the entrance, the 4000-square-foot house is beautifully finished. Handsome woodwork abounds in the principal rooms, especially in the wall paneling, beamed ceilings, fireplace, and entry-stair details. A curved bay with leaded transom windows in series dominates the dining room end wall.

William Gadsby House.

Blaine R. Smith House.

Blaine R. Smith (1908)
Ellis F. Lawrence

Combining a multitude of design influences in the house constructed for Blaine R. Smith, architect Ellis F. Lawrence, of the firm of McNaughton, Raymond and Lawrence, was able to satisfy his interests in the Arts and Crafts style (the first use of a catslide roof, descending from the upper ridge to the first floor porch), the Craftsman style (the two-story multi-gables), and the Bungalow style (shed-roofed dormers), as well as utilizing an array of Tudor style details. The Tudor details predomi-

nate in the design, described in the 1909 *Portland Daily Abstract* as "English half timbered" style. The steeply pitched gable ends with wide bargeboards, the cantilevered second floor, the fake half-timbering, and the banks of casement windows are all Tudor in nature. Inside, rooms radiate off the central hall, which is noted for its elliptically arched openings supported by paired pilasters. Finishes include dark stained crown molding and casings, art tile for the Tudor-arched fireplace, parquet floors, and the mahogany-paneled dining room with ornamental plaster ceiling. The extant, well-maintained house is located at 5219 SE Belmont Street in the Mount Tabor Addition to the city of Portland.

Rev. Charles Scadding (1911)
David C. Lewis

Notable architect David C. Lewis designed the imposing Tudor style house at 1832 SW Elm Street for Reverend Charles Scadding of Portland's Episcopal Church. The house was located just below the Diocesan Library, also built in 1911, and the 1889 Ascension Episcopal Chapel on Spring Street. (Lewis also designed the 1905 Trinity Episcopal Church, located on NW Nineteenth Street.) In the Scadding House, Lewis used well the Tudor vocabulary. Much like the Hart and Gadsby houses, the Scadding House has large intersecting gables with prominent bargeboards, and it combines brick construction at the main floor with half-

Reverend Charles Scadding House.

timbering at the second and attic floors. The entrance portico, more correctly Tudor than those of the other houses, has brick buttresses and, unfortunately now missing, crenellations in the balustrade above. The combined double gabled dormers reflect the Arts and Crafts style influence. Notable in the interior is the former chapel room, located to the left of the spacious entrance hall, with stained glass in its front-facing transom windows. The house was, and remains, remarkably well built.

Henry Miller (1911)
Ellis F. Lawrence

During the first decades of the twentieth century, the designs of the Tudor style mixed freely with those of the Craftsman and Arts and Crafts styles. The use of brick in Tudor homes was often combined with horizontal lap siding, or possibly both mixed with Tudor half-timbering effects. The Henry Miller House of 1911 designed by Ellis Lawrence combines all these elements.

Prominent in the design is the slightly curved two-story bay window, composed of banks of casement windows and with Tudor style transom windows at the first floor. The bay is protected by a triangular cantilevered gable, which has a wide but simple bargeboard. Other Tudor elements are the Tudor arch at the entry porch, with its chamfered and clustered columns. The balustrade above continues the large-scale timber appearance, in keeping with Tudor precedents. A component of Craftsman style influence is the brick terrace and railing, which wraps around the end of the house.

Located at 2439 NE Twenty-first Avenue, the house is in excellent condition, barring the now-painted brickwork and the porch roof balustrade, which has been replaced with one of wrought-iron.

Henry Miller House.

D. R. Munroe (1913)
Francis Jacobberger

The qualities of the Tudor style were remarkably flexible to the needs of residential architecture. Francis Jacobberger, architect son of Josef Jacobberger, designed a handsome house at 2709 SW Buena Vista Drive in 1913 that has great sculptural vitality, despite its basically rectilinear plan. From the large hipped roof, with intersecting gables at the ends, two prominent gabled extensions project out from the front facade, full

of Tudor detailing. The half-timbering, no longer painted in its striking dark and light color combinations, is framed by the wide, plain and decorated, bargeboards of the gables. Distinctive Tudor quatrefoil designs are located in the bottom panels of the second floor cantilevered polygonal bays. Most handsome is the entrance portal, centered on the main gabled extension. Its pediment is supported by scroll brackets on Roman Doric columns, and the entire composition includes leaded-glass sidelights and the large windows above it. The house originally had an open veranda within the volume of the house, and a sleeping porch above it, the latter introduced into house planning during this decade. Recent additions on the street facade obscure the house's original design integrity.

D. R. Munroe House.

Cameron Squires (1920)
Ellis F. Lawrence

As the Tudor style worked well for small city lots, it also worked in tying together the large, rambling designs of country estates. The stately residence designed by architect Ellis Lawrence for Cameron Squires in 1920 is one of the more handsome examples of well-conceived Tudor-inspired architecture. Of particular interest, and fundamentally Tudor in concept, is the two-story main stair tower, with its crenellated parapet and full, Tudor-arched leaded glass window. Likewise, the character-defining gable-ended front extension combines with a massive Tudor

Cameron Squires House.

style brick chimney, the combination being a favorite and repeated design feature of Lawrence-designed homes. Unusually, the house's entrance is located to the side of the central gable, under a curved eave, with the roof descending two stories to the entry portal. Lawrence unified the entire multi-winged house by the massive hipped central roof, off of which are several gabled and hipped extensions, some angled with the main block of the house. The large house exemplifies a lifestyle now long gone, and though the house was well maintained, today's more modest living has necessitated the removal of the large servants' wing.

Stanley C. E. Smith (1923)
Ellis F. Lawrence

By the 1920s, the English-inspired Arts and Crafts style was having a profound influence on house designs in Portland. The designs of Ellis Lawrence were affected by these changes, even when combining the spare detailing of the Arts and Crafts style with more established Tudor forms. In the house designed for Stanley C. E. Smith in 1923 at 01905 SW Greenwood Road in Dunthorpe, these two styles are successfully woven together. The remaining Tudor elements are the half-timbering, found mainly on the garden elevation, the characteristic large brick chimney, and a few leaded casement windows. The Arts and Crafts influence is represented by the simplicity of details, the use of stucco at the main floor, and the shingled second floor. Decorated bargeboards had all but disappeared by this time, although Lawrence had become fond of the arched eave, an English Cottage style influence used in many of his houses, and here found above the second floor balcony. For the first time, Lawrence also integrated garages in the architectural sculpture, here located straightforwardly off the circle of the main drive.

Stanley C. E. Smith House.

Architect Herman Brookman's sketch for the M. Lloyd Frank House.

M. Lloyd Frank (1924)
Herman Brookman

When quality residential architecture is considered in Portland, no house quite compares with Fir Acres, the monumental country estate of M. Lloyd Frank, heir to the fortunes of the Meier and Frank Department Store. Frank brought New York architect Herman Brookman to Portland to design and supervise construction of his massive house and gardens. This architect-client teamwork resulted in the creation of a superlative example of large-scale residential design and craftsmanship. The house,

in retrospect, embodies the "golden" decades of high style enjoyed by the well-to-do before the Great Depression and World War II.

In Portland, architect Herman Brookman had few peers. The energy that he committed to the mastery of architecture as an art, his sense of composition and site-planning, and the execution of joyously beautiful detail produced results as fine as could be found anywhere in the country. To those who knew and admired his work, Brookman was a master architect out of an older tradition. That older tradition was exemplified by the office in which he received his training, that of New York architect Harry T. Lindeberg, which designed many of the fabulous mansions found along the eastern seaboard. Brookman continued the grand tradition in Portland with his commission for Lloyd Frank, which he designed in the Tudor style, a favorite of wealthy eastern clients.

Brookman's design for the Frank residence was based on an irregular plan comprising two angled wings that meet at the gabled front projec-

Garden-side elevation, Frank House.

tion of the entrance hall and are oriented toward the rear gardens. The major hipped-roof wing to the left of the entrance contains the dining room, with the kitchen wing extending out; the massive living room is located in the other wing. An engaged turret, with bell-cast roof, is adjacent to the projected entrance gable. The garden side of the house, embracing the garden views, has large gable projections and, above the entrance-hall garden doors, an oriel window at the second floor. From the garden side, the massive hipped roof and chimneys give the appearance of a huge Norman farmhouse, another style name to which this house could be referred. Both Norman and Tudor architecture employed half-timbering, the Tudor style chimney, and windows with leaded panes, here found in abundance.

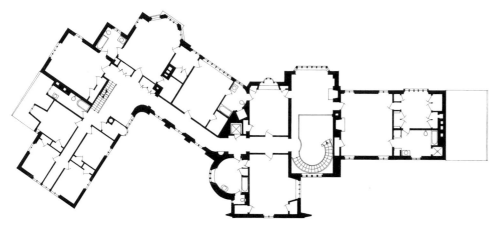

Second floor plan, Frank House.

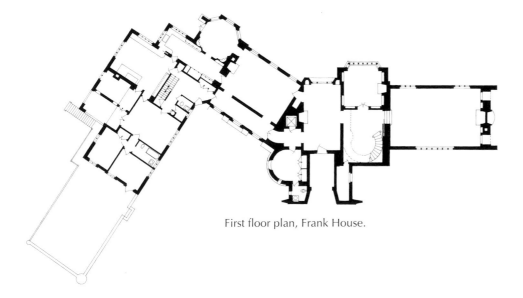

First floor plan, Frank House.

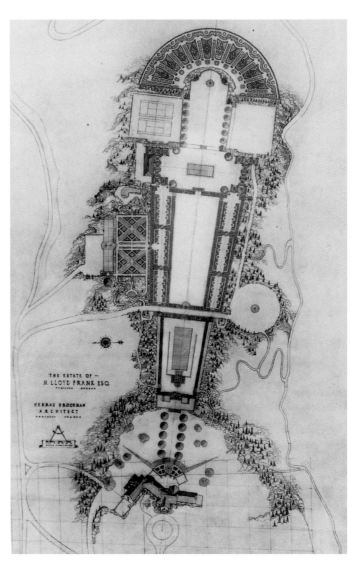

Brookman's sketch of the Frank estate and gardens.

Aerial photo of the Frank estate and gardens.

Interior wood-paneled walls and door, Frank House.

Interior stairway, Frank House.

At close observation, the house would truly seem to be a period piece of architecture. The ancient-looking brick, with a wide range of muted tones, is basically a salmon-pink color, and it complements the golden-brown slate roof. In addition, the Mankato sandblasted cut-stone, used for masonry trim, blends into the whole with a warm glow. All the millwork is mortised and pegged oak, left to weather, which adds to the house's ancient appearance, while the lead gutters and leaders are specially antiqued. Every material, in texture and execution, is treated like artwork, leaving the eye to find pleasure in the smallest detail.

The interiors continue the subdued but masterful use of materials. The entire entrance hall has hand-carved and finished wood-paneled walls and ceiling beams. A separate space for the hung stairway is lo-

Dining room, Frank House.

cated off the main hall, designed according to traditions established in the years following the American Revolution. Off the stair hall is the paneled library, in which huge leaded bay windows face the distant gardens, and the enormous living room, which runs the full width of the house. On the other side of the entrance hall, the dining room also has a beamed ceiling and is oriented toward the rear gardens. The polygonal breakfast room, setting a standard for Portland, is located off the dining room, connected through the pantry to the kitchen and the servants' hall.

All the major rooms look out toward the most amazing feature of the estate: the splendid gardens. They stretch down the hillside in formally arranged, axial terraces with fountains, paired gazebos, reflecting pools, and a raised semicircular terrace at the far end, all focusing on Mount Hood in the distance. A variety of structures line the mall formed by the gardens: greenhouses, swimming and eating pavilions, and side gardens, all with the background of the still-standing Douglas firs, after which the estate was named.

After the Frank family moved from the property, it was purchased as a campus for Lewis and Clark College, which, while adding a great variety of other campus buildings, has kept the main house, outbuildings, and gardens intact and beautifully preserved.

Dr. Zimmerman (1925)
Carl L. Linde

During the 1920s and 1930s, Tudor style houses continued to be designed by all the leading Portland architects, although the Tudor influences were readily combined with other architectural trends. The Dr. Zimmerman House designed by Carl Linde and located at 2260 NE Twenty-eighth Avenue reflects the Arts and Crafts style's basic concepts,

Dr. Zimmerman House.

yet it retains individual Tudor elements. The diagonally placed multiple flues of the brick chimney are decidedly Tudor, as are the half-timbering and the banks of casement windows. Yet, the windows are located in a Craftsman, or Bungalow, style shed-roofed dormer. The minimally detailed eave and the catslide roof, descending over the arched brick entry, are Arts and Crafts details. Linde, always inventive, combined the mass of the chimney with the brick front gable in a single plane, a concept new to Portland. Altogether, the general design bears some similarity to Ellis Lawrence's Blaine Smith House of 1908, with its telescoping roof at the entry porch. Each house reflects then-current architectural trends, which in turn influenced design standards for hundreds of other houses.

Thomas J. Autzen (1927)
Kirtland K. Cutter

One of the more remarkable houses in the Alameda District, and in all of Portland, is the large house designed by nationally recognized architect Kirtland K. Cutter for Thomas Autzen. Occupying an entire block at 2425 NE Alameda Drive, the house reflects the various angled street fronts in the arrangement of its plan. Tudor designs, which predominate at both the exterior and interior, are evident in the combined use of brick and half-timbering at the gabled extensions. Dressed stone is added in the polygonal south bay, complete with leaded glass and transom windows, and at the front elevation a handsomely carved wood lintel is placed above the main entrance portal.

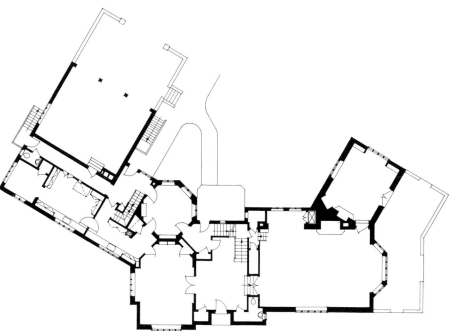

First floor plan, Autzen House.

Thomas J. Autzen House.

Interior elements are particularly fine. Unusually, the half-timbering continues to within the house. Hand-hewn woodwork is mixed with Tudor and Gothic details at doorways and fireplace mantels. Linenfold carving, a medieval tradition, is found in doors. Due to the various angles of the house, some rooms have angled corners, and the breakfast room is polygonal. Ceilings have coffered beams in the dining room and "king-post" trusses and rafters in the library. (A "king-post" is a vertical member that extends from the apex of the inclined rafters to the tie beam between the rafters at their lowest end.)

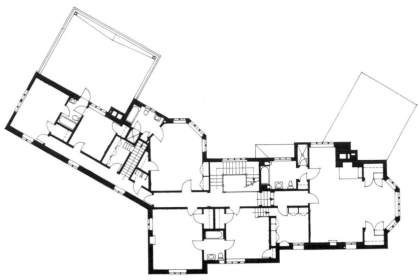

Second floor plan, Autzen House.

Carl C. Jantzen House.

Carl C. Jantzen (1930)
Charles Ertz

Located on Crazyman's Island in Lake Oswego, the Carl C. Jantzen estate is a most picturesque and attractively situated residence. Designed by Charles Ertz of the firm of Ertz and Burns Architects in 1930, the nearly 9500-square-foot house is sited on a knoll at the top of the island, and it is connected to the north shore of Lake Oswego by its own turreted stone and rustic-log bridge. Ertz designed a rambling house, primarily constructed of stone, with angled wings on either side of a hipped central volume with truncated gable. The gabled living room wing, extending to the right, has its fireplace on the front elevation, constructed of stone

and topped with multiple flues in the Tudor fashion. To the left is the hipped kitchen wing. Tudor elements, besides the chimneys, include the half-timbered bays of the living and dining rooms. The house is largely intact, though considerable alterations have been made to the interior.

Also on the island is a remarkable boathouse designed by Richard Sundeleaf in 1933. It is constructed of stone, offering sculptural turrets, wrought-iron gates, and exposed-beam interiors.

J. L. Easson (1931)
Ellis F. Lawrence (attributed)

The J. L. Easson House together with its neighbor to the immediate south, the Tudor style Rosenberg House of 1933, with their similar hillside sites and city views, make a handsome pair on a street already dominated by extraordinary houses. The Easson House, located at 1796 SW Montgomery Drive, is credited to architect Ellis Lawrence, as an identical house at 630 NW Alpine Terrace was designed by Lawrence for Isaac Neuberger in 1938. Displaying Lawrence's trademark detail, the house has a gabled and cantilevered attic over a rounded bay, with a catslide roof descending to the first floor. Lawrence enjoyed the utilization of prominent chimneys, and the one on the Easson House is a basic part of the front elevation. Brick walls are used at the first floor, and half-timbering is used for the remainder of the house. The house has a handsome entrance portico with a roof supported by heavy timber columns and curved brackets. On the mostly half-timbered city-facing elevation, two gabled extensions project from the hipped central roof. The house's back elevation is three-and-a-half stories high, much like the Rosenberg House, allowing for a handsome viewing from SW Vista Avenue below.

Roy Hunt (1932)
Richard Sundeleaf (attributed)

An early significant house in the Highlands Addition of Portland is the brick house built by Roy Hunt in 1932. Its architect is not known, but the design could be credited to Richard Sundeleaf, due to the turret and the similarity in detail to his other houses. More Norman farmhouse than Tudor, the materials used in the house's construction are common to both styles. Brick veneer and stone are combined in a romantic asymmetrical arrangement, as is seen prominently in the early photograph, with the stone of the gable end combining with the chimney.

Located at 4241 SW Torr Lane, the L-shaped house has a turret, which

Roy Hunt House.

J. L. Easson House.

contains the stair, at the intersection of the gabled living room wing and the wing that houses the covered entry porch. As in many residences with similar intersecting roofs, the wings extend from a hipped central mass, tying the structure into a unified whole. On the Torr Lane facade is a round-arched living room window and the truss projection of the vaulted ceiling behind it. A new era of high, vaulted living room ceilings, either beamed or constructed with handsome hand-hewn trusses, had begun.

Roy Gangware (1932)
Roscoe D. Hemenway

Roscoe Hemenway was considered one of the finest residential architects of his time. Even today, when a Hemenway house is sold, both realtors and prospective buyers find the Hemenway name adds value. The architect was known primarily for his Colonial Revival style homes, but those in the Tudor style are equally fine. One such home was designed for Roy Gangware, built in 1932 and located at 4848 SW Humphrey Boulevard. The large house is sited on a rise of land and surrounded by tall native firs. Its entrance court is defined by the main volume of the house and its intersection with the garage wing, which is connected to the main house by an open passage. In a gabled extension, the entrance portal is defined by a Tudor arch and a wide bank of multi-paned casement windows above at the second floor. Gabled dormers, multi-faceted brick chimneys, and an engaged exterior stair (located at the garage) are influences of the nineteenth-century tradition of English domestic architects, most notably Richard Norman Shaw. Interior details are equally attractive, with fine paneling and finish materials.

Roy Gangware House.

Dr. James J. Rosenberg (1933)
Henry Herzog

Long familiar to motorists on Vista Avenue, the half-timbered and brick residence of Dr. James J. Rosenberg commands an impressive location above downtown Portland. Located at 1792 SW Montgomery Drive, the house occupies a steep site between Montgomery and Vista, but such restraints were overcome by architect Henry Herzog, who created a spacious house with a fine plan and handsome elevations. The house exhibits the best of Tudor details, finished to perfection. Especially hand-some are the beautifully carved bargeboard at the main front entrance gable and the lintel above the recessed entrance. First-rate construction and a sense of permanence is evident in the lavish use of brick and stone construction, as well as in the hand-craftsmanship in details through-out the house. While the front elevation is mostly brick, the sides and the rear city-view side are half-timbered, and the strong light and dark con-trasts make the house so distinguished when viewed from Vista Avenue below. The house's interiors continue the excellence of design and crafts-manship shown on the exterior, with all major rooms opening to pan oramic eastern views.

Paul F. Murphy (1934)
Richard Sundeleaf

In 1934, Paul F. Murphy, developer of Westover Terraces, built his own house at 850 NW Powhatan Terrace, in the middle of the development. He hired Richard Sundeleaf, one of the few busy architects in Portland during the latter part of the Depression. The architect's designs at this time had followed the Arts and Crafts trend, but they still included major elements of medieval residential architecture. The Murphy House, constructed of used brick and having a massive roof descending to the first floor, might just as well be labeled Norman farmhouse style. Common to both Tudor and Norman are the leaded, diagonally paned

Dr. James J. Rosenberg House.

Paul F. Murphy House.

casement windows, the half-timbering, and the hand-hewn beams and posts. The entrance portal, hipped-roof dormers, and stair turret on the side elevation exemplify the Norman characteristics.

The interior has the typical Sundeleaf touches: finely crafted beamed ceilings, paneled walls, and sculptured newels and balustrades. A knotty-pine breakfast room, with pyramidal ceiling, is a delightful room, overlooking the city and mountain views.

Dean B. Webster (1936)
Richard Sundeleaf

A common feature of houses designed by Richard Sundeleaf with Tudor influences was a turret, or tower, carefully placed at the intersection of a gabled extension and the central structure of a house. In the Dean Webster House at 2050 SW Mount Hood Lane, built in 1936, he used the tower to enclose the circular staircase, somewhat as Herman Brookman did on a much grander scale at the 1924 M. Lloyd Frank Fir Acres estate. With its shingled conical roof and curved leaded windows, the tower is well balanced with the large brick chimney and with the library wing that projects forward. The house sits on a high promontory, and the major rooms overlook a sweeping city view. The half-timbering Tudor motif is used sparingly on the mostly brick facade, though it is found at a few of the gable ends and where the upper wall is set back on the front elevation between the tower and chimney. Sundeleaf was a great admirer of brick texture. On the Webster House, he employed clinker brick with an over-flowing mortar joint, giving the walls a very rough-hewn look. This brickwork continues in the garden walls that extend from the house and in the stairs leading down to the street.

Dean B. Webster House.

Wesley P. Steinmetz (1936)
Charles Ertz (attributed)

Overlooking Hoyt Park, and with a distant city view, is the 1936 Wesley P. Steinmetz House. Its architect is unrecorded, but the design shares many of the characteristics of the Carl Jantzen House designed several years earlier by Charles Ertz. Located on a ridge to maximize the views, the large residence successfully accommodates the asymmetrical combination of intersecting volumes with steep roofs and telescoping gables. The entrance-facade gable, centered over the arched and recessed stone entry, has an asymmetrical catslide roof. Side gables have beveled wood

Wesley P. Steinmetz House.

siding, contrasting with the house's brick walls. A dropped shed roof extends out over the three garage doors, with timbered posts and beams supporting it, and gabled dormers are located at the second floor. Tudor influences are found in the half-timbering at the main floor, the massive articulated brick chimneys, and the small-paned casement windows. The house is otherwise heavily influenced by the Arts and Crafts style, especially in the minimal eave detail.

CHAPTER 12

Jacobethan

Like most cosmopolitan centers, Portland has its examples of houses designed in the Jacobethan style. Jacobethan (or Jacobean) applies to the English houses of the early Renaissance during the first few decades of the seventeenth century. It is a marriage of Tudor and Elizabethan architecture, with considerable Renaissance detail. The Jacobethan period was the "great era of mansion building," beginning under the reign of Queen Elizabeth I (1558–1603) and flourishing during the reign of King James I (1603–1625). Some of England's most famous houses in the style, influencing later houses in the United States and Portland, include Hatfield House (1607–11) in Hertfordshire, Holland House (1607) in Kensington, and Charlton House (1607) in Kent. Constructed of brick with dressed-stone trim, these houses had, for the most part, symmetrical plans, polygonal bays with transomed banked windows, and flat roofs with stone balustrades. Portland's best examples in the style were influenced by the smaller Jacobethan houses, those which continued earlier Tudor and Elizabethan forms. Such houses, with multiple gable ends and extensions, reflected the earlier

"Hillside Vista Point," from *The Greater Portland Plan* by Edward H. Bennett, 1912.

293

English country estates, such as Lytes Cary Manor House (1343, with additions in 1450 and 1533) in Somerset, Great Chalfield (1450) in Wiltshire, and Compton Wynyates (1520) in Warwickshire. Though constructed of stone and not brick, as in the Jacobethan style, the forms were more appropriate to smaller residential and collegiate architecture. In Portland, the work of Albert E. Doyle was directly influenced by these structures. His Sallyport (1912) in the Reed College dormitories incorporated the entrance from Compton Wynyates exactly, including the arch, the crenellated roof, and even the sundial. Whitehouse and Fouilhoux used similar English precedents in their Uni-

Hatfield House, Hertfordshire, England, 1607–11.

Holland House, Kensington, England, 1607.

Lytes Cary Manor House, Somerset, England, 1343.

Great Chalfield, Wiltshire, England, 1450.

versity Club design of 1913. Since so many of the famous English colleges and schools were designed in the Tudor and Jacobethan styles, American architects considered these styles highly appropriate for the designs of new educational institutions in this country.

This English architectural style came to an end in the Stuart period (1625–1714), when the full Renaissance reached England with the construction of the Banqueting House (1621) in Whitehall Palace, London, and Queen's House (1618–35), Greenwich. Both structures, designed by Inigo Jones (1573–1652) for the wife of King James I, showed influences from the Italian architecture of Andrea Palladio (1508–1580).

Renewed interest in Gothic or Elizabethan forms emerged in England during the mid-eighteenth century. Leading examples include Horace Walpole's Strawberry Hill country estate (1753–78) and, later, the remodeling of his Fonthill Abbey in 1796–99. Various writers popularized the style in literature, including Sir Walter Scott, Goethe,

and Victor Hugo. Elaborate treatises on the style were written during the first half of the nineteenth century, laying the groundwork for the later revivals. In this country, Andrew Jackson Downing often referred to the Elizabethan style, and he believed it could be "adopted for

Compton Wynyates, Warwickshire, England, 1520.

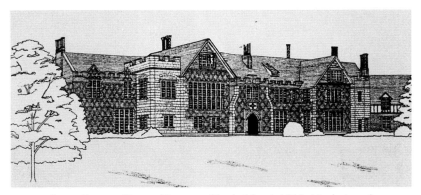
Stuart Duncan House, Newport, Rhode Island, 1912–18, designed by John Russell Pope.

country residences here in picturesque situations with a quaint and happy effect." In his writings, Downing illustrated houses that displayed what he considered Elizabethan details, commencing a considerable Gothic Revival vogue that competed actively with the then-predominant Greek Revival style. By the turn of the twentieth century, the Elizabethan and Jacobethan forms arrived in Portland along with the Tudor style, and the first examples certainly had these mixed influences. The Allen L. Lewis House (c. 1901) designed by David C. Lewis introduced the brick gable form, albeit with a more Classical Revival entrance. The Winslow B. Ayer House of 1903, a design of Whidden and Lewis, mixed a Classical pedimented entrance and shuttered windows with the Tudor-influenced high brick gable ends.

More authentic Jacobethan stylistic features were incorporated in the construction of the Cicero Hunt Lewis House of circa 1910. The deliberately rambling plan for the Lewis House re-created the fine design attributes of smaller Tudor and Jacobethan country estates, which often had been constructed over long periods of time and with numerous additions. The picturesque qualities were well suited to residential design, allowing the architect to develop practical plans that accommodated twentieth-century amenities, from advanced kitchen and bathroom layouts to adjacent garages. The latter feature would be directly addressed in practicality by having the garages attached to the main house, with conveniently covered access into the house proper.

A. E. Doyle designed the grandest Jacobethan houses in Portland. In 1917, Frank J. Cobb asked Doyle to design for him a magnificent home on Portland Heights. At that time, those who built such houses often had contacts with people who were constructing similar houses on the East Coast or in San Francisco. They also read such popular illustrated magazines as *Country Life*. The magazines portrayed the homes of the wealthy in affluent centers around Philadelphia, Long Island, New York, and Newport, Rhode Island. In them, it was observed that the country's most fashionable architects had adopted the Jacobethan style for lavish summer homes, such as the house for Stuart Duncan designed by John Russell Pope in 1912–18 in Newport. In Portland, Doyle's Cobb mansion incorporated the best of selected details within a masterfully balanced framework of gable-ended forms. The lavishly appointed house is of masonry construction (mostly brick

Typical Jacobethan style entrance hall from the Portland area.

Typical Jacobethan style dining room from the Portland area.

with dressed-stone trim) and incorporates appropriate Classical details, which define it as Jacobethan. Tudor elements are also found in the house, with half-timbering in the garden room extension and rough-cast stuccowork on the engaged tower and kitchen/garage wing. Doyle designed the garages to be attached to the house, as other architects were doing at the time, acknowledging the automobile as an essential consideration in home design, at least for the wealthy. The entire ensemble, including the circular drive at the entrance court, the gabled entry with its oriel windows, and the balustraded gardens, make the Cobb House one of Portland's most exceptionally designed homes.

Doyle's other major Jacobethan style house was designed ten years later for Aaron Holtz. It has many similar features with the Cobb House, though confined to a much smaller piece of property on King's Hill. It also is asymmetrical in its composition and incorporates both Elizabethan and Classical details. The Classical garden entrance portal is especially handsome in cast-stone, as are the balustraded terraces overlooking the lawns. As with the Cobb mansion, the house is constructed of brick, with dressed-stone trim at the windows, the parapets, and the quoined corners. A permanent slate roof covers the house, making it an especially durable and lasting house.

Other architects continued the Jacobethan forms up until the Great Depression. The Leon Hirsch residence (1922) on Portland Heights is a smaller interpretation of the style, but it incorporates a fine Tudor entrance, Classical arched openings off the living and garden rooms, and the best of brick and cast-stone detailing. Richard Sundeleaf used Jacobethan forms in his William Scott House of 1927, constructed in Greenhills. The site was difficult, but he managed a gracious sunken entrance court, rounded arches at the entrance, and multiple gables—somewhat more Arts and Crafts than Jacobethan, but definitely continuing the latter tradition. It was the last house constructed in the style in a period of exceptional architectural construction that ended abruptly with the Depression.

Jacobethan
CHARACTERISTICS

PLANS: asymmetrical, with entrance hall centrally located; engaged towers.

ROOFS: multiple steep gables on the front or sides, often with gables rising above the roof ridge; crenellations at flat-roofed entrance porticos; hipped-roof extensions; conical or bell-shaped tower roofs. Slate-covered roofs, with copper ridge cap.

EXTERIOR FINISHES: brick, with stone trim at windows, doors, or quoins. Half-timbering and rough-cast stuccowork also used.

CHIMNEYS: massive and tall, with multiple shafts set diagonally to main stack; multiple flues.

WINDOWS: rectangular casements in series, divided by stone mullions; transoms at larger first floor windows; oriel windows; polygonal bays with multiple casements; leaded or wood muntins.

WINDOW TRIM (exterior): minimal steel frames set in stone trim of brick walls.

ENTRANCE DOORS: recessed entry with Tudor or round arch. Classical details mixed with Tudor.

VERANDAS/PORCHES: recessed verandas, with round arches supported by Classical columns; crenellated porticos with Tudor arches. Balustrated terraces off first floor rooms.

INTERIOR FINISHES: ornamental plaster ceilings; plaster walls; paneled walls at stairwell or libraries. Hardwood floors.

INTERIOR TRIM: molded casings and baseboards, often dark stained oak.

STAIRS: oak tread and risers; substantial newels with finials and turned balusters.

FIREPLACE FRONTS: stone or cement surrounds, with Tudor arch; ceiling-high paneled overmantels. Openings are sized smaller than original Tudor designs.

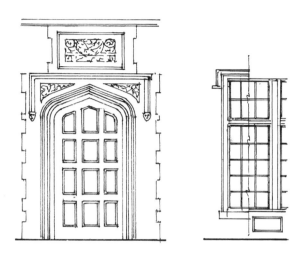

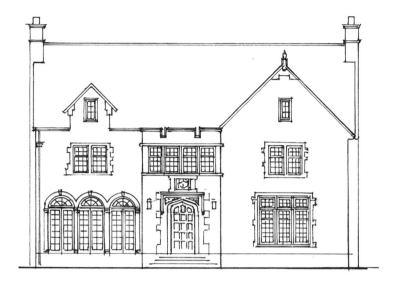

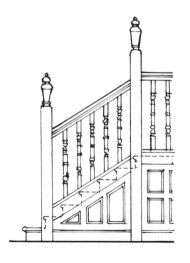

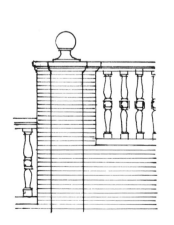

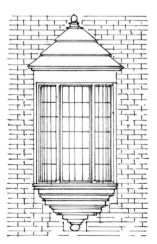

Entrance to the Frank J. Cobb House.

Jacobethan
HOUSES

c. 1901	Allen L. Lewis (David C. Lewis)	c. 1917	Daniel Kern (Ellis F. Lawrence)
1903	Winslow B. Ayer (Whidden and Lewis)	1917	Frank J. Cobb (Albert E. Doyle)
		1922	Leon Hirsch (Sutton and Whitney)
c. 1910	Cicero Hunt Lewis (attributed to David C. Lewis)	1927	Aaron Holtz (Albert E. Doyle)
		1927	William Scott (Richard Sundeleaf)

Allen L. Lewis (c. 1901)
David C. Lewis

One of the first houses in Portland to show influence of the Jacobethan style is that which Allen Lewis had constructed at 2164 SW Park Place to the designs of his architect brother, David C. Lewis. Most distinctive in the house is the prominent use of brick gable ends, with parapets, suggesting powerful masses and sculptural form. Architect Lewis designed a T-shaped plan, with the steep gables on major elevations. To this he added half-timbered gabled dormers on the blue-slate roof and Tudor-influenced transomed windows at major rooms. Other windows followed fashion, being one-over-one (1/1) panes and double-hung. Somewhat more Classical features are the flat-roofed eastern porch with rectangular wood columns, and the very handsome entrance. Here,

Allen L. Lewis House.

Entrance, Lewis House.

architect Lewis added a Colonial Revival doorway, complete with side-lights and an elliptical transom. The crowning feature is the wrought-iron canopy, domed with leaded curved lights and supported by wrought-iron scroll brackets. It surely is one of the most handsome entrances in the city and a remarkable example of craftsmanship at the turn of the century.

Winslow B. Ayer (1903)
Whidden and Lewis

Whidden and Lewis designed a most impressive house for wealthy lumberman Winslow B. Ayer. Located at 811 NW Nineteenth Avenue, the house was originally situated in what was then considered the most

Winslow B. Ayer House.

prominent area of the city, an enclave of the wealthy since Captain John Couch began selling off part of his 1850s land claim.

The Ayer House has a symmetrical central-hall plan, with the Jacobethan brick gabled extensions framing the recessed entrance. It was, in fact, a marriage of styles, combining the bold geometries of the Jacobethan with Colonial Revival detail. Medieval traits are further found in the brick chimneys and the transomed windows on the south-facing bay. Colonial Revival details are the shuttered 8/8 double-hung windows and the broken pediment over the entrance.

Much of the original architectural configuration was altered when the house was converted into offices, particularly by the additions to the side and rear. Interior spaces, while preserving some original rooms, are lacking the cohesiveness of the now-missing central stair.

Cicero Hunt Lewis (c. 1910)
David C. Lewis (attributed)

At the end of the first decade of the twentieth century, the district of Rivera was developed just south of the city and above the Willamette River, and many who had previously built homes in the northwest area of Portland built new homes there. The Cicero Hunt Lewis family was among the first to establish a palatial country estate, just a comfortable motoring distance from the city.

Judging from the details of the mansion, David C. Lewis was most likely the architect. The large house at 11645 SW Military Lane is arranged with an irregular, angled plan, with major rooms facing the gardens. Jacobethan elements include the brick gable ends, the jerkinhead roof gables, Tudor-arched openings and Tudor chimneys, half-timbering, and transomed windows. As with almost all the major houses in the

Cicero Hunt Lewis House.

style, sweeping masonry terraces provided a gracious transition between the main floor level of the house and the garden level about a half-dozen steps below.

In the decades to follow, Military Lane would be built up with fine Colonial Revival houses, creating one of the most attractive residential areas in the city.

Daniel Kern (c. 1917)
Ellis F. Lawrence

Formerly located on NE Fifteenth Avenue in what is now the heart of the Lloyd Center, the handsome brick house of Daniel Kern replaced his Queen Anne hilltop house on Powell Boulevard. Architect Ellis Lawrence provided a symmetrically planned house, combining some Jaco-bethan elements with those of the Colonial Revival. The handsome entrance portal was an almost exact replica of the Whidden and Lewis recessed portal on the Winslow Ayer House (1903) in northwest Portland, albeit in stone rather than wood. The side-gabled Kern House had single-story polygonal bays on the entrance facade, with transomed, wood-paned windows. Other casement windows were clustered between brick piers at the second floor, and the dormers on the slate-covered roof had round and pedimented gable fronts.

When the Lloyd Corporation bought the home from Gracie Kern, Daniel's daughter who inherited the house, she had architect Herman Brookman design her a new home on Portland Heights that incorporated the major elements of the interior woodwork and fireplace fronts.

Daniel Kern House.

Had the original Kern House remained, it would have provided a serious lesson of architectural character and quality among the bland towers of the new and ever-changing Lloyd Development.

Frank J. Cobb (1917)
Albert E. Doyle

No Portland home so completely evokes the aura of Jacobethan residential style more than the magnificent residence constructed by Frank
J. Cobb in 1917 at 2424 SW Montgomery Drive. The house is, assuredly,
a true masterpiece of native-born Albert E. Doyle, whose practice helped
give Portland its unusually distinctive architectural character. Situated
on a Portland Heights hillside between Vista Avenue above and Montgomery Drive below, the Cobb House incorporates the best of site planning, house design, and period craftsmanship, with the most gracious
appointments. The mansion is approached from Montgomery by a
curved and gated brick drive that culminates at the main floor level with
a circular turn-around, off of which are the house's main entrance and, to
the side, the garage wing. The gabled entrance projection has a recessed
Tudor-arched entry with a rounded oriel window above. To the right is
a Classically arched recessed gallery off the living room, with the garden
room wing projecting beyond. The massive, gabled central roof has
Tudor style chimneys at either end, and the angled kitchen wing and
garage extend to the left. To the immediate left of the entrance portal are
the large window of the central stairway and the large engaged tower
containing the library. Brick construction with stone dressing is the primary material, with stuccoed masonry and half-timbering at the lesser
wings. A richly hued gray slate covers the roof. The double-gabled rear
garden elevation has a projecting central polygonal bay and an arched

Frank J. Cobb House.

Rear garden elevation, Cobb House.

Windows of the main stairway, Cobb House.

Main stairway, Cobb House.

entrance portal, both with crenellated parapets. All the windows are banked, with stone piers, or muntins, structurally separating the major window divisions. Typical Tudor transom windows appear at the major first floor rooms. A favorite Portland design feature is the rounded breakfast room, usually enjoying morning sunlight and a view if possible. Doyle incorporated one in the Cobb House at the end of the formal dining room. Only breakfast was taken there, as the main noon and evening meals were served in the more formal dining room.

Despite the house's large size, the rooms are conveniently arranged. The large living room could be closed off, with the family using only the library and dining quarters. A central hall has openings to the living room and dining room and the garden terraces beyond. The main stair is also located in the hall, with typical Tudor detailing. Ceilings are beamed, the walls paneled, and wood floors predominate in the house. Massive fireplaces are at the far ends of the living room, dining room, and to the side of the library tower. The other major chimney is for the kitchen wing. The house exhibits the best of craftsmanship in every detail and has been considerably restored by its present owners. Especially attractive are the gardens; those off the garden room have a small reflecting pool and are surrounded by brick walls with balustrades at the top, a detail that is found in the perimeters of the property and at the swimming pool area of the garden. A favorite viewpoint of the house and property is from the top of a curved bifurcated stairway that reaches Vista Avenue. Most every stroller on Vista is inclined to stop and admire the uniquely fine architecture of the house and its terraced gardens. The house is a special Portland treasure, and fortunately it has survived intact.

Dining room, Cobb House.   Living room, Cobb House.

Breakfast room, Cobb House.

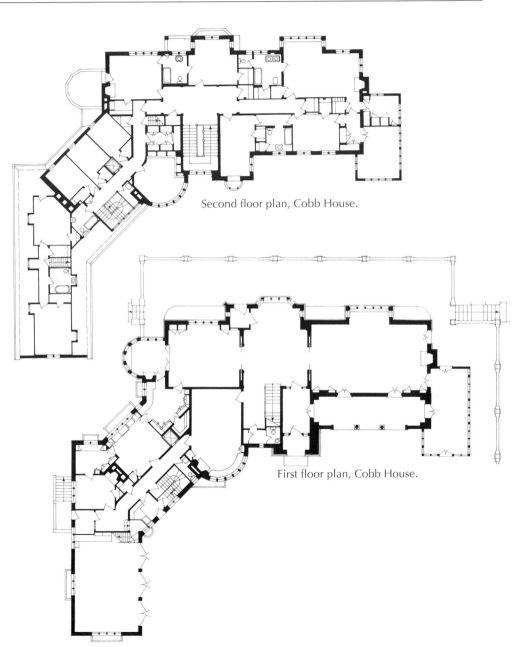

Second floor plan, Cobb House.

First floor plan, Cobb House.

Leon Hirsch (1922)
Sutton and Whitney

The prominent houses on the ridge above SW Montgomery Drive comprise some of the finest in the city, and every major style can be found there. They were favored properties because of the fine eastern views of city and mountains, and hence they were built on before much of the surrounding residential area. One house in the Jacobethan style is that designed in 1922 by Sutton and Whitney for Leon Hirsch at 1957 SW Montgomery Drive. Beneath its side-gabled slate roof, the house incorporates the full spectrum of Jacobethan details, including high gabled projections. The chimneys have the articulated flues favored in both

Leon Hirsch House.

Tudor and Jacobethan designs. Bearing similarities to Doyle's Cobb mansion, the main facade has a crenellated parapet above banked second floor windows and a Tudor-arched recessed entry. The arch is bordered with an ear-drip molding, a detail that is repeated on the large bank of windows of the dining room, to the right of the entrance portal. To the left, recessed Classical arches house French doors that open onto the east terrace. All windows are double-hung, except for the Tudor-inspired transomed windows.

Aaron Holtz (1927)
Albert E. Doyle

On the 200-foot frontage at SW Park Place as it approaches Washington Park, the Aaron Holtz mansion commands a fine lot in the residential area of King's Hill. The house, located at 2370 SW Park Place, was designed by A. E. Doyle, and it is one of his finest. Though the actual motor entrance is off SW Douglas, the entrance elevation most familiar to the public is on Park Place. The expansive side-gabled elevation has two prominent facade gables, under which are two-story polygonal bays with parapets. All the gables have cast-stone copings, leveling at the sides, where gutters abut them. Between the main elevation's gables, the arched entry, with stone voussoirs, is surrounded by Ionic stone pilasters. The architrave over the entry is decorated with scroll work and pyramidal finials in bas-relief. Leaded-glass casement windows predominate throughout the house, and the main floor windows are transomed. The superb brickwork, classic with its Flemish bond, is finished with dressed-stone details and corner quoins. The terraces, much like those of the Cobb mansion of 1917, have the Tudor style cast-stone balustrades.

Aaron Holtz House.

William Scott House.

William Scott (1927)
Richard Sundeleaf

With his typical architectural aplomb, Richard Sundeleaf created, in the heady years just before the Great Depression, one of his finest residences. Designed for William Scott in 1927, the house has all the charm of asymmetry inherent in the Jacobethan style, allowing a rambling asymmetrical plan with a wealth of handsomely created elevations and details. Situated on a difficult downhill site—which does offer lovely western views from terraced gardens—the large house is masterfully

Living room, Scott House.

accommodated within the confining parameters. The garages are discretely placed to the side, while the visitor descends into a lovely entrance court, complete with a fountain and surrounded by Tudor style cast-stone balustrades. The arched cast-stone entry is within one of the several gabled projections that make up the entrance facade. All construction is first rate, from the gray-blue slate roof to the garden amenities, and the landscaping is well integrated with the house.

Inside, Sundeleaf is at his best. Paneled walls, beamed ceilings, cast-stone fireplaces, and leaded windows in bays, all combine to provide a striking ambiance of rich detailing and innate comfort.

Wall paneling and fireplace details, Scott House.

Stairway, Scott House.

CHAPTER 13

French Renaissance

French architecture was a popular interest among upper-class circles in Portland in the last half of the nineteenth century. The city's first great mansions, such as those of Jacob Kamm (1871), Henry Failing (1873), and Henry W. Corbett (1874), had either mansard roofs or further details from the French Second Empire period. Some of the greatest of the San Francisco mansions of the same period, built by that city's new tycoons, employed the elegant French style with great abundance; and their owners were, no doubt, familiar with the fashions and grandiose lifestyle of Napoleon III and Eugénie. For the most part, it was a style for the very wealthy, although the mansard roof became a familiar fixture on numerous houses during the 1870s and 1880s. In the late nineteenth century, fabulously wealthy easterners, seeking to establish dynastic seats on the scale of the English and French nobility, found the style compelling as an aristocratic statement of their newly won position in society. Most every traveler is familiar with the legacy of Biltmore, one of the most ostentatious of the wealthy "chateaus," designed by Richard Morris Hunt for George W. Vanderbilt near Asheville, North Carolina,

Drawing of original proposed landscape for the Henry L. Pittock Mansion, by Thomas Hawkes, landscape architect.

311

in 1895. Architects designed many of the great mansions of Newport, Rhode Island, during its heyday in the style of the French Renaissance, as they did numerous grand houses nationwide, including the wealthy enclaves on the Peninsula, south of San Francisco.

It seemed only natural that Henry L. Pittock, Portland's wealthiest citizen in the first decade of the twentieth century, hire a prominent San Francisco architect, Edward T. Foulkes, to design his French Renaissance–inspired mansion on Imperial Heights, a magnificent site overlooking the city, mountains, and rivers. In the comfortable world of the great fortunes, the wealthy of Portland had many ties, both social and professional, with their peers in San Francisco; and they wished their homes to compare well with those of their friends in the more cosmopolitan city. Foulkes's plan for Pittock was more inspired by, rather than a copy of, French designs. Imperative to the design would be the very steep roof, used extensively by François Mansart in such works as the Orléans wing of Blois chateau (1635–38). Many of the ancient French chateaus were constructed on earlier castles, which still had their rounded battlement towers. The towers had steep conical roofs placed over them to match the main roof, and this became an established part of the French

Renaissance architecture, even when no tie was made to an earlier fortification. They symbolized the lasting authority of the aristocratic legacy of many centuries. Hence, Henry Pittock, or his architect Foulkes, had such towers included in the design of his Portland mansion. In keeping with such a gesture, the Pittock family arms were researched and diligently carved above the fireplace in the library. This was to be a statement of a Portland family that intended to leave its imprint and a permanent record of the Pittock name, much as Vanderbilt dreamed that he could leave a permanent dynasty.

The plan of Pittock Mansion bears little resemblance to any known French chateau. Its hallmark staircase has a Baroque magnificence to it, with curved bronze rails superbly crafted

George W. Vanderbilt Estate (Biltmore), Asheville, North Carolina, 1895, designed by Richard Morris Hunt.

Chateau de Fontainbleu, Paris, seventeenth century.

Louis XII Wing, Chateau de Blois, France, 1498–1504.

Montgeoffroy, Maine-et-Loire, France, 1772–75, designed by Nicolas Barre.

Azey Le Rideau, Indre-et-Loire, France, 1518–27, designed by Gilles Berthelot.

Interior stairway, Chateau d'Anet, Eure-et-Loire, France, 1547–50. Stair constructed by Duc de Vindôme in the 1680s.

Hotel, Rue du Cherche-Midi, Paris, late nineteenth century.

and monumental for a private home. The only other Portland homes known to have similar railings are the Hamilton Corbett home (1928) in Dunthorpe and that of A. J. Lewthwaite (1926). The Lewthwaite House is Portland's most authentically detailed French Renaissance style house, with inspiration dating from the eighteenth century. Of the countless French chateaus that defined the period, the one designed by Nicolas Barre for Maréchal de Contades, named Montgeoffroy (1772–75) at Maine-et-Loire, is a good example. Its superb proportions, elegant materials, and refined details are the source of the design for the Lewthwaite House. As in its French predecessor, Lewthwaite's home has elegant carvings gracing the tympanum of the pediment, its windows are shuttered, and graceful wrought-iron balconies decorate the entrance portal. Inside, all the details, including the stair, boiserie, and fireplaces, are in the French tradition of the eighteenth-century Montgeoffroy.

Other French Renaissance–inspired houses in Portland, though less grand than the French originals, are nevertheless well conceived and finished. The Philip L. Jackson House (c. 1927) by architect Jamieson Parker resembles a smaller French country house, rather than a grand chateau. Ellis Lawrence's Burt Brown Barker House of 1928 has the conically roofed tower and steep main roof typical of the style, but this house combines these elements with some Arts and Crafts traditions. Carl L. Linde designed the Gordon Barde House (1939) with tall, arched French doors and a miniature tower—a greatly reduced version of the French originals. As was the case with many of the historic period styles, the heyday of the French Renaissance style in Portland lasted until the 1929 financial crash, when the economic means and lifestyles changed dramatically.

French Renaissance
CHARACTERISTICS

PLANS: asymmetrical and symmetrical, with entrance hall centrally located; angled wings.

ROOFS: steeply pitched hipped, often with conically roofed engaged towers; facade or roof dormers with French-arched or hipped roofs. Tile, slate, or shingle covered.

EXTERIOR FINISHES: masonry appearance, either sandstone, brick, or stuccoed wood-frame.

CHIMNEYS: simple rectangular designs, with modest ornamental corbeling at top; no featured chimney pots, nor expressed multiple flues. Stone or brick.

WINDOWS: casements with transoms; three panes per casement; casement windows at dormers. Paired French doors, with arched transom and shutters to fit.

WINDOW TRIM (exterior): minimal wood trim set within masonry walls.

ENTRANCE DOORS: recessed entry with paired doors. Entrances in towers or porte-cocheres.

VERANDAS/PORCHES: little or no veranda or porch additions. Balustraded terraces off first floor rooms.

INTERIOR FINISHES: plaster walls and cornices; French-inspired Renaissance detailings. Rooms designed to various periods: Tudor library, Georgian dining room, Turkish smoking room, etc. Marble entry floors, and the remainder polished wood floors.

INTERIOR TRIM: molded casings and baseboards, or French boiserie.

STAIRS: bifurcated with landings; curved bronze or iron decorative railings.

FIREPLACE FRONTS: stone, cement, or marble surrounds, with elaborate overmantel. Often designs varied according to the style of the room—that is, Tudor fireplace in the Tudor library, Georgian fireplace in the Georgian dining room, etc.

4 5/8"

3 3/4"

Entrance to the A. J. Lewthwaite House.

French Renaissance
HOUSES

1914   Henry L. Pittock (Edward T. Foulkes)

1926   A. J. Lewthwaite (Albert Parr and
Francis Ward)

c. 1927 Philip L. Jackson (Jamieson K. Parker)

1928   Burt Brown Barker (Ellis F.
Lawrence)

1939   Gordon Barde (Carl L. Linde)

Henry L. Pittock (1914)
Edward T. Foulkes

Of all the great houses of Portland, the Henry Pittock mansion is the most well known as well as the most beloved, being one of the very few made into a museum and opened to the public. It typifies the success of the nineteenth-century American entrepreneurial spirit, which, with talent and enormous energy, was able to express itself in the construction of a mighty residence. Henry Pittock was one of Portland's most esteemed citizens and, indeed, one of its wealthiest. The house he chose to build, near the end of his lifetime, expresses his pleasures, hopes, and dreams, which the public now shares to its great enrichment.

Beginning in 1909, the huge mansion was constructed on the top of Imperial Heights, high above the Westover development. Its views are panoramic, and the angled plan is aligned with the distant mountains through its windows. With the city below, it is a truly breathtaking site, and now a major tourist attraction. The house originally was approached through Westover Terraces but now is accessed by its new entrance at 3229 NW Pittock Drive. The original road wound to the hilltop, past the gatekeeper's lodge, and circled back to the impressive portecochere, where the main entrance is located.

The Pittocks hired architect Edward T. Foulkes from San Francisco to design the house in the French Renaissance style. The architect planned two symmetrical angled wings toward the views, the intersections marked by twin engaged turrets with conical roofs. At this intersection and between the turrets is the large bay of the drawing room, with a terrace above off the master bedroom suite. A massive, red-tiled, hipped roof with prominent attic dormers sits above the central volume of the

Henry L. Pittock Mansion.

house. The axially placed central fireplaces and chimneys peak at the ridge. The house is constructed of dressed Bellingham sandstone, adorned with scrolled and modillioned cornices, a Greek meander entablature, pedimented garden doorways, and balustraded balconies. Renaissance detailing continues at the drawing room bay, where the angled sides are defined by piers framed by Roman Doric columns. All windows are casement with transoms above.

The most notable interior feature of the house is the grand stairway, the most impressive in the city—no expense was spared. The floating stair, aided by a concrete structure, hovers and flows in space, with marble treads and bronze railings of the finest craftsmanship. It bifurcates at its landing to the curved balustrade of the hallway above. All the major rooms of the house are located off of the curved stair hall, with the oval drawing room at the center; the oak-paneled Jacobethan library is to one side and the mahogany-paneled dining room to the other. A breakfast room is at the opposite end of the stair hall from the main entrance lobby. Upstairs, the Pittock master suite occupies the central location, sharing the same fireplace chimney as the drawing room below. To either side are suites of bedrooms, with individual sleeping porches at each wing. Henry Pittock's turreted bathroom is as noted for its dramatic views as it is for its deluxe period plumbing fixtures, especially the shower.

The grounds of the great house were planned to have a full presentation of Renaissance style gardens, unfortunately not installed by the time Henry Pittock and his wife, Georgiana, died. Descendants remained in the house until it was purchased by the city of Portland—and it is

Terrace and drawing room bay, Pittock Mansion.

now a jewel in the city's park system. With the handsome period furnishings, supplied and maintained by the Pittock Mansion Society, the house exemplifies the scale of living possible for the wealthy in the years after the turn of the century and before the First World War.

Entrance, Pittock Mansion.

Gatekeeper's lodge, Pittock Mansion.

Central stairway, Pittock Mansion.

Library, Pittock Mansion.

Drawing room, Pittock Mansion.

Dining room, Pittock Mansion.

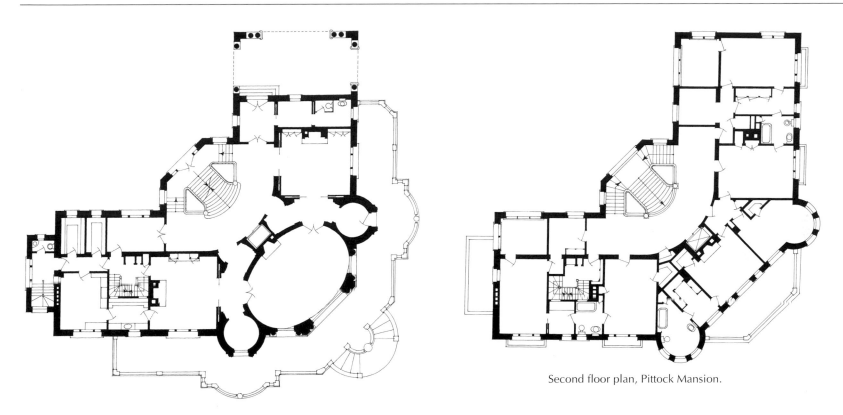

First floor plan, Pittock Mansion.

Second floor plan, Pittock Mansion.

A. J. Lewthwaite (1926)
Albert Parr and Francis Ward

Of the various French Renaissance style houses in Portland, the A. J. Lewthwaite home is one of the most distinguished, as well as one of the most authentic in detail. Its Louis XVI styling handsomely reflects a great period in world architectural history, where simplicity and beautiful proportions are enhanced by restrained decoration. Corner quoins and tall, shuttered, French windows are the only features, other than the elegant detailing at the projecting entrance extension, with its decorated tympanum, paired entry doors, and wrought-iron balcony. The major interior rooms continue the French detailing. Most handsome is the

A. J. Lewthwaite House.

curved stair and wrought-iron railings. Other French details are the raised panel-mold on the walls, the period fireplaces, and the tall French doors on the city side, originally opening onto terraces.

The Lewthwaites hired Albert Parr and Francis Ward to design the home for a San Francisco site. After the designs were completed, the Lewthwaites wished, instead, to return to Portland, where the designs were transplanted with some modifications for the site at 1715 SW Montgomery Drive.

Philip L. Jackson (c. 1927)
Jamieson K. Parker

Around 1927, Philip Jackson, editor of the *Oregon Journal*, constructed one of the finer houses in the Riverwood section of Dunthorpe, at 11522 SW Riverwood Road, with property to the banks of the Willamette River. Designed by architect Jamieson Parker, the style of the house imitates a small French country house of the eighteenth century, formal in plan. It includes the tall casement windows, steeply hipped central roof, and dormers so typical of the French Renaissance. The house's striking texture is a result of the whitewashed brick used in its construction. Details are relatively subdued—dentil brickwork at the cornice, simple headers over the doors and windows, and a slate roof—as the Jackson House relies on fine proportions to gain its imposing presence.

In siting and plan, the house is direct and axial throughout. The gated entrance drive, with rows of trees on either side, arrives at an entrance circle. A three-car garage to the right is distinguished by its arched French doors. The house's paired entrance doors, paneled in the French manner, are slightly recessed below a transom window. To the right is the kitchen wing.

Philip L. Jackson House.

Burt Brown Barker House.

Burt Brown Barker (1928)
Ellis F. Lawrence

When Ellis F. Lawrence interpreted the French Renaissance style, he did it in a way that clearly incorporated his interest in the current Arts and Crafts style. The steeply pitched hipped roof on the Burt B. Barker House is typically French, but its descent down to the first floor, on the right of the conically roofed turret, is an Arts and Crafts influence. The French turret is well used here as an entrance hall. Additional French influences are seen in the facade dormer windows, which bisect the eave line, one elongating into a tall stair window with a French style wrought-iron balcony at its sill. Windows have leaded glass in their casements, and the three windows of the living room, centered on a dormer above, have cast-stone panels above them. A lovely five-sided bay, also with a dormer above it, extends from the end of the living room.

Located at 3438 SW Brentwood Drive, the house is approached by a U-shaped drive, with the garages in a recessed wing to the right of the main structure. It enjoys views of both the city and the mountains, as well as outlooks to the side and rear gardens.

Gordon Barde House.

Gordon Barde (1939)
Carl L. Linde

In 1939, on property adjacent to his father's home—the Mediterranean style Jacob Barde House of 1926—Gordon Barde had constructed a fine French Renaissance style house, designed by his father's architect, Carl L. Linde. The architect met the challenges of an uphill property by creating an upper terrace, with garages at the street level, on which he placed an L-shaped residence, oriented toward the terraced garden. Washington Park is behind the house, providing an unusually attractive ambiance for in-city living. French architectural aspects of the house include the distinctive round-arched French doors, with arched fanlights and tall rounded shutters to fit the openings. The belt cornice above the first floor becomes an architrave as it extends into balconies off each end of the L. At the intersection of the two wings, an engaged turret houses the arched entrance portal and a wrought-iron balcony above. The second floor windows are casements with shutters. Exterior materials originally were entirely stuccoed brick; the first floor brick is now exposed. The house is located in the Ardmore Addition of King's Hill at 1055 SW Douglas Place.

CHAPTER 14

Mediterranean

The term Mediterranean would seem, off hand, to have little to do with Portland's more misty and verdant clime. But given the city's reasonably temperate climate, it follows that the location is well suited for Mediterranean-influenced residential architecture. In addition, the low hills of Portland's west side, resembling those rising above the Arno in Florence, and the presence of lush hillside gardens and handsome views would seem to make many house locations as promising as any of those in Florence. Of course, the humanistic scale of those Mediterranean cities, with their towers and visual adornments, would differ greatly with the scale of downtown Portland, where competition from high-rise office buildings walls up any possible views toward the east, particularly views of the nearby snow-capped mountains or of the Willamette and Columbia rivers. The Mediterranean style, however, was as aptly suited to Portland as were the Tudor, French Renaissance, Colonial Revival, or even Prairie styles.

To scholars of residential design, Italy, for one, offered many glorious examples of fine houses. From Roman days onward, Italian vil-

Proposed residence on Council Crest, designed by Carl L. Linde.

las and city homes comprised some of the world's most handsome architecture. The particular houses that influenced most Mediterranean style architecture in Portland were those fifteenth- through seventeenth-century Italian country villas or hill-town dwellings of Tuscany, Venetia, and Lazio (where Rome is located). None of the Portland examples are copies of the grander Italian villas. Few in the city also seem influenced by Spanish Mediterranean architecture, being located so far north from Spanish traditions, although examples can be found. Nearly all Mediterranean-influenced houses are distinguished by their low-pitched,

hipped, terra-cotta tiled roofs, the use of arched entrances or loggias, modest use of windows, and stuccoed, mostly painted white, exterior walls. Some have widely extended eaves, with rafter extensions, and others have more modest eaves with cornices. Each design adjusts its basic styling to prevailing architectural trends, from academic purity to Craftsman or Arts and Crafts influences. It is a potpourri, but one that offers some exciting residential architecture.

When influences are more direct, one could point to particular Italian precedents. The Whitehouse and Fouilhoux design for Dorothy H. Jacobson (1916) has a wonderful site at the foot of

Courtyard of the Palazzo Ricardi, Florence, Italy, 1430, designed by Michelozzo.

Villa Medici, Pincian Hill, Rome, 1485.

Villa Ambra, Poggio a Caiano, Italy, 1480, designed by Giuliano da Sangallo.

the Columbia Gorge cliffs at Bridal Veil, with fine overlooks to the Columbia River. Handsome terraces with Classical cast balustrades and fountains look over formal gardens. The house originally had a magnificent two-story, balconied main room, with a massive Renaissance fireplace and arched windows that looked out to the terraces and views. As in many Italian country villas, the casement windows have shutters, and some have wrought-iron balconettes or railings. At the entrance portal, the Ionic columns and pediment could be Italian, especially with the cartouche over the door, but

Villa Bombicci, Florence, Italy, c. 1560, designed by Santi di Tito.

instead seem more of the English Renaissance. For sheer spectacular location, and inclusion of *quatro cento* (fifteenth-century) details, the villa of Major Watson Eastman designed by Hollis E. Johnson in 1928 is one of the finest in the city. Its panoramic landscape terraces, high above the city, cannot help but remind one of the villas above Florence. On its city-side elevations are the familiar recessed loggias that can be found in the Villa Medici at Careggi (designed by Michelozzo di Bartolomeo in 1434), the Villa Ambra for Lorenzo de' Medici at Poggio a Caiano (designed by Giuliano da Sangallo in 1480), and lastly the Villa Bombicci near Florence (designed by Santi di Tito, c. 1560). The Eastman House has a roof-top belvedere, much like that of Villa Lante at Bagnaia, near Viterbo, Italy (see Chapter 3). The house also is graced by a magnificent entrance hall with groined vaults, the side arches of which frame garden doors, major rooms, stairs, and the entrance. Only the Town Club, a private Portland women's club on Salmon Street, can compare. The club, designed in 1931 by Johnson, Wallwork and Johnson, has the finest Italian, or Mediterranean, interior entrance hall and salon in the city, displaying the reserved elegance possible with fifteenth-century spatial layouts and details. For exterior loggias, the travertine-columned one at the

Joseph R. Bowles residence, designed by Albert E. Doyle in 1924, is especially handsome overlooking the city.

Architect Carl Linde designed numerous Mediterranean style Portland houses. Some were modest, such as the Cornwell and Perry Building Company residence, with its imitation-tile roof. Others exuded elegance, as in the case of the Jacob N. Barde mansion of 1926. Some strongly resembled miniature Italian hilltown houses. The Ward R. Bowles (1926) and Otho Pool (1928) houses have highly irregular plans and multiple projections, but they do have low-pitched hipped tile roofs, sparsely located windows, and white stuccoed walls. Another irregularly planned house is the Thomas Christianson House of circa 1928. A suggestion of castellated fourteenth-century Italian houses is found in the detailing over the garage doors. The *machicolations* are closely spaced cantilevered arches, which date from medieval times when they were used to aid the defense of castles and towns by helping to prevent scaling of the walls and through which heavy rocks, boiling oil, and other objects could be dropped on intruders or invaders.

Some of the earlier houses in Portland with Mediterranean inclinations are a mixture of styles. The Robert F. Lytle House of 1911 combines the Mediterranean roof with an Ionic columned entrance portico and French casement windows. In the David A. E. Rocky House (1913), a strong suggestion of Arts and Crafts detailing is felt in the banked second floor casement windows. Craftsman proportions are found in the Clarissa Inman House (1926), which also has an Ionic columned entrance portico. Although the bifurcated garden steps might be associated with the Italian Renaissance, the general proportions and sculpture of the house are more of local tradition than of those emanating from the Mediterranean. Noted architect Herman Brookman also mixed his styles. The Harry Green House, roofed with beautiful red tiles, has a plan that comes out of the English Arts and Crafts tradition. The handsome rear garden parterre and the medieval style columns and arches at the breakfast room windows all suggest Italian influences, while the decorative trim of the main garden door seems to be a mixture of Art Deco and Spanish Plateresque styles.

The Mediterranean style, beginning after the 1910s, did not survive the financial crunch of the Great Depression. During that relatively brief period of Mediterranean architectural influence, however, some of the finest and most gracious homes were added to the city's collection, well worthy of special note and preservation.

Mediterranean
CHARACTERISTICS

PLANS: asymmetrical and symmetrical, often with angled wings.

ROOFS: low-pitched central hipped, with hipped extensions and wings; often with rafter tails used for eave-extension support. Mediterranean tile roofs.

EXTERIOR FINISHES: stuccoed masonry or wood-frame; cast-stone, or concrete, dressing at entrance doors, cornices, or window sills.

CHIMNEYS: stuccoed brick, with detail at cap; often small roofed caps, with tile.

WINDOWS: casement and double-hung, set within masonry walls; arched fanlight transom windows, with arched mullions to carry through mullion pattern of doors. French doors opening onto first floor terraces. Dormers not used.

WINDOW TRIM (exterior): minimal trim in wood or iron, set within masonry walls.

ENTRANCE DOORS: paneled doors, primarily within arched openings; transom and sidelights.

VERANDAS/PORCHES: gabled entrance porticos, with arched openings; balustraded loggias or side porches, with arched openings.

INTERIOR FINISHES: plastered walls and ceilings, with texture approximating plastered stone walls. Unglazed terra-cotta and polished oak floors. Decorative tile work incorporated.

INTERIOR TRIM: molded casings and baseboards; paneled doors.

STAIRS: oak treads and risers; wrought-iron railing details.

FIREPLACE FRONTS: stone, cement, or marble surrounds, with elaborate overmantel. Carved travertine marble with Renaissance detailing.

Entrance to the O. L. Price House.

Mediterranean
HOUSES

1911	Robert F. Lytle (David L. Williams)	1926	Barbara Price (Herman Brookman)
1913	David A. E. Rocky (Folger Johnson)	1927	Dr. H. W. Howard (Bruce McKay)
1916	Dorothy H. Jacobson (Whitehouse and Fouilhoux)	c. 1927	Frank A. McGuire
1922	Cornwell and Perry Building Co. (Carl L. Linde)	1928	Otho Pool (Carl L. Linde)
		1928	Harry A. Green (Herman Brookman)
1924	Joseph R. Bowles (Albert E. Doyle)	1928	Major Watson Eastman (Hollis E. Johnson)
1926	Ward R. Bowles (Carl L. Linde)		
1926	Jacob N. Barde (Carl L. Linde)	c. 1928	Thomas Christianson
1926	Clarissa Inman (David L. Williams)	1928	O. L. Price (Ellis F. Lawrence)

Robert F. Lytle (1911)
David L. Williams

The Mediterranean style covers a broad spectrum. Its earlier derivations included Colonial Revival details along with the more traditional vocabulary of the Mediterranean influences. In the Robert F. Lytle House at 1914 NE Twenty-second Avenue, architect David L. Williams successfully combined these elements. The two-story entrance portico carries on the design approach of Whidden and Lewis from the Colonial Revival style Nahum A. King House of circa 1904, but it also includes the widely extended Mediterranean eave, complete with exposed rafter tails. With its Ionic columns and the curved front of the smaller porch within the portico, the entrance might suggest the marriage of a Roman villa with the front portion of a local temple. Romanic materials include the tile roof, the plain stuccoed walls, and possibly the paired eave brackets. The chimney is brick.

The house is symmetrical in plan, the major rooms located on either side of the large entrance hall. The living room has unusual French casement windows and doors, with segmental-arched tops projecting into the transoms, opening to a balustraded terrace at the garden level.

David A. E. Rocky (1913)
Folger Johnson

One of the earliest residences to be designed by Folger Johnson, of the firm of Johnson, Parker and Wallwork, is the David A. E. Rocky House at 10263 SW Riverside Drive. Johnson planned an axially symmetrical house on an eight-acre site, with two short wings projecting to form a

Robert F. Lytle House.

David A. E. Rocky House.

small open court on the river-oriented elevation and an entrance porte-cochere at the opposite end. The house has the familiar low-pitched hipped roof and stuccoed walls of the Mediterranean style. Its facade has a belt-cornice line, just below the banked second floor windows, and dramatic shouldered-arch openings, some of which have been infilled. On the north elevation, a wrought-iron and glass canopy covers the entrance, and bracketed iron balconies extend at the second floor windows. French doors with arched transoms open at the first floor to balustraded terraces.

Folger Johnson had pursued his architectural studies at Columbia University in New York, followed by studies at L'Ecole des Beaux Arts in Paris. The Rocky House displays much of that formal training, as does the Town Club of 1931, Johnson's most noted work, also in the Mediterranean style.

Small open court on the river-oriented elevation, Rocky House.

Front terrace and entrance canopy, Rocky House.

Dorothy H. Jacobson (1916)
Whitehouse and Fouilhoux

Having inherited a considerable fortune from her "tobacco king" father, Dorothy H. Jacobson and her second husband, Clarence S. Jacobson, sought property along the Columbia River Gorge as the perfect location for an elegant summer villa. The house was to be reminiscent of the handsome Mediterranean villas visited by Dorothy during her frequent European travels. The Jacobsons found the ideal property along the newly constructed, and breathtakingly beautiful, Columbia River High-

Dorothy H. Jacobson House.

Main entrance and arrival court, Jacobson House.

Entrance door, Jacobson House.

Original two-story living room, Jacobson House.

Library, Jacobson House.

way, just beyond the small lumber community of Bridal Veil and at the base of 171-foot Coopey Falls. At that time there were fine vistas of the Gorge, where the scenery of cliffs and river are quite spectacular. At an elegant party in Portland, the Jacobsons chanced to meet Morris H. Whitehouse, architect of Simon Benson's Columbia Gorge Hotel in Hood River, a fine and notable structure in the Jacobsons' favored Mediterranean style. With the bearing of a Roman patrician, Whitehouse seemed the perfect candidate to design the Jacobson villa. A graduate of M.I.T., he had spent some time at the American Academy in Rome and was fully versed in Classical architecture.

The remarkable villa that the Jacobsons and Whitehouse planned was sited high on the property, just below the cliffs and the falls. The white stuccoed house consists of a major two-story structure with flanking projections, all under a red-tiled, low-hipped roof. A dining room and kitchen wing behind the front volume forms a T-shaped plan. The central view-facing portion contains the spacious living room, with French doors opening to the raised terrace above the gardens. Originally a beamed, two-story space, but now altered to one story, the living room had balconies at each end and a massive Renaissance style fireplace. In the house's two projections are the paneled library to the east and the "Chinese" room to the west. Paintings from the Jacobson collection lined the walls, complementing the reproductions of Renaissance style furniture mixed with large upholstered lounge chairs and sofas.

The main entrance to the residence is located on the west side of the house. It centers on an arrival court, complete with reflecting pond. A winding drive ascends from the gated entrance on the highway, passing the gatekeeper's house. The three-car garage, toward the back of the house, originally housed the Jacobsons' twelve-cylinder Packard, a Locomobile, and a yellow sports Oldsmobile.

The Jacobsons lived in the house for only five years. Clarence Jacobson died suddenly of a heart attack in the fall of 1919, and Dorothy closed up the house and returned to New York. In 1926, the property was sold to the William C. Lawrence family, who used it for many years as a summer retreat. After several subsequent ownerships, the house passed to the Franciscan Sisters of the Eucharist in 1975, who have fully restored the house and grounds, using them for a Life Center.

Cornwell and Perry Building Co. (1922)
Carl L. Linde

A test of an excellent architect is what he or she can do with a smaller residence. Given a limited budget, can a first-rate design be created to match that budget? Carl Linde, many of whose prominent residences are recorded in this book, took on the task for the Cornwell and Perry Building Company, developers of residential property. The house he designed is located on a narrow lot at 1926 SE Twenty-third Avenue. Linde designed the house with a decidedly Mediterranean air, including extended eaves supported by rafter extensions and a prominently arched recessed entry. The entry received the most detailed consideration. Its arch and cast-stone pilasters are in the Roman Doric style. Much of the charm of the house comes from the unusual pattern of its brick. Dark colored headers alternate with light colored full-length bricks. The effect is bold and most enriching. Other features are subdued and inexpensive. The front elevation has only two pairs of casement windows, the smaller pair banked at the second floor. The only adornments are the window boxes on an extended window cornice, the scroll work at the second floor, and the pressed-tin roof tiles.

Cornwell and Perry Building Co. House.

Joseph R. Bowles (1924)
Albert E. Doyle

A prize commission for architect Albert E. Doyle was the Joseph R. Bowles residence at 1934 SW Vista Avenue. From its fine Portland Heights site, the house overlooks the city much as the Florentine villas overlook their city. Sited close to Vista Avenue, the house's gated drive passes through a porte-cochere, arcaded with elegant Florentine style travertine columns, handsome against the rusticated, unpainted stuccowork of the house. All materials, bronze, stucco, and travertine, are

Joseph R. Bowles House.

ancient but classic, giving the house its established appearance and a great sense of quality. First-rate details are found in the bronze grilles of the entrance doors and the wrought-iron lanterns. Doyle, however, combined the new with the old. His living room windows, overlooking the balustraded travertine terraces, have full-sized plate glass, with only travertine sills for detail. A highly refined space of the large house is its open cloistered court, away from public view. Here, the colonnades remind one of the early years of the Renaissance: simple, elegant, and timeless. It is A. E. Doyle at his best, and a great architectural jewel for the city of Portland.

Mediterranean style loggia, Bowles House.

Ward R. Bowles (1926)
Carl L. Linde

In the 1910s and '20s, an enormous variety of Mediterranean style houses were designed and constructed in Portland. It would seem that architect Carl L. Linde received the lion's share of commissions with clients who preferred the solidity and ambiance the style offered. In the Ward R. Bowles House at 2903 NW Cumberland Road in Westover Terraces, Linde indulged in his passion for sculptural form, creating one of the most unusual houses to be constructed in the style. It might also be termed Spanish or Spanish Colonial, as the characteristics were overlapping. On its exterior, the Bowles House exhibits the smooth stucco walls and the low-pitched hipped roof associated with the Mediterran-

ean. Its asymmetrical masses are reminiscent of a Mexican hacienda, particularly the chimney pots, which, with their tiled miniature roofs, considerably resemble dovecotes. Other Mediterranean influences are found in the wrought-iron railings and window grilles, as well as at the entry, which has free-standing columns supporting its plaster arch, and in its loggia, all of which can be found throughout the Mediterranean region.

Jacob N. Barde (1926)
Carl L. Linde

At the more elegant side of the spectrum, houses could be graciously formal in plan, elevations, and detail. Carl L. Linde designed the Jacob N. Barde residence at 2400 SW Park Place at one of most prestigious lo-

Ward R. Bowles House.

Jacob N. Barde House.

cations in the city, just at the entrance to Washington Park and originally across the street from the baronial Loewenberg mansion of 1891 with its magnificent stonework. In its design, the Barde home responded to the high level of its surroundings, though in the Mediterranean style and considerably smaller. Linde designed the house in much the way an Italian villa was planned; it has a central axis, two projecting extensions on either side, a central entrance loggia, and the low-hipped tile roof of the Mediterranean style. On the east side of the house is an arched porte-cochere, and on the west a wing with columned porch. Windows on the lower floor, and some on the upper floor, are casement windows with half-round transoms, contributing to the house's considerable grace. Classical balustrades top the loggia, side porches, and porte-cochere. The house is a first-rate piece of architecture throughout and remains beautifully maintained.

Clarissa Inman (1926)
David L. Williams

When Clarissa Inman enlisted David Lockheed Williams to design her new home, she asked him in particular to incorporate many of the formalities of her previous home, the house Williams had originally designed for Robert F. Lytle in Irvington in 1911. She named her Mediterranean-inspired house Ariel Terraces, and she had lavish sums spent on construction, making the home a showplace of the Westover Terraces development. Williams indeed did use many elements of the Lytle House, particularly the imposing two-story portico with groupings of fluted Ionic columns supporting the balustraded roof. In addition to its axial plan, the Inman House also has the same extended eave, with dentil work and paired support brackets, as is found in the Lytle House.

Other details are influenced by Classical architecture, making the house not only Mediterranean, but Roman. The elaborate exterior stairway, on axis with the entrance portico, is a smaller version of the Spanish Steps in Rome, offering bifurcated stairs, a central landing, and a fountain. Other Mediterranean features in the house and garage structures are the low-sloped tile roofs, the stuccoed walls, and the casement windows.

Inside, the major rooms emanate off the central entrance hall. Directly ahead of the hall, the living room is on axis with the portico. The music room runs the full width of the house on one side of the hall, while the other larger wing contains the dining room, solarium, and kitchen. A cross axis is established from the music room, through the living room, and into the dining room, making for a grand sequence of spaces. In the

Clarissa Inman House.

corner of the living room are the stairs to the second floor. All major rooms are enriched with embossed paneling, intricate fireplaces, French doors, and large multi-paned casement windows. A metal frame supports the solarium structure, which provides access to the garden. Its floor is green polished granite, and wrought-iron gates close over the French doors.

The house has been extensively restored, and thanks to the removal of overgrown plantings, it is once again visible from Cumberland Road below. Located at 2884 NW Cumberland Road, its prominent position and large structure make it one of the most impressive houses with Mediterranean influences in the entire city, and it is clearly a major work of architect David L. Williams.

Music room, looking across the living and dining rooms, Inman House.

Entrance portico, Inman House.

Master bedroom, Inman House.

Barbara Price (1926)
Herman Brookman

A superb house that does not conveniently ally itself with an exact style is the Barbara Price home at 2643 SW Buena Vista Drive. The hillside street, possibly the most attractive in the city, has closely grouped houses, partly because of the steep drop-off toward the city view. This was no limitation to architect Herman Brookman, who not only provided a screened garage, but also an attractive lowered entrance court beside it. Brookman's inevitable creativity solved the site problem with a split-level entrance and a sunken living room one-half-floor down. The interior effect has the charm of a small castle, with inventive use of space. For the exterior entrance design, Brookman provided his typical recessed

opening, supported by a carved wood lintel. Sculpted on the pediment of the living room bay, to the right, is Brookman's signature ram's head. On the view side, a large cantilevered bay balances handsomely with the large living room windows and the half-round balcony of the bedroom level. Fine wrought-iron grilles and lamp brackets give the stuccoed house its Brookman air of immaculate detail and craftsmanship.

Dr. H. W. Howard (1927)
Bruce McKay

When constructed, the new house of Dr. H. W. Howard was praised by the Sunday *Oregonian*, which stated "The stately residence is one of the most outstanding in the Eastmoreland District of beautiful homes." Dr.

Barbara Price House.

Dr. H. W. Howard House.

Howard's Dutch-born wife asked architect Bruce McKay to incorporate features of her native Holland. Most particular to the sixteenth-century style—when Spain ruled the Netherlands—are the stepped masonry gable ends rising above the red-tile roofs. Dutch influence, likewise, greets the visitor at the Dutch style divided entrance door, with a carved oak panel in the lower half depicting a typical sixteenth-century home interior. Inside, the Dutch influence is seen in the massive fireplace, nearly eight feet across and equally high below the ten-foot-high ceilings. Impressive wrought-iron work is found in the fire screen and tools, as well as in other details throughout the house. Further Dutch features are the Delft tiles found in the kitchen and bathrooms. Mahogany trim finishes the plastered interior walls. The home, located at 2916 SE Woodstock Boulevard, remains in excellent condition.

Massive fireplace, Howard House.

Carved panel of the entrance door, Howard House.

Frank A. McGuire (c. 1927)

Among the most handsome of the Mediterranean style homes is the Frank A. McGuire residence at 1108 SW Collina Avenue in Dunthorpe. First viewed from Palatine Hill Road, the house has a commanding presence, with asymmetrical gable-ended masses arranged around the arched entrance turret. White stuccoed walls, a red-tile roof, and multiple arched openings add to the image of a substantial Mediterranean villa. Cars approach the house from Collina Avenue above, through impressive entrance pylons, and descend, looping, to the arched entrance portal. Many of the upper windows have balconies with extensive wrought-iron railings, and the railings over the arched entrance and side loggias have turned balusters. A handsome wrought-iron stair railing runs along the interior entrance-hall stair. The living and dining rooms, off the entrance hall, face the mountain views. The living room is most impressive, with its high vaulted ceiling and tall Renaissance style fireplace. Above the room's entrance doors is an arched opening and balcony from the second floor hall. The house's architect is unknown.

Frank A. McGuire House.

Living room, McGuire House.

Otho Pool (1928)
Carl L. Linde

Architect Carl L. Linde was sixty-four years old and at the height of his creative life when he designed a house for Otho Pool in 1928. For the house's ridge location on King's Hill, at 506 NW Hermosa Boulevard, Linde chose a butterfly plan, which took full advantage of the exciting city and mountain views. The living and dining room wings embrace the views beyond. With all its angles, various tile roofs, and rustic stucco walls, the house has a highly romantic flavor. There are decided traces of Spanish architecture, particularly as it might apply to a picturesque mountainside village. Every room seems expressed on the exterior, as are the additional polygonal bays and sun rooms. A three-story tower with a belvedere at the top floor stands where the two back wings of the house meet. Below, at the terrace formed by the wings, the garden-access doors lie on axis with the tower and the sweeping garden stair descending to the swimming pool and lower terraced gardens. The interiors are equally rich, with tile floors, arched window openings, cast-stone fireplaces, beamed ceilings, niches, and paneled doors.

Harry A. Green (1928)
Herman Brookman

In the first two years after coming to Portland from New York, Herman Brookman had gained a considerable reputation for his architectural skill. He was by no means confined to the Tudor vocabulary of the M.

Otho Pool House.

Harry A. Green House.

Wrought-iron entrance gate, Green House.

Lloyd Frank estate, where he had achieved spectacular success. Brookman revealed his remarkable talents for other architectural directions when he designed the home for Harry A. Green at 3316 SE Ankeny Street in a rambling Mediterranean style. On a beautiful site overlooking Laurelhurst Park, the seventeen-room house shows Brookman's mastery of architectural form. The sweeping and curved low-pitched roofs of the Green residence have as an anchor a bell-cast entrance tower, which houses the curved stairway and a mirrored vestibule with magnificent wrought-iron work. Beside the tower is the massive fireplace chimney of the living room. Extending to the right off the spacious entrance hall that runs through the house, the huge formal living room opens to the landscaped parterre overlooking the park. To the left of the entrance hall

Rear facade and parterre, Green House.

is the dining room, with the kitchen and service areas in a curved wing, and garages beyond. Both the living room and dining room have large bay windows, the undulations of which create a rich backdrop to the parterre. Most unusual are the columned decorations around the French doors leading out from the entrance hall. Paired peacocks in cast stone sit atop the side columns, and other, almost Art Deco designs help give the house an exotic air. With the sculptural richness of the facade on one side, the beauty of Laurelhurst Park on the other, and the luxury of the formal gardens of the parterre in between, the private and intimate space is one of the most attractive in the city.

French doors leading to the parterre, Green House.

Interior stairway, Green House.

In its own way, the Harry Green House employs the materials and style of the Mediterranean. The walls are stuccoed, the roof is covered with a rich textured tile, and the windows are metal-framed casements with three panes vertically in each casement. Feature windows, such as in the breakfast room overlooking the park, have Moorish arched openings supported by columns. A colonnaded arcade provides access to the swimming pool to the west, and a pyramid-roofed bath house and the garden walls provide privacy from the street. Even these elements add to the unity of the entire architectural composition, giving a handsome facade to the public street, yet providing a great variety of private spaces behind the house and walled gardens to the rear. It is an exceptional house, and one of Herman Brookman's best designs.

Major Watson Eastman House.

Major Watson Eastman (1928)
Hollis E. Johnson

On the uppermost reaches of Portland's west hills are located some of the city's finest residences. From Council Crest on Portland Heights to Forest Park, numerous magnificent houses on magnificent sites offer spectacular vistas out toward the city and the famed mountain peaks of the Cascade Range. On King's Hill, below the Pittock Mansion, the Mediterranean style house of Major Watson Eastman truly commands its ridge at this most scenic location. The 10,000-square-foot house is approached from its uphill side by a steep walled drive off of NW Beuhla Vista, arriving at an entrance court with a circular drive passing through a porte-cochere. The house's unadorned but highly imposing stuccoed facade is actually constructed of poured-in-place concrete, given an exposed aggregate finish, and now displaying the patina of age. Across the facade are casement windows, four panes high, shuttered, and painted

Garden facade, Eastman House.

a soft gray-green, with only the red-tile roof for contrast. In general appearance, the house would seem to be an authentic Mediterranean villa, perched high on the hills above the Mediterranean Sea. In fact, the house's design was inspired by a villa in Monte Carlo once lived in by the Eastmans. A painting of the original villa and Monte Carlo still resides in the living room of the Portland Eastman House.

It was Portland architect Hollis E. Johnson who assembled the Eastmans' requirements for the "villa." The garden facade has the large wing

Living room, Eastman House.

Entrance hall, Eastman House.

Dining room, Eastman House.

of the living room projecting out toward the city. Arched windows frame the city view from the living room, and handsome doors open onto the terrace and lawns—now partially replaced by a swimming pool—seemingly at the very edge of a cliff. The main entrance hall, on axis with the porte-cochere, has its own French doors opening onto an arched exterior loggia, from which steps lead down to the garden. The remainder of the garden elevation houses the dining room, with kitchen and garage wings angling off toward the side of the hill. A true belvedere crowns the low-pitched hipped tile roof, with perimeter windows looking out toward the distant panorama and western hills.

On the interior, authentic details are in abundance. The long, groin-vaulted entrance hall is particularly handsome, with doors to all the major first floor rooms and, within one of its arches, the stair to the second floor. Extant are the original wall surfaces of lacquered colors and stencilwork, much in the Italian Renaissance tradition. Even some of the villa's original furniture remains in the house, making it quite possible to visualize the house and setting as it appeared just after construction. Each subsequent owner has carefully maintained the house, and today it appears in near-perfect condition, a tribute to its design as one of Portland's most handsome houses.

Thomas Christianson (c. 1928)

By the late 1920s, before the Great Depression, houses in the Mediterranean style tended to be simpler and more tailored. The extended eave, with its rafter extensions, disappeared almost entirely. The low-pitched tile roof came out only to the house's facade, and a gutter was applied. This use of minimal detail reflected, no doubt, the influence of the Arts and Crafts style, then concurrent with the Mediterranean style. Classical

Thomas Christianson House.

details continued, however, primarily in the treatment of the entrance. On the Thomas Christianson House at 2833 NW Cumberland Road, the paned-glass door is surrounded by a dramatically high cornice, which is supported by two cast-stone columns in the Corinthian style. The Baroque arch over the door and the flared keystone follow the cast-stone work. Other cast-stone features on the all-stucco house include small scrolls where the first floor side walls extend out slightly from the second floor corners. The simple proportions and shuttered windows of the front facade are continued on the garden side of the house, enhanced by a half-round bay capturing the city and mountain views to the east.

O. L. Price (1928)

Ellis F. Lawrence

The residential architecture of Ellis F. Lawrence underwent considerable changes in the late 1920s. In the O. L. Price House at 2681 SW Buena Vista Drive, Lawrence combined a tailored Mediterranean style with some fairly startling rectilinear modern forms on the house's towering city elevation. The asymmetrical front facade is simple but carefully balanced and sophisticated. More articulated detail is found in the gabled entrance extension. A cast-stone arch with staggered side quoins surrounds the paneled door, sidelights, and wrought-iron grilled transom,

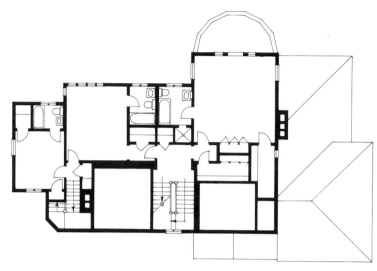

Second floor plan, Price House.

O. L. Price House.

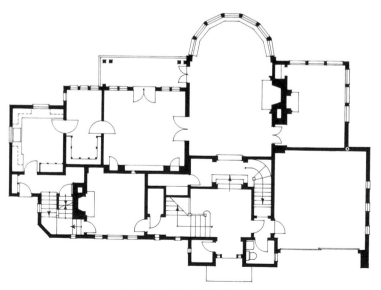

First floor plan, Price House.

and large scrolls buttress the portico. To the left of the entry, a tall stair window has a wrought-iron false balcony, the only other adornment. On the rear view side are multiple-level terraces and the handsome polygonal bay of the living room, which is lit by paired casement windows and transom lights. While exterior details are reserved and very sculptural, the interior features the full range of handsome finishwork. Carved wood decorations, paneling, tile floors, and a fine stair give the house high marks as one of Lawrence's best urban designs.

CHAPTER 15

English Cottage

While the Arts and Crafts and Tudor styles had a remarkable Portland following in the second and third decades of the twentieth century, a smaller, but no less distinct, group of houses were designed in the English Cottage style. Clearly as English in origin as the other two styles, the English Cottage style was tied to the smaller, romantic country dwelling, whether a cottage or inn. Charles Dickens described their many charms in the nineteenth century, as had countless other writers. In 1898, John L. Stoddard provided photographs of the smaller English cottages in his ten-volume leather-bound and amply illustrated set, found on the shelves of many of the more prominent private libraries. "What can be prettier and more picturesque," Stoddard asked, "than one of the quaint old English inns?" And who had not heard of, or seen pictures of, William Shakespeare's restored half-timbered home in Stratford-on-Avon. Always pictured with it was Anne Hathaway's thatch-covered farmhouse, typical of those dating from the reign of Queen Elizabeth. It was here that Shakespeare courted his wife-to-be, Anne Hathaway. The original rooms exist today, displaying their low ceilings beamed

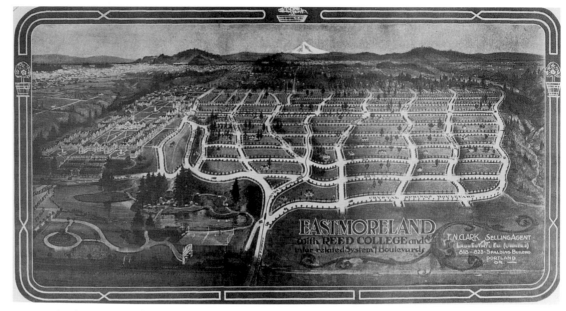

Eastmoreland District, Portland, circa 1911.

with heavy timbers and focusing on the large, open fireplace. Small-paned leaded windows look out on the lovely flower gardens. With the charm of rose-covered walls and inviting thatched roofs, these origins evolved into a style with impeccable historic credentials. For those constructing homes during the 1920s and seeking a less-than-ostentatious lifestyle, with, of course, more modern amenities, if not plenty of servants, the English Cottage style was the preferred choice.

The ancient houses on which the English Cottage style was based were either constructed of genuine half-timbering or of stone

Sixteenth-century "Rose-Covered Cottage," from *John L. Stoddard's Lectures*, "England," 1898.

with rough-cast stucco covering. The dominant thatched roof created its own aesthetic. By the necessities of the roof installation, the eaves of the thatching were clipped in rounded forms to a sharp edge, channeling rain water away from the walls of the house; gutters would be useless, even impossible to attach to the thatched roof. Gable ends had an arched peak at the ridge, a more practical and reasonable design given the material, or they had a thatched version of a jerkinhead. The thatching on facade dormers arched up and over the windows, creating one of the most discernible features of the style, appearing like a giant wig over the dormers.

While the libraries of Portland's architects undoubtedly included Sir Banister Fletcher's remarkable compendium of historic architectural styles, originally published in 1896, which included views of the more notable original English cottages, it was the published works of English architects such as Sir Edwin Lutyens (1869–1944) that most contributed to bringing the renascent English Cottage style to Portland. The famous and beautifully illustrated volumes of Lutyens's works show many examples of the thatched cottage, including a group of six cottages in the ancient village of Ashby St. Ledgers. The houses were grouped together, as duplexes or four-plexes are today, sharing common walls and fireplace chimneys. Lutyens's plan for the houses was practical for their 1909 construction, with rooms arranged in a manner close to what is found today, but their thatched roofs employed ancient roofing methods, as the thatching was cut at the eave to a sharp projection to throw the rain water away from the house. The facade dormers were constructed in the ancient manner as well, arching the thatching up and over the windows. Lutyens adapted separate roof dormers to the same aesthetic, with the thatching hooded over paired casement windows. All the windows were casements, following the historical tradition.

Anne Hathaway's cottage, England, early sixteenth century.

"An English Inn" from the sixteenth or seventeenth century, from *John L. Stoddard's Lectures*, "England," 1898.

Architect Albert E. Doyle purchased the leather-bound volumes of Lutyens's works for his professional architectural library. His design for the cliff-top country house of Edward Ehrman (1915) in the Columbia Gorge is a superlative example of the English Cottage style in the Portland vicinity, and it warrants comparisons with Lutyens's work as well as with the Elizabethan originals. The roof of the Ehrman House appears much as those of the early thatched cottages did, except that it is covered with shingles, carefully rounded at the eave to imitate thatching. Jerkinhead roofs are also evident, and the free-standing dormers have rounded forms, highly sculptural as in the Lutyens cottages and many old English originals.

Even the chimneys have the simple, curved-inward-at-the-top designs that are found in the Elizabethan models. The exposed, roughly laid stonework offers a particularly interesting comparison. In Lutyens's cottages, the stonework is romantically and casually installed at the base of the houses, as if the houses were constructed on previous foundations. Doyle repeated this theme exactly in the Ehrman House, with stonework revealed at the chimneys, under the bay windows, and prominently at the piers of the pavilion-style rear wings. Similar stonework carries over to the garden terraces and baths, informal in nature but constructed with carefully studied casualness.

Doyle continued his development of the English Cottage style in the Bert C. Ball House of 1921. The rounded eaves are even more pronounced in the Ball House, and they have extended beam supports to help hold them up. Jerkinhead gables are used on every elevation, with some of the roofs descending over open porches, much in the Arts and Crafts style. Particularly adaptive is the arched entrance porch, an approach used again two years later in Doyle's Wheeler House. The entire exterior of the Ball House is covered in rough-cast stucco, romantically softened with climbing vines in the English tradition. Equally English are the diagonally paned windows of the dining room bay, with the same simple details at the window trim as is found on old English inns. With

Cottage at Lustleigh, Devon, England, sixteenth century.

Group of six cottages, Ashby St. Ledgers, England, 1909, designed by Sir Edwin Lutyens.

the foundation plantings, the house could almost pass for one several centuries old. The Arts and Crafts floor plan and other details, such as the shed-roofed dormer, remind one that the house is a compilation of various influences, updated for twentieth-century convenience.

Other architects, as well as a great number of contractors, experimented with the style. Ellis Lawrence tried the rounded eaves, in a modest way, on his Paul Murphy House (1918). Josef Jacobberger used many of the features, including the jerkinhead gables, in the Rosenfeld House of 1922, and Carl Linde designed the Farrington House of 1924 with a highly pronounced imitation thatched roof, perhaps tending more toward the fairy tale than the romantic Anne Hathaway influences. Other houses, such as the Boutain and Frye houses, combined rustic brick with thatched-looking roofs. Dozens of non-architect-designed English cottages were built in the Alameda, Irvington, and Laurelhurst neighborhoods in the 1920s and '30s. The last architect-designed house in the style constructed in Portland, the Upshaw House by Morris Whitehouse, employed the rounded eave form in both the house and garage roofs, with one arched opening over the entrance door. Styles were changing abruptly during the later years of the Depression.

English Cottage
CHARACTERISTICS

PLANS: asymmetrical, with entrance hall centrally located.

ROOFS: central hipped with gabled extensions; rounded ridge, shoulders, or eyebrow raises over entrance portals to suggest English thatched cottages; jerkinhead at gables and facade dormers. Shingled roof, with irregular spacing and butts to imitate thatching.

EXTERIOR FINISHES: stuccoed masonry or wood construction, combined with half-timbering.

CHIMNEYS: stuccoed brick, with cap detailing.

WINDOWS: casement and double-hung; small wood panes, sometimes leaded decorative windows. Arranged in series, mostly groupings of three; five casements at polygonal bays. Some larger picture windows introduced.

WINDOW TRIM (exterior): small casing trim within stuccoed walls. When half-timbering used, window trim is integral with design.

ENTRANCE DOORS: paneled doors with glass panels and sidelights. Tudor arch, or arched thatched shed roof over entry.

VERANDAS/PORCHES: verandas enclosed under extensions of main roof; entrance porticos with arched projection or shed roof.

INTERIOR FINISHES: plastered walls and ceilings, with textured surfaces. Unglazed terra-cotta and polished oak floors. Beamed ceiling in feature rooms.

INTERIOR TRIM: molded casing and baseboards. Paneled doors.

STAIRS: oak treads and risers; wrought-iron railing details.

FIREPLACE FRONTS: cast-stone mantel, with tile surround.

3 1/2"

7 5/8"

Entrance to the Bert C. Ball House.

English Cottage
HOUSES

1915   Edward Ehrman (Albert E. Doyle)

1918   Paul F. Murphy (Ellis F. Lawrence)

1921   Bert C. Ball (Albert E. Doyle)

1922   Dr. James Rosenfeld (Josef
       Jacobberger)

1922   Max S. Hirsch (Ellis F. Lawrence)

1923   Coleman Wheeler (Albert E. Doyle)

1924   C. H. Farrington (Carl L. Linde)

1926   Frank Boutain

1930   J. O. Frye (J. O. Frye)

1935   Frank B. Upshaw (Morris H.
       Whitehouse)

Edward Ehrman (1915)
Albert E. Doyle

Architect Albert E. Doyle created a masterpiece in the country residence for Edward Ehrman. Located high on the cliffs above the Columbia River near Crown Point, the residence was designed in a handsome blend of English Cottage and Arts and Crafts styles. With its rolled eaves, without overhang, and its rusticated stonework combined with rough-textured stucco, the house had an immediate sense of character derived from centuries of tradition. As a country residence, with a spectacular view of the Columbia Gorge below, the Ehrman House featured a great hall—combining the living and dining rooms and complete with an open-trussed ceiling—which opened through banks of French doors to the terraces and views beyond. Above the great room was the central hipped roof, and two piered loggias projected out on the northern view side, one enclosed with French doors and the other open. Extending off the enclosed eastern loggia is a formal garden containing a reflecting pond and, originally, a vine-covered arbor, all taking full advantage of the Gorge views.

On the main, entrance side of the house, the bedrooms extended out on either side of the central entrance hall, with a kitchen wing on the western end. Various gabled facade dormers, jerkinhead side extensions, and roof dormers (one arched) provided architectural enrichment. Massive brick chimneys, with stone randomly placed at the corners, flanked both ends of the house, and two additional large chimneys served the fireplaces in the living and dining room great hall. Shortly after its construction, the Ehrman House appeared in the July 1919 issue of *Architect and Engineer*, which featured the work of Doyle and his spectacular contributions to Portland's architectural environment.

Edward Ehrman House.

View-side elevation, Ehrman House.

The Edward Ehrman House has suffered numerous indignities since it left private hands. Productively used as a church retreat, a large chapel now all but blocks the dramatic views from the main rooms, dominating the end of the point, and a carport has been insensitively placed at the front entrance, eliminating in its installation the elegant arched canopy over the stone entrance portal. The interiors, somewhat neglected, need considerable restoration. As a work of first-rate importance in association with a prominent Portland pioneer family and the remarkable talents of A. E. Doyle, the landmark house on a gorgeous site would hope for a brighter future.

Stonework at the chimney and bay window, Ehrman House.

Living room, Ehrman House.

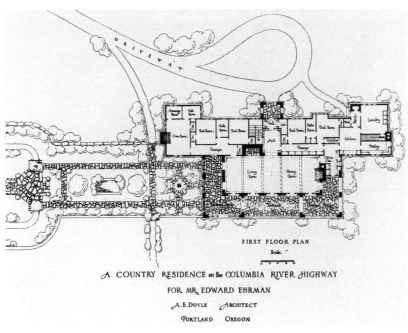

FIRST FLOOR PLAN
Scale

A COUNTRY RESIDENCE on the COLUMBIA RIVER HIGHWAY
FOR MR. EDWARD EHRMAN
A.E.DOYLE   ARCHITECT
PORTLAND   OREGON

Plans for the Ehrman House and grounds, by A. E. Doyle.

Paul F. Murphy (1918)
Ellis F. Lawrence

Architect Ellis Lawrence introduced to Portland his first design in the English Cottage style with the house for Paul F. Murphy, the developer of Laurelhurst. Located at 3574 East Burnside Street, a prominent property in the Laurelhurst district, the house has many of the characteristics associated with the style, mainly the curved edge of the roof at the eave line, imitating in shingles an English thatched cottage roof design. It has as well the jerkinhead at the main gable and the descending side roof covering an open porch. To it Lawrence added banked casement windows, in the Arts and Crafts tradition, a wrought-iron balcony, and a projecting arched cover above the entrance door, taken from the English domestic architecture of C. F. A. Voysey and Sir Edwin Lutyens. (Wade Pipes had introduced the entry roof detail in his Arts and Crafts John M. Pipes House of 1912.) The Murphy House was featured in the *Architectural Record* of November 1918, showing Lawrence's well-worked plan and his clever placement of the garage with a separate apartment above it. The house remains in excellent condition, although the shed-roofed dormer has been altered and the open porch enclosed.

Paul F. Murphy House.

Bert C. Ball (1921)
Albert E. Doyle

A wide interest in English Cottage architecture began to emerge in Portland by the late 1910s, probably beginning with the house that Ellis Lawrence designed for Paul Murphy in Laurelhurst. But the characteristics of the style were first clearly brought together by Albert E. Doyle in his house for Bert C. Ball on Portland Heights. The house at 2040 SW Laurel Street commands a full half-block site, still retaining some of the unique-to-Portland indigenous fir trees. Most unusual in Doyle's design is the rolled roof, hugging the house with its protective covering and extending down over several wings or open porches. In this case, the open porch (as per the Lawrence design) is off the library. The porch has large-

Garden elevation, showing the open porch, Ball House.

Bert C. Ball House.

Main stairway, Ball House.

scale stuccoed piers—matching the stucco covering of the house—supporting its roof at the eave. Another open porch is located at the back corner of the house, off the living and dining rooms. These porches are, in effect, outdoor rooms, suitable for comfortable summer outdoor living, and were enjoyed in that fashion, not needing screening in the Portland area. In addition to the hipped central roof with gabled extensions, all having rolled eaves to imitate thatching, the Ball House has a shed roof over the entrance porch, with its lower rolled eave arched in the center, a theme repeated in later houses with an English Cottage theme. Another attractive feature of the exterior is the rounded two-story bay at the dining room, with its diamond-paned windows with mullions enhancing the medieval thatched-cottage appearance.

In plan, major rooms surround the large central entrance-stair hall.

The dining room and its bay window are on axis with the entry. To the right of the hall is the living room, with windows on three sides, and to the left is the library and access to the butler's pantry, the kitchen, and the breakfast room. The breakfast room has corner windows that look out toward the lovely walled gardens in the back of the house. Upstairs, the large hall, with an open well to the entrance hall below, is surrounded by bedrooms, all having private bathrooms. A servants' stair off a back hall accesses the kitchen below. The functional aspects of the plan, as well as its appealing flow of spatial arrangements, make the Ball House one of Doyle's most significant works, clearly demonstrating his mastery of architectural form and residential planning. As a reflection of Doyle's amazing talents, the house has had successive caring owners who have maintained the residence's unique qualities in excellent condition.

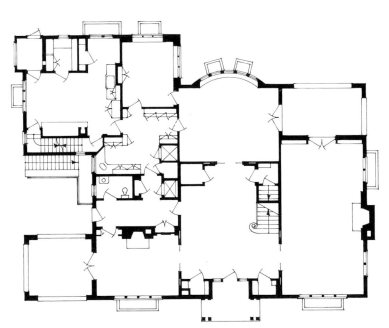

First floor plan, Ball House.

Second floor plan, Ball House.

Dr. James Rosenfeld (1922)
Josef Jacobberger

Located a few blocks north of the Ball residence is the Dr. James Rosenfeld House designed by Josef Jacobberger in 1922. The house developed the design themes of the English Cottage style, while adding some Tudor elements. Typical English Cottage characteristics are the jerkinheads at the gable ends and the rounded eaves imitating thatched roofs. On the south elevation is an open porch protected by its roof extension, much as is found in the Ball House. The gabled facade dormer and the arched cast-stone entrance below it represent more Tudor influences. The dormer is half-timbered and cantilevers out over modillions. Another

Dr. James Rosenfeld House.

unusual architectural element is the metal-roofed, rectangular bay window on the front elevation. It has the same small wood casement windows as are found elsewhere in the house. Below the bay is the garage, one of the first examples in residential design where the garage was included within the basic volume of the main house, and not in a separate or attached structure. Located at 2125 SW Twenty-first Avenue on a quarter-block site, the Rosenfeld House is adjacent to some exceptional homes in the Colonial Revival style.

Max S. Hirsch (1922)
Ellis F. Lawrence

Extraordinarily substantial houses were constructed throughout the decade preceding the great Wall Street economic crash of 1929. Portland Heights continued to be developed, either slowly replacing the existing Queen Anne houses or building new homes on still-vacant properties. The Max S. Hirsch House designed by Ellis Lawrence is sited on one of those long-vacant properties, which still enjoyed glimpses of the city view until subsequent houses and established gardens gradually blocked that view. The Hirsch House at 1770 SW Prospect Drive, just off Montgomery Drive, is completely surrounded by Prospect. A narrow front yard serves for entrance-drive access, and the main gardens are in the rear. Immediately adjacent to the drive is the massive main facade of the house. Substantial architecture is evident in the use of brick at the first floor, half-timbering at the second floor, and gray slate on the steeply pitched hipped roof. A half-timbered and brick stair tower projects from the front facade. Most of the house's details are Tudor influenced, but the arched eave over the half-timbered entrance porch and the small recessed eyebrow dormer above are definite English Cottage influences.

Max S. Hirsch House.

garages at the southwest corner of the home. Characteristically, the house has the English Cottage rolled eaves, as well as rolled ridges on its hipped roofs. The roof slopes descend to the first floor at the arched eave of the entrance porch and the glassed porch on the north side. A variety of materials cover the house. Stucco combines with shingle siding and half-timbering, and river rock is used for the piered roof supports. A two-story polygonal bay with a hipped roof projects from the front elevation. The interiors are more Classical, with details of the Colonial Revival style at the stair, fireplaces, and wood trim. All rooms enjoy the spectacular views of the city or of the terraced hillside gardens to the west.

Coleman Wheeler (1923)
Albert E. Doyle

On an amazing street of exceptionally well-designed residential architecture, Coleman Wheeler built a house at 1841 SW Montgomery Drive. The very typical English Cottage design was by A. E. Doyle, whose mastery of the idiom was equal to his mastery of most every other design form or style. Offering panoramic views, the house sits high on a ridge above Montgomery. The driveway accesses an angled wing housing the

Coleman Wheeler House.

C. H. Farrington (1924)
Carl L. Linde

Versatile architect Carl L. Linde designed an English Cottage style house for C. H. Farrington at 2208 NE Twenty-eighth Avenue. Linde could easily adapt his talents to changing architectural tastes, but he always added his own interpretation. The Farrington House is organized around its steeply pitched hipped central roof, with gabled extensions. A catslide roof descends from the front gable over the asymmetrical entrance. All eaves are rounded, as are the hips of the roof and the arched dormer

C. H. Farrington House.

roof. Instead of a jerkinhead at the major gable ends, the entire roof is rounded at that location, giving the house a somewhat storybook appearance. Linde used the traditional banked windows and the combination of stucco siding with half-timbering. Large picture windows, with leaded glass, are located on either side of the entrance on the front elevation. The side elevation includes the gabled extensions, a large half-timbered facade dormer, and an extended gable over the double garage doors. Garages, by this time a necessity, had become integral with the main structure of the house, and now usually were located immediately adjacent to the kitchen and service entrance.

Frank Boutain (1926)

The residential areas of Eastmoreland, with its winding streets following the undulations of the land, developed considerably in the 1920s and '30s. Not all the houses have the architect recorded, and some houses may not have been designed by architects. The Frank Boutain residence at 6633 SE Twenty-ninth Avenue is a large English Cottage style house displaying most of the major characteristics of the style, despite having no architect of record. The front elevation combines a large gabled extension off the central hipped roof and a massive chimney. Between them is the entrance porch, with an arched entry. Windows across the facade are multi-paned, some having diagonal leaded panes. The oriel window centered on the asymmetrical front gable has a rolled eave, in keeping with the rolled eaves throughout the house. Unusual for a design of this style is the use of multi-toned brick on the exterior, when most houses of the genre had a stucco finish. The Boutain House has been well maintained, though the lower gardens across from the Eastmoreland Golf Course have been sold and further developed.

Frank Boutain House.

J. O. Frye (1930)
J. O. Frye

English Cottage style picturesqueness reached its peak with the house designed by contractor J. O. Frye in 1930. Located at 2997 SW Fairview Boulevard on Arlington Heights, the house comes closer than any others to the storybook ambiance of old English cottages. Its steep, rolled roof is highly sculptural, incorporating both recessed and eyebrow dormers. The living room wing has a large fireplace chimney, and its vaulted ceiling has the well-noted "spider-glass" round window at the gable end, beneath the arched meeting of the rounded eaves. As in those on the

Farrington and Boutain houses, the gable jerkinhead blends completely into the roof. Despite the size of the house, the designer included the English Cottage style open porch, tucking it under the corner of the hipped central roof. It serves as a covered entrance for the single-car garage. The house is sided with textured brick of varying hue, accented by randomly spaced dark clinker bricks, giving it a distinctive surface texture. Though generally well maintained, the house's original and prominent shingled roof has been re-covered with composition shingles.

J. O. Frye House.

Frank B. Upshaw (1935)
Morris H. Whitehouse

When the Eastmoreland District was developed by the Ladd Estate Investment Company, Frank B. Upshaw worked for the company selling properties. On one of the corner lots, at 2923 SE Tolman Street, the Upshaws built their own home, designed by noted architect Morris Whitehouse. Whitehouse incorporated a few of the distinctive features of the English Cottage style popular during the 1920s. The house has extended rolled eaves, with beam supports, and the arched roof above the entrance used previously by A. E. Doyle. Reflecting the arched roof, the entry door and sidelights follow the half-elliptical shape. The size of the living room on the western side of the house is unusual, supposedly designed to the "golden rectangle" (a pleasing proportion that can be recreated by geometric design). It extends the full width of the house and was used for the frequent entertaining for which the Upshaws were noted. Other rooms are smaller in scale, such as the dining room and the upstairs bedrooms in the story-and-a-half house. Mrs. Upshaw was a woman of great taste, and she filled the house with her extensive antique furniture collection. Landscape architect L. M. Thielsen designed the original gardens.

Frank B. Upshaw House.

PART VI

Innovative American Forms
1900s–1930s

CHAPTER 16

Prairie

Though the Prairie style made a remarkable contribution to residential design in the Midwest, particularly in and around Chicago, it was a fairly short-lived style, and one that produced only a few noteworthy examples in Portland. Developed around the turn of the century and lasting until after the First World War, the style began with such houses as the substantially rectilinear William H. Winslow House (1893) in River Forest, Illinois, designed by Frank Lloyd Wright and heavily influenced by Wright's mentor, Louis H. Sullivan. Its basic box-like shape is capped by a low-pitched, centrally placed hipped roof. Below widely extended eaves, the second floor windows and frieze-like geometric decorations are framed between the eaves and a strong horizontal band at the sill line of the windows. The windows of the lower floor are set in the brick walls below the frieze, symmetrically arranged around a central entrance door. All the windows on the front facade are individually placed.

Several years later, in 1899, Wright designed another and much larger house, the Husser villa in the Buena Park section of Chicago, also influenced by earlier Sullivan designs. The massive

Portland, overlooking Ladd's Addition, circa 1915.

369

house, three stories in height, has many of the features that became associated with the Prairie style. Most prominent is the very low-pitched roof, with exceedingly wide eaves cantilevered four to five feet out from the wall of the house. The third floor is featured with windows and decorations set between the eave line and the prominent horizontal band surrounding the entire house. Windows are individually placed on the first and second floors, as in the Winslow House, or grouped in banks of architecturally framed casement windows. Additional features include the polygonal belvederes at the second floor, which are also covered by low-pitched

hipped roofs with widely extended eaves. The theme extends to the porte-cochere, a continuation of the carriage entrance of the 1870s now adapted for the advent of the automobile. In 1901, Frank Lloyd Wright designed what was probably his first true Prairie style home. The Frank W. Thomas House in Oak Park, Illinois, offers the characteristic wide eaves on a low-pitched hipped roof, and it further emphasizes the horizontal in its bands of windows with a continuous sill line and the dark band around the base of the rectilinear home.

As a result of the architectural publications of the day, the Husser House became widely

known across the United States. It most likely influenced the Portland house designed by architects Whidden and Lewis for Walter F. Burrell in 1901, only two years later. The three-story Burrell House has a similar low-pitched hipped roof, with multiple wings and extensions. The front entrance facade also has an open belvedere—plus a second one at the western end of the house—much as in the Husser House. The third floor windows of the Burrell House are defined between the eave and a strong horizontal band, exactly like the band in the Husser House, at the window sill line. Somewhat inconsistent are the second floor shuttered win-

William H. Winslow House, River Forest, Illinois, 1893, designed by Frank Lloyd Wright.

Joseph W. Husser House, Chicago, Illinois, 1899, designed by Frank Lloyd Wright.

dows in the Colonial Revival style, recognizing Portland's inclinations toward that style. The enthusiastic reception of the Colonial Revival style coupled with the apparent lack of interest in the Prairie style undoubtedly persuaded Whidden and Lewis that the most fertile fields in Portland had Colonial-bearing soil.

Starting in 1909, the firm of Bennes, Hendricks and Thompson embarked on a series of Prairie style homes in Portland. The first of these was the Marcus J. Delahunt House of 1909, with

W. W. Willits House, Highland Park, Illinois, 1902, designed by Frank Lloyd Wright.

Frank W. Thomas House, Oak Park, Illinois, 1901, designed by Frank Lloyd Wright.

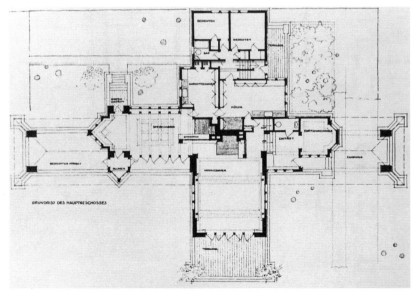

The Willits House plan by Frank Lloyd Wright.

John Virginius Bennes as chief designer. The precedents of Louis H. Sullivan and George G. Elmslie, as shown in the pages of the Chicago Architectural Club Catalogue of 1902, are clearly felt in the design. Bennes's own home of 1911 carries on the influences of the Chicago area. It is a house with a low-sloped hipped roof, banks of casement windows, and a front extension, also hipped against the house. Unusual was his addition of brackets, which appear to add support to the widely extended eaves. Bennes's masterpiece was the Aaron H. Maegley House of 1914 on Arlington Heights. In plan, the house demonstrates the interconnecting spatial qualities that are possible when major first floor rooms open onto one another. The asymmetrical plan takes much from the Chicago Prairie designs, even the massive piers at the outer corners of the house, particularly influenced by the house plans of Frank Lloyd Wright from the preceding decade.

The widely distributed *Western Architect* of 1915 printed illustrations of many such houses, including one designed by John S. Van Bergen in Chicago. A similar Portland house was designed by C. V.

Vanderpool for Emma McCauley (c. 1912), complete with the widely flared roof, banks of casement windows, and asymmetrical plan. All these houses had continuous horizontal bands that emphasize the horizontal qualities of the entire architectural structure: at the eaves, at the sill of the second floor windows, and often across the top of the first floor windows. One unusual house, yet ascribed to the Prairie style and designed by Vanderpool, is the Robert McBride House of 1912. The two-story house has the typical widely extended low-hipped roof, but it also features an arched projection with a heavily accented cornice across the front of the house. Flared side walls

and an arched central door add further to this original and imaginative design.

Portland is most fortunate in having a collection of houses designed during the early 1920s by the famed Minneapolis architect William Grey Purcell. Purcell had previously designed a remarkable series of houses in the Prairie style elsewhere in the country, some having widely extended gable ends and others with central hipped roofs. The Harold C. Bradley House of 1912 in Woods Hole, Massachusetts, had an extensive rectangular hipped roof, banks of second floor casement windows, and a striking horizontal emphasis. Purcell retired to Portland in 1920 for health reasons, but he continued a limited architectural practice. Some of his houses were adapted to Northwest traditions, mainly to the Portland version of the Arts and Crafts style, but they retained many of the stylistic characteristics that Purcell developed while practicing in the Midwest. Two Portland houses show particular hints of the Prairie style for which Purcell was famous: the Lilian K. Pollock and the Thomas Mostyn houses. The Mostyn House (1924) has a side-gabled roof, with a wide roof over-

Harold C. Bradley House, Woods Hole, Massachusetts, 1912, designed by Purcell, Feick & Elmslie.

hang, and the signature band of windows unified at the second floor. Where casement windows are not present in the band, the siding is smooth, providing contrast with the horizontal lap siding at the floor below. Under the second floor window sills, at the height of the balcony rail, is the typical strong horizontal band found in most Prairie style houses. Purcell's stay in Portland was not long, but the little-known series of notable houses is a substantial legacy in the city's rich history of residential design.

Prairie
CHARACTERISTICS

PLANS: asymmetrical and symmetrical.

ROOFS: prominent flat or low-pitched hipped, with widely extended eaves, sometimes supported by brackets. Tile or shingle roofs.

EXTERIOR FINISHES: stuccoed masonry or wood-frame construction. Brick and beveled horizontal siding also used.

CHIMNEYS: subdued designs, in keeping with horizontal emphasis; brick or stuccoed masonry.

WINDOWS: continuous bands of casement windows, mixed with some paned double-hung.

WINDOW TRIM (exterior): continuous trim to emphasize bands of casement windows, either above or below windows.

ENTRANCE DOORS: glass doors with sidelights.

VERANDAS / PORCHES: expansive covered porches with widely extended eaves.

INTERIOR FINISHES: plastered walls and ceilings, with textured surfaces. Unglazed terra-cotta and polished oak floors.

INTERIOR TRIM: stained wood trim and exposed beams in main rooms; painted trim elsewhere.

STAIRS: wide stairs, with landing over entrance vestibules. Extensive woodwork.

FIREPLACE FRONTS: Chicago-school influences, as well as Classical. Art-tile surrounds and hearths.

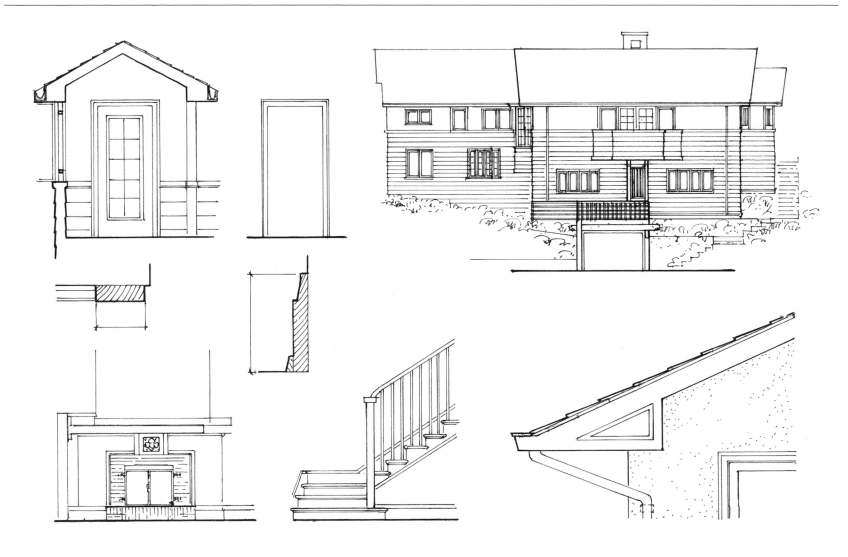

Entrance to the Thomas Mostyn House.

Prairie
HOUSES

1901	Walter F. Burrell (Whidden and Lewis)
1909	Marcus J. Delahunt (John Virginius Bennes)
1911	John Virginius Bennes (John Virginius Bennes)
1912	Carl M. Little (Bennes, Hendricks and Thompson)
1912	Robert McBride (C. V. Vanderpool)
c. 1912	Emma McCauley (C. V. Vanderpool)
1914	Aaron H. Maegley (John Virginius Bennes)
1921	Lilian K. Pollock (William Grey Purcell)
1922	C. Spies (A. R. Hossack)
1924	Thomas Mostyn (William Grey Purcell)

Walter F. Burrell (1901)
Whidden and Lewis

The Prairie style architecture emanating out of the Chicago area by the turn of the century had some effect in Portland, but only to the extent of a handful of houses. The old-guard firm of Whidden and Lewis, heavily involved with the Colonial Revival style at this time, did venture into some of the ideas being developed in the East with the Walter F. Burrell House of 1901. Strong horizontal elements were the chief characteristics of the developing style, and the Burrell House does exhibit this quality.

Walter F. Burrell House.

The prominent feature of the house is the widely extended, low-pitched hipped roof. To emphasize its hovering quality, the roof extends out over two open balconies at the third floor: one over the polygonal bay above the former dining room, and the other atop the west-facing side of the house. In addition, the low-hipped roof of the porte-cochere on the entrance facade has widely extended eaves and, typical of the Prairie style, large-scaled masonry piers. Other horizontal elements are found at the second floor, where some of the first floor rooms extend out beyond the second floor facade, emphasized by strong horizontal stucco banding at the balustrade and, above, at the continuous line under the third floor windows and balustrades. As a possible nod to Colonial Revival leanings, all the double-hung windows have shutters—not a feature found in the typical Chicago-area Prairie house.

In 1920, the large house, located at 2610 SE Hawthorne Boulevard, was purchased by Portland's pioneer funeral home, Holmans, who have maintained it in excellent condition for over fifty years. Some changes have been made to the porte-cochere to allow for present-day uses, but most other features, exterior and interior, are intact, including the handsome stair, fireplace, and woodwork details.

Marcus J. Delahunt (1909)
John Virginius Bennes

The architect most closely connected to the Prairie style in Portland is John Virginius Bennes. The firm of Bennes, Hendricks and Thompson, with Bennes as chief designer, was responsible for most of the Prairie style homes in Portland. The first of their homes in the style is the Marcus J. Delahunt House located at 1617 NE Thompson Street. All the defining Prairie features are represented. Its prominent, low-pitched hipped roof has widely extended eaves, with no bracket supports, and the wrap-around porch has the typical eave detail and is supported by large clusters of wood columns on masonry piers. The low flight of entrance stairs is in an extension of the covered porch, somewhat off center, but balanced with a Bennes-signature planter on a porch-level extension. Another feature of the Prairie style is the banks of casement windows. Here they are in clusters of three, adding to the horizontal qualities of the house. The house has all the attributes of an architecture designed for the mostly horizontal terrain around Chicago, and it is very much at home in its Irvington neighborhood.

John Virginius Bennes (1911)
John Virginius Bennes

When John Virginius Bennes designed his own home at 122 SW Marconi Avenue, it was one of the first houses in the developing Arlington Heights area of the city, above the old City Park, now Washington Park. The house originally had more space around it, now filled in with neighboring houses. In the design of his home, Bennes incorporated the strong horizontal features typical of the Prairie style, including the low-pitched hipped roof, though with the unusual addition of brackets supporting

Marcus J. Delahunt House.

John Virginius Bennes House.

the wide eaves. To reduce the two-story elevations of the house, he added another low-pitched roof covering an open porch in front of the house, as he had in the Delahunt House, and a bayed extension of the full-facade living room. The actual entrance to the house is on the side, covered with a glass and metal canopy. By locating the entrance there, Bennes made for a more practical central-entrance plan. Both the living and dining rooms, on either side of the hall, then looked into the side garden of the narrow property. A garage was later added at the property line, with the same low-pitched tile roof and stucco exterior as the main house. Two cast-concrete planter urns flank the wrought-iron entrance gates.

Carl M. Little (1912)
Bennes, Hendricks and Thompson

For a brief five-year period, the firm of Bennes, Hendricks and Thompson produced the most avant-garde architecture to be seen in Portland. Their influences were clearly the Prairie style masters, such as Louis H. Sullivan and Frank Lloyd Wright, and while it lasted, the firm produced some first-rate houses in that genre, all at a time when the Arts and Crafts style was just beginning its tremendous influence in the city. The Carl M. Little House at 3711 NE Davis Street continued the theme begun with the Delahunt House, but it dealt with a more restrictive site. Due to the narrowness of the site, the house is only one room wide, with the entry recessed back on the side. Instead of a flat-roofed wrap-around porch, a strongly horizontal bank of first floor casement windows, including a substantial horizontal cornice, is employed in this house to confront the two-story facade. The second floor, to continue the horizontal emphasis, has a full-facade bank of windows and a prominent, widely extended eave. Such radical departure in Portland, however, caused little stir, de-

Carl M. Little House.

spite the great inventiveness for the period and the promising possibilities of an entirely new aesthetic.

Robert McBride (1912)
C. V. Vanderpool

Although little is known of the designer C. V. Vanderpool, his houses in the Prairie style have considerable distinction. The house he designed for Robert McBride at 431 NE Laddington Court has strong influences of the Chicago school, mainly the work of George W. Maher. Maher's C. R.

Irwin House (1905) in Oak Park, Illinois, was almost certainly the inspiration for the McBride House. The Irwin House was exhibited by Maher at the Chicago Architectural Club in 1906, showing somewhat the influences of C. F. A. Voysey, strangely combined with those of the Austrian Succession designs.

Besides the widely extended hipped roof, the most notable feature of the McBride House is the arched roof extension at the front of the house, where the front entry is located. Other features are the coved cornice detail at the eave, the flared base of the stucco walls, and the arched canopy over the arched entry door. Changes to the windows detract from the clarity of the original design.

Emma McCauley (c. 1912)
C. V. Vanderpool

Another distinctive Prairie style house was designed by C. V. Vanderpool for Emma McCauley in Eastmoreland at 7808 SE Twenty-eighth Avenue. It combines both two-story and one-story elements, with the living room located in a one-story wing to the north of the entrance hall. A projecting, heavily piered entrance porch bridges the two masses. As with the previous houses in the style, strong horizontal lines are incorporated both above the first floor windows and below the second floor windows, where they become window boxes supported by articulated

Robert McBride House.

Emma McCauley House.

beam-like brackets. Above the window boxes are typical banked casement windows, and below, at the first floor, are large picture windows, an American architectural tradition since the Queen Anne style. A possible Bungalow or Craftsman influence is the high windows at the south elevation, presumably above a dining room buffet. The one-story portion of the house continues at the back of the house, where an arched gate connects to a double garage. Although examples of this style are rare in Portland, the few, including this one, are very well done, both in plan and basic sculpture.

Aaron H. Maegley (1914)
John Virginius Bennes

John Virginius Bennes clearly demonstrated his mastery of architectural form when he designed the Aaron H. Maegley House at 226 SW Kingston Avenue on Arlington Heights. It is a highly unique and compelling example of Prairie style architecture; unique in that it not only offers the hovering qualities of Prairie designs, but has in its detail some decidedly Classical features. Bennes combined the two brilliantly. In pure Prairie fashion, the house has the low-hipped roof, tiled in this case, and the banks of

Aaron H. Maegley House.

windows typical of the style. The horizontal main floor projections extend from the central mass of the house, with a hipped roof over the porte-cochere on the entrance elevation and over covered porches at the north and east elevations. With great inventiveness, Bennes used polygonal bays, or oriels, at the second floor, projecting out from, but protected by, the gen-

Porte-cochere detail, Maegley House.

Living room, Maegley House.

Interior stair detail, Maegley House.

erously wide eaves. Below the windows, and wrapping nearly around the entire house, is a horizontal stucco band, which not only organizes the facade, but gives the elevations their distinctive proportions.

The unusual siting of the house allows all major rooms to enjoy the city views to the east. A separate garage is located at the front of the property, and it has unusual details sympathetic with the house. Its sliding doors are glass paned, and an arched trellis spans the opening. For the house itself, Bennes combined a highly practical plan with graciously open interconnecting spaces. As was common in the Queen Anne style, interior rooms could be opened up to provide expanded and continuous spaces. The house has a classic central-hall plan, entered through a vestibule under the landing of the stair. Directly ahead, on axis with the

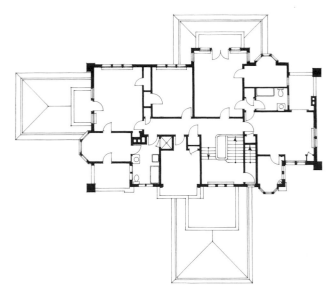

Second floor plan, Maegley House.

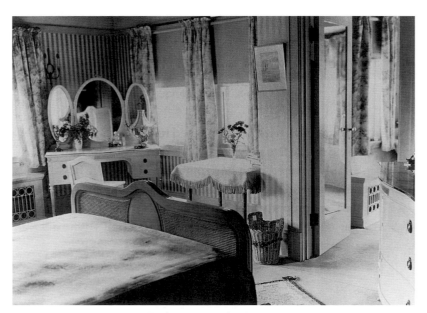

Bedroom, Maegley House.

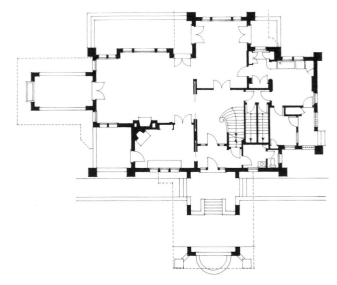

First floor plan, Maegley House.

city view over Washington Park, is the dining room, and on the left are the library and living room, which share a fireplace chimney and have covered porches off their north elevations. To the right of the entrance hall are the kitchen and service areas. Upstairs, five bedrooms are arranged around the central hall, with a separate servants' stair splitting off to the kitchen from the stair landing. Though the bedrooms share two bathrooms, major rooms have separate dressing rooms. Family sleeping porches are also provided, as it was believed they were more healthful than interior bedrooms. Other balconies are over the porte-cochere and roofed porches of the north and east sides of the house.

The exceptional Prairie style plan, the wonderful sculpture of the house, and the fine interior and exterior details rank this house not only as architect Bennes's finest work, but as an eminent example of residential architecture in the city.

Lilian K. Pollock (1921)
William Grey Purcell

When the nationally recognized Minneapolis architect William Grey Purcell retired to Portland because of ill health at age forty-one, he managed to continue his architectural practice in this city for several years. Though in a much smaller office than the famous Purcell and Elmslie firm of Minneapolis, Purcell designed a number of significant homes and buildings in the area, furthering his unique interpretation of the Prairie style of architecture. Two neighboring houses on Portland Heights attest to his great architectural talents. The first of these houses is located at 2666 SW Vista Avenue and was designed for Lilian K. Pollock in 1921. Sited at the foot of a hillside, the house has its main floor level two floors

Lilian K. Pollock House.

above the garage level. It has a low-pitched roof over the central gabled mass, with one distinctive polygonal bay extended to the full width of the eave. Simply covered with horizontal lap siding, the house gains distinction by its handling of the necessary but dominant street-level garage at the front property line. To minimize its presence, the garage is all but disguised behind a large-columned garden trellis, with a paved terrace as its roof.

C. Spies (1922)
A. R. Hossack

The only symmetrically planned house in the Prairie style in Portland is the house at 2424 NE Seventeenth Avenue constructed in 1922 for C. Spies. Little-known architect A. R. Hossack designed the house using the predominant horizontal emphasis for which the style was noted. Its wide eaves create the primary horizontal element, and they compare with those of the Prairie houses by Bennes, Hendricks and Thompson. In this house, massive brick piers, in a tan-buff color, are at each corner of the central structure, with projecting smaller piers framing the entrance portal. The flat roof slung between the piers of the entrance is continued over the banks of three casement windows on each side of the central entry, and again over the two one-story side extensions. A typical horizontal line, in cast concrete, is placed beneath both the second and first floor windows, making four major horizontal lines that give definition to the house. All windows are casements, in banks, and muntins are placed at the sides of each window so that they create squares in the corners. This window design was to repeat throughout Bungalow, Craftsman, and even some Mediterranean styles.

Thomas Mostyn (1924)
William Grey Purcell

The second of the two neighboring houses designed by William Grey Purcell on Portland Heights was for Thomas Mostyn at 2660 SW Vista Avenue. Originally located between towering Douglas fir trees, this house also has its main living level two floors above street level. Pri-

C. Spies House.

Thomas Mostyn House.

mary access is gained up a flight of steps at the right side of the house to a covered entrance porch, with a secondary entrance at the lower level left side and under a polygonal dining room bay. Evidence of Purcell's unique Prairie style is found in the predominantly horizontal accent of the house, the linear vertical porch supports, and the widely extended side-gabled roof with its boxed-in triangular detail at the eave. The central mass is symmetrical on its exterior, and a polygonal porch extends from the house. Its paired beams and posts, with vertical lattice between, are repeated at the right-side entrance porch. An angled wing for the

kitchen and bedrooms extends to the left. Inside, Prairie details abound. An angled fireplace, reflecting the angled wing, partially separates the open living and dining rooms, both of which have ample light from the abundant windows and French doors overlooking the hillside vistas beyond. The linear geometries continue through the stair, fireplace, and woodwork details. It is an exceptional house, despite its difficult site. Only the original railing above the concrete garage is missing in the otherwise intact home, and two additional support columns have been added to the character-defining second story cantilevered porch.

CHAPTER 17

Bungalow

One of the more amazing infatuations in residential design has been America's love affair with the Bungalow. Portland knows the latter phase of the style, in houses constructed roughly between 1900 and 1920. Actually, the origin of the name stretches back to the 1880s when India was a part of the British Empire. A dak bungalow was an Indian rest house that the government provided for travelers. "Bangla" is the Hindustani word meaning "belonging to Bengal." As a general description at that time, the individual guest houses were of one-story construction, had tile or thatched roofs, and were surrounded by a wide veranda. When the style came to Portland several decades later, as one facet of the Craftsman movement, various interpretations evolved. The early houses, always with widely extended eaves, reflected the Shingle style; others appeared to be adaptations of the houses designed by the Greene brothers around Pasadena, California. Some had a definite Swiss-chalet, or even Japanese, feel to them, and some appeared to be one-story versions of early Arts and Crafts houses. Others were much more rustic, sometimes log-cabin variations on the theme. The most predominant style features

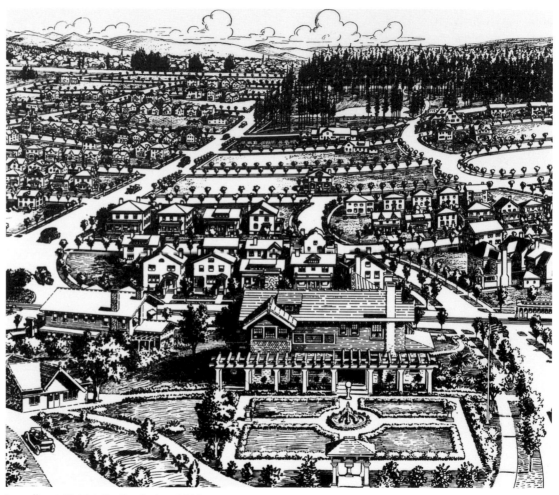

Laurelhurst District, Portland, circa 1916.

were the low-pitched, side-gabled roof, widely extended and supported by brackets, the banks of casement windows, and a prominent porch, often across the entire front of the house.

The phenomenal success of the Bungalow style, with houses constructed in nearly every corner of the country, owes much to the publications that promoted the style beginning just after the turn of the century. The greatest promoter of the style was Gustav Stickley. In his early years, Stickley opened a furniture shop with two younger brothers, Charles and Albert, before setting up his own shop in New York state. The furniture they produced was simple in design, comfortable, economical, and, though blocky, had good proportions and was well made. It was perfectly compatible with the Craftsman and Bungalow style houses produced after the turn of the century. Two other brothers, Leopold and J. George, established another furniture firm, L. and J. G. Stickley, that produced similar furniture in competition. It was Gustav, however, who visited England in 1898, where he met leaders of the Arts and Crafts movement. Back in the United States, Stickley established *The Craftsman* magazine. This immensely popular publication, first printed in 1901 and continuing until 1916, not only advertised his company's furniture, but featured house designs and presented a whole way of life.

Stickley hired professionals to draw a variety of one- and two-story houses, all having the practical layouts and design features that he believed would promote a more wholesome and healthy life. *The Craftsman* included plans with the price of the magazine, hence it was of great appeal to the successful laborer or middle-class businessman. Subscribers to *The Craftsman* "Home Builders' Club" were offered more than 200 plans over the years, plans for which construction cost varied between $2,000 and $15,000. Free modifications were made, via mail, for builders who wished to construct variations of the plans. For the women who ran the households, *The Craftsman* discussed built-in furniture, buffets, inglenooks, kitchen cabinets, and a variety of time- and space-saving advice. The advantages of step-saving, low-maintenance, and low-cost features appealed greatly to the household that could not afford hired help or simply desired more free time. Appliances to ease the burden were only just beginning to appear, but owners welcomed every hint on how to run a household with less drudgery. In addition, gone was the separate parlor reserved for guests, filled with Victorian knickknacks.

The house plans were as open as possible. The entry stair hall became a part of the living room, which in turn opened to the dining area, usually framed with bookcases and free-standing columns.

A "Bangla" house, or "A Bungalow in Ceylon," from *John L. Stoddard's Lectures*, "India," 1897.

Built-in bookcases with glass doors were placed on either side of the fireplace, and buffets often had pass-throughs to the kitchen, so the buffet could be serviced without leaving the kitchen. Hooded vents over the cooking stove were suggested for eliminating cooking odors and greasy residue. Iceboxes could be filled from the back service porch, and coolers were provided in cupboards so that the cooler air from outside would keep things fresher, away from the warmer interiors—in those days, it was not imperative to put everything in a refrigerator. Every room in the house was considered. The sleeping porch was widely acclaimed for its healthfulness. At that time, houses were generally heated by wood, gravity furnaces, or coal, but without much fresh-air intake. It was believed that a healthier life could be attained by sleeping on the porches, with full banks of windows providing ample amounts of circulating fresh air.

Staff member Harvey Ellis drew some of the finest plans for *The Craftsman* magazine between May 1903 and January 1904. The romantically appealing drawings presented the best of the attractive features of the Bungalow and Craftsman designs. Naturally, the simply designed Stickley furniture was featured, arranged in appealingly comfortable rooms, with beams overhead and appropriate wallpapers, floor coverings, and upholstery.

Several major California architects were introduced to readers through *The Craftsman*. The designs of Irving Gill in San Diego and those of Greene and Greene, centered around Pasadena, were particularly influential. Their designs demonstrated that the same principles of open planning, honest native materials, and simplicity of details could translate into the homes of the affluent. The houses designed by the Greene brothers were masterpieces. They too had shingled walls, exposed wood rafters,

"A European's Residence, Colombo," from *John L. Stoddard's Lectures*, "India," 1897.

Edhofer House, Brünig, Switzerland, 1682.

stone or brick foundations and piers, and a strong sense of Japanese architecture about them. The woodwork achieved magnificence, the furniture was perfectly coordinated, and fireplace tiles and art-glass windows were integrated with utmost artistry. Every feature was carefully considered, and each one depended on the others; nothing could be removed without disrupting the harmony of the whole. Such successful houses influenced countless other architects, who learned about the new designs primarily from a plethora of Craftsman magazines, such as *Architectural Record*, *Western Architect*, *House Beautiful*, *Good Housekeeping*, *Country Life in America*, and *The Ladies' Home Journal*.

Other promoters of the style and of the Craftsman philosophy became popular and highly influential. Elbert Hubbard was a grand promoter of the movement both in publications and in his architecture. His Roycrofters Inn and Campus in East Aurora, New York, and the Grove Park Inn in Asheville, North Carolina, were immensely attractive as high watermarks of the Craftsman ethic. Many publications featured examples of Bun-

galow houses. Harry H. Saylor's book entitled *Bungalow*, published in 1911, noted at least ten variants of American bungalows. All had versions of the ample front porch, the low-pitched roofs close to the earth, and open, rambling floor plans.

In Portland, Bungalow style houses appeared throughout the city. A major population increase, spurred by the successful and widely attended Lewis and Clark Centennial Exposition in 1905, necessitated a boom of residential building to house the new arrivals to the city. From North Portland though Eastmoreland, all the east-side neighborhoods experienced huge

"Cottage Design XI," from *Village and Farm Cottages* by Henry W. Cleaveland, William Backus, and Samuel D. Backus, 1856.

influxes of Bungalow houses; from Willamette Heights to Lake Oswego on the west side, a multitude of Bungalows were built, usually in already established neighborhoods. The best examples seem to be greatly influenced by the designs of Greene and Greene. Just outside Lake Oswego, in what was then countryside near the Willamette River, the Emma M. Austin House was built circa 1910. Massive stone piers support huge trusses and a low-pitched roof in multiple layers. Beam extensions, somewhat in the Japanese tradition, support the wide eave extensions. Similarly, the Wilbur Reid House (1914) has intersecting low-pitched gable roofs, massive stonework, trusses, and rafter extensions, all naturally stained and beautifully crafted. Francis Brown, the architect of the Reid House, is reported to have worked with Greene and Greene.

Another stone-piered house is the one designed for Gertrude Smith in Irvington in 1907. Exceptional details, following the Craftsman tradition, are found in the built-in buffet and the wonderful stair, which is open to the main floor rooms, well lit and inviting. The Swiss influence in Bungalow designs is represented by the Frederick Alva Jacobs House (1913) on Mount Tabor, designed by the firm of Johnson and Mayer. Swiss balconies, railing details, and rusticated stone give a welcoming effect to the board-and-batten covered house. An example of a house directly inspired by a Stickley plan from *The Craftsman* is the Lewis T. Gilliand home of 1910, the plan and elevation of which were redrawn for Gilliand by Ellis Lawrence. Bungalow features abound: the rambling, open plan, the spatial framing of the dining room with built-in bookcases, the pergola at the entrance, the roofed porch off the living and dining rooms, the shed-roofed dormers, and the banks of casement windows.

The more typical Bungalow designs are those with low-pitched bracketed roofs, often in multiple layers. Successful ones include the Ellison (1914) and Schegel (c. 1916) houses. They have suggestions of Japanese influence in the treatment of the roofs. The Ellison House employs roof forms much like those found on Japanese farm and tea houses. Bracketed eaves, of course, were expected in the local versions, as was shingle covering and, most likely, trim of a lighter color. The Schegel House is one of the smallest of the Bungalow designs, but it manages considerable cohesion of design and plan. It has the flared and shingled piers, supporting the porch roof, that are found in the great majority of Portland Bungalows. Porch supports were varied, however: stone or brick piers, clustered square posts, shingled piers, or various other combinations. Usually, the height of the porch railing was equal to that of the base on which the wood flared posts were placed. They had square block capitals, or none at all, and the framing, usually rectilinear beams and purlins, was profusely displayed, sometimes more decorative than purely practical. In many of these houses, an arbor-like trellis system was attached to the house at entrance areas or porte-cocheres, or above outdoor sitting areas adjacent to main floor living spaces.

The Bungalow houses represent some of Portland's most distinguishing architectural features. Many have fared well over the years, but others have had false siding added to their shingles, or the massive columns have been removed and replaced with inadequately scaled pipe or wrought-iron columns. They are, nevertheless, being restored in great numbers, particularly in areas like Ladd's Addition, and they will continue to define fine neighborhoods for some time to come.

D. B. Gamble House, Pasadena, California, 1909, designed by Greene & Greene.

Bungalow
CHARACTERISTICS

PLANS: asymmetrical and symmetrical, with extensive roofed porches. Free-flowing interior spaces.

ROOFS: low-pitched, gable-ended with widely extended eaves, supported by brackets or rafter extensions. Multiple shed, or gabled, dormers; wing extensions. Shingled.

EXTERIOR FINISHES: shingles, lap siding, or board and batten; rusticated foundations of stone or clinker brick. Porch piers of tapered wood (elephantine-shaped), stone, or brick. Sometimes shingled skirts for porches, resembling masonry in scale.

CHIMNEYS: rusticated stone or brick; sculpturally located as part of asymmetrical architectural composition.

WINDOWS: continuous banks of casement, or double-hung windows, often with small-paned glass.

WINDOW TRIM (exterior): simple, wide casings; continuous at tops of banks of casement windows.

ENTRANCE DOORS: glass-paned, with sidelights.

VERANDAS/PORCHES: expansive covered porches, under extension of main roof.

INTERIOR FINISHES: simple-paneled wainscoting with plate rail; plaster wall and ceilings in lesser rooms. Beamed ceilings. Wood floors.

INTERIOR TRIM: simple, wide-board casements and baseboards, varnished.

STAIRS: wood treads and risers, with inventive railings, usually rectangular balusters and newels.

FIREPLACE FRONTS: clinker-brick surrounds, with varnished wood mantels and details.

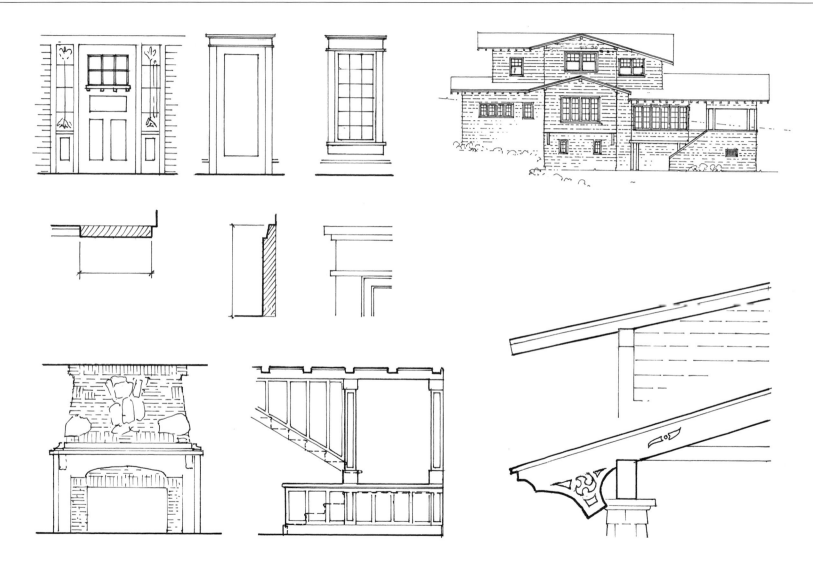

Garden gate of the Frederick Alva Jacobs House.

Bungalow
HOUSES

1906	Fred A. Shogren (attributed to Josef Jacobberger)
1906	G. W. Sherk (Dunlap Brothers Construction)
1907	Gertrude Smith (A. H. Faber)
1908	Woods Hutchinson (Josef Jacobberger)
c. 1910	Emma M. Austin (attributed to Josef Jacobberger)
1910	Catherine H. Percival
1910	Lewis T. Gilliand (Ellis F. Lawrence)
1911	M. C. White (George A. Eastman)
1912	H. P. Palmer (David L. Williams)
1912	Belle Ainsworth Jenkins (Root and Hoose)
1913	George A. Eastman (George A. Eastman)
1913	Frederick Alva Jacobs (Johnson and Mayer)
1914	Wilbur Reid (Francis Brown)
1914	E. J. Ellison
c. 1915	C. S. Jackson (attributed to Johnson and Mayer)
1916	William H. Hossack (attributed to A. R. Hossack)
1916	Bungalow "A"
c. 1916	H. E. Schegel (F. G. Quimby)

Fred A. Shogren (1906)
Josef Jacobberger (attributed)

Within the broad spectrum of Bungalow style houses, many could be equally labeled Shingle style, or Craftsman, depending on the date of construction, the details, or whether they are one story or two. Demonstrating the subtle transitions between styles, the Fred A. Shogren House at 400 NE Sixty-second Avenue would seem to span Shingle and Bungalow. The two-and-a-half-story house has many of the Shingle style features of the Heusner House designed by Edgar Lazarus in 1892, such as exposed beam and rafter tails, shingle siding, and the use of stonework for foundations and porch roof supports. Both houses have

Fred A. Shogren House.

rounded engaged turrets. Yet, the low-sloped roof, side gables, dormer, and recessed porch and pergola details of Shogren's house are more of the Craftsman or Bungalow style. The handsome Shogren House beautifully continues an evolving tradition that began decades earlier, while setting the stage for the new style of Bungalow. A prime candidate for the house's architect is Josef Jacobberger, as his design for the Woods Hutchinson House of 1908, and other Craftsman houses, bears many resemblances.

G. W. Sherk (1906)
Dunlap Brothers Construction

Among the earliest true Bungalow style houses in the city are the paired structures at 1710 SW Elizabeth Street on Portland Heights. Built by Dunlap Brothers Construction in 1906 for G. W. Sherk, the two one-and-a-half story houses sit high on the hillside and are reached by a bifurcated stair that meets in a pathway between the houses. On their level plateau, they enjoy the fabulous panorama of city and mountain views for which Portland's western hills are famous. The two houses are opposite in plan, and as such they have their pergola entrances facing each other. The pergolas are similarly proportioned, with shingled boxed piers, but have different roof designs. One has a gabled end, with expressed beams and a bargeboard, and the other is hipped, with angled bracket supports for the wide eave. Full porches, with open railings, stretch from the pergola across the rest of the facade to capture the views from the arched living and dining room windows. Both houses also have dormers: a hipped one on the left and a gabled one on the right. Most of the characteristics of the Bungalow style in various forms are expressed on the two houses.

G. W. Sherk House.

Gertrude Smith House.

Main interior stairway, Smith House.

Gertrude Smith (1907)
A. H. Faber

By 1907, the distinctive forms of the Bungalow style were well established. A house that captures the great charm and cohesiveness of the style is located at 1831 NE Brazee Street, built for Gertrude Smith and designed by architect A. H. Faber. The Smith House is a remarkably sophisticated, yet deceptively simple, solution to residential design. Its story-and-a-half rectangular volume has a basic side-gabled roof that extends down to cover the full-facade porch. The porch roof has rafter tails with a slight upward curve, and typical brackets are used at the side gables. A wide shed dormer is built into the roof, recessed suffi-

Dining room and buffet, Smith House.

ciently to provide a small balcony. Rounded river-rock piers at each end of the first floor porch support the porch roof, and similar material is used for the foundations as well as the chimney and garden walls. Shingles cover the entire house, with rich tonalities, and once covered the roof.

The interiors of the Smith House are beautifully conceived. Typical dark varnished wood trim brings an almost Japanese unity to the design. Because of the house's open plan, the stairway to the second floor is a part of the living room, and the dining room, with its built-in buffet, seems a part of one large space.

Woods Hutchinson (1908)
Josef Jacobberger

Shingle, Craftsman, and Bungalow style features blend in the picturesque Woods Hutchinson House designed by Josef Jacobberger in 1908 and located at 1435 NW Thirtieth Avenue on Westover Terraces. Concurrent with Jacobberger's Shingle style Lamson House (1908), the Hutchinson House departs from the tailored Shingle to the Bungalow style characteristics, such as the wide eaves supported by extended beams. Though the entrance to the house is currently off Thirtieth Avenue, it originally was off Quimby Street, and that side extension is now developed as a separate property. The great covered polygonal veranda had steps at its outer facet, toward a northeast view. A low hipped-roof polygonal tur-

Woods Hutchinson House.

ret is built within the porch, against the main front gable of the house. Rounded river-rock porch piers and foundations, shingle siding, diagonal-paned casement windows, and window boxes at the second floor all enhance the structure's picturesque qualities. The house's original color scheme was white trim against weathered shingles, which contrasted well with the river-rock piers and foundations. Architect Jacobberger, so talented in many directions, quickly adapted to changing tastes and here produced an excellent Bungalow house.

Emma M. Austin (c. 1910)
Josef Jacobberger (attributed)

One of the finest Bungalow style houses was designed as a summer home near the Willamette River, outside Lake Oswego. At 49 Briarwood Court, practically hidden from street view, the remarkable Emma Austin House has all the characteristics to make it so appealing and so timeless. Its rustic materials—shingles and river rock—keep the house in touch with its once-rural surroundings, making for an essential shelter, protected from warm summer sun as well as from the area's wetter seasons. Elemental to the design is the very low-pitched roof, which is supported by substantial beams, rafters, and rock piers. The wide covered veranda seemingly floats in space. The low-pitched gabled roof over the hovering second floor is perpendicular to the gabled porch roof. An arched high window on the first floor emphasizes the rustic masonry character. Inside, the rooms are comfortable and in keeping with the Bungalow details of dark wood beams, stone fireplaces, inglenooks, and bays, giving the house such appeal. Unfortunately, the house's architect is unrecorded, but it could be attributed to Josef Jacobberger, or possibly designer George Eastman.

Emma M. Austin House.

Catherine H. Percival (1910)

If we attribute style primarily according to the predominant roof configurations, the house at 2585 SW Montgomery Drive would clearly be Bungalow style. Seen from the street above, the symmetrical double gables projecting from a large side-gabled roof are beautifully designed. Between the facade gables, a large shed dormer visually penetrates the gables and appears with a small window at the sides of the two gable extensions. Typical bracket supports are found on all elevations, and window boxes are located at major windows. The house is accessed from the

Catherine H. Percival House.

Lewis T. Gilliand (1910)
Ellis F. Lawrence

One of the few Portland Bungalows in which the architectural ideas had clear precedent in the work of other architects is the house designed in 1910 for Lewis T. Gilliand at 2229 NE Brazee Street. Ellis F. Lawrence, the architect of the house, apparently must have seen the plans and perspectives in Gustav Stickley's *The Craftsman*. The Gilliand House shares numerous similar elements with a house presented in Stickley's magazine in April 1907: the side porch with low-sloped shed roof, the shed-roofed dormer, the banked casement windows with protective overhangs, the stone fireplace, piers, and footings, and the shingle siding.

Lewis T. Gilliand House.

street down a long flight of steps. It is entered directly on center into the large living room space that runs the full width of the house, with the main brick fireplace directly ahead. Stairs to the upper and lower levels are on either side of the fireplace, and additional sitting rooms and the master bedroom are situated to the left and right. Unusually, the dining room and kitchen, plus the servants' quarters, are located a full level down. Upstairs was originally a large open space, devoted to a private chapel. The original interiors have been altered, but the dining room woodwork remains, most notably the fine built-in sideboard.

Drawing of a house published in *The Craftsman*, April 1907.

The house's central-hall scheme, with two unequal gabled extensions, has the attractive feature of a small entrance court with a vine-covered pergola. Except for the configuration of the second floor and the side-hipped central roof, the plan of the Gilliand House is nearly identical to that of Stickley's design. Such basic concepts were, however, to have a powerful influence on other architects in Portland as well, as numerous similar houses were designed in the city. Then, as today, the architectural publications played an important role in the adaptation of new styles.

M. C. White (1911)
George A. Eastman

In the opening years of the century, countless Bungalow style houses were constructed throughout the city. The M. C. White home at 5620 NE Cleveland Avenue, in the Piedmont Addition, is an exceptional one. Architect George A. Eastman designed the house in 1911, and he employed the popular design idea of two symmetrical gables extending from a central hipped roof, with a covered porch between the gables. The porch, which is entered off Cleveland, is supported by two full river-rock piers. To the north, a low-pitched side porch is also supported by massive rock piers, and the same masonry appears at the chimney and at the piers

M. C. White House.

between the wrought-iron fences (originally a simple hung chain). Prominent on the gables are the strong bargeboards, supported by brackets, and the matching shed-roofed bays with banked casement windows. Rafter tails are visible, and the bargeboards have cut-out end designs. Until it was covered with artificial siding, the house was the prime example of the Bungalow style in the area, and one of George Eastman's best designs.

H. P. Palmer (1912)
David L. Williams

Another inventive Bungalow in the northeast section of the city is the house constructed by H. P. Palmer at 1908 NE Twenty-fourth Avenue in 1912. Architect David Lockheed Williams designed the two-and-a-half-story house using a combination of Bungalow and Craftsman style details. To the side-gabled roof, with exposed roof beams, Williams added impressive flat-roofed porches at the entrance and south elevations. Both porches are supported by massive clinker-brick piers, but while the front porch is open, the side porch is enclosed with cross-paned windows. The north elevation features a most interesting arrangement of intersecting forms, including an angled gabled projection, a turreted tower, and a polygonal bay window, all protected by wide eaves with beam extensions and exposed rafter tails. A rich textural effect is achieved by the use of rusticated brick up to the second floor and wide beveled siding over the second floor exterior. On the roof is a wide shed dormer with banked casement windows. The house has undergone restoration efforts, and previous alterations to the original structure have been removed, exposing a superlative Portland example of the style.

H. P. Palmer House.

Side elevation, Palmer House.

Belle Ainsworth Jenkins (1912)
Root and Hoose

With its considerable acreage, large house, stables, and outbuildings, the Jenkins' country estate, called Lolomi and located at 20950 SW Farmington Road, remains among the city's best examples of homes in the Bungalow style. Though the house is only a story-and-a-half in height, the ground floor area constitutes a substantial piece of architecture, much larger than any other Bungalow style house in the Portland area. Part of the considerable mass of the L-shaped plan is the spacious wraparound porch, which is recessed under the low-sloped roof. The side-

Decorative lantern at the entrance of the Palmer House.

Belle Ainsworth Jenkins House.

gabled house has two large gabled dormers on the front elevation. A back wing, itself with a sizable gabled dormer, is perpendicular to the front facade. Prominent features of the Bungalow style are the river-rock chimney and porch footings, the shingle siding, and the banks of casement windows. Colors on the house are original: brown shingles (originally weathered dark) and light cream trim, while the round porch columns are dark brown with cream capitals—a rustic log-cabin version of a Greek Doric column. Beautifully sited at the crest of rolling lawn, the house is a rare example from the firm of Root and Hoose.

George A. Eastman (1913)
George A. Eastman

Though not recorded as an architect in the *Architect Directory* of 1913, George A. Eastman was clearly an architectural designer with a flair. When he designed his own home in 1913, Eastman tackled a difficult hillside lot at 2628 NE Stuart Drive, just below the crest of Alameda. Although the house is three stories high on its lower side, Eastman managed to give the house the horizontal emphasis that characterizes the Bungalow style. He accomplished this by using numerous low-pitched gable roofs, which form various planes of deeply recessed eaves, by having the main, or middle floor, of the house cantilevered, and by employing horizontal courses of shingles. The sculpture of the house is what distinguishes it so greatly from the mass of Bungalows. Intersecting volumes, multiple projections, and open porches all contribute to create a satisfying sculpture for those who enjoy the art of architecture. Some of these sculptural qualities have been considerably altered by the addition of porches along the entire lower portion of the house at its meeting with the hillside.

George A. Eastman House.

Frederick Alva Jacobs (1913)
Johnson and Mayer

In a remarkably pristine and preserved state, the Frederick Alva Jacobs House at 6461 SE Thorburn Street, on Mount Tabor, represents an influence not often found in the Bungalow houses of the mid to late 1910s. While the plan and basic forms are pure Bungalow, the details of the 1913 house have a decidedly Swiss flavor. Instead of the typical plain design, the bargeboard is treated to some Swiss-inspired edge designs;

instead of the usual shingles, board-and-batten siding partly covers the house; and the porch and balcony railings have Swiss cut-out designs. And probably the most Swiss-like detail is the bracketed balconies projecting out at the second floor from the east and west gable ends (which have Swiss cut-out attic ventilator holes). In other details, we find typical Bungalow characteristics. Most obvious is the rusticated stone foundation surrounding the house, and the massive chimney. The low-pitched shed dormer on the roof in this case becomes a facade dormer, except where the roof extends down over the entry porch. The house has banked casement windows on all elevations, exposed rafter tails,

and a handsome and well-integrated polygonal bay on its south elevation. A small modification to this elevation was the partial infilling of the back-porch service entrance. Otherwise, the house is among the best preserved and maintained in the city. It is the only known residence designed by the firm of Johnson and Mayer.

It is a pleasure to enjoy the fine interiors of the Jacobs House. Spaces interlock with one another, a continuous development since the late 1880s. The living and dining rooms, the entrance hall, and the stair to the second floor are seemingly contiguous. All the woodwork is a wonderfully rich, dark stained fir, including the paired columns separating

Frederick Alva Jacobs House.

South elevation, Jacobs House.

Living room, Jacobs House.

Dining room, Jacobs House.

Main interior stairway, Jacobs House.

spaces, the built-in buffets and bookcases with art glass, the beamed ceiling, and the paneled fireplace. The latter has terra-cotta art tiles, some embossed with "Ter Ar DVM Prosim," which is translated as "May I be worn out provided I do good."

The Jacobs House is located slightly below street level at its Thorburn Street entrance elevation. On the south elevation, a driveway, which is entered through rusticated piers in the stone property wall, descends to the garage below. Mature trees now complement the house, but the views to the city beyond off the back terrace are still a feature of the house and property.

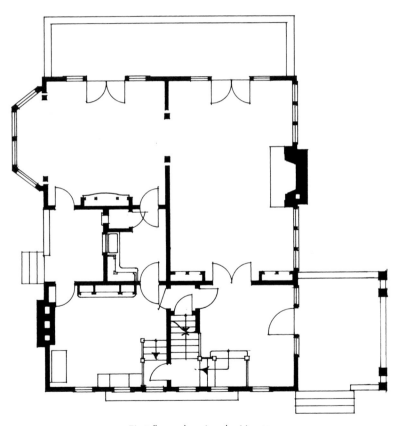

First floor plan, Jacobs House.

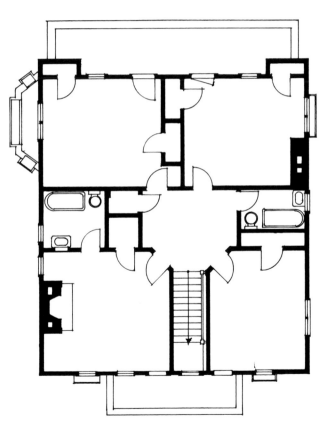

Second floor plan, Jacobs House.

Wilbur Reid (1914)
Francis Brown

Celebrated for years as the pre-eminent example of the Bungalow style in Portland, the Wilbur Reid House at 4775 SE Stark Street remains unsurpassed. The expansive house encompasses all the varied characteristics of the style, more so than any other house in the city. While its central gable fronts on Stark Street, other extensions, wings, porches, porte-cocheres, and dormers add a multitude of gabled layers, making the house seemingly hover over the property. A mighty roof-supporting truss, weathered with age, spans the entire front porch and is used as a monumental trellis for an ancient wisteria. The multi-column posts supporting the truss rest on river-rock piers and balustrade; unpainted shingles, beams, and bargeboards and a brick chimney comprise the other materials. Detailing of the wood structure carefully articulates the beams, rafter tails, and joinery, apparently without metal connections, much as in a Japanese temple. The designer of this handsome composition was California architect Francis Brown, reportedly once associated with Greene and Greene Architects.

E. J. Ellison (1914)

A mid-sized Bungalow with sophisticated features is the house at 1803 NE Thompson Street. Built for E. J. Ellison in 1914, the house offers the delightful complexities of interwoven architectural forms, which contribute to the hovering effect, primarily the telescoping facade and porch

Wilbur Reid House.

E. J. Ellison House.

gables. These particular characteristics give the house much of the effect of Japanese temple architecture, despite the truncated porch columns and heavily bracketed eaves, which are definitely not Japanese in nature, but which link it to Bungalow style designs. A house like this cost $8,500 in 1914, a goodly price at the time, but an astoundingly modest amount compared to today's prices for a typical-sized story-and-a-half home. What is amazing is the quality that was incorporated in the house: large covered porches with balustrades, a fireplace, banked casement windows, rafter extensions, quality shingle siding, a glassed-in trellised bay, and beautiful interior amenities. Despite the house's considerable architectural integrity, only the contractor, W. S. Macmeeken, is recorded on the building permit.

C. S. Jackson House.

C. S. Jackson (c. 1915)
Johnson and Mayer (attributed)

Once an idyllic summer retreat, the properties along the banks of the Clackamas River house a rich supply of residential architecture. In the years before the Depression and the Second World War, the river properties offered a rural, yet convenient, location for wealthy Portland families to spend the summer months. C. S. Jackson, founder and owner of the *Oregon Journal*, was one such Portlander. His retreat, located at 14999 Springwater Road in Carver, Oregon, was constructed of logs, especially appropriate for rustic, casual relaxation. It was not casually conceived, however. Its considerable Bungalow style design clearly demonstrates Jackson's sophisticated taste in architecture. Deceptively simple in general layout, the house has the well-proportioned low-hipped, gable-ended roof, with shed dormer, and the front porch, with rough-hewn log posts, that are well within the classic Bungalow idiom. Additional

stylistic features include the banks of paned casement windows and the Swiss-type balcony under the gable eaves at the second floor. Its handling suggests that Johnson and Mayer may have been the architects of the house, a firm noted for its Swiss-influenced Bungalow designs.

William H. Hossack (1916)
A. R. Hossack (attributed)

Several excellent designs were created with the theme of two gable-fronted wings flanking an entrance pergola or covered porch. The William H. Hossack House of 1916 at 5701 SE Yamhill Street is one of the most successful in applying this design approach, primarily because of the excellent proportions of its front elevation. Low-pitched, bracketed

William H. Hossack House.

roofs create a most welcoming facade, and the typical shed dormer for cozy second floor bedrooms is located between the two wings. Triangular brackets support the greatly extended bargeboard; this method had become popular during the 1910s and was in competition with beam extensions as the preferred means to support the wide eaves. Rafter tails were nearly universal, and they often had some decoration at their exposed ends. Bungalow features of the Hossack House extend to the casement windows, some of which have cross panes, which by this time were found frequently in the city. Trim and body colors appear to be original on the house. Brown shingles above and cream siding below, all outlined with white trim, was often seen in the Craftsman design books as exemplary colors for the proper Bungalow.

Bungalow "A" (1916)

In many ways typical, but clearly a notch above, the small Bungalow house at 1402 SE Reynolds Street is representative of the thousands of small, single-story houses constructed throughout the city in the second decade of the century. While modest in size, the house has considerable character. Low-sloped, gable-ended roofs form an interesting architectural composition, with both telescoping and perpendicular gables. Two solid-looking boxed columns, without flare, support the bracketed roof at the entrance portico. This feature came to define the vast majority of Bungalow style houses, and it appeared in countless variations. In this house, the columns sit squarely on a low, shingled balustrade, four steps

Bungalow "A" House.

above grade. The porch extends across the facade, repeating the shingles on the piers and with slat railings in between. A picture window, with sidelights, is the feature of the living room, as is the brick fireplace. Beyond is a dining room. The home's convenient plan offered practical living with comfortable Bungalow features. This clearly was a workingman's residence with considerable style and charm.

H. E. Schegel (c. 1916)
F. G. Quimby

The term "cottage" would be appropriate for the small, single-story house at 5537 NE Atlantic Avenue in North Portland. Though modest in width, being a single room wide, the house is well designed and has all the charm and appeal for which the Bungalow style is famous. Its front elevation consists of simply a central door flanked by multiple sets of transomed windows and a very fine low-pitched, gable-roofed central porch. Two tapered porch piers, often described as truncated obelisks or elephantine, support the beamed and bracketed porch roof. They are flared at the ground, as is the water-table at the bottom course of shingles covering the house. Shingle coursings alternate wide and narrow to give a more horizontal appearance. The walls are well protected by the wide side gables, which extend the same width as the porch gable, and

which are also supported with brackets or triangular knee braces. The careful composition, designed by F. G. Quimby, is enhanced by the use of white trim. With shingles painted a dark gray and the window sashes painted black, the house comes close to the quintessential appearance of the Portland Bungalow.

H. E. Schegel House.

CHAPTER 18

Craftsman

In national as well as local architectural histories, one style has been largely overlooked. The Craftsman style, not easily correlated with historical references, is a distinctively American style. Common to all Craftsman houses, particularly in Portland, was a moderately to steeply pitched roof with extensive eave projections. They rested on their structures much like a giant cap. The roofs were hipped or gabled, often supported by extensive brackets, modillions, or extended beams, sometimes revealing roof-rafter extensions, bargeboards, and dormers. In the J. S. Bradley House of 1906, the gabled roof has wrap-around eaves, which add to the illusion that the house is roofed by a giant cap. If no brackets or modillions were used, the underside of the extended eaves had applied siding, usually smooth tongue-and-groove boards. Both the Wells (1910) and Mills (c. 1911) houses display this more tailored eave design. Dormers represent another roof feature prominent in the design of the Craftsman house. Many dormers had roofs to match those of the main house, and others were partly recessed in the main roof slope, as in the John E. Wheeler House of 1907. Some dormers, such as on the Mills House, had small balconies.

Portland, overlooking Portland Heights, circa 1910.

The wrap-around porch was another trait typical of the Craftsman style house. The porches, generally a half-dozen steps above grade, were open terraces at the main floor level and covered only at the house's entrance, though in some the roofs extended over the entire wrap-around porch. If the terraces were of masonry construction, the railings often had pierced-brick patterns, capped by a cast-concrete rail. If they were of wood construction, the railings had open balustrades, with decorated open work, or large-scale vertical balusters. Most often these railings were combined with more solid-appearing corner piers constructed of masonry or shingled. These piers commonly supported the porch roof posts, helping to integrate all the elements. In some cases, the railings were covered entirely with shingles. Whatever the design, nearly all railings on Craftsman homes were designed purposely low, at approximately two feet above the terraces (today's railing must be three feet high). They were believed to be perfectly safe, and by and large they were. But they were also wider and much more substantial in appearance, clearly meant to be in scale with the houses. The crawl spaces under the terraces had shingled or brick skirts, or enclosures, with much the sculptural effect of a masonry terrace with walls. Whether front, side, or wrap-around, porches were an important part of the social life of the family. They not only provided a gracious tie to the garden level of the house, but they also accommodated social intercourse with neighbors during the warm-weather months, serving as predecessors to the back terrace, deck, or patio of later years.

The uniqueness of the Craftsman style was that it often freed itself completely of any other influences, including historical ones. Craftsman houses were not simply two-story bungalows, as their whole emphasis was more square-like and two-story, hence the term "four-square"

that is attached to some examples of this style. While they often had shingle siding, they did not have the clipped eave of the Shingle style, and hardly ever did they have the rounded bays and extensions exhibited by that style. The Craftsman style does have some possible design influences, however. The wrap-around eave, such as that in the Bradley House, was found in Japanese homes, tea houses, and temples. Japanese influences were very fashionable during this period. Fine quality Japanese prints were available in Portland in the early twentieth century, showing temples with similar roofs, and architectural publications often referred to the architecture of the Orient. Architect Edward Root designed entrance porches for his houses—such as the Stolte House of

William J. Hawkins House at 1827 SW Myrtle Street, Portland, 1910, designed by Richard Martin.

1910—that strongly suggest the beamed architecture of the Japanese Shinto shrines. Other houses had decidedly different influences. The basic Craftsman two-story house sometimes had suggestions of medieval influence, such as in the false half-timbering work in the gable ends; the Ainsworth House of 1907 reflects such medieval precedents. Likewise, the Schnabel House, also 1907, has half-timbering as well as extensive bargeboards, although its particular interpretation is far from true Tudor design. The extended gable ends of the Hahn House (1905) feature a more exact rendition of false half-timbering, and they even cantilever out in Tudor fashion over the bay windows beneath them. Cantilevers are very much a part of the Craftsman style, whether in gabled ends, second floor projections, or bay windows.

In other Craftsman houses, there is a distinct suggestion of influence from the Swiss chalet. For example, the massive Wheeler House has the arched bargeboards, with pointed tops, found in Bernese middle-land farmhouses. Other Swiss-influenced houses in Portland built during the same era had low-pitched roofs, still with widely extended eaves, supported with Swiss style brackets. Some of these were very authentic, despite the addition of locally available windows. Presumably, the style was thought eminently practical for Oregon's climate, particularly with the wide eaves.

Most of the families who owned the larger Craftsman homes purchased automobiles during this era and learned for the first time how to drive them. This adventurous spirit, open to new ideas and ways of living, translated to their residences. The Craftsman house, despite its competition with Colonial Revival, Tudor, and Bungalow styles, seemed best to exemplify the vitality and expansion of the city up until the advent of the First World War.

In plan, the Craftsman house was practical. The larger residences invariably had spacious central entrance halls, off of which were the major rooms—living and dining rooms, library, or music room—entered through wide sliding doors. Stairs were a feature of the entrance halls, almost always with multiple landings to break up their length, making the stair safer and easier to climb, as well as more interesting to experience. Landings were a favorite place to display large art-glass windows, or perhaps a built-in bench. Such landings, where the stair turned back around an opening, prevented visitors from viewing the upper floor hall and adjacent bedrooms from the first floor entrance hall. Even in the smaller homes, a fine stair was a prevalent feature, and they too had decorated stained-glass windows. In most of the houses, the woodwork was extensive and stained dark. Beautiful woods with perfect graining were selected and profusely displayed. Dining rooms had exotic woods, such as Oregon myrtle wood, now all but vanished from the market. Parlors, dining rooms, or libraries often were paneled in mahogany, with high wainscoting and picture rails, as in the Wells House (1910), or the woodwork was painted, as in the living room of the Ransom House (1908). Woodwork continued at the ceilings with beams, false or otherwise. Floors, constructed of polished oak, were often designed with inset perimeter patterns to surround the ubiquitous Oriental rugs. Fireplaces commonly had art tiles in earth colors, soft dark greens, mauves, or beiges.

Japanese tea-house.

Hall of the Butchers' Guild, Hereford, England.

Bernese middle-land farmhouse, Emmental, Switzerland.

Portland enjoyed a wide variety of Craftsman style houses in nearly every neighborhood under development during the first decade of the new century. Laurelhurst, Irvington, Eastmoreland, Willamette Heights, Westover Terraces, Portland Heights, Mount Tabor, and Ladd's Addition all have an abundance of Craftsman style houses. The finest ones were designed by noted architects such as Emil Schacht, William Knighton, Edward Root, Josef Jacobberger, Edgar Lazarus, and Bennes, Hendricks and Thompson. In addition, many houses with Craftsman influences were designed by lesser architects, and the vast remainder, usually the smaller homes, were probably built from standard plans available in contractors' offices, much as most new houses are designed today, where the cohesion and appearance of finer architectural design are neither desired nor paramount.

"House with court, pergolas, outdoor living rooms and sleeping balconies," from *The Craftsman*, January 1909.

Craftsman
CHARACTERISTICS

PLANS: asymmetrical, two-story houses; free-flowing interior spaces, tied to the exterior with wide and deep first floor balustraded terraces; cantilevered at second floor.

ROOFS: moderately to steeply pitched side gables, with multiple perpendicular extensions; widely extended eaves, sometimes supported with modillions, beam extensions, or brackets; gabled dormers or connecting double gables. Shingled.

EXTERIOR FINISHES: shingle, stucco, or stone; stone or brick foundations. Sometimes shingled skirts for porches, resembling masonry in scale, canted or with flared shingle courses at bottom of skirt.

CHIMNEYS: brick or stone facings; modest corbeled tops; exterior or interior locations.

WINDOWS: asymmetrically placed double-hung windows with mullions in upper sash, or casements in series (ribbon windows); picture windows in main rooms, single or multiple windows with transoms. Rectangular or polygonal cantilevered bays.

WINDOW TRIM (exterior): modest casings within shingle siding, or plain wide board casings. Window boxes sometimes at upper windows.

ENTRANCE DOORS: wide, single glass doors, with sidelights; often under gabled portico.

VERANDAS/PORCHES: extended gable-ended roofs, or balustraded flat roofs; heavy brick or shingle supports, or multiple square columns.

INTERIOR FINISHES: plaster walls and ceilings, with extensive varnished wood trim; paneled wainscoting with wallpaper above plate rail. Polished wood floors.

INTERIOR TRIM: wood cornices, window and door trim, and baseboards; wide plain casings with entablatures. Classical details mixed with Craftsman. Painted woodwork in parlor.

STAIRS: multiple landings, with semicircular openings to second floor. Wood risers and treads; paneled walls.

FIREPLACE FRONTS: art-tile surrounds, plain wood mantels and side trim. Craftsman or Classical details.

6"

9 ¼"

Entrance to the Sarah Rosenblatt House of 1915,
located on SW Twenty-first Avenue
in Portland Heights.

Craftsman
HOUSES

1895	C. A. Landenberger	1909	Amedee M. Smith (William C. Knighton)
1905	Henry Hahn (Emil Schacht)		
1906	Gustav Freiwald	1910	William Biddle Wells (John Virginius Bennes)
1906	J. S. Bradley		
1907	Belle and Maude Ainsworth (William C. Knighton)	1910	Dwight Edwards (attributed to William C. Knighton)
1907	Charles J. Schnabel (William C. Knighton)	1910	Dr. A. M. Stolte (Edward T. Root)
1907	John E. Wheeler	c. 1910	George H. Howell (Josef Jacobberger)
1908	Frank H. Ransom (Josef Jacobberger)	c. 1911	Emerson L. Mills
1909	W. F. Donahae		

C. A. Landenberger (1895)

While the Queen Anne and Eastlake styles were being eclipsed, and while the new Shingle and Colonial Revival styles were emerging, there appeared another entirely new stylistic direction in Portland, generally described as Craftsman. The architects who ventured into the new style sometimes added elements from the other current styles, but they veered eventually to a new, commonly shared set of architectural principles. One of the first houses in the city to clearly speak for the new direction was built for C. A. Landenberger at 1805 NW Glisan Street. Though the Landenberger House maintained relatively simple roof forms, the dynamic projection of the house's eaves and the continuation

Parlor, Landenberger House.

C. A. Landenberger House.

Dining room, Landenberger House.

of the main roof slope down over the entrance porch were unusual traits. These and other characteristics led to the Bungalow style, of which the Craftsman style is generally considered the two-story version. The early period of the Craftsman style had the stone foundations, shingle siding (without corner boards), telescoping roofs, and some transomed windows. The interiors of the Landenberger House, however, were handsomely Colonial Revival, with some of the finest detail in the city.

Henry Hahn (1905)
Emil Schacht

Architect Emil Schacht was one who experimented with the emerging Craftsman style. In his Henry Hahn House at 2636 NW Cornell Road, on Westover Terraces, Schacht combined Tudor style projecting twin gables with a central entrance and roofed entrance porch. The gable pediments cantilever out over two-story bays, one polygonal and the other round, much as appeared in some Queen Anne style houses. In this facade, however, the general proportions are much broader and more square. The proportions of the windows, either one-over-one (1/1) double-hung or transomed casements, add to the square-like forms. The entrance porch, which features groups of three columns over broad shingled piers and a low-pitched hipped roof, is also particularly squared. Craftsman brackets support the porch beams, which in turn support exposed rafter tails. The massive porch, with shingled sides to grade, projects across the facade, and the entrance is to the left. A pergola extends off the dining room on the south elevation. Inside, symmetry reigns; the large living room is on the north side of the entry hall and the dining room and kitchen are to the south. Craftsman and Colonial Revival details complement the interior.

Henry Hahn House.

Gustav Freiwald (1906)

As the Craftsman style gathered momentum, several houses designed in the early period do not fit conveniently as examples of a particular style. One of the most interesting is the Gustav Freiwald House at 1810 NE Fifteenth Avenue. At first glance, the house could be of the Queen Anne style, particularly with its corner polygonal three-story turret and wraparound covered porch. However, if roofs are the determining factor, then the house would be more of the Craftsman style. The turret roof, mod-

Gustav Freiwald House.

J. S. Bradley (1906)

By 1906, the new Craftsman style had been considerably codified, at least to the point where roofs would invariably be caps or lids over more horizontally or squarely proportioned two-story houses. Actually, a new style had been born, remarkably original in concept and very American. It competed vigorously with Colonial and Arts and Crafts style houses for some years, but then yielded as the more popular styles tended to dominate. In the J. S. Bradley House of 1906, located at 2111 SW Vista Avenue, the lid-cap roof style is clearly evident in the widely extended eave that wraps around at the gables. The massive roof dominates the house, extending out over polygonal and rectangular bays, and has a

J. S. Bradley House.

erately pitched with wide overhangs, the gabled dormers with porches at the attic level, and the main hipped roof speak much more to the coming fashion than to one that had been quietly eclipsed some fifteen years earlier. The Freiwald House has the more square proportions, the wider windows, and the curved eave of the Craftsman period, despite the addition of Colonial Revival detailing at porch columns, corner pilasters, and pediments. The present owners have completely refurbished the house, restoring it inside and out to near-original configuration. The restored dining room with coffered ceiling is particularly handsome.

distinctive horizontal aspect. This repeats in the low-sloped porch roof that stretches across the facade. Paired and grouped heavy posts on wide brick piers support the porch roof, and a low open balustrade runs between the piers. Main room windows are wide and transomed at the first and second floors; others are double-hung with 9/1 panes. A large gabled dormer, with the same wrap-around eave as the main roof, balances with the off-center front gable.

Belle and Maude Ainsworth (1907)
William C. Knighton

A premier house of the Craftsman style is the large residence designed in 1907 by William C. Knighton for Misses Belle and Maude Ainsworth, the daughters of John C. Ainsworth and granddaughters of Captain J. C. Ainsworth. Knighton ingeniously combined a central-hall plan with asymmetrical elevations. Basically, he designed telescoping front gables projecting from a side-gabled roof, with further wings for the kitchen and a polygonal "summer dining room." A semicircular sewing room with a semiconical roof sits over the rectangular kitchen wing. Other projections include the gable-roofed dormers, one of which is combined with a polygonal cantilevered bay on the front elevation. Originally, the massive gables had false-timber work supporting the bargeboard, but this was removed and replaced with triangular knee braces when the house was later remodeled by architects Root and Kerr. At that time, additional brick facing was added at the main floor, sleeping porches were filled in, and various windows were altered. The interior is just as beautifully conceived as the exterior, combining Classical details at the fireplace and stairway with Craftsman beamed ceilings and a built-in buffet. The house is located at 2542 SW Hillcrest Drive.

Belle and Maude Ainsworth House.

Charles J. Schnabel (1907)
William C. Knighton

A more typical William C. Knighton house is the handsome one he designed for Charles J. Schnabel at 2375 SW Park Place in 1907. The two-and-a-half-story house sits on a 50-by-100-foot lot in the heart of the King's Hill neighborhood. Despite the narrowness of the property, Knighton managed to provide a spacious and attractive plan with beautifully proportioned elevations. Basically, the house has a side-gabled roof and a gabled front projection just to the right, or east, of the entrance. This element, in turn, is balanced by the gable-roofed dormer and brick entry porch, now covered and enclosed with many windows. The first floor of the side projection now has a polygonal bay with windows to match those of the enclosed porch. Knighton's signature emblem is at the upper gable center, on the lower beam of the false half-timbering.

A convenient plan graces the interior. The spacious central entrance hall features an open stair and, at the landing, windows designed by the renowned Portland firm of Povey Brothers. The parlor and dining room are to the left of the hall, and the library and stair are to the right. In the back northeast corner is the kitchen.

John E. Wheeler (1907)

The dynamic Craftsman style house at 2410 SW Seventeenth Avenue on Portland Heights demonstrates the considerable originality and inventiveness possible within the style. The arched bargeboards, with pointed top, may be an interpretation of Swiss-chalet influences, particularly in light of the deep second floor porches and the railings. Or, perhaps, the house exhibits a latent influence from the Queen Anne style bargeboards of the early 1880s, such as that on the Senator Joseph Dolph House of 1891. In any case, the greatly extended eaves and the balconies contained within the arches are new interpretations in which the roof is the most at-

Charles J. Schnabel House.

John E. Wheeler House.

tractive element, and which can be viewed as a lid or cap on the structure. Many roof experiments were undertaken at this time, but they were not always as successful as the one on the Wheeler House. Other typical features include the shingle siding, the combination of multiple transomed windows, the cantilevered polygonal bay with large picture windows, and the porches off the major rooms. A large porch, now covered, remains on the north elevation, but the original porch on the west, or entrance, elevation has been removed.

Frank H. Ransom House.

Frank H. Ransom (1908)
Josef Jacobberger

In an inventive period of architectural design, Josef Jacobberger searched for new yet appropriate forms. Though not representative of Craftsman or Arts and Crafts styles, the Frank H. Ransom House at 2331 SW Madison Street on King's Hill expresses the solid, well-built architecture of the times. Its symmetrical and well-tailored design, lacking Craftsman beams or brackets, has a certain formal quality, appropriate to the neighborhood. Notable on the front facade are the symmetrical cantilevered second floor projections on either side of the entrance, each with a hipped roof extending out from the main hipped roof. Each projection extends over a three-window bay, which have transom windows. Symmetrically placed hipped-roof dormers reflect the same roof curve at the eave. While the attic balustrade has Tudor quatrefoil designs, the entrance porch is solidly Craftsman. Large brick piers support the low-hipped roof, with a somewhat Tudor styled bracket supporting the porch lintel. A photograph of the original interior shows Colonial detailing at the fireplace, as well as Craftsman built-in seating and bookcases.

Living room, Ransom House.

W. F. Donahae (1909)

Another unusual house outside of the architectural mainstream is the W. F. Donahae House at 5125 NE Garfield Street, built in 1909. Its massive side-gabled roof, with intersecting facade dormer and turret, bespeaks the Craftsman designs as practiced by architect Edgar Lazarus, or William Knighton, particularly in the curved treatment of the bargeboard ends. Identifying an architect would only be speculative, but whomever it was, he must have been interested in the products of the new Portland Miracle Dressed Stone Company, as the house is a stellar example of construction in that material, with its stone-like appearance. Lintels

W. F. Donahae House.

are also cast-stone with smooth dressing, as are the Ionic-design porch posts and balustrade of the wrap-around terraces. The cast-stone was used in a variety of houses around the city and in numerous small commercial buildings. Although it never became as popular as brick, and eventually was surpassed as a building material, the cast-stone material offered a durability that is amply demonstrated in the Donahae House. The house is well designed with Craftsman proportions, despite the presence of a decade-late Richardsonian-type tower.

Amedee M. Smith (1909)
William C. Knighton

One of the finest Craftsman style residences in the city is the large two-and-a-half-story Amedee M. Smith House at 10101 SW Riverside Drive, designed by William C. Knighton in 1909. Commanding an expansive property, the house is surrounded by brick walls and overlooks the Willamette River. It is approached by a winding drive to the crest of the property, where the house is located, entering a large porte-cochere that provides access to the front terraces and entrance hall. Garages, undoubtedly for a chauffeur, are located at the back of the property and exited to the side street. The house has all the elements of mature Craftsman designs: widely extended gable eaves; brackets supporting the bargeboard at the gabled entrance porch, the dormers, and the porte-cochere; cantilevered second floor bays beneath the main facade gable; expansive wrap-around terraces with pierced-board balustrades; and a side pergola. The house has a central stair hall, with living room to the left and dining room to the right. It was considered an outstanding country estate and appeared upon completion in the 1909 *Portland Architectural Club* publication.

Amedee M. Smith House.

William Biddle Wells House.

William Biddle Wells (1910)
John Virginius Bennes

Constructed at the peak of the period, the William Biddle Wells residence of 1910 represents the best of the Craftsman style of architecture in Portland. The house's architect was John Virginius Bennes, of the firm Bennes, Hendricks and Thompson. While also developing his abilities with the Prairie style, Bennes was clearly a master of the Craftsman style. The massive-appearing, beautifully proportioned house is located at 1515 SW Clifton Street, a Portland Heights site with panoramic views north and east to the city below and the distant mountains. The house sits high on its bank, the result of the cutting of the crest of the hill be-

tween Fifteenth and Sixteenth avenues to accommodate the construction of Clifton Street. No garage was provided with the house, until a later time, as a public trolley system was only blocks away, and many businessmen walked to and from work on Sixteenth Avenue, which descends directly to the city center.

The architect managed to create a design with considerable simplicity yet providing visual interest. A gabled extension, with open balcony above it (now enclosed), projects forward on the south-facing front elevation of the house. Across the entire facade is a balustraded open porch. The gable-roofed, brick-piered entrance porch is slightly off center, but it is carefully balanced with the long expanse of the side-gabled main roof and the two gabled dormers. An arched brick loggia, with balustraded flat roof, wraps around the back on the northeast corner of the house. Shingles are used as siding on the second floor exterior, while fine brickwork of varying dark hue and raked joints are at the first floor.

Bennes employed a central-hall plan with great inventiveness. Entered through a vestibule under the stair landing, the hall is dominated by the stair descending from the left. The music room opens to the right, offering eastern views on axis through a rounded bay window. To the left of the entrance hall, the dining room is projected forward of the entrance doors to capture the magnificent view. The dining room has fine woodwork and a beamed ceiling, and a fireplace backed to the kitchen. The library and living room share a fireplace chimney with the music room. Banked casement windows with art-glass panes look west and south. The kitchen, pantries, and service stair are located to the rear of the dining room.

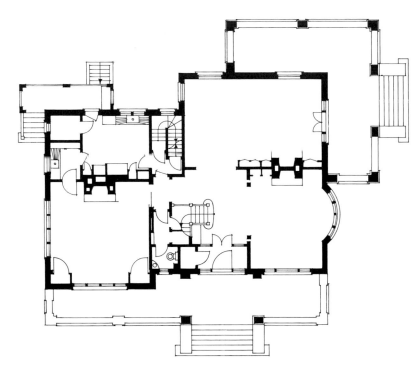

First floor plan, Wells House.

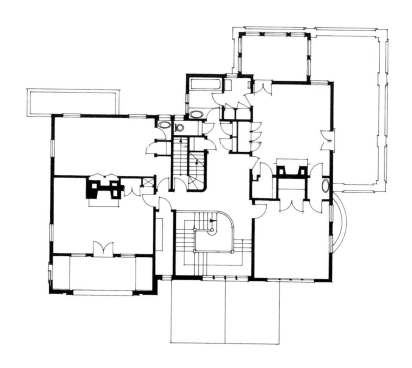

Second floor plan, Wells House.

Dwight Edwards (1910)
William C. Knighton (attributed)

The shingled volumes of the Craftsman houses took many forms, as architects were always experimenting with the endless variety of new roof forms. The Dwight Edwards House of 1910, the design of which is attributed to William C. Knighton, introduced a side-entrance plan, primarily to provide a central entrance that allowed the living room to be located on the view side of the house in the rear. The stair is located to the front of the entrance doors, with windows staggered up following along the stair rise. To accomplish this unusual plan and also create an attractive street facade, the architect introduced intersecting double gables over a front extension of the house, the roof of which continues

Dwight Edwards House.

the slope of the side-gabled main roof. The eaves are widely projected and supported with beam extensions, a decorative feature of the design. Shingles cover the house and originally the roof, making the entire house somewhat rustic in appearance, especially when left to weather a dark brown. White trim was the only accent, used on the windows, bargeboards, and rafter tails. The house remains today much as constructed, with painted shingles and traditional white trim. It is located at 1153 NW Thurman Street on Willamette Heights.

Dr. A. M. Stolte (1910)
Edward T. Root

After the first decade of the twentieth century, the Craftsman style was gradually replaced by the Arts and Crafts style, which slowly reduced the widely extended Craftsman eaves, eventually eliminating them altogether. One of the last of the fine houses in the full-bloom of Craftsman detailing is the Dr. A. M. Stolte House of 1910 at 1214 SE Sixtieth Avenue, located on a large lot with a sweeping driveway in the Mount Tabor neighborhood. Its architect was Edward T. Root, eminent practitioner of Craftsman and Bungalow style houses. His Stolte House has a symmetrical plan, complete with an all-but-symmetrical front elevation. The two second floor shingled projections are especially notable, one extended slightly farther than the other and both with gabled roofs intersecting the main side-gabled roof. Other details include the exposed rafter tails, definitive bargeboards, and brick-sided first floor walls. Typical of these designs is the gabled entrance porch, the eave of which is supported by beam extensions, and the beams are carried in turn by side clusters of three columns on brick pier bases. The low brick balustrades continue at the open side porches and the entrance stairs.

Dr. A. M. Stolte House.

George H. Howell (c. 1910)
Josef Jacobberger

In the residential areas of the northwest part of the city, among the lavishly decorated Queen Anne style houses, Craftsman houses filled vacant properties well into the first and second decades of the century. The George H. Howell House at 2637 NW Kearney Street fills its small city lot, and it offers considerable amenities. Architect Josef Jacobberger designed a straightforward side-gabled house, but he added angled corner windows looking back toward the city, a fine entrance porch, widely extended eaves showing rafter tails, and two fine attic dormer windows. The porch, now missing its central stair and side extension, is topped by a flat roof and a deck, which is surrounded with a somewhat Colonial style railing between shingled Craftsman style piers. Scroll brackets support the roof eave and porch beam. The entire house was shingled, attaining a rich, dark weathered appearance until it was subsequently painted. Inside, only the entrance hall and living room are on the Kearney Street elevation. A fireplace occupies the east wall of the living room, between the corner bay and the high windows. Toward the back, a polygonal bay with shed roof is a feature of the dining room.

George H. Howell House.

Emerson L. Mills (c. 1911)

With a plan all-but-identical to that of the Howell House, the Emerson L. Mills House at 7107 SE Seventeenth Avenue in Sellwood has a lot sufficiently large to allow for a garage behind the house. Cars were accommodated wherever possible, but the garage structure was not always attached to or part of the house architecture. To gain some variety in the front elevation, the architect of the Mills House introduced a cantilevered gable extension. Similarly, the dining room bay on the north elevation cantilevers out and has a small balcony above it. As in the Knighton-designed Schnabel House (1907), the balance of the facade was accomplished by adding a gabled dormer with balcony at the third floor and a gabled entry porch. Very stylish Craftsman truncated-obelisk piers support the porch roof. None of the roofs has expressed rafter tails or beam extensions. Instead, soffits are tailored with smooth siding. The shingled house appears today much as it did when constructed, in both its details and coloring. It is missing the front side-porch with turned balustrades and flared shingle skirting, which often were the victims of untreated wood or unventilated crawl spaces.

Emerson L. Mills House.

CHAPTER 19

Craftsman/Colonial

Scattered around Portland, a number of houses were built during the first two decades of the twentieth century in a style that could be ascribed to Craftsman/Colonial, a mixture of stylistic elements coming from the Craftsman tradition but having distinctive Colonial detailing. The meld had been developing in various forms since the 1880s, and the houses designed with this mixture of styles were contemporaneous with the large number of houses being constructed in each of the Craftsman and Colonial styles.

The distinguishing characteristics of these houses center on the roof forms and other details. Craftsman style roofs, with steep gables, are in evidence, but missing are the wide eave overhangs. The Craftsman fondness for porches continues in this style category, although nearly all the Craftsman/Colonial style porches are contained within the main roof and mass of the house. In extended porches, such as that on the Harmon House of 1908, roof coverings are designed as arbors, with posts, beams, and purlins supporting a flat roof. Columns, however, are decidedly Classical in design, usually of a nonfluted Doric, almost Tuscan, style. In addition,

"Proposed $125,000 Improvement of Vista Avenue on Portland Heights, Prepared by Olmstead Brothers."

the Craftsman style's love of masonry, either ashlar-bond stone or brick, is found in the chimneys, the main floor exterior walls, or the porch corner columns—this is seen particularly in the F. E. Bowman House of 1915.

Many other Colonial style details are included in the Craftsman/Colonial houses. Besides the columns of Classical inspiration, balustrades are sometimes designed with turned balusters in the celebrated urn pattern. Other railings are more inventive, almost lattice-like, while in some houses railings are not used at all. The favored window forms are double-hung, invariably with panes in the upper sash only, or banks of casement windows. It is not surprising to find Colonial shutters at some of the double-hung windows. Most dormers are of the shed-roof variety, with either banks of casements or double-hung windows. Some dormers come directly from the Colonial Revival tradition: pedimented dormers joined by shed-roof infilling between.

As with the more purely Craftsman forms, the Craftsman/Colonial style has as a prominent characteristic a variety of roof types. In the earlier phase of the Craftsman/Colonial style, the large, steeply pitched, side-gabled roof mass displayed elements of the Shingle style, particularly when combined with a large Palladian opening. The architects McKim, Mead and White used a Palladian window in a large, triangular-gabled dormer as early as 1879 in the Casino at Newport, Rhode Island. Later, many Shingle style architects employed similar concepts in their gable designs. New York architect Bruce Price used a Palladian window with diagonally paned sashes in his Chandler House (1885–86) in Tuxedo Park, New York. The celebrated Frank Lloyd Wright had a wider version in the design for his own home in Oak Park, Illinois, built in 1889, though one cannot imagine Wright giving credence to Andrea Palladio in his work. In Portland, the talented architect Justus Krumbein, designer of the Hochapfel

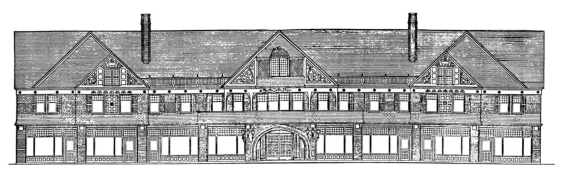

Street facade of the Newport Casino, Newport, Rhode Island, 1879–81, designed by McKim, Mead and White.

W. Chandler House, Tuxedo Park, New York, 1885–86, designed by Bruce Price.

Frank Lloyd Wright House, Oak Park, Illinois, 1889, designed by Frank Lloyd Wright.

Cyrus McCormick House, Richfield Springs, New York, 1881–82, designed by McKim, Mead and White.

House of 1907, was several years late in interpreting this style. Although Colonial Revival houses abounded with the Palladian motif, the Craftsman/Colonial houses used them more sparingly.

The gambrel has been an established roof form in this country since early Colonial times, used primarily by the Dutch settlers in an area centered around the Hudson River Valley, roughly from the middle of New York state south through New Jersey. It was not until about 1750, however, that Colonial Americans fully adopted the distinctive gambrel shape, with its steep sides and flattened upper slopes. Many of these houses had wide porches within the roof extensions, not at the gambrel gable ends. Such porch roofs had flared eaves, as is found later in the F. E. Bowman House in Portland. The gambrel roof continued in various forms throughout the nineteenth century, evolving into the Shingle style, especially in the New England summer resort towns. Architect John Calvin Stevens designed his own home (1883) and the James Hopkins Smith House (1885) with distinctive gambrel roofs in Portland, Maine, and Falmouth Foreside, Maine, respectively. An interesting house in Kennebunkport, Maine, the F. W. Sprague House, was designed by Henry Paston Clark and Ion Lewis in 1882, before the latter architect came to Portland in 1889 to form the renowned firm of Whidden and Lewis.

The return, or wrap-around, eave was used occasionally in Craftsman/Colonial houses, and it seems to have come out of the Shingle style. McKim, Mead and White, instigators of popular new styles, designed the Cyrus McCormick House (1881–82) in Richfield Springs, New York, just a few years before they designed the Portland Hotel. The McCormick House had an interesting return eave, as well as some almost Japanese-inspired rounded forms in the porch-support detailing. Hence, the firm may have been inspired by the then-fashionable taste for things Japanese. Japanese

John Calvin Stevens House, Portland, Maine, 1883, designed by John Calvin Stevens.

F. W. Sprague House, Kennebunkport, Maine, 1882, designed by Henry Paston Clark and Ion Lewis.

homes as well as temples often had return eaves at gable ends.

Portland's well-established architects employed these various elements of the Craftsman/Colonial style. At the end of an illustrious career, Justus Krumbein designed the Hochapfel House in 1907, the year he died. Emil Schacht was at the height of his career when he designed the Becker and Veness houses and many others similar in nature. Contractor F. E. Bowman designed a number of houses during this period, usually with very wide shed roofs over open, columned porches. Ellis Lawrence was also at the peak of his career when he designed the John L. Bowman House in 1916, which would be a fully Colonial Revival house were it not for the wrap-around eaves at the roof gables.

The Craftsman/Colonial houses in Portland combined two major design trends, seemingly finding comfort in elements of both styles. In the long tradition of roof forms in this country, contemporary trends were tied to those of our past—part of a long-evolving pattern, yet a step into the future.

Craftsman/Colonial
CHARACTERISTICS

PLANS: symmetrical; one-and-a-half stories. Free-flowing interior spaces, tied to the exterior with wide and deep first floor porches.

ROOFS: moderate to steeply pitched, with side gables and wrap-around rounded eaves; sometimes supported with modillions or beam extensions; wide shed, hipped, or combined gabled and shed-roofed dormers. Side-gabled gambrel roofs also used frequently. Shingled roofs.

EXTERIOR FINISHES: shingle siding, or stone at first floor and shingled at second; stone or brick foundations and chimneys.

CHIMNEYS: stone or brick construction, with simple chimney caps and terra-cotta flues expressed; exterior locations, usually at the gable ends, at the ridge line.

WINDOWS: symmetrically placed double-hung windows, with panes in the upper sash; some banked casements. Shuttered on many examples.

WINDOW TRIM (exterior): modest casings within shingle, stone, or brick siding.

ENTRANCE DOORS: wide doors with sidelights; small or glazed window in door.

VERANDAS/PORCHES: front extended; roofs supported by massive non-fluted Doric style columns, or by piers constructed of stone or shingle sided.

INTERIOR FINISHES: plaster walls and ceilings, with expansive varnished wood trim; paneled wainscoting with wallpaper above plate rail. Polished wood floors.

INTERIOR TRIM: wood cornices, window and door trim, and baseboards; wide plain casings with entablatures, or molded casings. Classical details mixed with Craftsman. Varnished wood in dining room, often painted in parlor.

STAIRS: multiple landings, with semicircular openings to second floor; wood risers and treads. Classical detailing in balusters and newels.

FIREPLACE FRONTS: Craftsman and Colonial style details; art-tile surrounds and hearths; Classical mantels and side trim.

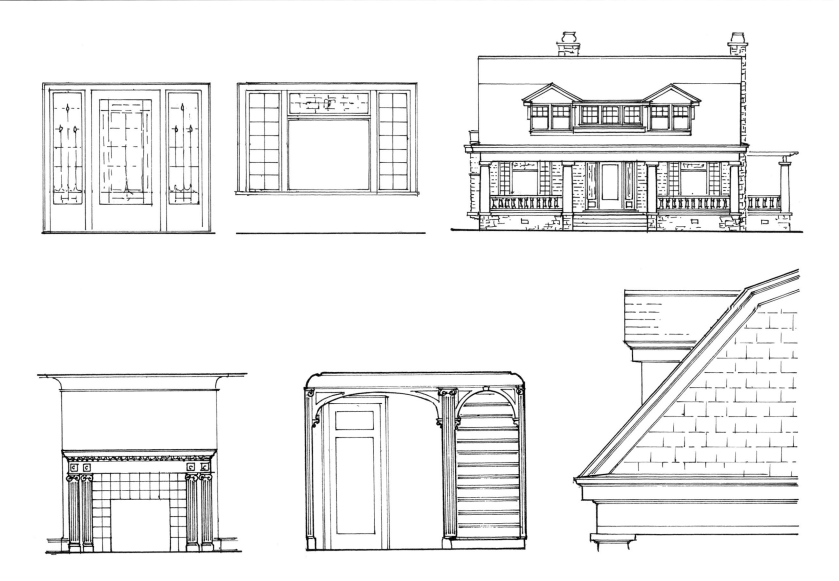

Entrance to the Edward L. Harmon House.

Craftsman/Colonial
HOUSES

1907   Edward C. Hochapfel (Justus F. Krumbein)

1908   Edward L. Harmon (Albert E. Doyle)

1909   Christine Becker (Emil Schacht)

1910   John A. Veness (Emil Schacht)

1915   F. E. Bowman

1916   John L. Bowman (Ellis F. Lawrence)

Edward C. Hochapfel (1907)
Justus F. Krumbein

In the first decade of the twentieth century, quite amazingly inventive approaches to residential architecture were attempted, combining various style elements, often with great success. One architect who felt no fear of changing tastes nor of invention was Justus F. Krumbein, a resident of the city of Portland since 1871. In 1907, after exercising his talents in Italianate, Romanesque, and Queen Anne style houses, he designed the one-and-a-half-story Hochapfel House with a completely original, high side-gabled roof. Still standing at 1520 SW Eleventh Avenue, though in dire need of repair, the handsome residence shows on the main floor

Architect's original drawing, front elevation, Hochapfel House.

Edward C. Hochapfel House.

Architect's original drawing, side elevation, Hochapfel House.

Krumbein's considerable skill in the practical use of space within a handsome form. Impressive is the narrow front facade, which has a dominating high roof that descends dramatically down over the veranda and wraps around the south-side elevation. A careful balance is achieved with the arched pediment of the entry portal and the large hipped-roof dormer above. The Classical detailing of the porch pediment and columns is continued on the north elevation, which boasts a dramatic second floor Palladian-arched porch. This unique house was Krumbein's last design.

Edward L. Harmon (1908)
Albert E. Doyle

With the symmetrical presentation of the Colonial Revival style and the details of the Craftsman style, the Edward L. Harmon House at 2642 NW Lovejoy Street is an excellent example of the handsome yet inventive architecture of the century's first decade. Architect Albert E. Doyle had just established his practice in the city—the beginning of a long and distinguished career—when he designed the house with the solid, wide proportions then in vogue. The segmental-arched and transomed windows, the solid porch columns, and the shed dormer were Craftsman elements, as is the wrap-around hip at the gable ends—an inventive, almost Japanese form that Doyle used in the famous Neahkahnie beach cottage of Harry Wentz, built in 1916 (see Chapter 23). Combined with

Edward L. Harmon House.

these details are the Classical brick quoins at the corners of the house, the flat modillions at the eaves, and the non-fluted Doric columns that support the covered entry pergola. And while the porch extension off the living room is a standard detail of the period, the crossed latticework of the railing is very unusual. The house has been well maintained, and a garage, originally not included, has been located discretely under the side porch.

Christine Becker (1909)
Emil Schacht

By 1909, the Colonial Revival in Portland was in full swing. One offshoot of the revival was the gambrel roof associated with Dutch Colonial architecture. When a Craftsman style porch was recessed under a side-facing gambrel roof, the marriage produced a unique and popular effect, repeated in numerous houses with considerable success. The handsome Craftsman/Colonial house at 1331 NW Twenty-fifth Avenue is a particularly distinguished example of this, a fine design by talented architect Emil Schacht. Schacht found that the gambrel form made for a practical roof on a smaller four-bedroom house, as it accommodated a second

Entrance hall, Becker House.

Christine Becker House.

Living room, Becker House.

floor without an expensive attic floor above. With so basic a form, the Christine Becker House gains considerable interest from its substantial non-fluted Doric porch columns and its dormer over the porch, which combines two gabled dormers with a shed-roofed infill. The handsome exterior as well as the interiors were featured in the September 1910 issue of *Northwest Architect*. The photographs show the arched openings and Ionic pilasters of the central entrance hall. Classical Revival details mix with Craftsman ones in the living and dining rooms.

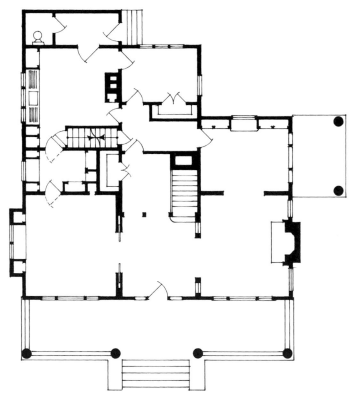

First floor plan, Becker House.

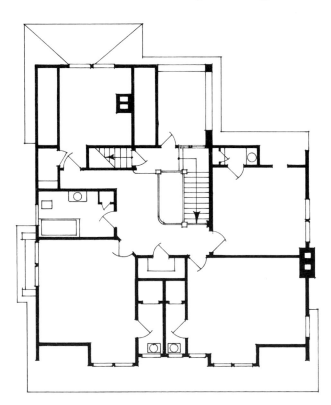

Second floor plan, Becker House.

John A. Veness (1910)
Emil Schacht

The houses of Emil Schacht were noted for their clarity of design: unified, simple statements, well conceived. The John A. Veness House located at 811 NW Twentieth Avenue exemplifies those qualities. The side-gabled central mass, with stone chimneys at either end of the roof ridge, is the base from which two matching gabled porticos extend at either side of the recessed entry porch. A wide shed-roofed dormer sits on the large expanse of the steep roof, and above that are recessed dormers, keeping the roof relatively simple. Schacht used the same wrap-around eave on the gabled side elevations as Doyle did on the Harmon House of 1908. This design function pulls the weight of this three-story house into a one-and-a-half-story appearance. Exaggerated non-fluted Doric columns support the extended porticos and the recessed porches at the front and back of the house. Plain shutters with cut-out designs originally adorned the side windows, and Colonial quarter-round attic windows flank the chimneys. In the back, a large wing extends at the northwest corner, the eave of which extends to the second floor line.

F. E. Bowman (1915)

The successful design concepts of the more prominent architects were often used by contractors who designed and built their own construction projects. F. E. Bowman and Company constructed numerous apartments and houses throughout the city, in addition to Bowman's own

John A. Veness House.

F. E. Bowman House.

home at 2732 NE Thompson Street. His house design incorporated architectural details used by Emil Schacht and others, including a side-gabled roof with stone chimneys at either end, massive non-fluted Doric columns across a recessed porch, and wide shed-roofed dormers. The house was constructed by Bowman in 1915 at a cost of $12,000. Clearly, that sum would procure for an owner a house of ample size as well as first-class construction. The Bowman House is finished with ashlar-bond tenino sandstone at the first floor and shingle siding at the second. To obtain the fashionable one-and-a-half-story appearance, the house has its gable designed as a large pediment, with the lower shingle courses flaring out over the beam extensions under the return cornice. These exposed beam ends are repeated in pairs over the front porch's stone corner piers and the massive columns between.

John L. Bowman (1916)
Ellis F. Lawrence

The larger homes that combined Craftsman and Colonial style details required a different approach than was used in the smaller homes. They became two-and-a-half stories in appearance, primarily because their greater depth would necessitate an overly high ridge line. Still, these houses had side-gabled roofs, with end chimneys, and expansive attic dormers across the front facade. The John L. Bowman House at 4719 NE Knott Street, designed in 1916 by the notable architect Ellis F. Lawrence, displays these features on a large structure. The wrap-around eaves at

the gable ends of the hipped roof combine effectively with the flat eave modillions and the Colonial Revival style louvered shutters at the double-hung windows. At the entrance portico, Lawrence used modified Roman Doric columns atop Craftsman style brick piers, an unusual mix of styles. The partial hipped roof of the porch actually contains a second floor balcony, shown with potted flowers in the early photograph. Inside, lavish woodwork prevails. Honduran mahogany is used throughout the main floor rooms in the carved moldings, coffered ceiling panels, and stair details. The dining room has oak wainscoting and a scenic fabric wallpaper above.

John L. Bowman House.

CHAPTER 20

Arts and Crafts

Of all the various styles of residential architecture in Portland during the period from 1850 to 1950, the Arts and Crafts style was the most prolific, spanning nearly the entire first half of the twentieth century. The first house in the city attributed to the style is the house Ellis Lawrence designed for his own family in the Irvington neighborhood. Stylistic influences in the house are varied, partly coming out of the preceding Craftsman style, but lacking its square, solid appearance. Extended eaves are carried over from the Craftsman, but they are only slightly extended, and some elements of false-timbering are added at the gable. The most notable difference is the Arts and Crafts style's more steeply pitched roof, descending at the sides to cover open porches. Some of these Arts and Crafts distinctions continued throughout the early period of the style, until the flush gable, first used by Josef Jacobberger in 1911 and then Wade Pipes in 1912, won acceptance. The flush gable dominated the Arts and Crafts period until the style's decline and ultimate replacement by the Northwest style in the 1950s.

Ida Catlin and Edwin T. Burke Houses on SW Hawthorne Terrace, Portland Heights.

The influences in the early Arts and Crafts period would all seem to trace back to England via the Philadelphia Exhibition of 1876, which had also profoundly influenced the development of the Queen Anne style. The Queen Anne style, and the British influences from the 1876 Exhibition, had become popular in Portland in the early 1880s and continued as late as 1890, as in the George H. Durham House. Heavy bargeboards reflected the early English precedents, such as Richard Norman Shaw's Leyswood (1868) in Sussex or Sir Edwin Lutyens's Crooksbury (1890). Both houses had considerable Tudor elements, particularly in their steep roofs, bargeboards, and prominent, articulated chimneys. Besides Shaw, other British pioneers in the Arts and Crafts movement were W. Eden Nes-field (1835–1888), George Devey (1820–1886), and Philip Webb (1831–1915). Webb's design for Red House of 1860, the home of William Morris in Kent, was considered highly influential.

After the home of Ellis Lawrence, several significant houses were designed in Portland during the early period of the Arts and Crafts style. Most notable was the work of Josef Jacobberger of the firm Jacobberger, Smith and Smith, one of the city's leading architects. Jacobberger's own home, built in 1906, has some of the same design treatments as Lawrence's home of that same year, mainly the use of false half-timbering in the steep gables. Jacobberger added, however, intersecting double gables on his front facade, an idea developed in England by Lutyens from earlier domestic examples. The asbestos shingle siding on the house also reflect Jacobberger's interest in Lutyens, appearing much like the slate shingles on Lutyens's early Crooksbury house. Lastly, the banks of casement windows and the wide-arched entrance portal all resemble Lutyens's work. Jacobberger continued his development of the Arts and Crafts style with the handsome Michael F. Brady House of 1911—which brought the first use of the clipped gable (that is, no bargeboard)—the Arts and Crafts "A" house of circa 1912, and the massive Dr. Andrew Geisy House of 1913. The latter gable-ended house also found inspiration in the works of C. F. A. Voysey in England, particularly the Julian Sturgis House (1896) in Surrey. Jacobberger's Alfred Smith House (1912) has the same jerkinhead

Red House, Kent, England, 1859–60, designed by Philip Webb.

Julian Sturgis House, Surrey, England, 1896, designed by C. F. A. Voysey.

Glen Andred, Sussex, England, 1866, designed by Richard Norman Shaw.

gable, with bargeboard, as Lutyens used in Crooksbury. Jacobberger's last house in the style, the Michael J. Walsh House of 1915, simplified and modernized much of the feel of the Arts and Crafts movement. Jacobberger truly pioneered the development of the style in Portland, employing original and highly inventive versions in his residential plans.

Wade Hampton Pipes began his illustrious architectural career in 1912 with his rendition of the Arts and Crafts style as expressed in the

John M. Pipes House. From 1907 to 1912, Wade Pipes studied in England at the famous Central School of the Arts and Crafts, where some of the most distinguished architects and teachers of the Arts and Crafts movement could be found, such as W. R. Lethaby, the school's first principal, and Charles Sidney Spooner. The chief influences for Pipes were three of the major architects of their time: Shaw, Voysey, and Lutyens. Features of the English Arts and Crafts movement adopted by Pipes in Portland

Broadleys, Lake Windermere, England, 1898, designed by C. F. A. Voysey.

The Deanery, Sonning, England, 1901, designed by Sir Edwin Lutyens.

included: (1) greatly simplified and tailored sculptured forms as compared to the Craftsman style homes; (2) horizontal surface materials separating the different floors (often rough-cast stucco or brick at lower floors), and a horizontal emphasis at windows and doors; (3) removal of ornament (no bargeboards, simplified gable ends); (4) long banks of casement windows, and transom windows in large bays with minimal trim; (5) asymmetrical plans and "Picturesque" massing reflecting the rationale of the plan; and (6) massive chimneys. Several early residences in England reflect the development

of the English Arts and Crafts ideas that influenced Pipes's work. The Glen Andred House, designed by Shaw in 1866 in Withyham, Sussex, has the clipped gable, cantilevering out over a second floor bay window, the division of materials at the first and second floors (brick below and slate shingles above), and the banks of casement windows on an asymmetrical facade. Voysey's Julian Sturgis House has massive, plain rough-cast walls with stone trim, banks of casement windows, prominent chimneys, and gable sides descending to the main floor. Another Voysey-designed house, Broadleys

Folly Farm, Berkshire, England, 1906, designed by Sir Edwin Lutyens.

Homewood, Knebworth, England, 1901, designed by Sir Edwin Lutyens.

Papillon Hall, near Market Harborough, England, 1902, designed by Sir Edwin Lutyens.

(1898) at Lake Windermere, uses hipped roofs and prominent flat-roofed bays, plus banks of casement windows and a massive chimney.

Several houses designed by Lutyens were clearly influential to Wade Pipes. Sullingstead (1896, with music-room addition in 1903), in Surrey, has the famous twin gables with horizontal lap siding at the second floor and brick below. The Deanery (1901) has the massive bay window so enjoyed by Pipes, and long banks of casement windows. In his design for Homewood (1901) in Knebworth, Lutyens continued his development of the twin-gable form, here using lap siding at the second floor and roughcast stucco at the first. Several of Pipes's houses take some direction from Lutyens's Papillon Hall of 1902.

Arts and Crafts
CHARACTERISTICS

PLANS: asymmetrical, with multiple single-room-wide extensions; L-shaped or "butterfly" plans. Second floors cantilevered over polygonal or curved bay windows.

ROOFS: multiple steeply pitched gables, some telescoping; hipped-roof and gabled dormers; conical roofs on engaged circular towers. Upper roofs often extended to cover first floor open porches and verand as; the roof often is eased, or flared out over the eave extension. Half-round gutters. Wood shingled.

EXTERIOR FINISHES: stucco or brick, combined with wide beveled wood siding or board and battens, mitered at corners. Often stuccoed first floor with wood siding in triangular second floor gables.

CHIMNEYS: large, dominant brick chimneys, with multiple flues expressed.

WINDOWS: small-scale casements with multiple leaded panes or wood mullions, or double-hung with small panes in upper sash. Feature casement windows in series, with transoms, or large bay windows with leaded panes, often under cantilevered second floor.

WINDOW TRIM (exterior): little or no trim; metal frames supporting leaded glass, set in brick or stucco.

ENTRANCE DOORS: vertical-board doors, recessed in arched openings. Decoratively carved beams above entry ways.

VERANDAS/PORCHES: entrance and side porches enclosed under extension of upper roof. Large-scale masonry piers carrying beamed roof supports.

INTERIOR FINISHES: plastered walls and ceilings, with wood trim; beamed ceilings in dining room; painted paneling in living room. Polished wood floors; terra-cotta tile floors in entrance hall.

INTERIOR TRIM: simple molded door and window casings (without cornices) and baseboards. Often dark stained vertical-grained fir.

STAIRS: varnished wood risers and treads, with iron rails. Often located in circular towers.

FIREPLACE FRONTS: chimney flush with interior wall. Marble or brick surrounds, with wood mantel and side trim.

Entrance to the Theodore F. Brown House.

Arts and Crafts
HOUSES

1906	Ellis F. Lawrence (Ellis F. Lawrence)		1926	Frank Robertson (Jacobberger, Smith and Smith)
1906	Josef Jacobberger (Josef Jacobberger)		1926	Caroline and Louise Flanders (Jamieson K. Parker)
1907	George W. Collins (Albert E. Doyle)			
1911	Michael F. Brady (Josef Jacobberger)		1926	Charles Green (Charles Green)
c. 1912	Arts and Crafts "A" (attributed to Josef Jacobberger)		1927	Ida Catlin (Wade H. Pipes)
1912	John M. Pipes (Wade H. Pipes)		1927	Edwin T. Burke (Wade H. Pipes)
1912	Alfred T. Smith (Josef Jacobberger)		1927	Joseph R. Gerber (Hollis E. Johnson and Harold W. Doty)
1913	Dr. Andrew J. Geisy (Josef Jacobberger)		1928	James Leland (Harold W. Doty)
1915	Michael J. Walsh (Josef Jacobberger)		1929	George Black (Jamieson K. Parker)
1918	T. H. Sherrard (Wade H. Pipes)		1929	Mary E. Parker (Morris H. Whitehouse)
1920	William Grey Purcell (William Grey Purcell)			
1922	C. P. Osborne (S. M. Stokes)		1929	George P. Berky (Roscoe D. Hemenway)
c. 1922	Woerner Lewis (William Grey Purcell)		1929	Charles Barker (Roscoe D. Hemenway)
1923	Purcell Residence (William Grey Purcell)		1930	Dr. Frank Kistner (Wade H. Pipes)
1923	George Pipes (Wade H. Pipes)		1931	Walter S. Zimmerman (Wade H. Pipes and Harold Doty)
1923	Theodore F. Brown (Wade H. Pipes)			
1924	Gatekeeper's Lodge, M. Lloyd Frank Estate (Herman Brookman)		1931	E. S. Beach (Ernest Tucker)
1925	John G. Edwards (Albert E. Doyle)		1937	E. T. Samuelson (Ernest Tucker)
1925	John A. Laing (Wade H. Pipes)		1939	Richard Sundeleaf (Richard Sundeleaf)
1925	Charles T. Ladd (attributed to Ellis F. Lawrence)		1940	Properties Unlimited (Lee Thomas)

Ellis F. Lawrence (1906)
Ellis F. Lawrence

Acknowledged as the first Arts and Crafts style house in the city, the residence Ellis F. Lawrence designed for himself in 1906 at 2201 NE Twenty-first Avenue in Irvington expresses some of the design directions exhibited by English architects of the end of the nineteenth century. Lawrence designed the house with an asymmetrical plan and steeply pitched roofs, the slopes of which continue down to the first floor eave line, extending over open porches at both sides of the house. Wide shed-roofed dormers are located above the porches. Though it appears as a large single house, the Lawrence residence is actually a double house, as an ample two-story home for Lawrence's mother was constructed adjacent to the main structure. To accentuate the entrance on his own half, Lawrence designed a false-timbered gable centered over the entrance portal, which is sheltered by a bracketed and beamed shed roof. Two high-backed Craftsman benches flank the entrance door and sidelights. Inside the house are extensive Craftsman details at the stair, the fireplace, and in the finish trim. Painted woodwork predominates, with high wainscoting trim to the plate rail surrounding wallpaper panels in the dining room.

Ellis F. Lawrence House.

Garden elevation, Lawrence House.

Dining room, Lawrence House.

Josef Jacobberger (1906)
Josef Jacobberger

In the same year as Lawrence's home was built, Josef Jacobberger built a residence for himself on a steep hillside property at 1502 SW Upper Hall Street. Jacobberger, a highly respected architect for well over a decade, designed his home reflecting the influences of English Arts and Crafts precedents as well. The main facade's interlocking, steeply pitched double gables is a prominent feature of those influences, as are the banked windows, the cantilevered second floor, and the arched recessed openings. Jacobberger still utilized the projecting eave—soon to disappear altogether—in addition to bargeboards and false half-timbering at the ridge. While the Craftsman-inspired wide shingles were typical, Jacob-

Living room, Lawrence House.

Josef Jacobberger House.

berger clad his home with gray cement-asbestos shingles (a Lutyens influence), still in good condition today. For the interior, the architect paid particular attention to detail. Handsome ceiling plasterwork with quatrefoil designs grace the living room, and Craftsman style built-in cases are features of the entry-hall openings and beside the living room fireplace. Art-glass doors, attributed to the Povey Brothers, front the cases, some bearing dogwood designs that are also found in the living room fireplace surround.

George W. Collins (1907)
Albert E. Doyle

When Albert E. Doyle returned to Portland from his extensive European travels, one of the first projects of his newly established architectural practice was a residence for George W. Collins. In the house, located at 1863 SW Montgomery Drive on Portland Heights, Doyle displays the same English Arts and Crafts influences that were adopted by both Lawrence and Jacobberger. The entrance, or city-facing, facade has interlocking double gables, in this case with roofs extending down to the first floor eave line and over open porches. It makes a handsome symmetrical facade, with two partially recessed shed dormers at each end and one between the two gable peaks where the central roof meets the front facade, above the second floor ceiling line. Doyle also divided the facade by using different materials at each floor level. At the first floor, the house is surfaced with brick, and from the top of the first floor windows up to the roof, shingles with wide exposure are used. This presented a simple triangular geometry to the facade, a device used later by other Portland architects, although all were directly influenced by the English domestic architecture of Sir Edwin Lutyens.

George W. Collins House.

Michael F. Brady (1911)
Josef Jacobberger

In a stroke of architectural genius, architect Josef Jacobberger designed one of the finest houses in the city of Portland. The Michael F. Brady House at 2210 NE Thompson Street captured the particular expression of the Arts and Crafts statement that makes the style so timeless and so appealing today. The Brady House was the first to reduce, or all but eliminate, the bargeboard and to make the intersection of roofing and wall surface as simple as possible. Though he used a plain surface stucco

Michael F. Brady House.

Arts and Crafts "A" (c. 1912)
Josef Jacobberger (attributed)

The theme of interlocking gable roofs was appealing to architects. It kept the ridge line lower, and hence the mass of the house lower, especially when one or more of the roof slopes extended down to near the line of the second floor. The house at 2442 NE Twenty-fourth Avenue further developed this gable theme, not on the front but on the side elevation. It appears to be the work of Josef Jacobberger. Certainly, the use of the interlocking gables, polygonal bays, and decorative oval windows are hallmarks of his designs. Though the extended eaves were passing out of fashion in Arts and Crafts structures, the house displays the new idea

siding, Jacobberger created a house that is nevertheless exceedingly rich in the balance and juxtaposition of its elements. As a work of sculpture, it is first rate. A large front extension projects from the straightforward side-gabled roof, as does a polygonal bay, the design of which is reminiscent of the one in the Craftsman style Knighton-designed Ainsworth House of 1907. A telescoping gable extends on the right side, and there is a porch extension on the left. The front entry portico, with a reduced roof slope and half-timbering, dynamically unifies the composition. For windows, Jacobberger combined double-hung with casements, the latter located at the cantilevered second floor rectangular bay.

Arts and Crafts "A" House.

Living room, Arts and Crafts "A" House.

John M. Pipes (1912)
Wade H. Pipes

In 1912, when *Pacific Architect* magazine published the just-completed John M. Pipes House, the architectural career of Wade Hampton Pipes was launched, a career that was to become remarkably impressive and productive in a time of expanding wealth and fine residential construction. Wade Pipes did not introduce the English Arts and Crafts style to Portland, but he became one of its most eloquent spokesmen. He did introduce a more restrained version of the style. While the Pipes House has the interlocking gables favored by leading residential architects, it displays minimal but elegant detail at the roof and side walls. And

of differing wall materials at different floors: brick at the first floor and shingles above the windows and up into the gables. A wide shed dormer, originally an outdoor sleeping porch, extends across the front elevation. The polygonal bay is an attractive feature of the living room. Open to the living room, but separated by massive square columns, the dining room has a built-in buffet and appealing built-up cornices. The excessive brush previously in front of the house has been removed and the house completely restored by its current owners.

John M. Pipes House.

though he also used different siding materials at the main and second floors, Wade Pipes furthered the new restraint in the use of stucco at the main floor and lap siding above to the gable ridge. The house bears comparison with Doyle's Collins House and with the houses by Sir Edwin Lutyens from which Pipes derived his inspiration, but on a much more modest scale. Although many residential architects in Portland were influenced by the extremely gifted Lutyens, Pipes's gift was his ability to adapt Lutyens's work to the local scene with great aplomb.

Alfred T. Smith (1912)
Josef Jacobberger

One of the most creative architects of his time, Josef Jacobberger always felt free to experiment with form, inventing novel ways of dealing with style and its ever-changing nature. For Alfred T. Smith, who commissioned Jacobberger to design a duplex with the appearance of a single residence, he designed a house clearly within the Craftsman mainstream, but auguring the breaking up of large masses, which was an integral part of the Arts and Crafts style. Yet, the house retained the use of bargeboards and extended eaves, some of which were bracketed. Located at 1806 SW High Street on Portland Heights, the house sits close to the sidewalk on its hillside site and offers a delight of sculptural form. The stair tower to the right of the entrance is tall and narrow, with a jerkinhead roof, and is balanced by a front extension that also has a jerkinhead. Stained-glass windows are found at the tower landings, and a round window with keystones is under the eave of the tower. For the entrance, Jacobberger brought an arched barrel-vault canopy into the composition, supported by scroll brackets. The house is stucco covered, with brick facing at the first floor.

Alfred T. Smith House.

Dr. Andrew J. Geisy (1913)
Josef Jacobberger

Architect Josef Jacobberger was at the height of his powers when he designed the Dr. Andrew J. Geisy House at 1965 SW Montgomery Place. He incorporated both the Craftsman and Arts and Crafts styles, creating an impressive combination of compelling stature. The massive house, two-and-a-half-stories high, offers not only unusually steep intersecting gabled roofs—descending to the back and side to cover an open porch and the kitchen side of the house—but also the widely extended eaves, or "hat" effect, favored in the Craftsman style. Unusual is the use of rough-textured stucco above the first floor brick siding. The stuccoed second floor cantilevers out on the side elevation and is supported by scroll brackets. For an elegant entrance, the architect added an arched-glass and wrought-iron canopy reminiscent of that on the Jacobethan style Allen Lewis House of 1901. The canopy was supported by elaborate wrought-iron scroll brackets, ceremonious in an age that was worthy of such a gesture. Seen from period photographs, the interiors reveal baronial spaciousness, impressive detail, and lavish furnishings. In the opulent pre-income-tax days, the Geisy House was indeed well done.

Entrance stair hall, Geisy House.

Dr. Andrew J. Geisy House.

Dining room, Geisy House.

Michael J. Walsh (1915)
Josef Jacobberger

Throughout his productive career, master architect Josef Jacobberger explored the evolving styles of architecture, finding new and valid expressions for residential design. In a house for Michael J. Walsh, he produced a design that well-belies its 1915 date of construction. Hardly seeming eighty-plus years old now, the design was years ahead of its time, despite the lingering traces of Tudor style bargeboards and chimney detailing. The entrance facade of the brick-sided house combines Jacobberger's interest in intersecting gables of the Arts and Crafts tradition with the quite-abstract arrangement of a two-story polygonal bay.

Michael J. Walsh House.

With the strong horizontal band of a shed-roofed hood, the bay balances with the two arched openings on the main floor, one being the entrance portal. Small brick buttresses with curved cast-stone caps are added to the sides of the front projection. Other cast-stone accents appear in the brickwork at the keystones and spring lines of the arches. Herringbone designs, diagonally set, decorate the infilling of the arches. The house is located at 2306 NE Siskiyou Street in Irvington.

T. H. Sherrard (1918)
Wade H. Pipes

Wade Hampton Pipes designed numerous houses that reflected specific houses designed by famous residential architects in England. The white stucco house constructed for T. H. Sherrard in 1917, located at 13100 SW Riverside Drive, combines concepts used in several houses designed by Sir Edwin Lutyens, most notably Papillon Hall and Marsh Court, both constructed just after the turn of the century. Lutyens, in turn, was strongly influenced by the remodeled Chesters, a design of architect Richard Norman Shaw in Northumberland. Thus the tradition of opposing wings off an angled central entry, roughly in the shape of a butterfly, continued in Portland. Papillon Hall is reflected in the diagonal central entry and the two side chimneys, and Marsh Court in the distinctive hipped roofs and the eave extension over polygonal bays. Architect Pipes was to further develop this roof form, combined with polygonal bays, on houses throughout the remainder of his career. In the Sherrard House, the floor plan centers on the entry, radiating to the living and dining rooms and a glassed-in study overlooking the winding Willamette River far below the house's dramatic cliff-top location.

T. H. Sherrard House.

William Grey Purcell (1920)
William Grey Purcell

William Grey Purcell brought a unique architectural talent to Portland when he retired here in 1920, and the city is blessed with a series of houses designed by the internationally recognized architect. Coming to Portland from Minneapolis, where his firm of Purcell and Elmslie had received remarkable recognition for their Arts and Crafts and Prairie style architecture, Purcell constructed his own home on Portland Heights at 2649 SW Georgian Place, on a hillside overlooking tree-clad western views. In the design of the house, Purcell utilized much of his Prairie style background, but he added to it contemporary themes of the Arts and Crafts tradition. The house is sited parallel to the street, having a large side-gabled central roof. On the entrance elevation are telescoping front gables and an open-gable entrance porch with extended support beams. Classic banked windows are found in the main rooms of the stucco-clad house, and a quite remarkable tall, narrow window is on the living room end wall. Off the window is a small balcony supported by two large wood brackets. Purcell had a masterful sense of balance, and all the elevations of the house reveal his inventive and unique sense of design.

William Grey Purcell House.

C. P. Osborne (1922)
S. M. Stokes

The C. P. Osborne House of 1922 used the Arts and Crafts theme of intersecting gables very effectively, handsomely arranged with an asymmetrical catslide roof over the entrance door. The house at 2240 SE Twenty-fourth Avenue combines a hipped central roof, with "gablets," and the double gables. Upper floor casements and the living room banked casement windows are centered around the prominently dis-

played upper roof downspout and central chimney. The second floor is cantilevered out on the banked casement windows of the front elevation, creating a wide polygonal bay. While the house has the typical beveled lap siding and popular mullioned windows, its innovative arrangement for a small lot gives it notable distinction. The apparent size of the house is increased because of the smaller-than-usual size of the windows. The architect of the house is S. M. Stokes, about whom little is known but who created this finely crafted house for the modest sum of $5,000.

Woerner Lewis (c. 1922)
William Grey Purcell

Another of the excellent designs William Grey Purcell constructed during his years in Portland is the Woerner Lewis House at 2903 NE Alameda Drive. One of the more exciting and original Portland designs in the Arts and Crafts mode, the house has three telescoping gables on its front elevation off the central hipped roof. The lower one has a wrap-around hipped eave (sometimes referred to as a hipped roof with truncated gable) extending out over the large, round porch support columns. A partial wrap-around eave uniquely extends over the banked second floor windows on the right, or east, side of the front elevation. Taking from the same source of English Arts and Crafts inspiration as Wade Pipes did in the Sherrard House of 1917, Purcell employed the triangular stuccoed gable over a polygonal bay, seen on the middle telescoping gable. To the west, or left, is the living room wing, complete with large banked windows on the entrance facade and a dramatic peaked window, Palladian fashion, on the end wall of the high-ceilinged room. The large chimney of the fireplace is located at the roof peak.

C. P. Osborne House.

Woerner Lewis House.

Purcell (1923)
William Grey Purcell

One of William Grey Purcell's most unusual, but still masterfully crafted, houses was the one he designed at 2534 SW Arden Road on Portland Heights. The architect used low-sloped intersecting gable ends in a highly sculptural way, with extended side wings to enclose the kitchen and garages at the opposite ends of the house. The gables meet at the corner of the house and combine with shed-roofed dormers. Some in-

fluences from English domestic architecture are evident, such as from the houses of Lutyens, as well as influences from the recently constructed houses of Wade Pipes in the same neighborhood. In addition to the Arts and Crafts characteristics, some fairly exotic elements were introduced into the design, such as the Gothic pointed arch of the recessed entrance portal and the tall, narrow windows of the winding stair. Throughout the exterior and interior, asymmetrical designs dominate, with ever-changing vistas and intriguing intersections. The house remains in excellent condition, clearly well appreciated for its special qualities.

Purcell House.

George Pipes (1923)
Wade H. Pipes

The abundant abilities of architect Wade Hampton Pipes were called upon with great frequency during the second decade of his career. For his brother George Pipes, he designed a small but imposing house at 2526 SW St. Helens Court, on Portland Heights. Its design heavily reflected Wade Pipes's fascination with the English architect Sir Edwin Lutyens, particularly Lutyens's design for Homewood, a 1901 country estate that has similar curved roofs on one-story wings to either side of a two-story central entrance facade. However, this was the only feature of

George Pipes House.

the English house that Pipes used, and he unified this smaller structure by adding flanking chimneys at each end of the side-gabled house as well as third story dormers. He also greatly simplified materials by using only textured stucco walls and a wood-shingle roof. The George Pipes House, which cost only $6,000, not only achieved well-considered architecture on the exterior elevations, but it reflected a practical central-hall plan, both commodious and handsomely arranged. Living and dining rooms accessed a central rear terrace with a bifurcated stairway descending to gardens below.

Theodore F. Brown (1923)
Wade H. Pipes

The Theodore F. Brown House is a medium-sized residence designed by Wade Pipes with an asymmetrical plan and front elevation. It incorporates the intersecting gables and long descending roofs so often found in Portland houses of the Arts and Crafts style. Like many of Pipes's houses, it is of wood-frame construction covered with stucco. The central hipped roof has multiple gabled extensions. The garden elevation, toward which the major rooms are oriented, has paired triangular gables extending over polygonal bays, making for an exceptionally handsome facade. The front elevation achieves its balance from the arrangement of the forward-projecting intersecting gables, with the main mass of the house behind and a garage wing to the right. The convenience of having direct access to kitchens was being developed by architects, but with kitchens still discretely placed so as not to be distracting from the entrance. Pipes designed the arched entry to be incorporated under an extension of the upper roof. The house is located on one of the most handsome streets in the city, at 2769 SW Buena Vista Drive.

Theodore F. Brown House.

Rear elevation, Brown House.

Gatekeeper's Lodge
M. Lloyd Frank Estate (1924)
Herman Brookman

At the entry to Fir Acres, the luxurious Tudor country estate of M. Lloyd Frank in Dunthorpe, architect Herman Brookman designed discrete stone walls and incorporated them into the gable-ended stone residence for the estate's gatekeeper. Brookman had just returned from England, where he must have viewed the residential architecture of Lutyens, particularly Folly Farm, which had similar heavy flared piers supporting the roof over an open loggia on the rear garden side of the house, and the gabled stone additions to Lambay, an Irish castle on an island of the same name in the Irish Sea. Lutyens's works were widely published between 1914 and 1925 and were available to Portland architects in hand-

Gatekeeper's Lodge, M. Lloyd Frank Estate.

An early photograph of the Frank Estate Gatekeeper's Lodge.

somely bound volumes. The Gatekeeper's Lodge was as beautifully constructed as the estate's main house, with fine stone-masonry walls and a slate-covered roof. Gabled and recessed dormers grace the house, and leaded casement windows have hand-hewn lintels. The side gables have wide-exposure horizontal lap siding, dark stained and weathered. The left side of the house extends into the entry-gate wall, affording privacy for the house.

John G. Edwards (1925)
Albert E. Doyle

The large estate of Welsh-born John G. Edwards, "Sheep King of the West," occupies a prominent knoll on Portland Heights, with panoramic views to the west, north, and east. Called Pen-y-Brin, meaning "Crest of the Hill," the estate is located at 2645 SW Alta Vista Place, and the land-

scaped property is surrounded on three sides by Buena Vista Drive. Edwards employed A. E. Doyle to design the house. Doyle used a combination of Arts and Crafts and Norman farmhouse design elements. He placed the angled house around a circular drive, at the culmination of what is now Alta Vista Place. The arched brick front entrance, located in the main hipped volume, is protected by a half-round glass and iron canopy. Garages are located in the slightly angled west wing. Besides the Welsh slate roof, the house is covered entirely with rough-hewn stucco, with some half-timbering at the north-side bays. Steeply pitched gabled extensions are found on all elevations, and shed dormers are located at the second floor and attic levels. The spacious interiors continue the reserved taste of the exterior, incorporating imported Welsh carvings on fireplace fronts.

John G. Edwards House.

John A. Laing (1925)
Wade H. Pipes

One of Wade Pipes's most classic houses, and one of the finest in the Arts and Crafts style in Portland, is the large home for John A. Laing, constructed in 1925 at the height of an era of affluence. Located at 12526 SW Edgecliff Road in Dunthorpe, the stately house is approached by a circular drive lined with old cobbles from Portland streets. The entrance facade is centered on the hipped roof and two connected, slightly projecting gables. The large, broad gables are covered with horizontal lap siding from the ridge down to the heads of the first floor windows, providing dramatic contrast with the stucco-covered main floor, much in the tradition of Lutyens's Homewood of 1901. All the leaded casement windows, some in pairs, are centered around the arched brick entrance portal, which is enlivened by the contrast of its white mortar joints with the brick. Windows and dormers are small in scale, giving the house the appearance of being larger in size, as does the steep pitch of the roof. To the far left, in a wing extending from a side volume of the main house, the discretely placed garage is located conveniently near the kitchen entrance of the house.

Charles T. Ladd (1925)
Ellis F. Lawrence (attributed)

Attributed to the designs of Ellis F. Lawrence, the Charles T. Ladd residence at 01649 SW Greenwood Road is an unusually large rendition of

John A. Laing House.

Charles T. Ladd House.

the Arts and Crafts style house. It was constructed in 1925 at the height of the Arts and Crafts period, when most architects partook of the fashionable design trend. Although the house is somewhat unusual for a Lawrence design, it would seem to have elements similar to his Tudor style Cameron Squires House of 1920 and Stanley C. E. Smith House of 1923. The Ladd House combines stuccoed lower walls with horizontal lap siding, and it incorporates a few of the Tudor half-timbering details found in those earlier houses. Unusual is the great variety of roof forms, which lack extensive eaves. From the hipped central mass, so prevalent in Arts and Crafts houses, project jerkinhead gable extensions, and even a catslide roof descends over the front entrance porch. Other details include the paned casement windows, banked at the large bay and expanded at the sizable window of the stair landing. The prominent brick chimney was a favorite design device of Lawrence, though he usually had them featured on the front elevation.

Frank Robertson (1926)
Jacobberger, Smith and Smith

In a remarkable departure from previous architectural work, Josef Jacobberger, of the firm Jacobberger, Smith and Smith, designed an Arts and Crafts style house with the newly fashionable detail of nonextended eaves and with sweeping roof lines quite unlike any other house in the city. Such low-pitched, asymmetrical, gable-fronted roofs had not been used since the 1880s, particularly in the Shingle style summer residences along the East Coast. Jacobberger adapted such designs in a house for Frank Robertson in 1926, located on a hillside site at 2687 NW Cornell Road. The Westover property is below street level, making the roofs unusually prominent when viewed from the entrance level. The simplicity

Frank Robertson House.

of the roof forms is reflected in the reserved use of windows and the broad shingle siding, now weathered to a deeply rich dark brown. A similarly shingled fence enclosure extends out to the sidewalk. Paired entrance gates are located in the fence, with steps beyond descending to the main entrance level below. Major rooms on both floors look northeast out over the Giles Lake district.

Caroline and Louise Flanders (1926)
Jamieson K. Parker

After selling the large Italianate style family home to Temple Beth Israel, the two daughters of Captain George Flanders, Caroline and Louise, hired architect Jamieson K. Parker to design for them a much smaller home, which is still standing at 2421 SW Arden Road. Parker's design for the Flanders sisters demonstrates his interest in the English Arts and Crafts traditions. The straightforward side-gabled central mass and projecting gabled extensions are unadorned except for tight bargeboards against the textured stucco walls. Some of the scaled-down leaded casement windows, designed in pairs or banked, have expressed wood headers, originally stained. At the large windows of the living and dining rooms, upper sashes have transoms in the Tudor tradition. All windows are modestly trimmed to emphasize the house's false-masonry appearance. Reflecting the less-then-ostentatious nature of the structure, the main entrance is located under a simple shed roof. The sisters brought with them several fireplaces and bookcases from the original Italianate Flanders mansion, which were carefully incorporated by Parker into the Arden Road house.

Charles Green (1926)
Charles Green

The small house at 3401 NE Thirty-third Avenue, in the Alameda District, was designed by its owner, Charles Green, chief designer for Doyle and Associates before his departure from the firm. Green's abilities are clearly evident in the compact but handsomely arranged house, situated with its main rooms facing the city view to the west and with a very private entrance facade located only a few feet behind the front property line. A handsome pine tree graces the narrow front yard. For a small house on a small lot, it achieves a great deal of architectural interest by its careful arrangement of facade elements: a stair turret with conical roof to the right of a small recessed entry, a high side-gabled central roof,

Caroline and Louise Flanders House.

Charles Green House.

and the perpendicular gabled addition of a single-car garage to the right, which is linked to the house with a connecting portion of the main roof. Though the floor-and-a-half house is narrow, the residence is enhanced by the steeply pitched shingle roof and by the partially exposed stuccoed gable revealed behind the turret, the roof of which descends down over the arched entrance. The exterior is stucco covered and with beveled lap siding at the gables.

Ida Catlin (1927)
Wade H. Pipes

Two handsome Arts and Crafts houses designed by Wade Hampton Pipes, both constructed in 1927, are neighbors on their Portland Heights properties. The first of these, at 1727 SW Hawthorne Terrace, was built by Ida Catlin, and though the smaller of the two, it is replete with Arts and Crafts detail. Typical of the English architectural traditions of Sir Edwin Lutyens, and of Wade Pipes's Portland interpretations of them, the Catlin House incorporates simple, unadorned gabled forms and depends upon proportion, fine craftsmanship, and careful detailing to achieve its effect. Typical Lutyens-inspired triangular gables over polygonal bays, cantilevered second floors over bays, and small-scale casement windows are all found in the house. In this case, the two-story polygonal bay, with triangular gable above, is scaled down to cleverly enclose the stair tower (which offers a small round window as it descends to the basement). The house has been well maintained, with the present paint scheme true to the original Pipes colors of dark cedar horizontal siding contrasting with light-colored stucco. New shingles, to match the originals, have been installed on the steep sloping roof.

Ida Catlin House.

Edwin T. Burke (1927)
Wade H. Pipes

The second of the two adjacent houses designed by Wade Pipes on Portland Heights is located at 1707 SW Hawthorne Terrace. It was built for Edwin T. Burke and complements the Catlin House by repeating the matching gable-fronted extensions. The two extensions off the main hipped-roof volume are closely arranged around the recessed central entrance, now somewhat hidden by the later addition of a fence at the property line. To keep the roof of the east wing lower than the main ridge, Pipes used double truncated gables to reduce the ridge height.

Edwin T. Burke House.

Other features that create a unity with the Catlin House are the use of horizontal lap siding at the second floor and stucco walls at the first, as well as the small-scale casement windows. Casements are paired at the second floor and are paired in banks at the left gabled extension. On the east side, with access from SW Seventeenth Avenue, the garages are discretely located off the entrance front but convenient to the main floor kitchen above. With their handsome appearance, splendid views to the city, and striking conceptual unity with each other, the Catlin and Burke houses are exceptional examples of Wade Pipes architecture and of the Arts and Crafts style in Portland.

Joseph R. Gerber (1927)
Hollis E. Johnson and Harold W. Doty

A particularly successful Arts and Crafts style house in Portland was designed by Hollis Johnson and Harold Doty for Joseph R. Gerber in 1927. Located on Arlington Heights, at 2875 SW Fairview Boulevard, the story-and-a-half house features a massive, steeply pitched, side-gabled roof, with a large, cantilevered front-gabled extension, plus a gabled dormer located over the entrance doors. Original finish materials have been maintained, with replacement shingles on the main roof. The triangular gable ends of the house are sided with wide-exposure, beveled lap siding, and shingle siding covers the first floor. A massive Tudor style brick chimney dominates the front elevation, carefully balanced with the gabled extensions, and has typical groupings of flues,

Joseph R. Gerber House.

revealing the number of fireplaces in the house. Now that attractive plantings are nearly up to the eave line, the lower floor banked casement windows are barely visible. Other paned casement windows appear in the gable ends. The interior features fine carvings at the fireplace mantel, paneling, and stair details. Subsequent owners have maintained the home in excellent condition.

James Leland (1928)
Harold W. Doty

In a similar, but larger, house designed by architect Harold Doty, the Arts and Crafts style reached another high watermark. The James Leland House, built in 1928 at 5303 SW Westwood Drive, adroitly combines two adjacent gabled extensions off a central hipped roof and balanced with a tall facade chimney. One projecting gabled extension is stucco covered, unpainted, and the other has half-timbering. To the east, the upper roof descends over an open porch. Above the twelve-paneled entrance doors is a handsomely carved decorative lintel. Windows are metal casement. Fine wrought-iron work is found in lanterns, decorative planters, and gates. Clearly, Harold Doty had exceptional talents, which are revealed throughout the Leland House. With great skill, Doty balances proportions and differing materials, always with the restraint of a master. All interior and exterior detailing is exceedingly well done. On the garden, or view, side, he created a fine terrace, defining the connection between windows of the main rooms and the distant views of the city and mountains. Skillfully restored by its present owners, this is Harold Doty's finest work.

George Black (1929)
Jamieson K. Parker

Although his clients thought of him mainly as skilled in the Colonial Revival style, Jamieson K. Parker created one of his best houses in the Arts and Crafts style. His house for George Black has all the elegant restraint that makes these houses so compelling. The masses of intersecting gabled projections are well handled. They are simply sided with horizontal lap siding at the second floor and plaster at the first. The telescoping front gable is also stuccoed. Until recently, the entrance featured superb hand-carved doors in the English tradition and, with the decorative lintel, stated quality architecture without fanfare. Unfortunately, the carved paired doors have been removed and replaced with a stock, off-the-shelf paneled door. Steel casements are set in the walls,

James Leland House.

George Black House.

Living room, Black House.

Original entrance doors, Black House.

Dining room, Black House.

small in scale to help create the impression of a much larger house. The large living room wing to the right has a stuccoed chimney at its end wall. As in the best of the homes, the roof retains its original shingles. Inside, Parker included details typical of the style: painted paneling in the living room, stained-fir woodwork in the other major rooms. The dining room ceiling beams are stained, as is the paneling of the library at the half-landing of the main stair. In all, the house is an exceptional Parker design.

Mary E. Parker (1929)
Morris H. Whitehouse

Eastmoreland still contained vacant properties in the late 1920s when Mary E. Parker chose one directly across from Reed College on which to build her large brick home. She hired Morris Whitehouse to be the architect, and he created a house with many of the elements common to the Arts and Crafts style. His roof is steeply pitched and central hipped, with a hipped front extension. The upper roof of this extension descends via a catslide over the entrance portal. As with many of the Arts and Crafts houses, a fine decoratively carved lintel spans the opening. All the woodwork is darkly stained, making for a strong contrast with the warm tones of the brick. Massive brick chimneys are located toward the back of the house, on the north side. The original gardens were designed by landscape architect Florence Holmes Gerke, and many original trees and shrubs survive today. Although the spacious property was subsequently divided, the house still maintains sufficient space around it, allowing one to visualize its once-rolling lawns down toward the Eastmoreland Golf Course. The address today is 2840 SE Woodstock Boulevard.

Mary E. Parker House.

George P. Berky (1929)
Roscoe D. Hemenway

Roscoe Hemenway designed primarily in the Colonial Revival style, and his few houses in the Arts and Crafts style are little known. One of the largest of these was designed for George P. Berky on Greenhills at 4311 SW Greenleaf Drive. Hemenway placed the house at the back edge of property, where the property falls away to SW Humphrey Boulevard below, keeping in the process some of the huge native trees that dotted the spacious lawns in front of the house. With the trees long ago removed, the circular entrance drive is once again fully revealed. To the right of the house, the angled garage wing offers a combination of garages and open carports, unusual for the time. Directly ahead along the driveway, the main house is distinguished by a hipped central roof, side extensions, and a slightly projecting gabled entrance. Above the glass entrance doors is a recessed balcony with an arched opening in the brick, possibly influenced by Herman Brookman's design for the entrance to M. Lloyd Frank's Fir Acres estate (1924). An open loggia off the main rooms extends to the left of the entrance, and there is a small oriel above. Originally, the house contrasted brick with horizontal lap siding; it is now all painted white.

Charles Barker (1929)
Roscoe D. Hemenway

A great challenge for any architect is the small house. Charles Barker, furniture maker and house developer, hired architect Roscoe Hemenway to find a solution for the hillside property at 2362 SW Madison Street, still undeveloped in 1929 in the long-established Ardmore Addition to the city of Portland (now King's Hill). Hemenway designed a home in the Arts and Crafts tradition, adding a stuccoed engaged turret that serves to house a circular stair. For further interest, he incorporated

George P. Berky House.

Charles Barker House.

a rather massive brick chimney with three prominent terra-cotta chimney flues. A small hipped-roof dormer sits atop the single-car garage. The remainder of the house has more typical Arts and Crafts details. Side and back elevations are covered with wide-exposure lap siding, and the small-paned casement windows are grouped at major rooms. The back, or south, side has a cantilevered second floor with exposed rafters. The triangular upper section of the side gable on the steeply pitched roof is also extended out for window protection. Hemenway repeated this successful house design in 1931 for a house in Lake Oswego, at 16847 Greenbrier Road.

Dr. Frank Kistner (1930)
Wade H. Pipes

Master architect Wade Hampton Pipes designed one of his best works for Dr. Frank Kistner. The large 10,800-square-foot house is sited at 5400 SW Hewett Boulevard on the southern slopes of the Greenhills Addition among tall native and first-planting trees. The circular drive approaches from the east, descending into the courtyard space of the multi-angled (butterfly plan) house. Dominating the entrance space are the massive hipped projection of the stair tower, with its large windows designed in the English traditions of Edwin Lutyens, and the arched entrance porch, which appears under a catslide from the second floor roof. To the right is the angled library wing, and to the left is the wing of the garages. The steeply pitched roof is accented by hipped facade dormers interrupting the gutter line. Most of the house is constructed of structural brick walls, lightly whitewashed, though the upper floors of the angled wings are covered with wide-exposure, horizontal lap siding. Only a few of the original copper gutters and leaders remain on the

Dr. Frank Kistner House.

Garden elevation, Kistner House.

house. Trim is stained dark, handsomely contrasted with the bronze, multi-paned casement windows. Similar treatment is afforded on the south elevations, where the two angled wings open from the central hall of the house onto the southern sunlight and views. It is perhaps the more remarkable facade, truly inspired by Lutyens. The massive roof descends over an expansive porch between the brick side wings and is supported by brick piers. Recessed and surface hipped-roof dormers protrude from the central roof. Originally constructed of wood shingles, the roof is now covered with composition shingles. Pipes, always one to consider the complete indoor-outdoor experience, provided a spacious lawn on the valley-view side of the house, with a semicircular stone stairway descending gracefully to the gardens.

In the house's plan, the virtues of the butterfly layout are evident, providing for every interior room at least two exterior walls allowing natural light. At the center of the plan is the long central hall, apsidal at each end, which connects the living room and library wing with the dining room, kitchen, and service wing. The fine stair is on the east end, and banks of French doors are located at the south, garden-facing wall. Examples of the superb craftsmanship on which Pipes insisted are found throughout the house. Mahogany doors and woodwork, brass hardware, exposed beams, fine fireplace details, and library paneling provide a tasteful ambiance, without opulence.

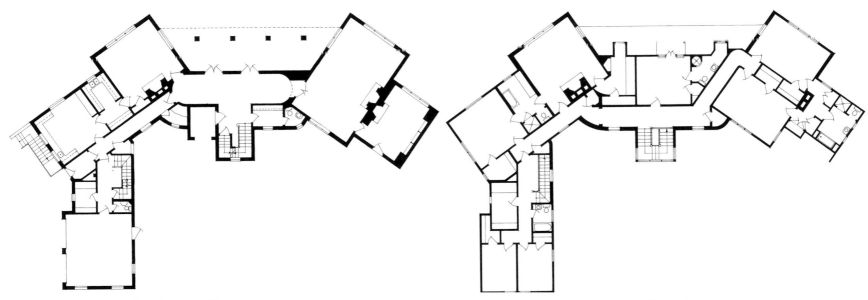

First floor plan, Kistner House.   Second floor plan, Kistner House.

Walter S. Zimmerman (1931)
Wade H. Pipes and Harold W. Doty

Though the Great Depression restricted general construction, Wade Pipes managed to continue his career and indeed designed some of his best architecture during this period, including the Walter S. Zimmerman House on a spectacular Portland Heights panoramic-view property. For the large commission, Pipes turned to his former associate in business, Harold W. Doty (associated from 1922 to 1926), whose name appeared along with Pipes's on the architectural drawings. The Zimmerman House, located at 1840 SW Hawthorne Terrace, commands its ridge location, facing the city views on its north, or entrance, side and

Garden elevation, Zimmerman House.

Walter S. Zimmerman House.

Interior stairway, Zimmerman House.

facing south on the garden elevations. Two massive gabled projections, steeply pitched and shingle covered, frame the arched entrance porch, which is recessed under the continuation of the central roof. One of the projections is covered with brick up to the lap siding of the slightly projecting triangular attic gable; the other has lap siding above the first floor. Both wings have spectacular iron-and-glass curved bay windows, unique with their arched center panes. The upper floor windows are leaded casements in banks of two and three pairs. Detailing is elegantly simple, including minimal articulation at the eave. Only the finest ma-

terials are used. The brickwork is exceptional, as it often was during this period. The Flemish-bond patterned brick, in a warm range of coloring and yellow-brown wide joints, seems to have followed the Fruit and Flower Nursery, which was designed by Frederick Fritch in 1928 and is considered by his peers the finest example of brick artistry in the city (see Chapter 21). The beautiful work continues on the garden elevations, where a major L extends along the garden on the west side of the house. Its hipped roof, with truncated gable, descends a floor-and-a-half down to the garage level. On the south side, the conical-roofed engaged turret

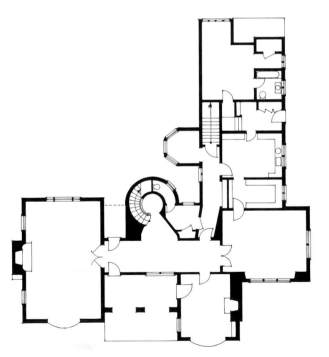

First floor plan, Zimmerman House.

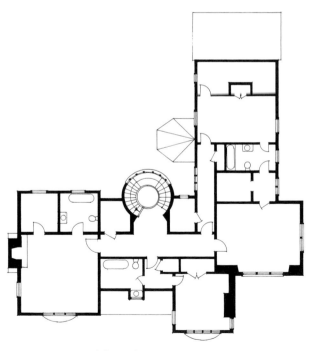

Second floor plan, Zimmerman House.

of the main stair is handsomely articulated with rounded, leaded case-ment windows in diagonal patterns. The garden, framed by the house and wings, typically is tied to the windows of the major rooms. The polygonal bay of the breakfast room, adjacent to the kitchen, looks into this private garden from its eastern and southern exposures. The interi-ors are equally fine. Simple moldings, fine materials, and elegant fire-place and stair details all combine to reflect a great era of residential ar-chitecture in Portland, when architects and their contributions were an essential part of the cultural life of the city.

E. S. Beach (1931)
Ernest Tucker

Respected architect Ernest Tucker produced numerous fine residences, most designed in the Arts and Crafts tradition. One of his finest was constructed at 4343 SW Fairview Boulevard for E. S. Beach in 1931. The large house is distinguished by its steeply pitched gables, intersecting and projecting from the central hipped roof, and by the angled wings that follow the drive and provide entry focus. At the intersection of the wings is a large brick chimney, articulated at the upper portions. The lightly whitewashed brick continues along the shed-roofed entrance projection and at the first floor walls. Above, to the peak of the gables, Tucker used wide board-and-batten siding in impressively long (though no longer available) vertical grain cedar. The second floor cantilevers out over first floor bay windows, which have leaded casements, some with leaded transoms. Banks of casement windows, six panes each, are at the second floor, and some false-timbering is revealed at the dormer between the front gables and the chimney. The house is well maintained, now partially screened by abundant growth in the surrounding gardens.

E. S. Beach House.

E. T. Samuelson (1937)
Ernest Tucker

One of the largest homes designed by Ernest Tucker was for E. T. Samuelson at 3737 SW Council Crest Drive. In the design for the house, Tucker used multiple gabled extensions off a large side-gabled roof. The gables are of various sizes and materials. Whitewashed brick, somewhat similar to that in the E. S. Beach residence, is used at the first floor and for the gabled extension that accents the slightly recessed entrance doors. The gables all have the same detail of the side eave, which projects out about a foot to hold the gutters and is slightly rounded at the ends. This detail had been used extensively by Wade Pipes, who, like Tucker and others, was influenced by the residential architecture of Voysey and Lu-

E. T. Samuelson House.

The house Sundeleaf designed for himself at 16715 Phantom Bluff Court is oriented toward the lake view. It has gabled extensions that create an L-shaped house and provide a small recessed court at the entrance. The house is styled in the Arts and Crafts tradition, with traces of Tudor intermingled. Arts and Crafts influences are evident in the details of the gabled roofs, especially the triangular end-gable designs. Sundeleaf added his own version of Tudor half-timbering by including brick in-filling at the gabled extension that encloses the main stair. Helping to distract attention away from the garage doors, Sundeleaf included a small polygonal bay window with diagonal leaded panes. The interiors include extensive woodwork, some ironwork, and carved panels by wood sculptor Gabriel Lavare. California landscape architect Tommy Thompson assisted with the garden layout and plantings.

tyens. In the English precedents, this eave detail was usually designed for a stuccoed stone structure, and the bottom was curved, not soffited. Other details in the Samuelson House are more typical: horizontal lap siding at the upper floors, banks of casement windows, some leaded, and massive chimneys. Unusual in this typically Arts and Crafts design is the entrance cornice, which is supported by Classical brackets.

Richard Sundeleaf (1939)
Richard Sundeleaf

As the Great Depression eased in the late 1930s, Richard Sundeleaf was one of the few busy and prosperous architects. At the time, it must have been quite unusual for an architect to build his own home, especially at such a spectacular location as high on a cliff overlooking Lake Oswego.

Richard Sundeleaf House.

Properties Unlimited (1940)
Lee Thomas

The main thrust of the Arts and Crafts era in Portland subsided in the late 1930s, and by 1940 the style had all but been eclipsed. With the Depression and the impending conflicts in Europe, architects veered toward new expressions for difficult times. One of the last Arts and Crafts style houses of note was built for a development firm, Properties Unlimited, and was designed by Lee Thomas and constructed on a corner location on Council Crest, at 4201 SW Council Crest Drive. The house Thomas designed combined a two-story volume, capped with a truncated-gable roof and wrap-around eave, and a story-and-a-half section, which is fronted with a tall brick chimney. Banked casement windows are used extensively around the entrance and major rooms, most cleverly at a diagonally placed second floor bay window, angled toward a distant mountain view. The hipped-roof garage, attached to the house by a covered walkway, has a slight bell-cast eave. Thomas created a house that is inventive within the Arts and Crafts style: unusually sculptured, well suited to its site, and attractive in appearance.

Properties Unlimited House.

PART VII

Early Modern
1930s–1950s

THE opportunities of a wartime economy awoke Portland in 1940 from the doldrums of the previous decade. At the end of the 1930s, planners had expected that Portland would only slowly break free from the stagnation caused by the Depression. A stable population and economy were expected to last for at least another generation. Predominately white and middle class, Portland was unprepared for the social changes brought on by World War II.

Shipbuilding for the war effort brought extraordinary growth to Portland. Before the war ended, Portland-area shipyards had produced over a thousand ocean-going vessels. Aluminum production and merchant shipping also added to the city's prosperity. Industrialists built three aluminum plants to take advantage of the cheap hydropower from Bonneville Dam on the Columbia River. As a result of the military demands placed on other West Coast ports, Portland soon became the leading merchant port, with civilian tonnage second only to that of New York City.

The wartime industries attracted large numbers of new workers, altering the ethnic makeup of the city and severely straining housing and other public facilities. Over 140,000 people worked in defense-related employment in Portland during the war, and half of these workers came from outside of Oregon. Among the new migrants were 13,000 African-Americans. Since Portland's prewar black population was less than 2,000 and was concentrated in the Albina District, the major influx was met with open hostility and demands for segregated housing. In fact, the shortage of housing confined most African-Americans to defense-industry housing projects, such as Vanport, physically isolated from the city.

Built by shipping mogul Edgar Kaiser in 1943 to house shipyard workers, Vanport contained 10,000 housing units on a square mile along the Columbia River flood plain just beyond the city limits. At its peak, Vanport housed 35,000 residents and had its own post office, schools, fire and police station, theater, library, hospital, parks, and commercial buildings. By the end of the war, the poor quality of the hastily constructed housing began to show, and many people were worried that the area would quickly become a vast slum. The massive Columbia River flood of 1948 solved, in a sense, the problem of what to do with postwar Vanport—without warning, on 30 May, flood waters breached the dike protecting Vanport and quickly laid waste to the entire community. At least 14 people drowned and over 18,000 were left homeless. (It later became an industrial area.)

Wartime demands on housing and public services caused direct strain on Portland's political system and planning capabilities. The city's leaders worked out solutions to pressing housing needs and postwar reconversion of industry largely on an ad hoc basis. At the urging of Edgar Kaiser, these leaders hired New York City's Parks Commissioner, Robert Moses, to prepare a postwar plan. By the end of 1943, Moses had produced a plan for the massive public works that would bridge the gap between the end of the war and the full resumption of peacetime private business activity. The heart of Moses' program called for major highway construction to create a freeway loop around the central business core and for the development of a civic center. He also recommended improvements to the sewage system, docks, airport, and parks. The major legacy of the Moses plan was the highway element, including the Stadium Freeway, the Fremont Bridge, and the I-5 east-bank alignment. Moses' plan ignored regional planning concerns, however, and offered no solution to the pressing social welfare needs. Highways and public buildings would provide short-term jobs during postwar demobilization, but no direction for the community's long-term growth needs.

Portland entered the postwar period with great ambivalence. Should it return to the old, conservative slow-growth mentality of the past, or embrace a new, rapid-changing openness to the future? Portland did change, if ever so slowly, in the late 1940s. New industries appeared—metal working, chemicals, and electronics—enticed by cheap electricity rates and a steady labor force. Greater social diversity came with the enlarged African-American community. By the 1950s, however, the economy turned stagnant, and the old habits of cautious business decisions and unimaginative politics in combination with a conservative populace led to a period of drift. Planning initiatives, civic-center bonds, and housing renewal proposals all failed at the polls.

The destruction of the Portland Hotel in 1951 symbolized the end of an old era and the uncertainty of a new one. The Portland Hotel—a seven-story Queen Anne chateau with a courtyard, built in the 1880s—reflected the solid, steady growth ushered in by the arrival of the transcontinental railroad at the end of the nineteenth century, whereas the concrete and asphalt parking garage that replaced the hotel represented the extensive and destructive impact of the automobile on the urban fabric. Over the years, the old Portland Hotel had come to embody the basic character of the city: solid in structure and rich in detail, yet modest in scale and unostentatious in appearance. The stark, utilitarian parking structure, on the other

Original view of the Portland Hotel, circa 1881.

Destruction of the Portland Hotel, 1951.

hand, came to reflect what unthinking reliance on the automobile meant: aimless motion and unplanned regional expansion that hollowed out the urban core.

The fate of the Portland Hotel presaged the future of so many of the city's nineteenth-century downtown buildings. Over the next twenty years, many fine but empty cast-iron structures would be replaced with surface parking lots. In time, a counter-movement of historical preservationists would staunch the loss, but not before most of the architecturally and historically significant buildings were demolished.

CHAPTER 21

Stripped Traditional/Transitional

The late 1920s and 1930s saw the introduction of a variety of new architectural expressions, leading ultimately to the emergence of the Moderne, International, and Northwest styles. Little recognized is the transitional period, during which the designers of Portland's residential architecture explored greater simplification of basic form and detail. For Georgian or Colonial style homes, most of the decorative detail was removed or modified to its simplest suggestion. The traditional gable-ended or hipped roofs were used extensively, but generally they were devoid of extended eaves or decorative eave details. Herman Brookman, Morris Whitehouse, J. Andre Fouilhoux, Frederick Fritch, and Richard Sundeleaf were the architects who explored these directions, all fully knowledgeable of traditional design and detail, yet bending to the changing architectural trends.

Nonresidential structures led the way in the development of new forms. Fred Fritch was one of the first to design in the stripped, more simplified styles. While working in the office of Sutton, Whitney, Aandahl and Fritch, he created designs for the Masonic Temple (1924) on the South Park Blocks and the nearby Fruit and

Original perspective drawing of the Lee S. Elliot House by Herman Brookman.

Flower Nursery (1928) on SW Eleventh Avenue that were avant-garde and well outside the Classical Revival mainstream of the time. Historical "correctness" was not nearly as important to Fritch as was a fresh or creative interpretation. In 1926, A. E. Doyle developed a Modernistic skyscraper design for the Terminal Sales Building at Twelfth Avenue and Morrison Street, followed in 1927 by Herman Brookman's design (with Whitehouse and Church) for the monumental Temple Beth Israel on NW Flanders Street, with its superb sculpture and somewhat Art Deco decorations. A few years later, the Whitehouse office produced the U.S. Federal Courthouse (1930) on SW Main Street and the Sixth Church of Christ Scientist (1931) on the South Park Blocks, bold expressions of Art Deco and Moderne forms, respectively. One other major commercial building was the much

celebrated Charles F. Berg Building of 1930 on SW Broadway, designed by the Grand Rapids Design Service. Art Deco was taken to extravagant heights in the elegant terra-cotta work and the black, aquamarine, cream, and gold glazes on its lively decorations. It was buildings such as these, produced by the city's major architects, that provided the commercial ambiance that led to new directions in residential work.

Morris Whitehouse was among the first to impart the sense of "stripped traditional" to his residential designs. The Elizabeth Clarke House in Oregon City would, at first glance, appear to

be a traditional Georgian style house, complete with side-gabled roof, brick facade, and paned windows. Yet, the exaggerated entrance portal, with rustication suggesting a massive, stone flat arch, is a pure abstraction of Classical architecture, imparting only a sense of an entrance to the house. Herman Brookman was adventuresome with his own home in Eastmoreland, built in 1931. Using a well-balanced combination of hipped and gable-ended roofs, he produced a charming plan with multiple levels oriented on a back courtyard. His innovations were further abstractions of Classical

Masonic Temple, Portland, 1924, designed by Sutton, Whitney, Aandahl and Fritch.

Fruit and Flower Nursery, Portland, 1928, designed by Sutton, Whitney, Aandahl and Fritch.

detailing, especially the pedimented dormer over the entrance to his office. Art Deco effects were achieved with the cornucopia carvings in the pediment and the suggestions of fluting at the door sides, achieved by angling bricks in vertical rows at 45 degrees. The same sense of bold geometries is shown in the arched side of the dormers of the second floor master bed-

room, making a strong statement in the ab-stracted flat-topped segmental arch that gives life to the front elevations. In his design for the Elliot House of 1934, Brookman added a simi-lar detail in the multiple-arched entrance por-tico, bold with its strong combination of Mod-erne geometries and Classical ram's-head and swag designs. The east elevations of the house

are among Brookman's most innovative in combining traditional (Tudor, in this case), Art Deco, and International styles. While the main facade has gabled roofs, dormers, and other typical Tudor elements, the siding is arranged in up-pointing arrow designs, pure abstrac-tions for decorative effect. The stair and porch railings may have been inspired by the Inter-

Temple Beth Israel, Portland, 1924, designed by Herman Brookman with Morris H. Whitehouse.

U.S. Federal Courthouse, Portland, 1930, designed by Morris H. Whitehouse and Associates.

national style "ship railings"—combinations of rounded corners, a cantilevered stair, posts, and strong horizontal bars. Its design is elegantly simple, and definitely of a nontraditional nature, clearly anticipating the future rather than harking back to the past.

Brookman's experimentations with the hipped roof were also important in the transitional phase. There is no doubt that his hipped-roof

forms with truncated gables, especially in his design for Julius Meier's Menucha (1926), were inspirational to later architects. Pietro Belluschi used some of these forms in his own house designed in the Northwest style in 1936. This design concept, possibly of Oriental influence, had also appeared in various houses designed by A. E. Doyle at the turn of the century, most notably the Harry Wentz beach cottage at

Neahkahnie on the Oregon Coast. In some respects, Brookman's scheme would seem to span the gap between the Wentz cottage and the Belluschi residence. Brookman also used hipped roofs successfully on his Savaria House of 1932, with its octagonal windows, simplified cornices, and horizontally emphasized railings, and on the home for Kenneth Eckert three years later. The bold use of horizontal siding accents

Sixth Church of Christ Scientist, Portland, 1931, designed by Morris H. Whitehouse and Associates.

Charles F. Berg Building, Portland, 1930, designed by Grand Rapids Design Service.

was carried across the facade, including in its design accommodations for windows, garage doors, and other features, much as John Yeon was to do with vertically emphasized paneled plywood siding several years later.

Other transitional designs by Brookman were more in the Stripped Traditional mode. His Baruh House (1936) took a Tudor-inspired gable-ended elevation, removed all detail such as cornices and window trim, and relied on superb materials, proportions, and simplified details. Only the windows, which are casements with horizontal mullions only, suggest more contemporary modern trends. Similarly, Brook-man's Arnsberg House of 1942 could be a Georgian design, particularly with its abstracted ogee-scroll pediment, yet there are no window-trim or cornice details, and the metal casement windows have the same horizontal mullions as those of the Baruh House. The railings combine Greek fret designs, in a somewhat Moderne tone, and handsome cast-stone rails supported on abstractions of a ram's horns. Brookman, the inventor, stretched his vocabulary to the very door of the Moderne and Northwest style designs.

Other architects followed suit. The Drake House (1937), by Sutton, Whitney and Aandahl, carried on Fred Fritch's tradition from the Fruit and Flower Nursery. Abstracted dentil work at the cornice and implications of quoins, combined with Greek meander insets, give the house a traditional air, yet no particular element was to be found in traditional designs. Richard Sundeleaf's work is included in the transitional designs, as his Tudor-inspired houses were stripped of all traditional design features, leaving just the basic forms and simple detailing. He would later evolve his designs considerably and explore the Northwest style.

Stripped Traditional/Transitional
CHARACTERISTICS

PLANS: symmetrical and asymmetrical.

ROOFS: low to steeply pitched gabled or hipped roofs. Dormers, if any, are flat roofed; cantilevered metal entry canopies; no eave extension. Some verandas under main-roof extension. Shingle or slate roofs.

EXTERIOR FINISHES: brick combined with Moderne style board-and-batten patterns; horizontal flush siding with streamlined horizontal accents. Moderne sculptured decorations; simplified dentil work or quoins in brick.

CHIMNEYS: prominent brick chimneys, sculpturally arranged within house design.

WINDOWS: small-scale casements with multiple leaded or wood mullions, or double-hung.

WINDOW TRIM (exterior): minimal steel or wood-frames, without trim, set in brick.

ENTRANCE DOORS: wood doors made of vertical boards, with small center window. Moderne or highly stylized Classical entrance pediments with recessed door. Minimal use of entry porches, but cantilevered metal canopies used.

VERANDAS/PORCHES: limited use of front or side porches and verandas; the front or wrap-around terrace had disappeared by this period.

INTERIOR FINISHES: plaster walls and ceilings, with wood trim; paneling in feature rooms; paneled entrance halls. Wood or tile floors.

INTERIOR TRIM: Moderne influences in door trim, window casings, and baseboards.

STAIRS: varnished wood risers and treads, with iron rails.

FIREPLACE FRONTS: modified traditional details, with marble or stone surrounds, wood mantel and side trim. Moderne trend to designs.

Entrance to the Lee S. Elliot House.

Stripped Traditional/Transitional
HOUSES

1926 Julius Meier (Herman Brookman)

1930 Elizabeth Clarke (Morris H. Whitehouse)

1931 Herman Brookman (Herman Brookman)

1932 Leon Savaria (Herman Brookman)

1934 Lee S. Elliot (Herman Brookman)

1935 Kenneth Eckert (Herman Brookman)

1936 Johns-Manville (Richard Sundeleaf)

1936 Leon H. Baruh (Herman Brookman)

1937 Donald M. Drake (Sutton, Whitney and Aandahl)

1942 Adrienne Arnsberg (Herman Brookman)

Julius Meier (1926)
Herman Brookman

Little noticed in the chronicles of architectural history is the Julius Meier country estate, named Menucha. The massive house, with extensive outbuildings and guest cottages, is located high on a point above the Columbia Gorge. It was designed by Herman Brookman and constructed in 1926, replacing an earlier log structure designed by A. E. Doyle. Offering the same dramatic views up and down the Columbia River as the site's previous structure, the Meier House also exhibits some of the design character of the earlier house, mainly in the huge baronial hall surrounded by service and guest rooms, all of which is covered by a hipped roof with truncated gables. This somewhat Oriental-influenced

design concept was used previously by A. E. Doyle in the Wentz Cottage of 1916 and would influence the Northwest style Pietro Belluschi House of 1936, though neither was in any way Moderne on the exterior. In the Meier house, the massive interior fireplace, however, exhibits features of the style in an exaggerated, almost Mannerist interpretation of Classical designs. Constructed of ashlar-bond stone, it has a massive firebox opening and a dressed-stone reversed-curve arch and high mantel. The hall itself has heavy-timber trusses, supported by Brookman's signature ram's head brackets. The perimeter balcony is somewhat in the mode of the National Park Service's Timberline Lodge (1936) on Mount Hood.

While the house itself exemplifies the gracious living of a country retreat, the grounds of the Meier estate must have equally amazed the guests. Down the sloping lawns to the cliff's edge, the swimming pool is

Julius Meier House.

Living room, Meier House.

sited on axis with the spectacular views of the upper Columbia River to the east. The view, masterfully planned by Brookman, is one of the finest in the state of Oregon. Other amenities surround the pool, such as a massive outdoor fireplace for evening entertaining and dressing rooms discretely placed below the cliff-edge terraces. Today, the house and grounds are used as a retreat and conference center.

Elizabeth Clarke (1930)
Morris H. Whitehouse

In the 1930s, the reserved and distinguished, Classically inspired architecture of Morris H. Whitehouse veered toward the emerging Moderne style. The house he designed for Elizabeth Clarke at 812 John Adams Street in the McLoughlin neighborhood of Oregon City demonstrates the bridge between Whitehouse's phases. The rectangular, side-gabled brick house has a basically Georgian appearance, with chimneys at the gable ends and eight-over-eight (8/8) and eight-over-twelve (8/12) paned windows. Yet, the wonderful detail at the entrance could be called a Moderne interpretation of a rusticated Classical flat arch. It gives the entrance and front facade considerable distinction, and it reflects well the beautifully conceived and practical floor plan. Inside, the major rooms are arranged to take full advantage of the garden in back. A shed-roofed piazza is located off the living room. The garage wing is connected to the kitchen by a back porch. Among Whitehouse's many distinguished projects, this small house was considered by the architect himself to be one of his three best works. The Clarke House was included in the 1932 listing of the "Finest Architectural Work in Portland, Oregon," and it received an award from *House Beautiful* magazine in 1935.

Elizabeth Clarke House.

Herman Brookman (1931)
Herman Brookman

When Herman Brookman designed his own home in 1931, he too ventured into Moderne elements. Located at 3680 SE Glenwood Street in the Reed Garden Homes section of Portland, the Brookman House originally had a U-shaped plan around a rear garden courtyard. Brookman's designs always considered the setting and the garden orientation, and he was noted for his sensitivity in landscaping. On the front elevation is a covered entry porch, with paired narrow columns, and a small side

Herman Brookman House.

Studio entrance, Brookman House.

wing that served as Brookman's office. The separate office entrance has a handsome pediment with Moderne or Art Deco carvings, a diagonally paneled door, and angled-brick side pilasters. Additional details incorporate Brookman's love of fine craftsmanship and decorative artwork. There are carved ram's heads, fine fireplace details, and wrought-iron railings and weathervanes. The high-ceilinged master bedroom is located in the upper part of the hipped roof, with an arched dormer and balcony overlooking the back garden. Changes have been made to the house over the years. A large skylight has been added, and a family room now occupies the courtyard.

Leon Savaria (1932)
Herman Brookman

The search for new and appropriate architecture during the 1930s produced many highly unusual designs. On a difficult hillside site, Herman Brookman designed a multi-faceted house displaying a combination of Classical and Northwest style elements. The house's strong horizontal cornice has Classical precedents, but the interconnecting roof forms were new and inventive for the time. Hipped roofs intersect one another in varying planes, and they are balanced by the dominating brick chimneys. Brookman placed the garage within the bank, under

Leon Savaria House.

the house, but he disguised it with a protruding balcony. The main level of the house is one floor above the street and opens to side gardens. Craftsmanship is evident in the careful window detailing, the second floor's curved dormer window, and the more Moderne balcony railing. Windows are casement with horizontal mullions only. This development of the 1930s soon became prevalent and added to the preferred tendency to emphasize horizontal design elements. The house, designed for Leon Savaria, is located at 2960 SW Montgomery Drive, in a neighborhood of exceptionally fine homes.

Lee S. Elliot (1934)
Herman Brookman

Clearly a Herman Brookman masterpiece, the Lee S. Elliot House is one of the most handsome and superbly constructed homes in all of Portland. In every respect, from siting to the smallest detail, the home exhibits Brookman's great skill in the basic qualities of architecture. The house is located at 1475 SW Vista Avenue, with access off Prospect Drive into a circular turnaround, and it enjoys a wide panorama of city and mountain views. All major rooms are on the view side, with the living room extending from the side-gabled central volume. Brick chimneys are located at the gable ends, flush with the outside walls. A second, one-story wing projects on the entrance side to form an entrance courtyard. On this court is the projecting entrance vestibule, distinguished by its notable cast-stone carvings of a ram's head and swag. It has an unusual roof composed of three parallel barrel vaults. The effect is Moderne, with exaggerated renditions of the Classical motif combined with the great simplicity of geometric masses found in the house. On the view side, a three-story rounded bay has fine paneled details that create a continuity with the leaded casement windows, some of which have Tudor-influenced transoms. The designs in the upper gables are streamlined and Moderne and relate to the linear, open railings of the terraces. At the northeast corner of the house is a polygonal breakfast room bay, reminiscent of the one Brookman designed for M. Lloyd Frank ten years earlier. All the wood siding and trim was originally a blue-green color (it is now tan), providing a strong contrast with the slightly salmon-colored brick.

The practical and gracious interiors also capture the Moderne elements of design. The wrought-iron stair railing has chevron-type designs, and the cornice replaces a crown molding with horizontal bands of reeding. The reed-

Interior stairway, Elliot House.

Lee S. Elliot House.

ing parallel lines continue on the living room ceiling, where they are combined with rows of acanthus leaves, somewhat in the manner of a Corinthian column. Other Classical details are found in the Georgian style fireplace mantel and are mixed with Moderne elements at the stair risers. The blocks formed by the treads and risers blend into the horizontal designs on the walls. Such detailing continues throughout the house, inventive in form, perfectly balanced in scale, and permeating a quality now unheard of and little appreciated. The Brookman attention to detail was masterful and of the "old school."

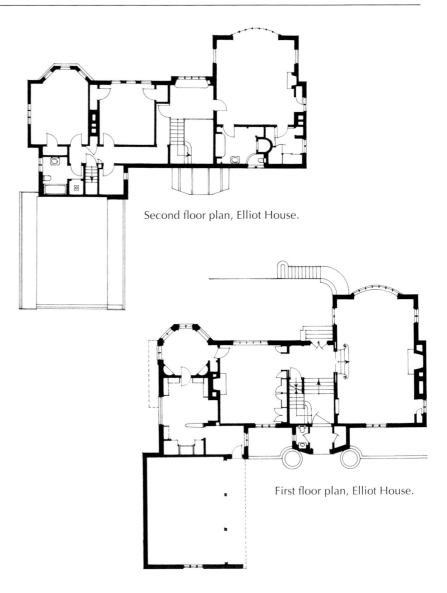

Second floor plan, Elliot House.

Living room ceiling detail, Elliot House.

First floor plan, Elliot House.

Kenneth Eckert (1935)

Herman Brookman

By the mid-1930s, Herman Brookman, of all the Portland architects, had explored the furthest in developing new forms of architectural expression. Moderne stylings took various directions but mostly added detail to already accepted design. In the Kenneth Eckert House of 1935, located at 3510 SE Tolman Street, Brookman designed a hipped-roof house of familiar forms, but in three intersecting masses. Most remarkable about the house is the division of the exterior walls into four horizontal bands of flush siding, each separated by a trim board. The bands surround the entire house, including the garage door. Windows are restricted within the bands, and the bands become mullions at the window divisions. The top band, at the gutter line, extends over the entrance door in a half circle. Although this approach is by no means a trait of the International style—which would not reach the city for another five years—it does foreshadow the arrival of that style with its strong horizontal emphasis. Here, it is more a combination of traditional roofs and Moderne elements. As such, it is unique and transitional, a distinguished house on the path toward a more contemporary style.

Kenneth Eckert House.

Living room, Eckert House.

Johns-Manville (1936)
Richard Sundeleaf

A part of the direction toward simplicity and the modern movement was to strip traditional designs of all but the most essential sculptural elements. Richard Sundeleaf did this to some extent with his design for the Johns-Manville model home, still standing at 420 SW Tenth Street in Lake Oswego. The house has a Tudor style side-gabled roof and a gabled projecting wing on the front. Details are extremely simple at the connection of the roof and the brick of the gable, and the lead-sheathed oriel window has the most reserved of half-round designs. As a result, the basic sculptural form of the house is straightforward and devoid of fur-

Johns-Manville House.

ther ornament. It is considerably enriched, however, by the use of Roman brick to cover the exterior walls and almost smooth asbestos shingles on the roof. Though the plain surfaces are broad, they are never lacking in visual richness. Only a slight curve at the gutter side of the gables, a chimney cap, and mullions in the windows could be considered superfluous design elements. From this stripped Tudor design, Sundeleaf ultimately broke away from traditional architecture completely. The Johns-Manville House was a first step.

Leon H. Baruh (1936)
Herman Brookman

During the 1930s, architectural styling tended to move in the direction of Stripped Traditional. Herman Brookman's Leon H. Baruh House at 3131 SW Talbot Street on Portland Heights incorporates much of the reserved massing and detail articulation that gave houses of the style their distinction. Acknowledged as one of Brookman's finest houses, the Baruh House relies greatly on fine materials, careful attention to proportions, and exacting tailoring. Its plan is a basic rectangle with two matching gabled extensions, plus a garage wing with a combined gable and shed roof. The front facade of the main volume is perfectly symmetrical, balancing a central recessed entrance portal, covered by a curved metal-hooded canopy, with the casement windows across the facade. Windows on the gabled extensions are stacked, and decorative brickwork ornaments the panel between. The windows are metal framed, have no vertical mullions, and are set with minimal trim in the Roman-brick walls. The plan of the house is as symmetrical as the facade, with a handsome well-lit gallery connecting the living room on the north with the dining room on the south.

Leon H. Baruh House.

Donald M. Drake (1937)
Sutton, Whitney and Aandahl

The use of abstracted Classical forms can be seen in the Donald M. Drake residence located at 1490 SW Clifton Street. A simplified cornice in brick resembles Classical dentil work, as do the indications of corner quoins. Likewise, slightly recessed brickwork around the main floor metal casement windows suggests a more Classical trim. This abstracted look could be called Moderne. It is the same aesthetic that was used by Frederick Fritch in the famous Fruit and Flower Nursery, and the Drake House continues that design idea, although by now the firm was working under the name of Sutton, Whitney and Aandahl after Fritch's un-

timely death. As with the Fruit and Flower Nursery, the Drake House's plan and elevations are symmetrical, formal, and cleanly detailed. A central half-round canopy covers the recessed entry, much like that in the Baruh House, and an octagonal window is centered above. The brickwork is of the same quality as is found in the Fruit and Flower Nursery, which was considered by many architects to be the most beautiful example of brick coloring and patterning to be found in the city. The Drake House cost, in 1937 prices, an amazingly little $14,000.

Donald M. Drake House.

Adrienne Arnsberg (1942)
Herman Brookman

One of the last houses of the Stripped Traditional or Moderne approach was the house designed by Herman Brookman for Adrienne Arnsberg at 1136 SW Davenport Street on Portland Heights. House details are simplified to create an extremely elegant statement, with no adornment other than the elaborate broken pediment over the recessed entry. This broken pediment is an inventive abstraction by Brookman, with his unique thin column proportions and the combination of a straight and ogee-scroll pediment. A Classically inspired carved pineapple, symbolizing hospitality and welcome, is located between the two scrolls. The facade of the side-gabled main volume of the house is entirely symmetri-

Adrienne Arnsberg House.

Entrance door, Arnsberg House.

Original perspective sketch by Herman Brookman, Arnsberg House

cal, coordinated on axis with the low-walled entrance terrace. The side wing, which has a slightly cantilevered second floor, extends to the east. Lap siding and stucco cover the wing, while the main house structure has a brick facing to match the entrance wall. Moderne design elements are found in the slightly Greek-inspired metal railing of the east-wing terrace and front entrance gate. Brookman's signature ram's heads, in abstraction, support the cast-stone cap of the front terrace railing.

CHAPTER 22

Modernistic/International

Only a handful of examples of houses designed in the Modernistic or International style exist in Portland. The Modernistic style had a brief flowering in the 1930s and early 1940s, as isolated houses were constructed from Seaside on the Oregon Coast to Pendleton in eastern Oregon. Portland's best-known Modernistic houses were built during this period, and they were closely aligned with the development of the streamlined ocean liners, airplanes, and automobiles of the time. Some will remember the "air-stream" designed automobiles, such as the 1937 Chrysler, where body details, such as fenders and covered spare tires, suggested the smooth flow of air over the vehicle without resistance. Portland's Modernistic houses, much like the Chrysler, ship, or airplane designs, incorporated smooth surfaces, curved corners, and considerable horizontal design emphasis. This was the era that gave birth to the ship-inspired "Porthole" and "pipe railing," still popular features of contemporary design. The whole house, in fact, seemed to be taken from the bridge of a large Moderne liner of the '30s. Though not particularly nautical, glass block was employed in the Modernistic style, as were

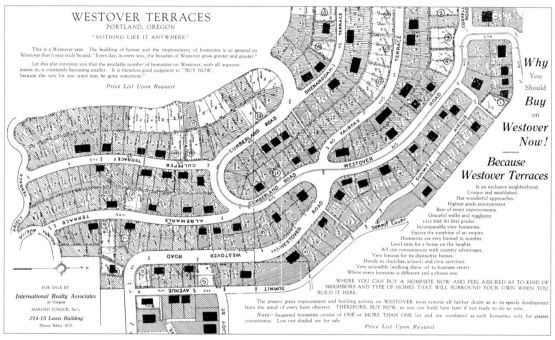

Promotional advertisement for the Westover Terraces development in Northwest Portland.

large expanses of industrial-style metal windows, often along the curve of a major room. Flat horizontal roofs were an essential element of the aesthetic, even in Portland where the efficient removal of rain and snow is central to a practical roof design. The houses were not large, but they were conveniently planned and well designed to their respective sites. None received special architectural note at the time. Van Evera Bailey, Roscoe D. Hemenway, and Hubert A. Williams are among the recorded architects in the Modernistic style.

The International style houses in Portland, on the other hand, are often tied to nationally known architects and can be more readily assessed. Richard J. Neutra designed the Jan De Graaff and William H. De Graaff houses in 1940, followed almost ten years later by Pietro Belluschi's Dr. D. C. Burkes House. Neutra's De Graaff houses hit conservative Portland like a lightning bolt. The owners were a wealthy young couple, he from the Netherlands and she from the fabulously wealthy New York City family that owned Macy's Department Store. Having come to Portland to establish a bulb farm in the fertile farmland east of the city, the De Graaffs brought their international collection of contemporary paintings, furniture, and artwork with them. Equally knowledgeable in architecture as in the other arts, they turned to Richard Neutra, pioneer of the International style on the West Coast. The 1929 Philip Lovell House in Los Angeles had brought Neutra great success and acclaim. The design for the De Graaffs' homes was remarkably similar in spirit to the Lovell House and many of Neutra's California and Texas houses, making extensive use of cantilevers, broad bands of windows,

and volumetric compositions of which the structural support was not entirely clear. The only remarkable difference in the Portland houses was the use of vertical tongue-and-groove siding in place of stuccoed exterior wall surfaces. This accommodation was encouraged by local supervising architect Van Evera Bailey, who was aware of the warm reception that had been given the first Northwest style houses of Pietro Belluschi and John Yeon only a few years earlier. Natural hemlock flooring or cedar siding, rough-side-out and unpainted, was especially attractive, adapting beautifully to the Japanese quality of the evolving Northwest landscape around Portland.

It should be remembered that in the later years of the Depression, before the Second World War, a sense of the strong need for social change haunted the land. Exhausted by the slow recovery of the nation's financial structure, people yearned for a new and better social order, one that would ensure survival for the country at a higher level of dignity than it was then experiencing. Integral to these debates were the ardent discussions of Socialism, Communism, and Unionism, all of which riveted the attention of those so deeply affected. Those restless aspirations, fed by the extremes of the social disorder, the extremes in wealth and poverty, found expression in architectural terms. Hence, when the new architecture stripped structures of all but the most essential functional elements, it had a social meaning and, to many, highly desirable qualities. Le Corbusier's Villa Savoie (1928–30) at Poissy, France, could exemplify that philosophy. The famous villa was, essentially, a white rectangular block, set on pilotis or round columns, squarely sculptural on

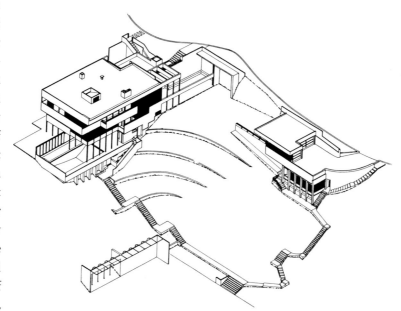

Philip Lovell House, Los Angeles, California, 1929, designed by Richard J. Neutra.

its barren site, and totally devoid of the usual amenities of softened edges, surface texture, ornamental enrichment, or plantings that could soften its impression. With its plain plastered walls and banks of metal windows, it became the embodiment of Le Corbusier's famous dictum: "a machine for living." This approach, which has greatly influenced one direction in American architecture for over sixty years, was a startlingly new intrusion in Portland in the 1930s. It would be years before the International style could become a part of the Portland architectural scene, and even then only with its more humanizing surface textures, such as cedar siding and the lavish use of Northwest plantings and gardens.

The De Graaff houses, therefore, represented isolated extremes in Portland for the next decade. It was Pietro Belluschi who next advanced the style when he designed the Burkes House in 1949. Again, it was unique, and one of Belluschi's few flat-roofed houses in the city, but it did lead to many other houses designed by other architects after the 1950s. The Burkes House wisely added the great enrichment of siding to its exterior walls and added it luxuriously to all interior walls and ceilings. As far as its structural system, the house followed the typical Northwest frame construction, sheathed and covered with the siding. Although much of the aesthetic was similar, the Burkes House bore no resemblance to Le Corbusier's concrete

Villa Savoie. The siting was also pure Northwest, with the gardens immediately accessible from the main floor ground level. Villa Savoie, by contrast, was a level above grade, with no direct garden access.

The International style in Portland offers some handsome examples by nationally recognized architects. The examples were tempered in their design and finish by the local environment and by respecting the regional penchant for wood architecture. The Northwest's great love affair with its gardens also influenced the design of the residences, nestling the house comfortably among the local firs and luxurious plantings. What the houses lost to purity of style, they gained in greater local acceptance.

Walter Dodge House, Los Angeles, California, 1915–16, designed by Irving Gill.

Villa Savoie, Poissy, France, 1928–30, designed by Le Corbusier and Pierre Jeanneret.

Modernistic/International
CHARACTERISTICS

PLANS: asymmetrical, connecting with gardens and landscapes. Interior spaces are interconnected and are not contained rectangles; open kitchen, dining room, living room, den, entry, and other spaces.

ROOFS: flat or low-sloped, usually with extensive cantilevered eaves, appearing as a thick horizontal plane supported by the sculptural mass; minimal use of columns, no visible beams. Built-up roofs with gravel surface.

EXTERIOR FINISHES: smooth and uniform wall surfaces, predominately tongue-and-groove vertical or horizontal siding. Roman brick or horizontal field-stone walls. Exposed concrete terraces with cedar dividers.

CHIMNEYS: field-stone or Roman brick. Low rectangular masses without articulation.

WINDOWS: ribbon windows, flush with the exterior wall plane; continuous bands with evenly spaced, thin, vertical mullions; horizontal mullions only at tops of doors to support large panes above. Walls of glass to the floor line, with minimal detail. Glass stopped directly into the columns.

WINDOW TRIM (exterior): the simplest possible detail, without visible trim or accent.

ENTRANCE DOORS: simple, flush wood or glass doors, without sidelights, transom, or decorative detail; located at perpendicular corners or wings. Often within modular ribbon windows, or covered with house siding.

VERANDAS/PORCHES: none, per se, but covered outdoor spaces located under the cantilevered roofs. Arbor trellises define exterior spaces and are attached to the house and landscape.

INTERIOR FINISHES: tongue-and-groove vertical siding, flush-side-out. Plaster or gypsum-board walls are smooth finished; almost invariably painted white. Flush ceilings, walls, and details, without trim. Exterior finishes, such as brick floor pavers, brought within the interior. Cork, wood, concrete, or tile floors.

INTERIOR TRIM: none.

STAIRS: minimal, as most houses of this style are one story, without a basement.

FIREPLACE FRONTS: simple rectangular openings in white plaster or field-stone surrounds. Sometimes open corners; pipe columns; raised hearths; and rectangular openings for storing wood. Metal canopy chimneys against a masonry wall, with raised hearth. Sometimes a minimal marble surround (more horizontal than vertical), with shelf substituting as a mantel.

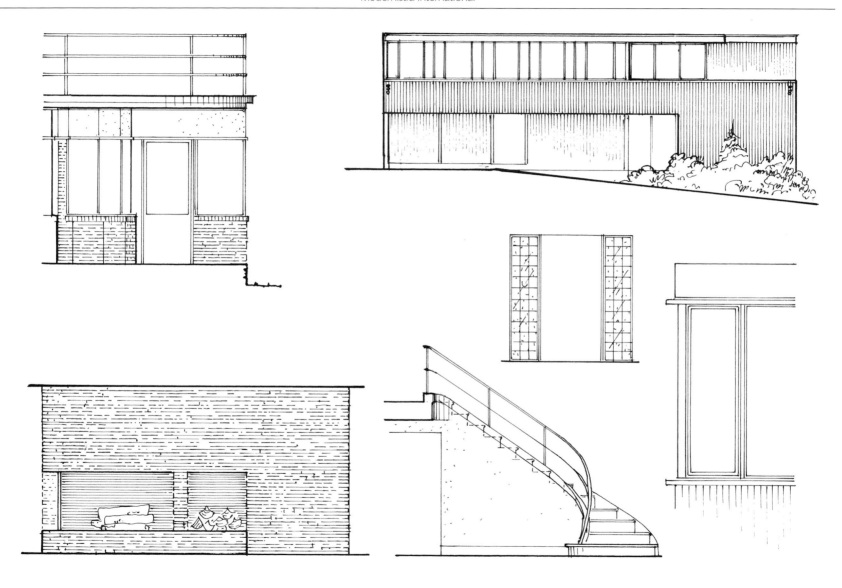

Entrance to the George J. Turner House.

Modernistic/International
HOUSES

1937　George J. Turner (Barrett and Logan)

1937　Harvey S. Hudson (attributed to Roscoe D. Hemenway)

1939　Thaddeus B. Bruno (Van Evera Bailey)

1940　Jan De Graaff (Richard J. Neutra)

1940　William H. De Graaff (Richard J. Neutra)

1946　R. J. O'Donnell (Hubert A. Williams)

1946　Keith Gilbert Powers (Herman Brookman)

1949　Dr. D. C. Burkes (Pietro Belluschi)

George J. Turner (1937)
Barrett and Logan

Modernistic architecture most often was an expression of the possibilities inherent in concrete construction. Windows, for instance, could easily be located at corners in concrete construction, with the concrete slightly cantilevered out above and below, or included as very wide expanses of glass. Northwest interpretations of the style attempted to suggest the concrete aesthetic in wood construction. Basically wood-framed houses were sheathed with stucco, to suggest smooth finished concrete, or with wood siding approximating the appearance. In the George J. Turner House, located at 5000 SW Humphrey Boulevard, vertical siding covers the rectilinear masses. Wood construction tends to sag with time,

however, and does not cantilever in the way that concrete does. Hence, corner windows and long stretches of horizontal windows required additional support. In the Turner House designed by Barrett and Logan Architects in 1937, this additional support is minimally expressed at the curved two-story bay and corner windows. In all other respects, the house has the typical characteristics of the Modernistic style.

Harvey S. Hudson (1937)
Roscoe D. Hemenway (attributed)

Though the style was relatively short-lived and produced only a few houses in Portland, the Modernistic style houses constructed in the city compare well with those built in other areas of the country. The Harvey

George J. Turner House.

Harvey S. Hudson House.

S. Hudson House, located at 3905 SW Viewpoint Terrace, displays many of the spartan characteristics for which the style is known, and its design is attributed to Roscoe Hemenway. Most prominent is the curve-ended second floor balcony, strongly resembling the flying bridge of a 1930s ocean liner. The remainder of the house is composed of intersecting stucco-covered rectilinear forms, with all wall surfaces, including the rectilinear windows, in the same plane, without relief. The windows are single paned, except for those that provide ventilation. All roofs, including those over the projecting porches, are flat. Beyond the recessed garage located beneath the house, the house's entry door is located under the "flying bridge." Above it, in turn, is a similar curved roof to protect the balcony. Though the house sits high on its bank above the street, main rooms have leveled garden areas. Most original details are intact, except for the various changes of sliding doors and windows on the back side.

Thaddeus B. Bruno House.

Thaddeus B. Bruno (1939)
Van Evera Bailey

Versatile architect Van Evera Bailey had the fortunate commission of designing a new multi-level home for Thaddeus B. Bruno on a spectacular bluff site, high above Oswego lake, with distant views of the Cascade Mountains, and fronting on the newly developed Oswego Country Club golf course. Bailey took full advantage of the opportunities. The house he designed was in the Moderne style, sided with a Roman-brick facing and having metal casement windows, but it bowed to the Northwest style with its slightly sloped hipped roof. The entrance foyer is on the street level, off the front garden, and stairs are located to the side, behind a curved glass-block wall. The entry landing opens to the stairway

Original sketch of street elevation by Van Evera Bailey, Bruno House.

Original sketch of the garden elevation by Van Evera Bailey, Bruno House.

Living room, Bruno House.

Curved porch, Bruno House.

with a Moderne style railing, and both open fully to the living and dining rooms below, all facing the cliff-top terraces above Lake Oswego. Curves abound on both the interior and exterior. Exterior roof lines and projecting decks and overhangs are curved. Inside, the fireplace wall and the fireplace front are also curved. Even the bar, quintessential for the 1930s, is located behind a hidden curved sliding door. The house is located at 1700 Ridgecrest Drive.

Jan De Graaff (1940)
Richard J. Neutra

In 1940, the International style arrived abruptly in the conservative Northwest when the celebrated Los Angeles architect Richard Neutra designed a house for Jan De Graaff, extant at 01900 SW Palatine Hill

Side view, Jan De Graaff House.

Jan De Graaff House.

Living room, Jan De Graaff House.

Road. The owners were avid admirers of contemporary architecture, and they sought out Neutra, who enjoyed an international reputation. He would design for them Portland's first residence in the style, which would house the impressive De Graaff collection of modern art and furnishings. The design that Neutra presented, in association with local architect Van Evera Bailey, has all the International style characteristics. Its flat roof, smooth walls, and continuous banks of windows are completely shorn of ornament. Detail is simplified to the extreme to obtain the tight-skinned, box-like appearance that was a quality of the style. The exterior emphasizes long horizontal bands of windows and similar expanses of vertical tongue-and-groove siding. House design had become an abstract art, relying on floating planes of varying irregularity to achieve the asymmetrical balance. Unfortunately, this most significant house, designed by an internationally recognized architect, has been remodeled so extensively that it has lost the qualities of design for which this architect was famous.

William H. De Graaff House.

William H. De Graaff (1940)
Richard J. Neutra

Richard Neutra was called upon to design another De Graaff home, this one for William H. De Graaff. It was constructed at 6308 SE Twenty-eighth Avenue, across from the Eastmoreland Golf Course. The house exhibits similar qualities of the International style as the Jan De Graaff House, primarily the continuous, tight-skinned exterior, composed of horizontal bands defined by the roof, the windows, and the siding under the windows. The floating roof plane extends out on the entrance, or western, elevation to provide protection from late-afternoon summer sun, an important design objective of many architects of the period. In addition to providing sun protection, the extended roof covers an open outdoor seating area, and to the back of the property, it covers an open carport. The house includes a second floor, which also has a projecting roof for sun protection. It is anchored by a chimney, constructed of Roman brick, that extends about two feet above the roof. As one of only two examples of the International style by the world-famous Neutra in Oregon, it is regrettable that its significance, not to mention its appearance, has been "remuddled" beyond recognition. Sadly, Portland has allowed its Neutra heritage to be destroyed.

R. J. O'Donnell (1946)
Hubert A. Williams

The last of the Moderne houses in Portland, as distinct from those more in the international Modernistic style, was that designed by Hubert A. Williams for R. J. O'Donnell in 1946. The house is located at 2708 NE Seventy-second Avenue in the Gregory Heights Addition to the city. Moderne elements abound in the house. Similar to the other Portland houses in the style, it has intersecting masses of one and two stories, horizontal corner windows, and a rounded extension with wrap-around windows off the living room. In addition, glass block is used in the O'Donnell House in the smaller entry windows and as sidelights to the main entrance door. Other windows have vertical and horizontal mullions, but they favor the horizontal emphasis, even where they continue around the curve of the living room walls. The house is of wood-frame construction covered with a stucco finish and painted off-white. Roofs, typically, are flat, with no parapet. These various elements are visually tied together by a cantilevered projection, or sun screen, above the entrance door and living room windows.

Keith Gilbert Powers (1946)
Herman Brookman

Using an amazing mixture of stylistic influences, Herman Brookman designed a handsomely conceived residence for Keith Gilbert Powers on a spectacular hillside site with panoramic views northward. The house

R. J. O'Donnell House.

Keith Gilbert Powers House.

Porch and balcony, Powers House.

combines Northwest style low-pitched and hipped roofs, International style influenced flat-roofed bays and projections, and even Moderne style steamship balconies and terraces. Such terraces are reminiscent of those on Brookman's Moderne Lee S. Elliot House (1934), and even of Van Evera Bailey's Bruno House of 1939. Surprisingly cohesive, despite the diverse style elements, the Powers House is tied together by its banks of casement windows, and by the Roman-brick siding at the first floor combined with the Northwest style tongue-and-groove flush wood siding at the gable ends and view-side elevations. Inward-curving walls, somewhat Moderne, announce the grilled entrance door, and additional curved walls are used for the garden border. Inside, the archetypal pe-

Side view, Powers House.

riod kitchen has rounded corners and islands, providing additional spatial flow. Brookman designed all the interiors complete with furniture, supplying a curved sofa near the floor-to-ceiling living room windows overlooking the city view. The house is located at 287 NW Cumberland Road, in the Westover Addition to the city.

Living room, Powers House.

Kitchen, Powers House.

Dr. D. C. Burkes (1949)
Pietro Belluschi

Though the number of International style houses in Portland before 1950 is limited, those constructed were notable. Pietro Belluschi designed a house for Dr. D. C. Burkes at 700 NW Rapidan Terrace, in Westover Terraces, that displays much of the style's characteristics. It has the hovering flat roof, the bands of glass windows, the walls of windows between structural components, and the interwoven interior spaces of an open floor plan that were an integral part of the style. Yet, the house departs from the white stuccoed walls and skin-tight planes found in eastern and European examples of the International style. The ceilings and walls are smooth hemlock siding, the floors are cork, and the fireplace mass is constructed of handsome, horizontally laid stonework. The same masonry continues at the kitchen stove and is used extensively in the garden walls, which tie the private courtyard space behind the garage to the main living spaces. The distant view of eastern mountains can be seen from the courtyard through the living room. This important house was purchased by the Belluschis following their return from the East Coast.

Dr. D. C. Burkes House.

Living room, Burkes House.

CHAPTER 23   Northwest Style

In the fifteen-year period from 1936 to 1951, Portland experienced the birth and development of what has become known as the Northwest style of architecture. During that brief time, it proved worthy of national attention, bringing considerable fame to its chief exponents, of which the city remains justifiably proud. John Yeon and Pietro Belluschi were the primary architects of the new style, the former an Oregon native and the latter born in Ancona, Italy.

The origins of the style have a wonderful tie to Oregon's unique architectural traditions. During the 1930s, Yeon and Belluschi, like other young architects during the Depression, spent considerable time discussing design philosophy and sketching under the tutelage of Harry Wentz, respected artist and teacher at the Portland Museum Art School and known also for his keen appreciation and knowledge of architecture. They traveled for sketching and architectural explorations to Wentz's cottage on the Oregon Coast, built in 1916 at Neahkahnie, a remarkable, isolated community on the meadowed southern slopes of Neahkahnie Mountain. It was remarkable not only for its splendid scenery of

Barn, Aurora, Oregon.

long stretches of coastal beaches and rough headlands, but for the people that the community and scenery attracted. They were a small group made up of a combination of Portland professionals, members of Portland's old families, mostly from New England, and an interesting segment of its old intelligentsia. Architecture would seem to have been a common interest and bond. As a community, they built their architecturally cohesive "cottages" much in the traditions of the New England Shingle style prior to the turn of the century. Among the first architectural features, directly on the rocky shore, were the shingled Neah-Kah-Nie Tavern and Inn and a cottage for Elizabeth Cadwell, both designed by Ellis Lawrence in the Arts and Crafts style in 1912. Concurrently, Albert E. Doyle designed cottages for Mary Francis Isom of the Portland Library (1912), the Doyle family (1915), Anna Belle Crocker, Curator of the Portland Art Museum (1916), and lastly, the Wentz cottage (1916). Though the cottages had similar roofs, banks of casement windows, and natural siding all in common, it was the Wentz studio that was considered the most important in the discussions over the future of residential architecture. Essentially, the cottage is composed of a large, attractive studio room, with large north windows, an ex-posed-truss interior ceiling, and a balcony/bedroom over a small kitchen at one end. The natural use of materials, a clearly expressed structure, the direct tie with the landscape, the banks of casement windows, and the open interior planning were all attractive features of the Wentz cottage. As quoted by Jo Stubblebine in her 1953 work, *The Northwest Architecture of Pietro Belluschi*, Belluschi said of the Wentz cottage: "It has function, appropriateness, harmony, materials, setting, orientation; it is modern, emotional, beautiful." As later years were to reveal, both Belluschi and Yeon would draw considerable inspiration from Wentz and his handsome retreat at Neahkahnie.

Homage must also be paid to the continuing and evolving architectural tradition around the city of Portland. A. E. Doyle had apprenticed as a youth in the Portland architectural offices of Whidden and Lewis. It was outdoorsman William Whidden who, in the very year his famous partnership with Ion Lewis began, designed the Cloud Cap Inn (1889) for William S. Ladd and Col. Erskine Scott Wood at the 6,000-foot level on Mount Hood. Its butterfly plan, following the contours of the hilltop below Cooper Spur, opens to the full views of the mountain. Constructed of logs from the site, the inn has large banks of casement windows, extensive overhangs, and a massive stone chimney and foundations. Today, the ruggedly handsome lodge seems as much a part of the ever-evolving Northwest style as any other source. It could have been designed yesterday, for its convenience of layout, use of native materials, and superb sense of siting. All these qualities were to become integral to the Northwest style when it emerged full-blown some forty years later.

It has been suggested that a major influence on the Northwest style may have been the indigenous rural architecture of Oregon: the barns, outbuildings, and utility structures that are found throughout the state. Indeed, they well could have been an inspiration, and Belluschi's churches often reflect some of the best qualities of those structures. The large wooden buildings, often having a magnificent structural system, were indeed handsome. They were architecturally sculptural in the most enjoyable sense, and they had the simplicity of statement that was so essential to the new architecture. The straightforward forms often used hipped roofs with truncated gables, or they employed the more direct gable-ended style, which both Belluschi and Yeon used. Likewise, the buildings often had intriguing assemblages of multiple volumes, all of which could be used where residential design needed flexibility. Covered with board-and-batten siding and shingle roofs, they wore an appropriate coat for Oregon's blustery winter weather. In addition, Japanese influences seemed to contribute to the emerging local architectural style.

In his lecture at the Portland Art Museum in 1941, Belluschi summed up well the basic approach that would define his interpretation of the practice of residential architecture for the future. He discussed twelve basic elements that were to define the future of residential design:

(1) the architect, (2) the client, (3) their relationship, (4) the surrounding country, (5) the orientation, (6) the climate, (7) surrounding buildings, (8) methods of construction, (9) materials at hand, (10) budget, (11) physical requirements, and (12) mechanical equipment. When all these were unified, he stated, "then we have modern architecture." Belluschi was quick to not allow himself to be labeled of either the International or Modernistic styles. He, therefore, summed it up with an acceptance of "Regionalism" as the term with which he felt most com-

fortable. Since that time, the term Regional has remained, but the general architectural term Northwest style has become most accepted.

Yeon and Belluschi were the vanguard of the new style, but several other architects also made a considerable contribution, especially during the searching transition years. Wade Pipes and Herman Brookman, the old-guard architects of the city, had spent years exploring more regional interpretations of their designs. Both Yeon and Belluschi had ties with Brookman, and they must have been familiar with

Harry Wentz Cottage, Neahkahnie, Oregon, 1916, designed by Albert E. Doyle.

Cloud Cap Inn, Mount Hood, Oregon, 1889, designed by William M. Whidden.

his remarkable concern for detail. His roof-form design for Julius Meier's Menucha in 1926 was to be utilized by both architects. Later, Brookman's W. R. Scott (1942), Ben Freedman (1946), and Keith Gilbert Powers (1946) houses were radical departures from traditional design and broadened the realm of possibilities for new residential design. Walter Gordon, who was working in San Francisco at the World's Fair in 1939, came to Portland after hearing great praise for Yeon's Watzek House. After establishing himself in Portland, Gordon worked for Belluschi (whose name replaced A.

E. Doyle and Associates in 1943) during the early 1940s before establishing his own practice in 1947. He produced a handsome series of houses reflecting the features of the new Northwest style. Van Evera Bailey became a major practitioner of the style, adding his own unique structural gymnastics and innovations with low-cost structures. His work was widely publicized, and he had an avid following of young families who wished to construct homes after the Second World War. He was noted for his "stilt houses" on difficult hillside sites and for his adventuresome roofs, sometimes appearing

without structural rationale. Though successful with his designs and clients and prolific in his outpouring of work, Bailey never was accepted on quite the same plane as Belluschi and Yeon.

Landscaping took a decided turn toward outdoor living during the era of the Northwest style houses. Brookman proved to be the first of the great architect-landscapers. His solution for the M. Lloyd Frank gardens at Fir Acres produced Portland's finest residential landscape, with magnificent terraced gardens on axis with Mount Hood in the distance. Brookman designed all of his own landscapes and helped se-

Ise Shrine, Naiku, Japan, archaic period (third century).

Katsura Imperial Villa, Katsura, Kyoto Prefecture, Japan, early seventeenth century, design attributed to Enshu Kobori.

lect and set the brick or stonework and the plants and trees, all toward creating beautiful outdoor spaces, or "exterior rooms." John Yeon inherited this mantle of architect-landscaper. The lovely work he did for his mother's home in 1935 was, according to Wallace K. Huntington, "both underivative and unhistorical," using circular brick walls, pools, trellised terraces, and openings to city views. Yeon continued this interest in plant material, championing the use of native plants and trees. The landscaping of the Watzek House grounds was exceptional in 1937. Rarely had there been such a dramatic connection between interior rooms and the views from the house, as well as between the house and the magnificent neighboring hills. The entire landscape became a unified experience, from the most distant mountains to the most immediate small-scale plantings. In the courtyard of the house, Yeon created a magical, private place where one could reflect on quiet lily pools, dogwoods, hanging wisteria, and southern magnolia. Even the mosses between the courtyard pavers were a part of the total experience.

Other names also became known in the landscaping profession. Arthur Erhfeldt, John Grant, Florence and Walter Gerke, Barbara Fealy, and Bill Roth were all landscape architects who lent their skills to developing the Northwest's gardens. A classic garden was constructed for Belluschi's John W. S. Platt House of 1941, developed by the owners over a long period of time. Belluschi incorporated into his design an outdoor room that centered on an elaborate rockery of native shrubs, all looming beneath a giant Northwest style portico. Here, the garden was an intimate part of the outdoor living area, as well as of the immediately adjacent living and dining rooms of the house.

The early phase of the Northwest style was abruptly altered in 1950 when Pietro Belluschi was appointed Dean of the School of Architecture and Planning at M.I.T. At the same time, after his brilliant plans for the Lawrence Shaw House, John Yeon effectively retired from residential design. A new group of young architects had come to the city, including John Storrs, Fletcher and Finch, Marvin Witt, and C. Gilman Davis—and all would contribute to the full flowering of the Northwest style. Hundreds of homes were constructed in the style over the next decades, many exhibiting the finest features of the style. Few homes, however, would offer the excitement elicited by the early works of Yeon and Belluschi.

Northwest Style
CHARACTERISTICS

PLANS: asymmetrical, connecting with gardens and landscapes. Interior spaces interconnected; open kitchen, dining room, living room, den, entry, and other rooms, without rectangular volumes.

ROOFS: low pitched, gable ended, or hipped, sometimes with truncated gables (Japanese influences). Open gable ends supported by posts. Recessed shed dormers. Shingled.

EXTERIOR FINISHES: smooth and uniform wall surfaces, predominately covered with tongue-and-groove wood siding; plywood panels used under modular window system. Roman brick or field-stone walls. Exposed concrete terraces with cedar dividers.

CHIMNEYS: field-stone or Roman brick. Low rectangular, without articulation.

WINDOWS: ribbon windows, flush with the exterior wall plane; continuous bands with moduled, thin, vertical mullions; horizontal mullions only at tops of doors to support large panes above. Walls of glass to the floor line, with minimal detail. Glass stopped directly into the columns.

WINDOW TRIM (exterior): the simplest possible detail, without visible trim or accent.

ENTRANCE DOORS: simple, flush wood or glass doors, without sidelights, transom, or decorative detail; located at perpendicular corners or wings. Often within modular ribbon windows, or covered with house siding.

VERANDAS/PORCHES: none, per se, but covered outdoor spaces under roof over-hangs supported by posts. Supported gable extensions also often used to provide out-door living spaces.

INTERIOR FINISHES: tongue-and-groove vertical siding, flush-side-out. Plaster or gypsum-board walls are smooth finished; almost invariably painted white. Flush ceilings, walls, and details, without trim. Exterior finishes, such as brick floor pavers, brought within the interior. Cork, wood, concrete, or tile floors.

INTERIOR TRIM: none.

STAIRS: minimal, as most houses of this style are one story, without a basement.

FIREPLACE FRONTS: simple rectangular openings in white plaster or field-stone walls. Sometimes open corners; pipe columns; raised hearths; and rectangular openings for storing wood. Metal canopy chimneys against a masonry wall, with raised hearth. Sometimes a minimal marble or stone surround (more horizontal than vertical), with shelf substituting as a mantel.

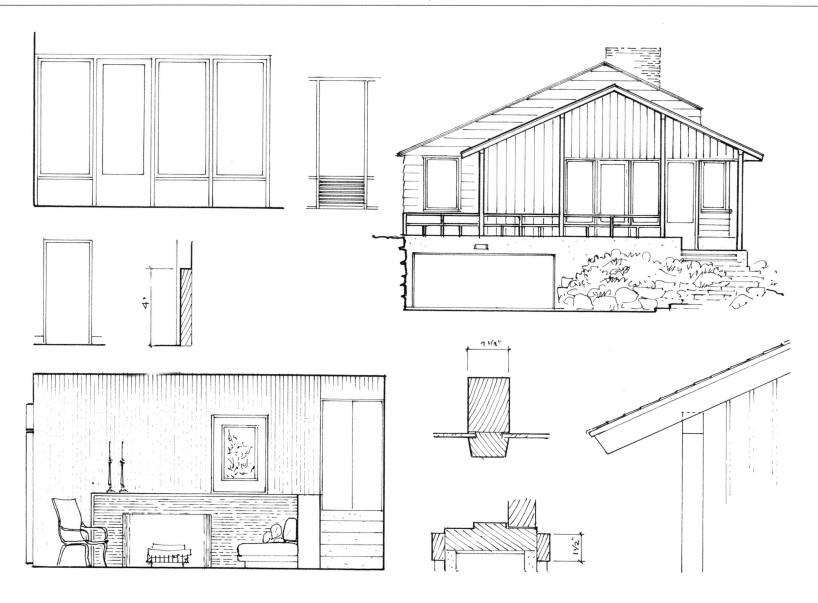

Entrance courtyard to the Aubrey R. Watzek House.

Northwest Style
HOUSES

1936	Pietro Belluschi (Pietro Belluschi)	1948	Dr. Merle Moore (Pietro Belluschi)
1937	Aubrey R. Watzek (John Yeon)	1948	William W. Wessinger (Walter Gordon)
1938	Jennings R. Sutor (Pietro Belluschi)	1948	E. W. Van Buren (John Yeon)
1939	Victor Jorgensen (John Yeon)	1949	Dr. Kenneth C. Swan (John Yeon)
1941	John W. S. Platt (Pietro Belluschi)	1950	Dr. James Rosenfeld (Wade H. Pipes)
1942	W. R. Scott (Herman Brookman)	1950	Allen Meier (Walter Gordon)
1946	Ben Freedman (Herman Brookman)	1950	George Cottrell (John Yeon)
1947	Lee Hawley Hoffman (Van Evera Bailey)	1950	P. L. Menefee (Pietro Belluschi)
1948	David Eyre (Van Evera Bailey)	1950	Lawrence Shaw (John Yeon)

Pietro Belluschi (1936)
Pietro Belluschi

As A. E. Doyle's cottage for Harry Wentz at Neahkahnie is believed seminal to the birth of the Northwest style, Pietro Belluschi's own home, built in 1936, would seem to pay homage to that cottage. The basic form, the hipped roof with truncated gables, the bay windows with upper transom panes, and the beveled lap siding, all find their parallels in the Wentz cottage. A bay window tucked under the eave was hardly a new idea, but banks of windows without panes, as is used on the house's front facade and on the rounded rear bay window, were to become a hallmark of the Northwest style. In plan, the small Belluschi House pivots around the central living/dining room. Two bedrooms, with baths, and a kitchen extend out toward the east on either side of the main room, forming a small country yard in the back of the house. A screening trellis, off the pre-existing garage, and terrace garden walls create a delightful outdoor room, visible from the curved dining room bay. The fireplace is located at the end of the living area, confined within a slightly protruding masonry rectangle. Original furnishings were somewhat Moderne, though

Pietro Belluschi House.

simpler and appropriately scaled to the room. The house has had numerous but sympathetic additions over the years.

Garden elevation, Belluschi House.

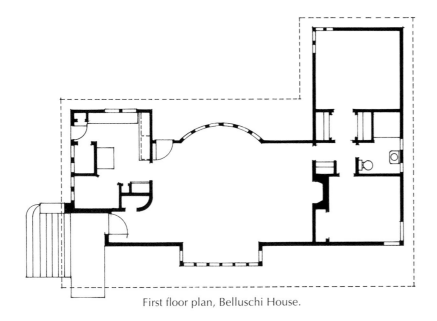

First floor plan, Belluschi House.

Living/dining room, Belluschi House.

Aubrey R. Watzek (1937)
John Yeon

The classic Northwest style was well launched with the construction of a magnificent house for Aubrey R. Watzek, located at 1061 SW Skyline Boulevard. Designed in 1937 by Oregon native John Yeon, then working in the office of A. E. Doyle and Associates, the handsome house remains one of Yeon's finest architectural designs. The house is planned around a central garden court. To enter the house, one is led under an open loggia, past the side of the court, to the entry door. Inside, a long gallery opens to the major rooms. The hilltop site commands views of the eastern mountains as well as the Tualatin Valley to the west, and the rooms surrounding the court all enjoy the panoramic views. The living room is on direct axis with Mount Hood. Looking out from wrap-around transomed windows, the views are framed by the posts of the open portico, an extension of the gable-ended roof. Such open-gable porticos were to become an accepted element of the Northwest style, used in varying forms by most architects in the style. Other traits of the Northwest style are found in the natural, unpainted siding, the transomed bay windows, and the flat field-stone foundations and garden walls.

Aubrey R. Watzek House, garden facade.

Entrance facade, Watzek House.

Stone wall and steps, Watzek House.

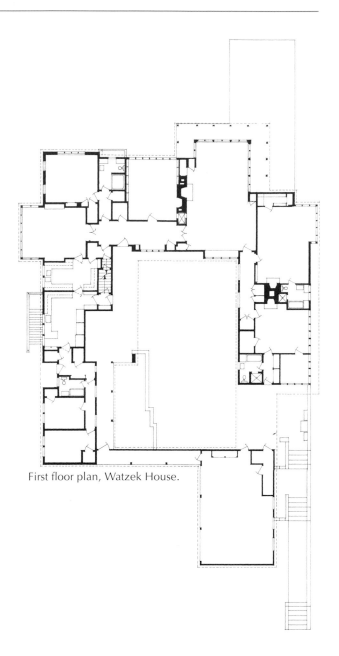

First floor plan, Watzek House.

Living room, Watzek House.

Dining room, Watzek House.

Most unlike the Wentz cottage are the Classically proportioned gable ends of the house, without any eave overhang. The restraint is remarkable. Details are handsome and simple, achieving maximum quality from excellent materials and careful proportioning. All exterior walls are covered with flush tongue-and-groove siding, rough-side-out to accept stain. The native-stone chimney, foundation, and garden walls and the shingled roof provide texture, all in concert with the Yeon-designed gardens. Rectangular stone patterns in the lawn tie the house module to the garden terraces. The entire landscape design was by Yeon, utilizing mostly native plantings and creating a handsome effect with the firs extant on the property.

The superb exterior detailing continues throughout the interior of the house. Wood is used extensively on the walls and on the coffered ceiling of the living room. Where the casement windows do not open, ventilation is achieved with paneled ventilators beneath the windows. Such paneling, combined with modular windows, was to be used extensively in Yeon's later houses.

Jennings R. Sutor (1938)
Pietro Belluschi

Pietro Belluschi, still operating in 1938 under the firm of A. E. Doyle and Associates, designed the Jennings Sutor House at nearly the same time that John Yeon designed the Aubrey Watzek House on a neighboring property, with only Skyline Boulevard between them. Both houses are among each architect's best works, and they would seem to acknowledge each other from their respective porticos. The Sutor House, located at 1100 SW Skyline Boulevard, is classic in Northwest style terms in that it exemplifies the simplicity and restraint that was believed an essential element of good architecture. The portico, so beautifully proportioned and perfectly scaled, in particular suggests the simplest of statements about the basic rectilinear plan and wood construction. It is presented in the most straightforward terms: posts, beams, purlins, and roof decking combining the structural harmonies of barn structure with the sophistication of ancient Japanese residential architecture. Echoes of the Wentz cottage are found in the bedroom bay, the continuous banks of windows, and the dark stained, horizontal beveled siding. The first impression of the house is gained from the approach drive, which enters into a double garage under the entrance terrace. Lush native plants, particularly mugo pines, which in the early years were of modest size, now screen the house from public view. At the main entrance terrace, located under the front portico, the banks of windows meld with the glass doors,

Jennings R. Sutor House.

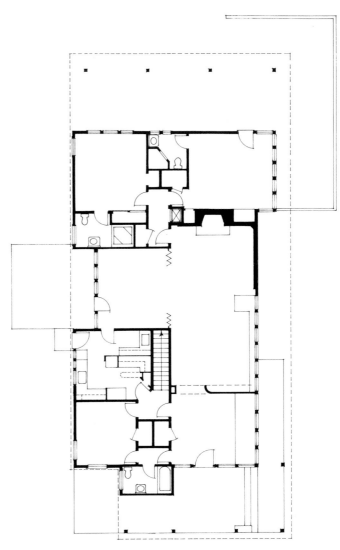

First floor plan, Sutor House.

Living room, Sutor House.

Dining room, Sutor House.

one of which, discretely, is the entrance door. The raised part of the house protrudes from the portico roof, separating house proper from porch.

The Sutor House is much smaller than the Watzek House, although both were designed for bachelors, and the Sutor House has only two bedrooms. A maid's quarters is adjacent to the kitchen. Main rooms are continuous, most notably the living and dining rooms, which are combined in various seating arrangements and form a T shape. These rooms are the center of the house, with bedrooms immediately to the east. A curved wall next to the fireplace is covered with an exotic "flex-wood" skin. The original furniture was designed by the architect, using large, comfortable, somewhat Moderne forms of rectilinear and drum-style shapes. The furniture is now long removed, but the house remains, due to successive respectful owners, in excellent condition.

Victor Jorgensen (1939)
John Yeon

After the success of the Watzek House, John Yeon gained numerous fine commissions. Among them is the Victor Jorgensen home, on a deeply wooded site at 4305 SW Dogwood Lane. Yeon took full advantage of the almost Japanese setting, placing the house back on the property and with a covered walkway connecting the house and the garage. The walkway consists of a rising series of intersecting hipped roofs, with an ingenious interconnecting structural system. The L-shaped volume of the house also has intersecting hipped roofs, the higher ones above the tall living room space. On the facade, Yeon used his theme of fixed windows, in series and with louvered ventilators beneath them, combined with plywood siding. Batten spacing is the same as that between the window mullions. Inside, the main living and dining space looks out to

Victor Jorgensen House.

both front and back garden views. At the fire-place end of the room, Yeon introduced a built-in seat to the side and a partial stair behind it accessing the north bedrooms. Another innovation of the room is a pull-out table from the kitchen to the dining area, with built-in bay seating.

Living room, Jorgensen House.

Covered entrance walkway, Jorgensen House.

John W. S. Platt (1941)
Pietro Belluschi

One of Pietro Belluschi's most successful houses is the John W. S. Platt House of 1941 at 4550 SW Humphrey Boulevard. As with other residences in the Northwest style, the house includes gardens that are integral with the house design, and the Platt gardens are exceptional. The site was originally an orchard; old apple trees blend with new exotic plantings, creating outdoor garden spaces that are among the most celebrated in the city. The original L-shaped plan of the house forms an en-

John W. S. Platt House.

Living room, Platt House.

Dining room, Platt House.

Garden terrace, Platt House.

trance court, now altered by garage additions. Hipped roofs with truncated gables and open porticos are combined in the house's basic structure. The open portico extends from the dining/living room, creating a wonderful outdoor room focused on an elaborate hillside rock garden. The interiors are deceptively simple. An interconnected living and dining room is separated from the entry hall by a screen. Exterior brick pavers extend into the entrance hall area, and the high ceilings are textured with patterned wood, suggesting Japanese influences. Unusually, the house has been furnished with exceptional antiques, handsome against the unadorned walls.

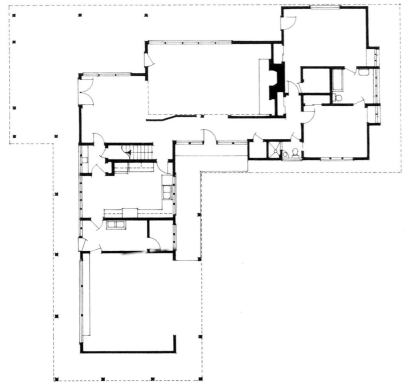

First floor plan, Platt House.

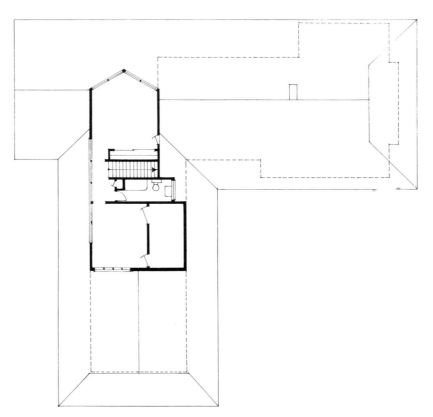

Second floor plan, Platt House.

W. R. Scott (1942)
Herman Brookman

The new departures in the Northwest style influenced all major Portland residential architects, including Herman Brookman, whose masterpieces generally had traditional styling. Brookman quickly adapted to the new fashion, designing for W. R. Scott an excellent home with Northwest characteristics. Located at 933 SW Davenport Street on Portland Heights, the house has an L-shaped plan, with an entrance space formed by a garage wing off the gable-roofed main volume. Its low-pitched roofs lack eave overhangs, somewhat as in Yeon's Watzek House. A telescoping gable, extending toward the street, articulates the end elevation. Brookman's signature ram's head sculptures are found in the carved-wood ends of the main portico's roof support beams, where they dynamically herald the entrance. Although from the street the house appears to be only a single story, stairs descend a half level down from the entrance hall to the living/dining room level and ascend up to the bedroom level. Dramatic views of the city and Oregon's famous mountains are enjoyed from all the major rooms.

Ben Freedman (1946)
Herman Brookman

Versatile Herman Brookman designed his Northwest style houses with a variety of roof forms. In the house he designed for Ben Freedman at 3636 SE Oak Street, just south of Laurelhurst Park, he used a hipped roof

W. R. Scott House.

Ben Freedman House.

with truncated gables, somewhat as he did for the Julius Meier country estate, Menucha. As in the latter house, the Freedman House has widely extended eaves, making the roof appear as a giant cap on the story-and-a-half house. The low hovering roof, telescoping at the front, also has a recessed dormer, but one that maintains the integrity of the roof form. Only the top of the dormer protrudes above the roof plane. Contrasting with this dormer, another one on the east side of the house is partially hidden behind two giant brick chimneys. The house is sided with brick at the first floor, and the truncated gables have vertical tongue-and-groove siding. Bands of fixed glass windows extend in a short bay on the front elevation. Individual casements, in pairs, extend across the other elevations and in the gable ends. A garage is accessed by a side drive along the western property line. To the east of the house is an enclosed garden.

Lee Hawley Hoffman House.

Lee Hawley Hoffman (1947)
Van Evera Bailey

Competing in popularity with Pietro Belluschi and John Yeon was Van Evera Bailey. His often-published houses, sometimes impulsive but always imaginative in their design and construction, found a welcome audience. After the Second World War, young families were anxious to hire Bailey, whose designs were economical as well as straightforward and practical. For Lee Hawley Hoffman, Bailey designed a well-constructed residence at 445 NW Hilltop Lane in an enclave of the Hoffman family, on property that was first used as a summer retreat at its ridge-top location. The house has several angled wings, one of which has a large picture window recessed under a triangular gable extension. Bailey employed gables, with clipped detail at the eave, out of the Arts and

Crafts tradition, somewhat in the manner of Wade Pipes, but with less of a slope to the roof. Horizontal beveled siding, a most popular material, is used here. The roof of the other wing extends out over a garden terrace, providing an attractive, view-oriented outdoor living area. The house is beautifully maintained and is lived in by Hoffman descendants.

David Eyre (1948)
Van Evera Bailey

Van Evera Bailey enjoyed wide popularity with his innovative Northwest style houses. Inevitably, his work is compared with that of others in the field, especially when he was so clearly influenced by others in his designs. The idea of creating an open portico under an extended gable-roof projection was developed, if not invented, by Yeon and Belluschi. Bailey employed this concept in the David Eyre House of 1948, nearly a decade after it was first used by Yeon and Belluschi. Instead of a symmetrical end gable, he designed an asymmetrical roof with different slopes on each side of the roof and with one side extending considerably farther out. The result cannot compare with Yeon's and Belluschi's classic sense of proportion, but it demonstrates Bailey's restless sense of invention. The roof itself is inventive, constructed out of decking—an economical solution for covering large roof expanses. While it provided a very thin roof structure with minimal cost and materials, it proved difficult to insulate. Other details in the house are clearly in the Northwest tradition. The post-and-beam construction, the banks of fixed windows, and the vertical siding are typical features of the style.

Dr. Merle Moore (1948)
Pietro Belluschi

By the later 1940s, Pietro Belluschi's houses had a great tailored clarity to them, well conceived in plan and balanced in their elevations. One such house was designed for Dr. Merle Moore on a point high above the city, at 2020 SW Fifteenth Street. The house was angled from the open "car shelter," and through a small courtyard, the main living/dining room wing of the house was aligned with the views of the city and mountains. The east elevation had a triple bank of windows protected under the wide overhang of the roof. Only the beam supports and exposed rafters added detail to the house's smooth-faced tongue-and-groove vertical siding. All other details were minimal. Entrance to the house was gained under a covered extension of the gabled roof along a brick walkway bor-

David Eyre House.

Dr. Merle Moore House.

dering the master bedroom wing of the house. A glass screen within small-scale supports separated the "car shelter" from the courtyard. Inside, the house had a considerable sense of spaciousness, further enhanced by the open living/dining room. With its gabled end overlapping the garage roof, the second story of the house had a small window under the roof ridge. The house was demolished in 1997 in preparation for the erection of a much larger house on this spectacular site.

William W. Wessinger (1948)
Walter Gordon

When Walter Gordon established his practice in Portland, the homes he designed exhibited the best of the Northwest style features. Displaying elegant restraint and careful detailing, the design for the William W.

William W. Wessinger House.

Wessinger House at 321 NW Hilltop Drive is clearly one of Gordon's best. The character-defining elevation is the open-gabled portico, the roof of which is supported by two posts with beams extended to the outer edge. The elevation is well balanced and harmonized with the house's angled side wings. The widely extended eave fully protects the large banks of windows from afternoon sun. The cap-like roof hovers over the house, and it is detailed in such a manner that the roof slab over the portico is thinner than the roof structure over the living space, as can be seen by the raised portion of the roof. Minimal casing details are found in the banked windows, and the chimney reflects the house's simplicity in its rectangular brick mass, clearly expressed against the low-pitched roof. The Wessinger family has beautifully maintained the house, having lived there for nearly fifty years.

E. W. Van Buren (1948)
John Yeon

On a small rise of land at 4273 SW Council Crest Drive, the E. W. Van Buren residence was designed by John Yeon in 1948. Except for the luxuriant plant growth, the house remains unchanged from Yeon's original design, including the interior furnishings. As in other Yeon houses, this one has a private walled-in garden, here behind the side-gabled main structure. A garage completes the enclosure at the extension of the garden wall. Because the house's owners are descendants of the owners of the Hidden Brick Works in Vancouver, Washington, the house is constructed primarily of brick, which structurally enclose the kitchen and bedroom blocks of the house and separate them from the living/dining room. The brick is expressed on the outside of the blocks as well as on

E. W. Van Buren House.

Garden elevation, Van Buren House.

Living/dining room, Van Buren House.

their interior walls. The nonstructural walls that separate the blocks have continuous banks of windows, repeating the modular theme of the non-brick walls. Louvered ventilators, as used on Yeon's previous houses, are located beneath the windows. The plywood siding of the house, and its modular battens, are painted two tones of the famous "Yeon-blue" color scheme.

Dr. Kenneth C. Swan (1949)
John Yeon

The Dr. Kenneth C. Swan residence, located at 4645 SW Fairview Boulevard, was built on basically the same ridge as the Watzek and Sutor houses. Designed by John Yeon and constructed in 1949, it has a design

Dr. Kenneth C. Swan House.

concept similar to Yeon's Jorgensen House of ten years earlier. At the street level, a covered walkway connects the house with the garage. The main space of the house, the living/dining room, is the center from which separate wings or blocks pinwheel in various directions. There are two bedroom wings and a kitchen wing, the latter opening to the covered walk to the garage. The walls between the blocks have Yeon's tall, moduled windows. As he had done in the Jorgensen and Van Buren houses, Yeon designed the living room of the Swan House a half level down from the bedroom wings, accessed by a small flight of stairs behind the built-in seating to the side of the living room fireplace. The interior is sided entirely with unfinished tongue-and-groove smooth hemlock, which attains a satin-like warm glow with age. Outside, the walls are board and batten, in twelve-inch modules with the windows.

Dr. James Rosenfeld (1950)
Wade H. Pipes

Wade Hampton Pipes was in the final decade of his remarkable architectural career when he designed a house in the Northwest style for Dr. James Rosenfeld at 6427 SW Hamilton Street. The previous Rosenfeld House on Portland Heights (an English Cottage style house built in 1922) had been designed by Josef Jacobberger. Although the newer Rosenfeld House has the simple, unadorned restraint typical of the Northwest style, it reflects Pipes's career-long fascination with the English Arts and Crafts style. Though their pitches are low, the roofs have his favored gable ends, extended out over multi-paned, metal casement bay windows. Unusual for a Pipes design, the extended gables are covered with board and batten, contrasting with the vertical tongue-and-groove siding of the main floor walls. The theme continues around the house,

Living room, Swan House.

Dr. James Rosenfeld House.

Allen Meier House, garden elevation.

even at the gabled entrance porch located between the two wing extensions of the front elevation. Because it is a one-story house with an expanded ground footprint, the roof appears quite large, dominating the central space of the gardens that surround the house. The house, plants, and gardens are completely integrated.

Allen Meier (1950)
Walter Gordon

Located on the site of two previous houses, the Allen Meier House at 2011 SW Carter Lane is an exceptional residential design by architect Walter Gordon. Gordon had the challenging task in 1950 of designing a new house on the foundations of the previous residence, which had been designed by A. E. Doyle in the Tudor Style in 1916, also for Allen

Meier. The Northwest style house kept the entrance adjacent to Carter Lane, but it accommodated a new double garage. The original stone garden walls (built around 1890) were curved in by Gordon to provide garage access at street level. As understated as the garage was the main entrance door, discretely tucked under a stairway bay window and covered in vertical siding to match the adjacent walls; the door has since been altered to a more conventional design. On the garden elevation, a more direct relationship was established between the house's living/dining areas and the spacious existing gardens, still encompassing some of the huge native fir trees. Gordon employed the open portico of the Northwest style, and he also designed a raised terrace with broad steps that descend gracefully to the garden level. Meier descendants still live in the house, accommodating it to current needs.

George Cottrell (1950)
John Yeon

The last of the impressive houses to be constructed, nearly in series, along SW Skyline Boulevard was the George Cottrell House of 1950. John Yeon's distinctive style is evident in the house, particularly his ability to adapt a residence to unusual or difficult sites. To capture eastern views, the house is sited on the top of a knoll, well above the entrance drive and garages. An exterior stair rises from the drive to the house's entrance at the main level. Off the main entry is the central living room, with Yeon's pinwheel of room blocks emanating from the space. As in his other houses, Yeon provided built-in seating next to the main living room fireplace, separating the living area from stairs to a slightly higher floor level. In addition to housing the master bedroom, the higher level accommodates the dining room and kitchen. Another level off the entry

contains additional bedrooms. Outside, a wrap-around trellis provides sun protection on the eastern elevation. The entire house is covered with flush horizontal siding, except at the moduled window walls between the various blocks and at other window locations.

P. L. Menefee (1950)
Pietro Belluschi

Several years before Pietro Belluschi sold his Portland practice and accepted his new position at M.I.T., he designed one of the finest houses of his career, built for P. L. Menefee. Belluschi designed a rambling ranch house near Sheridan, Oregon, over forty miles southwest of Portland. Wood pylons at the entrance fence welcome visitors to a large courtyard. Enclosing the court is the guest house, the ranch office, a carport, utility rooms, and the main rooms of the house, which surprisingly includes

George Cottrell House.

P. L. Menefee House.

only one bedroom. The living and dining rooms face east, and they are protected by an open-ended portico, a classic of the Northwest style. Four posts support the roof over the large area, with a crosstie between the two center posts. As is typical for the style, roof beams extend to the edge of the roof and slightly beyond, in the Japanese manner. The house's massive roof, with fully extended eaves, is hipped, except at the open gable ends; all components of the roof are low pitched. Belluschi designed all the furniture for the interior, as well as the huge open fireplace, which has no side enclosure but rather has a massive copper hood with a relief sculpture by Frederick Littman, a favorite artist of Belluschi's.

Lawrence Shaw (1950)
John Yeon

One of John Yeon's last, and possibly finest, residences was designed for Lawrence Shaw at 12800 SW Goodal Road. Handsome on its eight-acre meadowland, the house offers a unique blend of Classical form and contemporary design. In basic structure, the central rectilinear mass has a low-hipped roof and is surrounded by several flat-roofed additions. The entire house, both outside and throughout the inte-

Lawrence Shaw House.

Front elevation, Shaw House.

Living room, Shaw House.

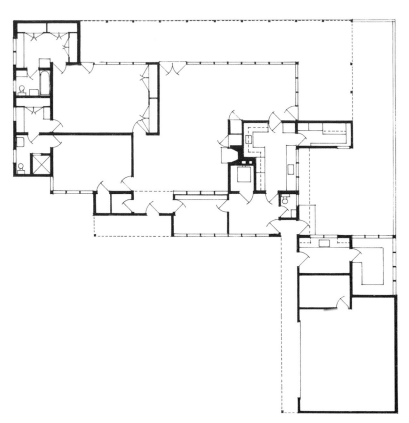

First floor plan, Shaw House.

rior, is sided with Yeon's typical three-foot modular plywood paneling, creating a marvelously unified architectural statement. Though the entrance elevations are more enclosed, with few windows and a covered entry porch, the meadow-side elevations are opened by a full wraparound piazza, Classically proportioned and elegantly detailed. The interiors were finished to every detail by Yeon, who used his special blend of contemporary tastes and his connoisseur's knowledge of antique furnishings. This special house was heralded in a 1953 issue of *House Beautiful*, which stated "The house illustrates in one superb design, the union of function and form, delight and performance. Like life, it works and plays. It has mood and warmth and vitality." Unfortunately, the house has been altered beyond recognition.

The Architects of Portland's Classic Houses

Van Evera Bailey

Thaddeus B. Bruno, 1939, Modernistic/International

Lee Hawley Hoffman, 1947, Northwest Style

David Eyre, 1948, Northwest Style

Barrett and Logan

George J. Turner, 1937, Modernistic/International

Pietro Belluschi

Pietro Belluschi, 1936, Northwest Style

Jennings R. Sutor, 1938, Northwest Style

John W. S. Platt, 1941, Northwest Style

Dr. Merle Moore, 1948, Northwest Style

Dr. D. C. Burkes, 1949, Modernistic/International

P. L. Menefee, 1950, Northwest Style

John Virginius Bennes

Marcus J. Delahunt, 1909, Prairie

William Biddle Wells, 1910, Craftsman

John Virginius Bennes, 1911, Prairie

Carl M. Little, 1912, Prairie (with Bennes, Hendricks and Thompson)

Aaron H. Maegley, 1914, Prairie

Leslie M. Scott, 1917, Colonial Revival—Second Phase

Herman Brookman

M. Lloyd Frank, 1924, Tudor

Gatekeeper's Lodge, M. Lloyd Frank Estate, 1924, Arts & Crafts

Barbara Price, 1926, Mediterranean

Julius Meier, 1926, Stripped Traditional/Transitional

Harry A. Green, 1928, Mediterranean

Herman Brookman, 1931, Stripped Traditional/Transitional

Leon Savaria, 1932, Stripped Traditional/Transitional

Lee S. Elliot, 1934, Stripped Traditional/Transitional

Kenneth Eckert, 1935, Stripped Traditional/Transitional

Leon H. Baruh, 1936, Stripped Traditional/Transitional

Adrienne Arnsberg, 1942, Stripped Traditional/Transitional

W. R. Scott, 1942, Northwest Style

Keith Gilbert Powers, 1946, Modernistic/International

Ben Freedman, 1946, Northwest Style

Francis Brown

Wilbur Reid, 1914, Bungalow

Elwood M. Burton

H. C. Hoyt, 1858, Gothic Revival (attributed)

Dr. J. A. Chapman, 1864, Italian Villa (attributed; with William W. Piper)

E. J. Jeffrey, 1868, Second Empire (attributed)

William S. Ladd, 1869, Second Empire

William Wadhams, 1873, Italian Villa

Henry W. Cleaveland

Simeon G. Reed, 1873, Second Empire

Henry W. Failing, 1873, Second Empire

Senator Joseph N. Dolph, 1881, Queen Anne

Harrison Corbett

James G. Gault, c. 1914, Colonial Revival—First Phase

Kirtland K. Cutter

Theodore B. Wilcox, 1919, Colonial Revival—Second Phase

Thomas J. Autzen, 1927, Tudor

Harold W. Doty

Paul C. Carey, 1925, Colonial Revival—Second Phase

Joseph R. Gerber, 1927, Arts & Crafts (with Hollis E. Johnson)

James Leland, 1928, Arts & Crafts

Walter S. Zimmerman, 1931, Arts & Crafts (with Wade H. Pipes)

Albert E. Doyle

George W. Collins, 1907, Arts & Crafts

Edward L. Harmon, 1908, Craftsman/Colonial

Mayor H. Russell Albee, 1912, Colonial Revival—First Phase

Edward Ehrman, 1915, English Cottage

Frank J. Cobb, 1917, Jacobethan

Bert C. Ball, 1921, English Cottage

Coleman Wheeler, 1923, English Cottage

Joseph R. Bowles, 1924, Mediterranean

John G. Edwards, 1925, Arts & Crafts

Aaron Holtz, 1927, Jacobethan

George F. Durham

George H. Watson, 1910, Colonial Revival—First Phase (attributed)

J. W. Creath, 1914, Colonial Revival—First Phase (attributed)

George A. Eastman

M. C. White, 1911, Bungalow

George A. Eastman, 1913, Bungalow

Charles Ertz

Carl C. Jantzen, 1930, Tudor

Wesley P. Steinmetz, 1936, Tudor (attributed)

A. H. Faber

Gertrude Smith, 1907, Bungalow

Edward T. Foulkes

Dr. Ami Nichols, 1913, Colonial Revival—First Phase

Henry L. Pittock, 1914, French Renaissance

J. O. Frye

J. O. Frye, 1930, English Cottage

Walter Gordon

William W. Wessinger, 1948, Northwest Style

Allen Meier, 1950, Northwest Style

Charles Green

Charles Green, 1926, Arts & Crafts

Absolom B. Hallock

Captain John C. Couch, 1850, Greek Revival (attributed)

Thomas J. Carter, 1850, Greek Revival (attributed)

Captain J. C. Ainsworth, 1850, Greek Revival (attributed)

General Stephen Coffin, 1852, Gothic Revival

Henry W. Corbett, 1854, Greek Revival (attributed)

T. J. Holmes, 1858, Gothic Revival

W. C. Hull, c. 1858, Gothic Revival (attributed)

Captain J. C. Ainsworth, 1862, Italian Villa

Henry J. Hefty

Henry J. Hefty, 1892, Shingle/Richardsonian

Roscoe D. Hemenway

Dr. D. C. Burkes, c. 1928, Colonial Revival—Second Phase

George P. Berky, 1929, Arts & Crafts

Charles Barker, 1929, Arts & Crafts

Roy Gangware, 1932, Tudor

Harvey S. Hudson, 1937, Modernistic/International (attributed)

Theodore B. Wilcox, 1950, Colonial Revival—Second Phase

Henry Herzog

Dr. James J. Rosenberg, 1933, Tudor

Isaac Hodgson, Jr.

Isaac Hodgson, Jr., 1891, Shingle/Richardsonian

Julius Loewenberg, 1891, Shingle/Richardsonian

A. R. Hossack

William H. Hossack, 1916, Bungalow (attributed)

C. Spies, 1922, Prairie

Francis Jacobberger

D. R. Munroe, 1913, Tudor

Josef Jacobberger

Fred A. Shogren, 1906, Bungalow (attributed)

Josef Jacobberger, 1906, Arts & Crafts

R. B. Lamson, 1908, Shingle/Richardsonian

Woods Hutchinson, 1908, Bungalow

Frank H. Ransom, 1908, Craftsman

Emma M. Austin, c. 1910, Bungalow (attributed)

George H. Howell, c. 1910, Craftsman

Michael F. Brady, 1911, Arts & Crafts

Arts and Crafts "A", c. 1912, Arts & Crafts (attributed)

Alfred T. Smith, 1912, Arts & Crafts

Dr. Andrew J. Geisy, 1913, Arts & Crafts

Michael J. Walsh, 1915, Arts & Crafts

Dr. Lawrence Selling, 1918, Colonial Revival—First Phase

Iva L. McFarlan, 1921, Colonial Revival—First Phase

Dr. James Rosenfeld, 1922, English Cottage

Frank Robertson, 1926, Arts & Crafts (Jacobberger, Smith and Smith)

Johnson and Mayer

Frederick Alva Jacobs, 1913, Bungalow

C. S. Jackson, c. 1915, Bungalow (attributed)

Folger Johnson

David A. E. Rocky, 1913, Mediterranean

Hollis E. Johnson

Joseph R. Gerber, 1927, Arts & Crafts (with Harold W. Doty)

Major Watson Eastman, 1928, Mediterranean

Albert H. Jordan

Ben Holladay, c. 1870, Italian Villa (attributed)

Judge John W. Whalley, 1879, Italianate (attributed)

M. W. Fechheimer, c. 1880, Italianate (attributed)

William C. Knighton

Belle and Maude Ainsworth, 1907, Craftsman

Charles J. Schnabel, 1907, Craftsman

Amedee M. Smith, 1909, Craftsman

Dwight Edwards, 1910, Craftsman (attributed)

Justus F. Krumbein

Jacob Kamm, 1871, Second Empire

Justus F. Krumbein, c. 1880, Italianate

George V. James, 1882, Italianate

Captain George Flanders, 1882, Italianate

Richard B. Knapp, 1882, Queen Anne (attributed)

Justus F. Krumbein, 1884, Queen Anne

John B. Bridges, 1884, Eastlake (attributed)

Rodney Glisan, 1885, Queen Anne (attributed)

Levi White, 1886, Eastlake

Edward C. Hochapfel, 1907, Craftsman/Colonial

Ellis F. Lawrence

Ellis F. Lawrence, 1906, Arts & Crafts

Blaine R. Smith, 1908, Tudor

James E. Wheeler, 1910, Colonial Revival—First Phase (McNaughton, Raymond and Lawrence)

Lewis T. Gilliand, 1910, Bungalow

Henry Miller, 1911, Tudor

Riverview Cemetery Caretaker's House, 1914, Colonial Revival—First Phase

John L. Bowman, 1916, Craftsman/
  Colonial
Daniel Kern, c. 1917, Jacobethan
Paul F. Murphy, 1918, English Cottage
Cameron Squires, 1920, Tudor
Max S. Hirsch, 1922, English Cottage
Stanley C. E. Smith, 1923, Tudor
Charles T. Ladd, 1925, Arts & Crafts
  (attributed)
William P. Hawley, 1927, Colonial
  Revival—Second Phase
Burt Brown Barker, 1928, French Ren-
  aissance
O. L. Price, 1928, Mediterranean
J. L. Easson, 1931, Tudor (attributed)

J. Irving Lawson
Dr. John P. Cleland, 1936, Colonial
  Revival—Second Phase

Edgar M. Lazarus
Friedlander Residence, c. 1890,
  Shingle/Richardsonian
Frederick V. Holman, 1890, Shingle/
  Richardsonian
George F. Heusner, 1892, Shingle/
  Richardsonian

David C. Lewis
Allen L. Lewis, c. 1901, Jacobethan
David T. Honeyman, 1907, Colonial
  Revival—First Phase
Cicero Hunt Lewis, c. 1910, Jacobethan
  (attributed)
Rev. Charles Scadding, 1911, Tudor

Carl L. Linde
Cornwell and Perry Building Co.,
  1922, Mediterranean
C. H. Farrington, 1924, English
  Cottage
Dr. Zimmerman, 1925, Tudor
Ward R. Bowles, 1926, Mediterranean
Jacob N. Barde, 1926, Mediterranean
Otho Pool, 1928, Mediterranean
Gordon Barde, 1939, French Renais-
  sance

William F. McCaw
Martha S. Thorton, c. 1885, Queen
  Anne
Commanding Officer's Quarters, Fort
  Vancouver, 1886, Queen Anne

Bruce McKay
Dr. H. W. Howard, 1927,
  Mediterranean

**McNaughton, Raymond and
Lawrence** (see also Ellis F. Law-
rence)
James E. Wheeler, 1910, Colonial
  Revival—First Phase

Richard Milwain
Richard Milwain, c. 1881, Italianate

Richard J. Neutra
Jan De Graaff, 1940, Modernistic/
  International
William H. De Graaff, 1940, Modern-
  istic/International

Jamieson K. Parker
Milton Markewitz, 1924, Colonial
  Revival—Second Phase
Edward D. Kingsley, 1926, Colonial
  Revival—Second Phase
Caroline and Louise Flanders, 1926,
  Arts & Crafts
Philip L. Jackson, c. 1927, French
  Renaissance
George Black, 1929, Arts & Crafts
William Haseltine, 1935, Colonial
  Revival—Second Phase
Donald McGraw, c. 1940, Colonial
  Revival—Second Phase

Albert Parr
A. J. Lewthwaite, 1926, French Renaissance (with Francis Ward)

William W. Piper
Dr. J. A. Chapman, 1864, Italian Villa
  (attributed; with E. M. Burton)
A. H. Johnson, 1873, Second Empire
  (attributed)

Wade H. Pipes
John M. Pipes, 1912, Arts & Crafts
T. H. Sherrard, 1918, Arts & Crafts
George Pipes, 1923, Arts & Crafts
Theodore F. Brown, 1923, Arts &
  Crafts
John A. Laing, 1925, Arts & Crafts
Ida Catlin, 1927, Arts & Crafts
Edwin T. Burke, 1927, Arts & Crafts
Dr. Frank Kistner, 1930, Arts & Crafts
Walter S. Zimmerman, 1931, Arts &
  Crafts (with Harold W. Doty)

Dr. James Rosenfeld, 1950, Northwest
  Style

George M. Post
William T. Waerner, 1927, Colonial
  Revival—Second Phase

William Grey Purcell
William Grey Purcell, 1920, Arts &
  Crafts
Lilian K. Pollock, 1921, Prairie
Woerner Lewis, c. 1922, Arts & Crafts
Purcell Residence, 1923, Arts & Crafts
Thomas Mostyn, 1924, Prairie

F. G. Quimby
H. E. Schegel, c. 1916, Bungalow

Edward T. Root
Dr. A. M. Stolte, 1910, Craftsman
Belle Ainsworth Jenkins, 1912,
  Bungalow (Root and Hoose)
Samuel Rosenblatt, 1915, Colonial
  Revival—First Phase

Emil Schacht
Emil Schacht, 1902, Shingle/Richard-
  sonian
Henry Hahn, 1905, Craftsman
William Gadsby, 1908, Tudor
Christine Becker, 1909, Craftsman/
  Colonial
John A. Veness, 1910, Craftsman/
  Colonial

Shepley, Rutan and Coolidge
Abbott Mills, 1908, Colonial Revival—
  First Phase

Lewis H. Mills, 1916, Colonial Revival
—Second Phase

Joseph Sherwin
George H. Williams, 1881, Queen
Anne

Glenn Stanton and Associates
Ernest Haycox, 1940, Colonial Revival
—Second Phase

S. M. Stokes
C. P. Osborne, 1922, Arts & Crafts

Richard Sundeleaf
William Scott, 1927, Jacobethan
Roy Hunt, 1932, Tudor (attributed)
Paul F. Murphy, 1934, Tudor
Dean B. Webster, 1936, Tudor
Johns-Manville, 1936, Stripped Tradi-
tional/Transitional
Richard Sundeleaf, 1939, Arts & Crafts

Sutton and Whitney
Leon Hirsch, 1922, Jacobethan

Sutton, Whitney and Aandahl
Donald M. Drake, 1937, Stripped
Traditional/Transitional

Lee Thomas
J. C. Braly, 1926, Colonial Revival—
Second Phase
Properties Unlimited, 1940, Arts &
Crafts

Ernest Tucker
E. S. Beach, 1931, Arts & Crafts
E. T. Samuelson, 1937, Arts & Crafts

C. V. Vanderpool
Robert McBride, 1912, Prairie
Emma McCauley, c. 1912, Prairie

Francis Ward
A. J. Lewthwaite, 1926, French
Renaissance (with Albert Parr)

William Whidden (*see also* Whidden
and Lewis)
Lucien W. Wallace, 1888, Colonial
Revival—First Phase

Whidden and Lewis
Charles B. Bellinger, 1889, Colonial
Revival—First Phase
H. C. Campbell, c. 1890, Shingle/
Richardsonian (attributed)
Theodore B. Trevitt, 1890, Colonial
Revival—First Phase
Winslow B. Ayer, 1890, Colonial
Revival—First Phase
Zera Snow, 1891, Colonial Revival—
First Phase
Dr. Kenneth A. J. Mackenzie, 1892,
Shingle/Richardsonian
Henry J. Corbett, 1892, Shingle/
Richardsonian
William Honeyman, 1893, Shingle/
Richardsonian
Theodore B. Wilcox, 1893, Shingle/
Richardsonian
Judge Wallace McCamant, 1899,
Colonial Revival—First Phase
Frank E. Hart, 1900, Tudor
Walter F. Burrell, 1901, Prairie

William E. MacKenzie, 1902, Colonial
Revival—First Phase (attributed)
Isom White, 1903, Colonial Revival—
First Phase
Winslow B. Ayer, 1903, Jacobethan
Nahum A. King, c. 1904, Colonial
Revival—First Phase
Dr. Henry Coe, c. 1905, Colonial
Revival—First Phase (attributed)
Philip Buehner, 1908, Colonial
Revival—First Phase

Morris H. Whitehouse
Max H. Hauser, 1908, Colonial
Revival—First Phase (attributed)
Osmond B. Stubbs, 1915, Colonial
Revival—First Phase (Whitehouse
and Fouilhoux)
Raymond Wilcox, 1916, Colonial
Revival—Second Phase
(Whitehouse and Fouilhoux)
Dorothy H. Jacobson, 1916,
Mediterranean (Whitehouse and
Fouilhoux)
Mary E. Parker, 1929, Arts & Crafts
Elizabeth Clarke, 1930, Stripped
Traditional/Transitional
Frank B. Upshaw, 1935, English
Cottage

David L. Williams
Robert F. Lytle, 1911, Mediterranean
H. P. Palmer, 1912, Bungalow
Clarissa Inman, 1926, Mediterranean

Hubert A. Williams
R. J. O'Donnell, 1946, Modernistic/
International

Warren H. Williams
Parish House, Trinity Episcopal
Church, 1874, Gothic Revival
Henry W. Corbett, 1874, Second
Empire
Ralph and Isaac Jacobs, 1880, Italian-
ate
Morris Marks, I, 1880, Italianate
(attributed)
Morris Marks, II, 1882, Italianate
Charles P. Bacon, 1882, Italianate
Blaise and Antoine Labbe, c. 1885,
Queen Anne
George H. Weidler, 1885, Queen Anne

John Yeon
Aubrey R. Watzek, 1937, Northwest
Style
Victor Jorgensen, 1939, Northwest
Style
E. W. Van Buren, 1948, Northwest
Style
Dr. Kenneth C. Swan, 1949, Northwest
Style
George Cottrell, 1950, Northwest Style
Lawrence Shaw, 1950, Northwest Style

APPENDIX B   Portland's Classic Houses by Neighborhood

Examples of classic residential architecture extend throughout the greater Portland area. Although the expansion of the downtown business core meant the demolition of many of the earliest classic houses in the area, most of Portland's residential neighborhoods feature fine houses of the city's rich architectural history. Fortunately, thanks to owners past and present who value this legacy, a significant number of the classic houses are still standing, most remaining true to the integrity of the original designs.

The houses featured in this book are presented here according to their location in the Portland metropolitan area. Although a city's architecture is an art to be enjoyed and celebrated by all, the majority of the houses remain in private hands as family homes, just as when they were constructed fifty or one hundred years ago. For that reason, we ask that you respect the privacy of these homes and their residents.

Address	Original Owner	Architect	Date of Construction	Style
Southwest Portland				
Downtown and Inner Southwest				
1134 SW 12th Ave.	Morris Marks, I	Warren H. Williams (attributed)	1880	Italianate
1520 SW 11th Ave.	Edward C. Hochapfel	Justus F. Krumbein	1907	Craftsman/Colonial
1423 SW Columbia St.	John B. Bridges	Justus F. Krumbein (attributed)	1884	Eastlake
1500 SW Taylor St.	Frederick V. Holman		1890	Shingle/Richardsonian
1425 SW 20th Ave.	Jacob Kamm	Justus F. Krumbein	1871	Second Empire
King's Hill				
2182 SW Yamhill St.	Howard Stratton		c. 1894	Shingle/Richardsonian
931 SW King Ave.	Theodore B. Wilcox	Whidden and Lewis	1893	Shingle/Richardsonian
2164 SW Park Pl.	Allen L. Lewis	David C. Lewis	c. 1901	Jacobethan
2138 SW Salmon St.	George H. Durham		1890	Queen Anne
2165 SW Main St.	Milton Markewitz	Jamieson K. Parker	1924	Colonial Revival—Second Phase
1046 SW King Ave.	Judge Wallace McCamant	Whidden and Lewis	1899	Colonial Revival—First Phase
1131 SW King Ave.	William E. MacKenzie	Whidden and Lewis (attributed)	1902	Colonial Revival—First Phase
1150 SW Kings Ct.	James G. Gault	Harrison Corbett	c. 1914	Colonial Revival—First Phase
2331 SW Madison St.	Frank H. Ransom	Josef Jacobberger	1908	Craftsman
2362 SW Madison St.	Charles Barker	Roscoe D. Hemenway	1929	Arts & Crafts

Address	Original Owner	Architect	Date of Construction	Style
King's Hill (continued)				
2359 SW Park Pl.	Samuel Rosenblatt	Edward T. Root	1915	Colonial Revival—First Phase
2370 SW Park Pl.	Aaron Holtz	Albert E. Doyle	1927	Jacobethan
2375 SW Park Pl.	Charles J. Schnabel	William C. Knighton	1907	Craftsman
2400 SW Park Pl.	Jacob N. Barde	Carl L. Linde	1926	Mediterranean
1055 SW Douglas Pl.	Gordon Barde	Carl L. Linde	1939	French Renaissance
733 SW Vista Ave.	Emil Schacht	Emil Schacht	1902	Shingle/Richardsonian
1111 SW Vista Ave.	Hardy C. Wortman		1896	Shingle/Richardsonian
Portland Heights and Council Crest				
933 SW Davenport St.	W. R. Scott	Herman Brookman	1942	Northwest Style
1136 SW Davenport St.	Adrienne Arnsberg	Herman Brookman	1942	Stripped Traditional
1501 SW Harrison St.	Morris Marks, II	Warren H. Williams	1882	Italianate
1502 SW Upper Hall St.	Josef Jacobberger	Josef Jacobberger	1906	Arts & Crafts
1490 SW Clifton St.	Donald M. Drake	Sutton, Whitney and Aandahl	1937	Stripped Traditional
1515 SW Clifton St.	William Biddle Wells	John Virginius Bennes	1910	Craftsman
2011 SW Carter Ln.	Allen Meier	Walter Gordon	1950	Northwest Style
2033 SW Jackson St.	William P. Hawley	Ellis F. Lawrence	1927	Colonial Revival—Second Phase
2040 SW Laurel St.	Bert C. Ball	Albert E. Doyle	1921	English Cottage
1832 SW Elm St.	Rev. Charles Scadding	David C. Lewis	1911	Tudor
2417 SW 16th Ave.	James E. Wheeler	McNaughton, Raymond and Lawrence	1910	Colonial Revival—First Phase
2410 SW 17th Ave.	John E. Wheeler		1907	Craftsman
1710 SW Elizabeth St.	G. W. Sherk		1906	Bungalow
1707 SW Hawthorne Terr.	Edwin T. Burke	Wade H. Pipes	1927	Arts & Crafts
1727 SW Hawthorne Terr.	Ida Catlin	Wade H. Pipes	1927	Arts & Crafts
1840 SW Hawthorne Terr.	Walter S. Zimmerman	Wade H. Pipes and Harold W. Doty	1931	Arts & Crafts
1806 SW High St.	Alfred T. Smith	Josef Jacobberger	1912	Arts & Crafts
1728 SW Prospect Dr.	David T. Honeyman	David C. Lewis	1907	Colonial Revival—First Phase
1770 SW Prospect Dr.	Max S. Hirsch	Ellis F. Lawrence	1922	English Cottage
1715 SW Montgomery Dr.	A. J. Lewthwaite	Albert Parr and Francis Ward	1926	French Renaissance
1792 SW Montgomery Dr.	Dr. James J. Rosenberg	Henry Herzog	1933	Tudor
1796 SW Montgomery Dr.	J. L. Easson	Ellis F. Lawrence (attributed)	1931	Tudor
1841 SW Montgomery Dr.	Coleman Wheeler	Albert E. Doyle	1923	English Cottage
1863 SW Montgomery Dr.	George W. Collins	Albert E. Doyle	1907	Arts & Crafts
1942 SW Montgomery Dr.	Frank E. Hart	Whidden and Lewis	1900	Tudor
1957 SW Montgomery Dr.	Leon Hirsch	Sutton and Whitney	1922	Jacobethan

Address	Original Owner	Architect	Date of Construction	Style
1965 SW Montgomery Pl.	Dr. Andrew I. Geisy	Josef Jacobberger	1913	Arts & Crafts
1975 SW Montgomery Dr.	Max H. Hauser	Morris H. Whitehouse (attributed)	1908	Colonial Revival—First Phase
2132 SW Montgomery Dr.	Edward D. Kingsley	Jamieson K. Parker	1926	Colonial Revival—Second Phase
2424 SW Montgomery Dr.	Frank J. Cobb	Albert E. Doyle	1917	Jacobethan
2585 SW Montgomery Dr.	Catherine H. Percival		1910	Bungalow
2960 SW Montgomery Dr.	Leon Savaria	Herman Brookman	1932	Stripped Traditional
2526 SW St. Helens Ct.	George Pipes	Wade H. Pipes	1923	Arts & Crafts
2111 SW 21st Ave.	Raymond Wilcox	Whitehouse and Fouilhoux	1916	Colonial Revival—Second Phase
2125 SW 21st Ave.	Dr. James Rosenfeld	Josef Jacobberger	1922	English Cottage
2228 SW 21st Ave.	Dr. Lawrence Selling	Josef Jacobberger	1918	Colonial Revival—First Phase
1475 SW Vista Ave.	Lee S. Elliot	Herman Brookman	1934	Stripped Traditional
1934 SW Vista Ave.	Joseph R. Bowles	Albert E. Doyle	1924	Mediterranean
1961 SW Vista Ave.	Dr. Ami Nichols	Edward T. Foulkes	1913	Colonial Revival—First Phase
2111 SW Vista Ave.	J. S. Bradley		1906	Craftsman
2660 SW Vista Ave.	Thomas Mostyn	William Grey Purcell	1924	Prairie
2666 SW Vista Ave.	Lilian K. Pollock	William Grey Purcell	1921	Prairie
2645 SW Alta Vista Pl.	John G. Edwards	Albert E. Doyle	1925	Arts & Crafts
2643 SW Buena Vista Dr.	Barbara Price	Herman Brookman	1926	Mediterranean
2681 SW Buena Vista Dr.	O. L. Price	Ellis F. Lawrence	1928	Mediterranean
2709 SW Buena Vista Dr.	D. R. Munroe	Francis Jacobberger	1913	Tudor
2769 SW Buena Vista Dr.	Theodore F. Brown	Wade H. Pipes	1923	Arts & Crafts
2421 SW Arden Rd.	Caroline and Louise Flanders	Jamieson K. Parker	1926	Arts & Crafts
2534 SW Arden Rd.	Purcell Residence	William Grey Purcell	1923	Arts & Crafts
2572 SW Arden Rd.	Paul C. Carey	Harold W. Doty	1925	Colonial Revival—Second Phase
2649 SW Georgian Pl.	William Grey Purcell	William Grey Purcell	1920	Arts & Crafts
2728 SW Greenway Ave.	Theodore B. Wilcox	Roscoe D. Hemenway	1950	Colonial Revival—Second Phase
3131 SW Talbot Rd.	Leon H. Baruh	Herman Brookman	1936	Stripped Traditional
3366 SW Talbot Rd.	George Black	Jamieson K. Parker	1929	Arts & Crafts
3438 SW Brentwood Dr.	Burt Brown Barker	Ellis F. Lawrence	1928	French Renaissance
3728 SW Beaverton Ave.	Pietro Belluschi	Pietro Belluschi	1936	Northwest Style
3737 SW Council Crest Dr.	E. T. Samuelson	Ernest Tucker	1937	Arts & Crafts
4201 SW Council Crest Dr.	Properties Unlimited	Lee Thomas	1940	Arts & Crafts
4273 SW Council Crest Dr.	E. W. Van Buren	John Yeon	1948	Northwest Style

Address	Original Owner	Architect	Date of Construction	Style
Arlington Heights				
122 SW Marconi Ave.	John Virginius Bennes	John Virginius Bennes	1911	Prairie
226 SW Kingston Ave.	Aaron H. Maegley	John Virginius Bennes	1914	Prairie
2875 SW Fairview Blvd.	Joseph R. Gerber	Hollis E. Johnson and Harold W. Doty	1927	Arts & Crafts
2997 SW Fairview Blvd.	J. O. Frye	J. O. Frye	1930	English Cottage
Sylvan and Greenhills				
4343 SW Fairview Blvd.	E. S. Beach	Ernest Tucker	1931	Arts & Crafts
4645 SW Fairview Blvd.	Dr. Kenneth C. Swan	John Yeon	1949	Northwest Style
1430 SW Barrow Ln.	Wesley P. Steinmetz	Charles Ertz (attributed)	1936	Tudor
4241 SW Torr Ln.	Roy Hunt	Richard Sundeleaf (attributed)	1932	Tudor
1060 SW Skyline Blvd.	George Cottrell	John Yeon	1950	Northwest Style
1061 SW Skyline Blvd.	Aubrey R. Watzek	John Yeon	1937	Northwest Style
1100 SW Skyline Blvd.	Jennings R. Sutor	Pietro Belluschi	1938	Northwest Style
4311 SW Greenleaf Dr.	George P. Berky	Roscoe D. Hemenway	1929	Arts & Crafts
4465 SW Greenleaf Dr.	William Scott	Richard Sundeleaf	1927	Jacobethan
4550 SW Humphrey Blvd.	John W. S. Platt	Pietro Belluschi	1941	Northwest Style
4700 SW Humphrey Blvd.	Ernest Haycox	Glenn Stanton and Associates	1940	Colonial Revival—Second Phase
4848 SW Humphrey Blvd.	Roy Gangware	Roscoe D. Hemenway	1932	Tudor
5000 SW Humphrey Blvd.	George J. Turner	Barrett and Logan	1937	Modernistic/International
5400 SW Hewett Blvd.	Dr. Frank Kistner	Wade H. Pipes	1930	Arts & Crafts
3703 SW 52nd Pl.	Theodore B. Wilcox	Kirtland K. Cutter	1919	Colonial Revival—Second Phase
6427 SW Hamilton St.	Dr. James Rosenfeld	Wade H. Pipes	1950	Northwest Style
4305 SW Dogwood Ln.	Victor Jorgensen	John Yeon	1939	Northwest Style
Outer West Hills and South				
2050 SW Mount Hood Ln.	Dean B. Webster	Richard Sundeleaf	1936	Tudor
5303 SW Westwood Dr.	James Leland	Harold W. Doty	1928	Arts & Crafts
1020 SW Cheltenham Ct.	Gov. George L. Curry		c. 1865	Italian Villa
3905 SW Viewpoint Terr.	Harvey S. Hudson	Roscoe D. Hemenway (attributed)	1937	Modernistic/International
8421 SW Macadam Ave.	Riverview Cemetery Caretaker's House	Ellis F. Lawrence	1914	Colonial Revival—First Phase
2542 SW Hillcrest Dr.	Belle and Maude Ainsworth	William C. Knighton	1907	Craftsman

Northwest Portland

Nob Hill Area

Address	Original Owner	Architect	Date of Construction	Style
1153 NW Thurman St.	Dwight Edwards	William C. Knighton (attributed)	1910	Craftsman
1805 NW Glisan St.	C. A. Landenberger		1895	Craftsman

Address	Original Owner	Architect	Date of Construction	Style
1808 NW Johnson St.	Winslow B. Ayer	Whidden and Lewis	1890	Colonial Revival—First Phase
811 NW 19th Ave.	Winslow B. Ayer	Whidden and Lewis	1903	Jacobethan
233 NW 20th Ave.	George F. Heusner	Edgar M. Lazarus	1892	Shingle/Richardsonian
311 NW 20th Ave.	Isom White	Whidden and Lewis	1903	Colonial Revival—First Phase
2233 NW Flanders St.	Friedlander Residence	Edgar M. Lazarus	c. 1890	Shingle/Richardsonian
2347 NW Flanders St.	Theodore B. Trevitt	Whidden and Lewis	1890	Colonial Revival—First Phase
2370 NW Flanders St.	Henry Noble		c. 1895	Shingle/Richardsonian
2381 NW Flanders St.	Lucien W. Wallace	William Whidden	1888	Colonial Revival—First Phase
615 NW 20th Ave.	Dr. Kenneth A. J. Mackenzie	Whidden and Lewis	1892	Shingle/Richardsonian
2039 NW Irving St.	Lewis H. Mills	Shepley, Rutan and Coolidge	1916	Colonial Revival—Second Phase
733 NW 20th Ave.	Abbott Mills	Shepley, Rutan and Coolidge	1908	Colonial Revival—First Phase
811 NW 20th Ave.	John A. Veness	Emil Schacht	1910	Craftsman/Colonial
2637 NW Kearney St.	George H. Howell	Josef Jacobberger	c. 1910	Craftsman
2642 NW Lovejoy St.	Edward L. Harmon	Albert E. Doyle	1908	Craftsman/Colonial
1205 NW 25th Ave.	William Gadsby	Emil Schacht	1908	Tudor
1331 NW 25th Ave.	Christine Becker	Emil Schacht	1909	Craftsman/Colonial

Westover Terraces and Willamette Heights

1611 NW 32nd Ave.	R. B. Lamson	Josef Jacobberger	1908	Shingle/Richardsonian
1435 NW 30th Ave.	Woods Hutchinson	Josef Jacobberger	1908	Bungalow
2687 NW Cornell Rd.	Frank Robertson	Jacobberger, Smith and Smith	1926	Arts & Crafts
2636 NW Cornell Rd.	Henry Hahn	Emil Schacht	1905	Craftsman
2846 NW Fairfax Terr.	J. C. Braly	Lee Thomas	1926	Colonial Revival—Second Phase
700 NW Rapidan Terr.	Dr. D. C. Burkes	Pietro Belluschi	1949	Modernistic/International
287 NW Cumberland Rd.	Keith Gilbert Powers	Herman Brookman	1946	Modernistic/International
1315 NW Cumberland Rd.	Dr. D. C. Burkes	Roscoe D. Hemenway	c. 1928	Colonial Revival—Second Phase
2833 NW Cumberland Rd.	Thomas Christianson		c. 1928	Mediterranean
2884 NW Cumberland Rd.	Clarissa Inman	David L. Williams	1926	Mediterranean
2903 NW Cumberland Rd.	Ward R. Bowles	Carl L. Linde	1926	Mediterranean
850 NW Powhatan Terr.	Paul F. Murphy	Richard Sundeleaf	1934	Tudor
506 NW Hermosa Blvd.	Otho Pool	Carl L. Linde	1928	Mediterranean
3229 NW Pittock Dr.	Henry L. Pittock	Edward T. Foulkes	1914	French Renaissance
321 NW Hilltop Dr.	William W. Wessinger	Walter Gordon	1948	Northwest Style
445 NW Hilltop Ln.	Lee Hawley Hoffman	Van Evera Bailey	1947	Northwest Style
NW Beuhla Vista	Major Watson Eastman	Hollis E. Johnson	1928	Mediterranean

Address	Original Owner	Architect	Date of Construction	Style
Northeast Portland				
Irvington Neighborhood				
1810 NE 15th Ave.	Gustav Freiwald		1906	Craftsman
1526 NE Thompson St.	J. W. Creath	George F. Durham (attributed)	1914	Colonial Revival—First Phase
1617 NE Thompson St.	Marcus J. Delahunt	John Virginius Bennes	1909	Prairie
1803 NE Thompson St.	E. J. Ellison		1914	Bungalow
2210 NE Thompson St.	Michael F. Brady	Josef Jacobberger	1911	Arts & Crafts
2116 NE 16th Ave.	Leslie M. Scott	John Virginius Bennes	1917	Colonial Revival—Second Phase
2424 NE 17th Ave.	C. Spies	A. R. Hossack	1922	Prairie
1831 NE Brazee St.	Gertrude Smith	A. H. Faber	1907	Bungalow
2229 NE Brazee St.	Lewis T. Gilliand	Ellis F. Lawrence	1910	Bungalow
2201 NE 21st Ave.	Ellis F. Lawrence	Ellis F. Lawrence	1906	Arts & Crafts
2439 NE 21st Ave.	Henry Miller		1911	Tudor
1914 NE 22nd Ave.	Robert F. Lytle	David L. Williams	1911	Mediterranean
2306 NE Siskiyou St.	Michael J. Walsh	Josef Jacobberger	1915	Arts & Crafts
1908 NE 24th Ave.	H. P. Palmer	David L. Williams	1912	Bungalow
2442 NE 24th Ave.	Arts and Crafts "A"	Josef Jacobberger	c. 1912	Arts & Crafts
2215 NE 25th Ave.	Iva L. McFarlan	Josef Jacobberger	1921	Colonial Revival—First Phase
2208 NE 28th Ave.	C. H. Farrington	Carl L. Linde	1924	English Cottage
2260 NE 28th Ave.	Dr. Zimmerman	Carl L. Linde	1925	Tudor
2732 NE Thompson St.	F. E. Bowman		1915	Craftsman/Colonial
Alameda District				
2425 NE Alameda Dr.	Thomas J. Autzen	Kirtland K. Cutter	1927	Tudor
2815 NE Alameda Dr.	Harold T. Prince		1916	Colonial Revival—First Phase
2903 NE Alameda Dr.	Woerner Lewis	William Grey Purcell	c. 1922	Arts & Crafts
2628 NE Stuart Dr.	George A. Eastman	George A. Eastman	1913	Bungalow
3401 NE 33rd Ave.	Charles Green	Charles Green	1926	Arts & Crafts
3231 NE U. S. Grant Pl.	William Haseltine	Jamieson K. Parker	1935	Colonial Revival—Second Phase
4206 NE Alameda Dr.	William T. Waerner	George M. Post	1927	Colonial Revival—Second Phase
Outer Northeast and North Portland				
431 NE Laddington Ct.	Robert McBride	C. V. Vanderpool	1912	Prairie
3711 NE Davis St.	Carl M. Little	Bennes, Hendricks and Thompson	1912	Prairie
4719 NE Knott St.	John L. Bowman	Ellis F. Lawrence	1916	Craftsman/Colonial
5125 NE Garfield St.	W. F. Donahae		1909	Craftsman

Address	Original Owner	Architect	Date of Construction	Style
5537 NE Atlantic Ave.	H. E. Schegel	F. G. Quimby	c. 1916	Bungalow
5620 NE Cleveland St.	M. C. White	George A. Eastman	1911	Bungalow
400 NE 62nd Ave.	Fred A. Shogren	Josef Jacobberger (attributed)	1906	Bungalow
2708 NE 72nd Ave.	R. J. O'Donnell	Hubert A. Williams	1946	Modernistic/International
4036 N Overlook Terr.	George H. Watson	George F. Durham (attributed)	1910	Colonial Revival—First Phase
4314 N Mississippi Ave.	John Palmer		1890	Eastlake

Southeast Portland

Laurelhurst

3316 SE Ankeny St.	Harry A. Green	Herman Brookman	1928	Mediterranean
3360 SE Ankeny St.	H. Russell Albee	Albert E. Doyle	1912	Colonial Revival—First Phase
3574 E Burnside St.	Paul F. Murphy	Ellis F. Lawrence	1918	English Cottage
3636 SE Oak St.	Ben Freedman	Herman Brookman	1946	Northwest Style
4272 SE Washington St.	John Sheffield		1866	Italian Villa

Mount Tabor Area

4775 SE Stark St.	Wilbur Reid	Francis Brown	1914	Bungalow
5219 SE Belmont St.	Blaine R. Smith	Ellis F. Lawrence	1908	Tudor
5701 SE Yamhill St.	William H. Hossack	A. R. Hossack (attributed)	1916	Bungalow
1214 SE 60th Ave.	Dr. A. M. Stolte	Edward T. Root	1910	Craftsman
6461 SE Thorburn St.	Frederick Alva Jacobs	Johnson and Mayer	1913	Bungalow
5511 SE Hawthorne Blvd.	Philip Buehner	Whidden and Lewis	1908	Colonial Revival—First Phase
722 SE 54th Ave.	William E. Brainard		c. 1888	Queen Anne

Hawthorne District and Ladd's Addition

1706 SE 12th Ave.	James B. Stephens		c. 1864	Italian Villa
1728 SE Belmont St.	J. Duthie		c. 1865	Italian Villa
1824 SE 23rd Ave.	Osmond B. Stubbs	Whitehouse and Fouilhoux	1915	Colonial Revival—First Phase
1926 SE 23rd Ave.	Cornwell and Perry Building Co.	Carl L. Linde	1922	Mediterranean
2240 SE 24th Ave.	C. P. Osborne	S. M. Stokes	1922	Arts & Crafts
2610 SE Hawthorne Blvd.	Walter F. Burrell	Whidden and Lewis	1901	Prairie

Eastmoreland, Sellwood, and Brooklyn Neighborhoods

6308 SE 28th Ave.	William H. De Graaff	Richard J. Neutra	1940	Modernistic/International
7808 SE 28th Ave.	Emma McCauley	C. V. Vanderpool	c. 1912	Prairie
2840 SE Woodstock Blvd.	Mary E. Parker	Morris H. Whitehouse	1929	Arts & Crafts
2916 SE Woodstock Blvd.	Dr. H. W. Howard	Bruce McKay	1927	Mediterranean

Address	Original Owner	Architect	Date of Construction	Style
Eastmoreland, Sellwood, and Brooklyn Neighborhoods (continued)				
6633 SE 29th Ave.	Frank Boutain		1926	English Cottage
2923 SE Tolman St.	Frank B. Upshaw	Morris H. Whitehouse	1935	English Cottage
3510 SE Tolman St.	Kenneth Eckert	Herman Brookman	1935	Stripped Traditional
3680 SE Glenwood St.	Herman Brookman	Herman Brookman	1931	Stripped Traditional
6209 SE 13th Ave.	John M. Pipes	Wade H. Pipes	1912	Arts & Crafts
1402 SE Reynolds St.	Bungalow "A"		1916	Bungalow
3040 SE McLoughlin Blvd.	Johan Poulsen		1890	Queen Anne
7107 SE 17th Ave.	Emerson L. Mills		c. 1911	Craftsman

Lake Oswego and Dunthorpe

Address	Original Owner	Architect	Date of Construction	Style
49 SW Briarwood Ct.	Emma M. Austin	Josef Jacobberger (attributed)	c. 1910	Bungalow
250 SW Stampher Rd.	Socrates H. Tryon		1850	Greek Revival
420 SW 10th St.	Johns-Manville	Richard Sundeleaf	1936	Stripped Traditional
1700 Ridgecrest Dr.	Thaddeus B. Bruno	Van Evera Bailey	1939	Modernistic/International
16715 Phantom Bluff Ct.	Richard Sundeleaf	Richard Sundeleaf	1939	Arts & Crafts
Crazyman's Island	Carl C. Jantzen	Charles Ertz	1930	Tudor
Lewis & Clark College	M. Lloyd Frank	Herman Brookman	1924	Tudor
Lewis & Clark College	Gatekeeper's Lodge, M. Lloyd Frank Estate	Herman Brookman	1924	Arts & Crafts
1108 SW Collina Ave.	Frank A. McGuire		c. 1927	Mediterranean
01900 SW Palatine Hill Rd.	Jan De Graaff	Richard J. Neutra	1940	Modernistic/International
01649 SW Greenwood Rd.	Charles T. Ladd	Ellis F. Lawrence (attributed)	1925	Arts & Crafts
01860 SW Greenwood Rd.	Cameron Squires	Ellis F. Lawrence	1920	Tudor
01905 SW Greenwood Rd.	Stanley C. E. Smith	Ellis F. Lawrence	1923	Tudor
11522 SW Riverwood Rd.	Philip L. Jackson	Jamieson K. Parker	c. 1927	French Renaissance
01845 SW Military Ln.	Donald McGraw	Jamieson K. Parker	c. 1940	Colonial Revival—Second Phase
11645 SW Military Ln.	Cicero Hunt Lewis	David C. Lewis (attributed)	c. 1910	Jacobethan
10101 SW Riverside Dr.	Amedee M. Smith	William C. Knighton	1909	Craftsman
10263 SW Riverside Dr.	David A. E. Rocky	Folger Johnson	1913	Mediterranean
13100 SW Riverside Dr.	T. H. Sherrard	Wade H. Pipes	1918	Arts & Crafts
12526 SW Edgecliff Rd.	John A. Laing	Wade H. Pipes	1925	Arts & Crafts
12800 SW Goodal Rd.	Lawrence Shaw	John Yeon	1950	Northwest Style
20950 SW Farmington Rd.	Belle Ainsworth Jenkins	Root and Hoose	1912	Bungalow

Address	Original Owner	Architect	Date of Construction	Style

Oregon City and Canemah

Address	Original Owner	Architect	Date of Construction	Style
19130 Lot Whitcomb Dr.	Captain J. C. Ainsworth	Absolom B. Hallock (attributed)	1850	Greek Revival
619 6th St.	Francis Ermatinger		1845	Greek Revival
713 Center St.	Dr. John McLoughlin		1845	Greek Revival
719 Center St.	Dr. Forbes Barclay		1849	Greek Revival
812 John Adams St.	Elizabeth Clarke	Morris H. Whitehouse	1930	Stripped Traditional
13030 S Clackamas River Dr.	Hiram Straight		1856	Gothic Revival
14343 S Clackamas River Rd.	Dr. John P. Cleland	J. Irving Lawson	1936	Colonial Revival—Second Phase
708 S McLoughlin Blvd.	Painter Residence		c. 1859	Gothic Revival
902 S McLoughlin Blvd.	Francis Xavier Pacquet		c. 1852	Gothic Revival

Vancouver, the Columbia Gorge, and Other Locations

Address	Original Owner	Architect	Date of Construction	Style
Fort Vancouver, Vancouver, Wash.	Chief Factor's House, Hudson's Bay Company		1838	Greek Revival
Fort Vancouver, Vancouver, Wash.	Commanding Officers' Quarters, Fort Vancouver		1849	Greek Revival
Marshall House, Officers Row, Vancouver, Wash.	Commanding Officer's Quarters	William F. McCaw	1886	Queen Anne
Near Crown Point	Edward Ehrman	Albert E. Doyle	1915	English Cottage
Bridal Veil	Dorothy H. Jacobson	Whitehouse and Fouilhoux	1916	Mediterranean
Columbia Gorge	Julius Meier	Herman Brookman	1926	Stripped Traditional
13901 NW Howell Park Rd., Sauvie Island	James F. Bybee		1856	Greek Revival
14999 Springwater Rd., Carver, Ore.	C. S. Jackson	Johnson and Mayer (attributed)	c. 1915	Bungalow
Sheridan, Ore.	P. L. Menefee	Pietro Belluschi	1950	Northwest Style

Glossary of Terms

Acroterion: An ornament or crowning adorning a pediment, such as on a temple.

Arch: A curved, flat, or pointed structure used to span an opening.

Architect: (from Greek *archi*, meaning chief, and *tekton*, worker or carpenter) "A person skilled in the art of building, who forms and estimates designs of edifices, directs the workmen, conducts the work, and measures and values the whole" (*Architect and Engineering Dictionary*, 1835).

Architecture: "The art of forming dwellings, or erecting buildings of any kind" (*Architect and Engineering Dictionary*, 1835).

Architrave: The lowest of the three main parts of a Classical entablature, below the cornice and the frieze. Also, an ornamental molding around openings such as doors or windows.

Balcony: A projecting balustrated platform before a window or door.

Balloon Frame: Introduced in the 1830s, a system of framing a building in which wood studs extend in one piece from the top of the foundation sill-plate to the top roof plate; floor joists are nailed to the studs and supported by horizontal boards.

Baluster: A short pillar or other upright that, in series, supports a handrail. *See* balustrade.

Balustrade: A series of balusters connected by a top rail or hand rail, as on staircases, balconies, or porches. Also, the railing connecting the balusters.

Bargeboard: An ornamental board placed on the incline of a gable to conceal rafter ends.

Baroque: The style of art and architecture that emerged in Italy and later spread throughout Europe during the seventeenth century. It was characterized by dynamic lines and masses and the free use of Classical motifs.

Barrel Vault: A semicircular-arched ceiling or roof.

Bay Window: A windowed alcove, with perpendicular or angled sides, that extends out from the exterior wall of a room and is supported by a foundation attached to the house.

Belt Cornice: An exterior trim located between floors of a structure. It is similar to a roof cornice, but usually smaller.

Belvedere: A tower or turret built for the purpose of giving a view.

Bifurcate: Divided or separated in two branches, as in a bifurcated stairway that meets at the head and/or foot.

Blinds (Weather): Rectangular frames of wood used to cover the whole or part of the sashes of a window. Now considered synonymous with shutters, the term "blinds" originally referred to exterior window closures, while "shutters" referred to interior closures.

Board and Batten: A form of wood siding for exterior walls, consisting of long vertical boards and thin strips, or battens, which extend over adjacent boards or joints (the spaces between adjacent surfaces).

Boiserie: A wood covering for interior walls, divided into decorative panels with stiles (vertical strips).

Bracket: A projecting support under eaves or overhangs. These can be plain or decorated.

Canopy: A decorative projection over a doorway or niche.

Cantilever: A beam or other structure projecting from a wall and supporting an extension to a building, as on a cantilevered balcony or upper story.

Capital: The upper portion of a column on which lies the entablature.

Cartouche: An ornamental panel or tablet, usually oval or scroll-like in shape.

Casement: A window frame that opens on vertical hinges. A casement window contains two such vertical-hinged windows, separated by a mullion.

Casing: The visible molding or framework around an opening such as a door or window.

Castellated: Built with battlements and turrets, in imitation of castles.

Chamber: A private living space commonly used as bedrooms in the late nineteenth century.

Classical: In the style of the ancient Greeks or Romans and their derivatives, especially in the use of orders.

Clinker Brick: A brick impregnated with a considerable quantity of niter, or saltpeter, that is placed next to the fire in the kiln to be thoroughly burned.

Coffer: A decorative feature formed by recessed panels, as in coffered ceilings.

Colonnade: A line of columns used to support an entablature or roof.

Column: A vertical, usually circular pillar, generally used as a support for a beam or other structure, such as an entablature.

Conservatory: A glass-enclosed room or greenhouse used for the purpose of cultivating and displaying plants.

Console: An ornamental, often scroll-shaped bracket used to support a door covering, shelf, cornice, etc.

Corbel: An ornamental projecting bracket, sometimes serving as a support for a cornice or other structure. Corbelling is often found on walls and chimney stacks.

Corinthian Column: A Classical fluted column characterized by an ornate capital decorated with stylized acanthus leaves.

Cornice: The upper projection of a Classical entablature. Also, a projection along the top of a wall.

Crenellation: A decorative element that simulates the square notches and spaces (battlements) of a parapet.

Cresting: A decorative ridging along the top of a screen, wall, or roof.

Cross Gable: A gable that is perpendicular to the main gable or ridge of a roof.

Cupola: A small domelike structure on top of a roof or tower.

Dado: The part of the interior finishing found on the lower portion of a wall, often a decorative panel or border that serves to contrast with the material used on the rest of the wall.

Dentils: A series of small, projecting square blocks, as on many cornices and moldings.

Dog Ear: In Greek Revival architecture, the extensions on either side of the upper casing on a door or window. It is in imitation of the carved stone borders found in ancient Greek architecture.

Doric Column: A Classical order characterized by a heavily fluted column with a plain capital.

Dormer: A window projecting from the slope of a roof and containing a sloped roof of its own. Eyebrow dormers have rounded roofs, resembling an eyelid in appearance.

Double-Hung Window: A window with two sashes, each movable by uses of sash cords and weights.

Dressed Stone: Stonework involving surface preparation by hand or machine. Hard stone is hammer-dressed, and soft stone is hewn or chiseled.

Drip-Molding (Eared): A projecting molding over doors, windows, and archways to direct rain away from the opening. The "eared" extensions at the head casing trim approximate stone details found in Greek and Roman Classical architecture.

Eave: The edge of a roof projecting beyond the walls.

Egg and Dart: A decorative molding composed of alternating egg-shaped and dart-shaped elements.

Entablature: In Classical architecture, the part of a building supported by the columns and composed of the cornice, frieze, and architrave.

Exedra: A semicircular covered porch or space.

Facade: A principal face or elevation of a building, usually the front.

Facade Dormer: A dormer whose front face is an extension of a facade wall.

Finial: An ornament that tops a gable, spire, pinnacle, or other architectural feature.

Flat Arch: An arch with a flat underside.

Flemish Bond: An arrangement of bricks in which the headers and stretchers alternate in each course, with the center of each header—a brick laid with its width exposed—projecting over the center of the stretcher—a brick with its length exposed—directly below it.

Flute, Fluting: Vertical grooves or concave channels, as on fluted columns or pilasters.

Fresco: A technique of painting in which paint, generally watercolors, is applied on fresh wet stucco or plaster, with the colors being absorbed into the surface.

Frieze: The middle section of a Classical entablature. Also, a decorative horizontal band along the wall of a room.

Gable: The triangular end of an exterior wall, formed by the sloping ends of a ridged roof.

Gambrel Roof: A roof with a double slope on each of its two sides.

Half-Timbering: A method of construction in which the spaces between the vertical structural timbers are filled with brickwork or plaster.

Hipped Roof: A roof with four equally sloped sides.

Horseshoe Arch: A style of rounded arch common to Islamic architecture. The lower part of the arch angles in toward the center, above the column supports, much like the shape of a horseshoe.

Inglenook: A recessed space adjacent to a fireplace. Also known as a chimney corner.

International Style: The style of architecture that emerged in Europe shortly before the First World War, and is still prevalent. It emphasizes function and rejects traditional decorative motifs.

Ionic Column: A Classical order characterized by the opposing spiral volutes on the capital.

Jerkinhead Roof: A gable roof that is truncated or clipped at the apex.

Keystone: The wedge-shaped stone found at the center of an arch.

Lancet Window: A long narrow window with a sharply pointed arch.

Lattice: An openwork structure of crossing laths or thin strips of wood or metal.

Lintel: A horizontal structural member over an opening, usually supporting the weight of the load above it.

Loggia: "A roofed open gallery. It differs from a veranda or a porch in being more architectural and in forming more decidedly a part of the main edifice" (*Architect and Engineering Dictionary*, 1835).

Lunette: A semicircular or crescent-shaped opening that serves as a decorative relief above doors or windows or on tympanums or other surfaces.

Mansard (Roof): A roof having two slopes on each of its four sides; the lower slope is steeper than the upper.

Modillion: An ornamental block or bracket used in series to support the overhang in Corinthian orders.

Molding: A continuous decorative band; it can be employed on both the interior and exterior of a building.

Mullion: A vertical bar on a window or door that divides and supports the panes or panels.

Muntin: A thin strip of wood or metal that holds the panes within a window.

Newel: The post at the top or bottom of a stairway, supporting the handrail.

Nogging: Brickwork in which bricks are used to fill in the spaces or crevices of a frame wall, such as between wooden panels.

Ogee: A semicircular arch that forms a point at its crown.

Oriel Window: A bay window supported by brackets or corbels and usually located on an upper story.

Overmantel: A panel, mirror, or the like placed over the mantelpiece.

Palazzo: An Italian palace, or any large extravagant building of a similar style.

Palladian Window: A window composed of a central arched sash flanked on either side by smaller rectilinear windows.

Parapet: A low wall or protective railing, as along the top of a building or a balcony.

Parlor: A room used for entertaining guests.

Pediment: A triangular section used as a crowning element over doors, windows, entryways, etc.

Pendule: A hanging ornament suspended from a roof or overhang.

Piazza: A veranda or open space.

Picket: A pointed stake or pale used in fences.

Pilaster: A rectangular column or shallow pier projecting from a wall.

Polygonal Bay: A projecting bay window of three or more sides.

Porch: A covered entrance or partially enclosed space projecting from the facade of a building.

Portal: A doorway or entrance, especially one that is large and impressive.

Porte-Cochere: A covered entrance or gateway extending across a driveway or entrance road through which vehicles may drive.

Portico: A large roofed porch or walkway, with a pedimented roof supported by columns.

Purlin: A horizontal beam used to support roof rafters between the roof ridge and the eave.

Quatrefoil: A Gothic architectural design consisting of four stylized converging arcs, as in the style of four-petaled flowers or four-lobed leaves.

Quoin: A large stone, brick, or wood block laid in vertical series to decorate the corners of a building.

Rafter: A structural wooden board or plank extending from the ridge of a roof to the eaves, serving as support.

Ribbon Windows: A continuous horizontal row or band of windows separated by mullions.

Romanesque: The style of art and architecture following Carolingian and preceding Gothic, prevalent in Europe during the eleventh and twelfth centuries. It is characterized by the use of massive masonry and thick proportions, round arches, and vaulting (first the barrel vault, then groined, and finally, the rib-vault).

Roughcast: A stucco exterior finishing in which newly applied stucco is bespattered with a finish coat, and the whole sets together.

Round Arch: A semicircular arch. Also called a Roman Arch.

Rustication: A type of masonry in which the stone blocks are separated by deeply grooved joints.

Segmental Arch: An arch formed by an arc or segment of a circle.

Shouldered Arch: A flat arch in which the horizontal is supported by corbels or brackets.

Shutters: Solid blinds hinged from either side of a window and which close over it.

Sidelight: A narrow vertical window, usually flanking the full height of a door or wall.

Spindle, Spindlework: A short decorative turned piece, such as a baluster or newel, often used in and around porch openings and sometimes forming an entablature.

Stencil: A pattern or design that is applied to a wall or other surface using a thin sheet that has the pattern cut into it, and through which paint or ink is applied.

Stucco: An exterior wall covering consisting of a mixture of cement, sand, lime, and water or of cement, sand, and hair.

Terra-Cotta: A fine-grained fired clay, often used for ornamenting building exteriors. It may be glazed or unglazed, and colors range from white to reddish brown.

Tracery: A style of ornamental openwork that is found in the upper part of Gothic windows.

Transom (Window or Light): A horizontal glass opening above a door or window. May be operable.

Triglyph: In the frieze of a Doric entablature, a rectangular block that has three vertical strips formed by two grooves.

Tudor Arch: A pointed arch often composed of four centers. Commonly constructed in fifteenth- and sixteenth-century Tudor England.

Tuscan Column: A Classical order distinguished by non-fluted and unadorned columns.

Tympanum: The recessed, usually triangular face of a pediment that is formed by the slanting cornices and is often ornamented.

Venetian Window: A window composed of three separate openings, the center of which is the tallest and has a round-arched top.

Veranda: An open space attached to the exterior wall of a building, usually with a roof supported by columns or posts.

Villa: A house in the country, often large and luxurious. Also, a middle-class suburban house.

Volute: A spiral scroll-like ornament commonly found on Ionic or Composite (combined Ionic and Corinthian) capitals.

Wainscoting: A wood lining or paneling on the walls of a room, usually at the lower part of a wall and especially when the upper part is finished in a different material.

Water Table: A ledge or molding that projects from the first floor level of a building to protect the foundation from rain water.

W.C. (Water Closet): A room equipped with a toilet or other fixture used for the disposal of human waste; also, the fixture itself.

Weatherboard: A narrow horizontal board, thicker at its bottom edge, used as wood siding. Also called clapboard.

Widow's Walk: An observation platform, usually with a railing, built on the roof of a house; especially found on coastal houses for the purpose of overlooking the sea.

Bibliography

Abbott, Carl. *Portland: Planning, Politics, and Growth in a Twentieth-Century City*. Lincoln: University of Nebraska Press, 1983.

Bosker, Gideon, and Lena Lencek. *Frozen Music: A History of Portland Architecture*. Portland, Ore.: Oregon Historical Society Press, 1985.

Clark, Kenneth. *The Gothic Revival: An Essay in the History of Taste*. 3rd ed. London: John Murray, 1962.

Clark, Rosalind. *Oregon Style: Architecture from 1840 to the 1950s*. Portland, Ore.: Professional Book Center, 1983.

Clarke, Ann Brewster. *Wade Hampton Pipes: Arts and Crafts Architect in Portland, Oregon*. Portland, Ore.: Binford and Mort Publishing, 1986.

Current, William R., and Karen Current. *Greene & Greene: Architects in the Residential Style*. Fort Worth, Tex.: Amon Carter Museum of Western Art, 1974.

Demuth, Kimberly. "Josef Jacobberger." Registration Form, Daniel J. Malarkey Residence. National Register of Historic Places, 1992.

Donovan, Sally, and Sharr Prohaska. "Folger Johnson." Registration Form, Ernest G. Swigert Residence. National Register of Historic Places, 1990.

Fletcher, Sir Banister. *A History of Architecture on a Comparative Method*. New York: Charles Scribner's Sons, 1929. 20th edition, Oxford, England: Butterworth-Heinemann, 1996.

Fletcher, Farr, and P. C. Ayotte. "John Virginius Bennes." Registration Form, L. B. Menefee Residence. National Register of Historic Places, 1993.

Gaston, Joseph. *Portland: Its History and Builders*. Portland, Ore.: S. J. Clarke Publishing, 1911.

Grow, Lawrence. *Classic Old House Plans: Three Centuries of American Domestic Architecture*. New York: Sterling Publishing Co., 1990.

Hamlin, Talbot F. *Greek Revival Architecture in America*. New York: Oxford University Press, 1944.

Hawkins, William John, III. "Justus Krumbein: Architect (1847–1907)." *Portland Friends of Cast-Iron Newsletter*, June 1980.

———. "Warren Heywood Williams: Architect (1844–1888)." *Portland Friends of Cast-Iron Newsletter*, December 1980.

———. "Absolom B. Hallock: Architect, Engineer, Surveyor (1826–1892)." *Portland Friends of Cast-Iron Newsletter*, October 1981.

———. "E. M. Burton: Architect (1817–1887)." *Portland Friends of Cast-Iron Newsletter*, April 1982.

———. "David Lockheed Williams." Registration Form, Senator Rufus Cecil Holman House. National Register of Historic Places, 1990.

Hawn, Arthur W. "Two Portland Houses by Henry Cleaveland." *Journal of Interior Design Education and Research*, Vol. III, no. 1 (Spring 1977).

Hitchcock, Henry-Russell. *Architecture: Nineteenth and Twentieth Centuries*. Baltimore, Md.: Penguin Books, 1958. Revised edition, New Haven, Conn.: Yale University Press, 1977.

Holly, Henry Hudson. *Holly's Country Seats and Modern Dwellings: Containing Lithographic Designs for Cottages, Villas, Mansions, etc., with Their Accompanying Outbuildings*. 1860. Reprint, Library of Victo-rian Culture, Watkins Glen, N.Y.: American Life Foundation and Study Institute, 1977.

———. *Modern Dwellings in Town and Country*. 1878. Reprint, Library of Victorian Culture, Watkins Glen, N.Y.: American Life Foundation and Study Institute, 1977.

Lloyd, Seton, et al. *World Architecture: An Illustrated History*. New York: McGraw-Hill Publishing Company, 1963.

MacColl, E. Kimbark. *The Shaping of a City: Business and Politics in Portland, Oregon, 1885–1915*. Portland, Ore.: The Georgian Press Company, 1976.

———. *The Growth of a City: Power and Politics in Portland, Oregon, 1915–1950*. Portland, Ore.: The Georgian Press Company, 1979.

MacColl, E. Kimbark, and Harry H. Stein. *Merchants, Money, and Power: The Portland Establishment, 1843–1913*. Portland, Ore.: The Georgian Press Company, 1988.

Marlitt, Richard. *Nineteenth Street*. Portland, Ore.: Oregon Historical Society Press, 1978.

———. *Matters of Proportion: The Portland Residential Architecture of Whidden & Lewis*. Portland, Ore.: Oregon Historical Society Press, 1989.

McAlester, Virginia and Lee. *A Field Guide to American Houses*. New York: Alfred A. Knopf, 1984.

McMath, George A. "A. E. Doyle." Registration Form, A. E. Doyle Cottage. National Register of Historic Places, 1990.

———. "Emil Schacht, Architect." Registration Form, Henry Hahn House. National Register of Historic Places, 1993.

Morin, Roi J. "Fred Fritch of Portland: An Appreciation of a Rare Spirit in the Profession." *Pencil Points*, March 1936.

Nelson, Lee H. "Architects of Oregon: Piper and Williams," *The Call Number* 20, no. 2 (Spring 1959).

Norman, James B. *Oregon's Architectural Heritage: The National Register Properties of the Portland Area*. Salem, Ore.: The Solo Press, 1986.

O'Donnell, Terence, and Thomas Vaughn. *Portland: An Informal History and Guide*. 2nd ed. Portland, Ore.: Oregon Historical Society Press, 1984.

O'Hara, John Michael, and William J. Hawkins, III. "William W. Piper." *Portland Friends of Cast-Iron Newsletter*, January 1983.

Oregon Historical Society. Manuscripts Department. Historic American Buildings Survey, 1934 (MSS3100). Oregon Collection, City of Portland.

Poppeliers, John, et al. *What Style Is It?: A Guide to American Architecture*. Washington, D.C.: The Preservation Press, Division of the National Trust for Historic Preservation, 1978.

Powell, John Edward. "Edward T. Foulkes." *Fresno Past & Present: The Journal of the Fresno City and County Historical Society* 25, no. 1 (Spring 1983).

Powers, David W., III. "Albert H. Jordan (ca. 1820–1872)." Presented at the meeting of the Northwest Coast Chapter of the Society of Architectural Historians, San Jose, Calif., November 9, 1985.

Rifkind, Carole. *A Field Guide to American Architecture*. New York: New American Library, 1980.

Ross, Marion D. "Architecture in Oregon, 1845–1895." *Oregon Historical Quarterly* 57, no. 1 (March 1956).

Sackett, Patricia Lynn. "A Partial Inventory of the Work of Emil Schacht: Architect in Portland, Oregon, from 1885 to 1926." Master's Thesis, University of Oregon, 1990.

Saint, Andrew. *Richard Norman Shaw*. New Haven, Conn.: Yale University Press, 1983.

Scully, Vincent J., Jr. *The Shingle Style: Architectural Theory and Design from Richardson to the Origins of Wright*. New Haven, Conn.: Yale University Press, 1955. Reprint 1971.

———. *The Architecture of the American Summer: The Flowering of the Shingle Style*. The Temple Hoyne Buell Center for the Study of American Architecture, Columbia University. New York: Rizzoli International Publications, 1989.

Shellenbarger, Michael, ed. *Harmony in Diversity: The Architecture of Ellis F. Lawrence*. Eugene, Ore.: University of Oregon Books, 1989.

Stickley, Gustav. *Craftsman Homes: Architecture and Furnishings of the American Arts and Crafts Movement*. New York: Dover Publications, 1979.

Stubblebine, Jo, ed. *The Northwest Architecture of Pietro Belluschi*. New York: F. W. Dodge, 1953.

Sutton, Robert K. *Americans Interpret the Parthenon: The Progression of Greek Revival Architecture from the East Coast to Oregon, 1800–1860*. Niwot, Colo.: University Press of Colorado, 1992.

Tess, John, and Richard Ritz, FAIA. "Richard William Sundeleaf." Registration Form, Clarence Francis Residence. National Register of Historic Places, 1992.

———. "Morris H. Whitehouse." Registration Form, Henry Ladd Corbett Residence. National Register of Historic Places, 1990.

Turville, Jane. "For Beauty's Sake: The Life and Work of Herman Brookman" (unpublished).

Vaughn, Thomas, and Virginia Guest Ferriday, eds. *Space, Style and Structure: Building in Northwest America*. Portland, Ore.: Oregon Historical Society Press, 1974.

Vaughn, Thomas, and George A. McMath. *A Century of Portland Architecture*. Portland, Ore.: Oregon Historical Society Press, 1967.

Weaver, Sir Lawrence. *Houses & Gardens by E. L. Lutyens*. New York: Charles Scribner's Sons, 1925. Reprint, Antique Collectors' Club, 1981.

Whiffin, Marcus. *American Architecture Since 1780: A Guide to the Styles*. Cambridge, Mass.: M.I.T. Press, 1969.

Withey, Henry F., and Elsie R. Withey. *Biographical Dictionary of American Architects (Deceased)*. Los Angeles: Hennessey & Ingalls, 1950; facsimile edition, 1970.

Index

Illustration Credits

page 79: Josiah Failing House. Courtesy Oregon Historical Society (ORHI#47116).

page 80: Captain J. C. Ainsworth House. From an 1865 Portland Panorama. Courtesy Oregon Historical Society (ORHI#5492).

page 80: James B. Stephens House. Courtesy Oregon Historical Society (ORHI#75590).

page 82: Frank Dekum House. Courtesy Oregon Historical Society (ORHI#39174).

page 84: Dr. J. A. Chapman House. Courtesy Oregon Historical Society (ORHI#38982).

page 84: James F. Failing House. Courtesy Oregon Historical Society (CN#021846).

page 85: Entrance hall, Failing House. Courtesy Oregon Historical Society (ORHI#56836).

page 85: Parlor, Failing House. Courtesy Oregon Historical Society (ORHI#56835).

page 86: William J. Van Schuyver. Courtesy Oregon Historical Society (CN#018288).

page 87: Governor George L. Curry House. Courtesy Oregon Historical Society (CN#020115).

page 87: J. Duthie House. Photo by William J. Hawkins, III.

page 88: John Sheffield House. Photo by William J. Hawkins, III.

page 89: Ben Holladay House. From the collection of William J. Hawkins, III.

page 89: William Wadhams House. From a lithograph entitled "Beautiful Homes of Portland." From the collection of William J. Hawkins, III.

page 90: Captain Charles Holman House. Courtesy Oregon Historical Society (ORHI#25679).

page 90: Interior, Holman House. Courtesy Oregon Historical Society (ORHI#62459).

Chapter 4, Second Empire

page 93: Portland, at Sixth Avenue and Yamhill Street, circa 1878. Courtesy Oregon Historical Society (ORHI#759).

page 94: Hotel de Ville extension, Paris. Lithograph from circa 1840.

page 94: Pavillon Richelieu, the Louvre, Paris. Photo by William J. Hawkins, III.

page 95: State, War and Navy Building, Washington, DC. Reproduced from Hitchcock 1958.

page 96: Charles Crocker Mansion, San Francisco. Reproduced from Thomas Aidala, *The Great Houses of San Francisco*, Alfred A. Knopf, New York, 1974.

page 97: A Second Empire style design, from *Holly's Country Seats* by Henry Hudson Holly, 1860.

page 97: "French Cottage," from Bicknell and Comstock's *Specimen Book of One-Hundred Architectural Designs*, 1880.

page 97: "Suburban House Design," from Bicknell and Comstock's *Specimen Book of One-Hundred Architectural Designs*, 1880.

page 98: Another Second Empire design from Bicknell and Comstock's *Specimen Book of One-Hundred Architectural Designs*, 1880.

page 100: Entrance to the Jacob Kamm House. Photo by Harriet Park Cramer. Courtesy Oregon Historical Society (ORHI#60338).

page 101: E. J. Jeffrey House. Courtesy Oregon Historical Society (ORHI#75617).

page 102: William S. Ladd House. From the collection of William J. Hawkins, III.

page 103: Jacob Kamm House. Postcard from the collection of William J. Hawkins, III.

page 103: Interior, Kamm House. From the collection of William J. Hawkins, III.

page 104: Simeon G. Reed House. Courtesy Oregon Historical Society (ORHI#38373).

page 104: Parlor, Reed House. Courtesy Oregon Historical Society (CN#010346).

page 105: Henry W. Failing House. Courtesy Oregon Historical Society (ORHI#4000).

page 106: Entrance hall, Failing House. Courtesy Oregon Historical Society (ORHI#37872).

page 106: Library, Failing House. Courtesy Oregon Historical Society (ORHI#37879).

page 107: Dining room, Failing House. Courtesy Oregon Historical Society (ORHI#37880).

page 108: A. H. Johnson House. Courtesy Oregon Historical Society (ORHI#57401).

page 108: The Johnson estate. Courtesy Oregon Historical Society (ORHI#38232).

page 108: Parlor, Johnson House. Courtesy Oregon Historical Society (ORHI#57409).

page 109: Henry W. Corbett House. *The Sunday Oregonian*, 30 August 1936. Photo courtesy Donald R. Nelson.

page 110: Side facade, Corbett House. Courtesy Oregon Historical Society (ORHI#42913).

page 110: Parlor, Corbett House. Courtesy Oregon Historical Society (ORHI#87861).

page 110: Drawing Room, Corbett House. Courtesy Oregon Historical Society (ORHI#73050).

page 111: Dining room, Corbett House. Courtesy Oregon Historical Society (ORHI#73045).

page 111: Master bedroom, Corbett House. Courtesy Oregon Historical Society (ORHI#73049).

Chapter 5, Italianate

page 113: Portland, the South Park Blocks, circa 1882. *West Shore* magazine, 1882. Courtesy Oregon Historical Society (ORHI#734).

page 114: New Market Theater, Portland. Drawing by William J. Hawkins, III.

page 114: Smith and Watson Building, Portland. Drawing by William J. Hawkins, III.

page 115: Palazzo della Consulta, Rome. Etching by Giambattista Piranesi. From the collection of William J. Hawkins, III.

page 116: Villa Albani, Italy. Etching by Giambattista Piranesi.

page 116: Villa Giulia, Rome. Courtesy British Architectural Library, RIBA, London. Reproduced from Fletcher 1996.

page 117: Palazzo Farnese, Rome. Courtesy British Architectural Library, RIBA, London. Reproduced from Fletcher 1996.

page 120: Entrance to the second Morris Marks House. Photo by William J. Hawkins, III.

page 121: Judge John W. Whalley House. Courtesy Oregon Historical Society (ORHI#47115).

page 122: M. W. Fechheimer House. Courtesy William Fletcher.

page 122: Entrance hall, Fechheimer House. Courtesy William Fletcher.

page 123: Dining room, Fechheimer House. Courtesy William Fletcher.

page 123: Library, Fechheimer House. Courtesy William Fletcher.

page 123: Parlor room, Fechheimer House. Courtesy William Fletcher.

page 123: Drawing room, Fechheimer House. Courtesy William Fletcher.

page 124: Ralph and Isaac Jacobs Houses. Photo by Minor White. Courtesy Oregon Historical Society (ORHI#9308).

page 125: Ralph Jacobs House. Courtesy Oregon Historical Society (ORHI#28112).

page 125: Isaac Jacobs House. Photo by Minor White. Courtesy Portland Art Museum, PAM #42.29.4.

page 125: Side entrance, Isaac Jacobs House. Photo by Minor White. Courtesy Portland Art Museum.

page 126: Entrance hall, Jacobs Houses. Photo by Minor White. Courtesy Portland Art Museum, PAM #42.29.45.

page 126: Ceiling fresco, front entrance hall, Jacobs Houses. Photo by Minor White. Courtesy Portland Art Museum, PAM #42.29.48.

page 127: Domed skylight and ceiling frescoes over the stairway, Jacobs Houses. Photo by Minor White. Courtesy Portland Art Museum.

page 127: Oriental parlor, Jacobs Houses. Photo by Minor White. Courtesy Portland Art Museum, PAM #42.29.62.

page 128: Drawing room, Jacobs Houses. Photo by Minor White. Courtesy Portland Art Museum, PAM #42.29.50.

page 128: Bedroom, Jacobs Houses. Photo by Minor White. Courtesy Portland Art Museum.

page 130: Justus F. Krumbein House. Rendering by William J. Hawkins, III, of architect's original sketch.

page 132: Morris Marks House, I. Photo by William J. Hawkins, III.

page 133: Morris Marks House, II. Photo by William J. Hawkins, III.

page 133: Richard Milwain House. Courtesy Oregon Historical Society (ORHI#45014).

page 134: George V. James House. Courtesy Oregon Historical Society.

page 135: Captain George Flanders House. Photo by B. C. Towne. Courtesy Oregon Historical Society (ORHI#73272).

page 135: Charles P. Bacon House. Courtesy Oregon Historical Society (ORHI#26566).

Chapter 6, Queen Anne

page 139: Portland, circa 1888. *West Shore* magazine. Courtesy Oregon Historical Society (ORHI#10740).

page 140: Old House, Brunswick, England. Courtesy British Architectural Library, RIBA, London. Reproduced from Fletcher 1996.

page 141: Leyswood, Sussex, England. *Building News*, 31 March 1871.

page 141: Hopedene, Surrey, England. *Building News*, 8 May 1874.

page 142: F. W. Andrews House, Newport, Rhode Island. From Henry-Russell Hitchcock, *The Architecture of H. H. Richardson and His Times*, New York, 1936.

page 142: William Watts Sherman House, Newport, Rhode Island. *New York Sketchbook of Architecture*, May 1875.

page 142: T. G. Appleton House, Newport, Rhode Island. *American Architect and Building News*, January 1876.

page 143: House at Medford, Massachusetts. *American Architect and Building News*, 1877.

page 143: "A Modern Villa Residence," from Bicknell and Comstock's *Specimen Book of One-Hundred Architectural Designs*, 1880.

page 146: Entrance-stair newel of the Richard B. Knapp House. Photo by Minor White. Courtesy Portland Art Museum, PAM #42.30.72.

page 147: Senator Joseph N. Dolph House. *West Shore* magazine, June 1882. Courtesy Oregon Historical Society (ORHI#91856).

page 147: The Dolph House in its prime. Courtesy William Failing.

page 148: The Dolph House shortly before demolition. Courtesy Oregon Historical Society (ORHI#019909).

page 148: The "Napoleon" drawing room, Dolph House. *Northwest Architect*, 1910. Photo courtesy Arthur Hawn.

page 148: Master bedroom, Dolph House. *Northwest Architect*, 1910. Photo courtesy Arthur Hawn.

page 150: George H. Williams House. Courtesy Oregon Historical Society (ORHI#3791).

page 150: Cicero Hunt Lewis House. Courtesy Oregon Historical Society (CN#020551).

page 151: Drawing room, Lewis House. Courtesy Oregon Historical Society (ORHI#11091).

page 152: Richard B. Knapp House. Courtesy Oregon Historical Society (ORHI#4515).

page 153: Knapp House chimney. Photo by Minor White. Courtesy Portland Art Museum, PAM #39817.

page 153: Main entrance doors, Knapp House. Photo by Minor White. Courtesy Portland Art Museum, PAM #25678.

page 154: Entrance hall, facing east, Knapp House. Photo by Minor White. Courtesy Portland Art Museum, PAM #42.30.75.

page 154: Entrance hall, Knapp House. Photo by Minor White. Courtesy Portland Art Museum, PAM #42.29.62.

page 155: Main interior stairway, Knapp House. Photo by Minor White. Courtesy Portland Art Museum, PAM #42.29.70.

page 155: Dining room, Knapp House. Photo by Minor White. Courtesy Portland Art Museum, PAM #42.30.77.

page 156: Library, Knapp House. Photo by Minor White. Courtesy Portland Art Museum, PAM #42.30.21.

page 156: Bedroom, Knapp House. Photo by Minor White. Courtesy Portland Art Museum, PAM #42.30.25.

page 158: Justus F. Krumbein House. Courtesy Oregon Historical Society (CN#020347).

page 159: Martha S. Thorton House. Rendering by William J. Hawkins, III, of architect's original sketch.

page 160: Rodney Glisan House. Courtesy Oregon Historical Society (ORHI#6040).

page 161: Blaise and Antoine Labbe Houses. Courtesy Oregon Historical Society (ORHI#12903).

page 162: George H. Weidler House. Courtesy Oregon Historical Society (ORHI#9701).

page 162: Commanding Officer's Quarters, Fort Vancouver. Courtesy Doug Magedanz Collection.

page 163: Commanding Officer's Quarters (Marshall House) today. Photo by William J. Hawkins, III.

page 163: Parlor, Commanding Officer's Quarters. Photo by William J. Hawkins, III.

page 164: William E. Brainard House. Courtesy Oregon Historical Society (CN#021075).

page 164: Frederick Bickel House. Courtesy Oregon Historical Society (ORHI#9769).

page 165: George H. Durham House. Photo by William J. Hawkins, III.

page 166: Johan Poulsen House. Courtesy Oregon Historical Society (ORHI#54128).

Chapter 7, Eastlake

page 167: Portland, overlooking the King's Hill District, circa 1891. Courtesy Oregon Historical Society (ORHI#81552).

page 168: Sottile House, Charleston, South Carolina. Photo by George McMath.

page 168: Horseshoe arch, Islamic Empire, circa 480.

page 168: Chateau de Chenonceaux, France. Postcard from the collection of William J. Hawkins, III.

page 169: Tower, Chateau de Pierrefonds, France. Photo by William J. Hawkins, III.

page 169: Sixteenth-century house, Le Mans, France. Postcard from the collection of William J. Hawkins, III.

page 170: Siena Cathedral, Italy. Postcard from the collection of William J. Hawkins, III.

page 170: Mark Hopkins Mansion, San Francisco. Reproduced from Thomas Aidala, *The Great Houses of San Francisco*, Alfred A. Knopf, New York, 1974.

page 174: Entrance porch of the John B. Bridges House. Courtesy Oregon Historical Society (ORHI#019906).

page 175: John B. Bridges House. Courtesy Oregon Historical Society (CN#007266).

page 175: Parlor, Bridges House. Courtesy Oregon Historical Society (CN#007267).

page 176: William W. Spaulding House. Courtesy Oregon Historical Society (ORHI#87858).

page 177: Levi White House. Courtesy Oregon Historical Society (ORHI#68313).

page 178: C. M. Forbes House. Courtesy Oregon Historical Society (ORHI#3792).

page 178: Forbes House. Courtesy Oregon Historical Society (CN#023192).

page 179: John Palmer House. Photo by William J. Hawkins, III.

page 180: Bernard L. Stone House. Postcard from the collection of William J. Hawkins, III.

page 180: Hon. William S. Mason House. Courtesy Oregon Historical Society (ORHI#11962).

Chapter 8, Shingle/Richardsonian

page 181: Portland, overlooking the King's Hill District, circa 1892. Courtesy Oregon Historical Society (ORHI#25595).

page 182: Trinity Church, Boston, Massachusetts. From Mariana G. Van Rensselaer, *Henry Hobson Richardson and His Works*, Boston, 1888.

page 182: Newport Casino, Newport, Rhode Island. Photo courtesy of the Stanhope Collection, Newport, Rhode Island. Reproduced from Scully 1955.

page 183: Ames Gate Lodge, North Easton, Massachusetts. From Henry-Russell Hitchcock, *The Architecture of H. H. Richardson and His Times*, New York, 1936.

page 183: Plan for the Ames Gate Lodge by H. H. Richardson. *American Architect and Building News*, 1885.

page 183: Isaac Bell House, Newport, Rhode Island. T. Schubert, delineator, for the Historic American Building Survey.

page 183: M. F. Stoughton House, Cambridge, Massachusetts. From George W. Sheldon, *Artistic Country Seats*, vol. I, New York, 1886.

page 184: Lionberger House, Chicago. Photo by William F. Willingham.

page 185: John J. Glessner House, Chicago. Photo by William F. Willingham.

page 185: Dunsmuir Castle, Victoria, British Columbia. *West Shore* magazine, June 1889. Courtesy Oregon Historical Society (ORHI#59384).

page 188: Entrance to the Dr. Kenneth A. J. Mackenzie House. Photo by William J. Hawkins, III.

page 189: James C. Van Rensselaer House. Courtesy Oregon Historical Society (ORHI#11073).

page 190: Quinn House. Courtesy Clackamas County Historical Society, Permanent Collection.

page 190: Friedlander House. Postcard courtesy Doug Magedanz.

page 191: H. C. Campbell House. Courtesy Oregon Historical Society (CN#023210).

page 191: Frederick V. Holman House. Courtesy Doug Magedanz Collection.

page 192: Side elevation, Holman House. Courtesy Doug Magedanz Collection.

page 192: Parlor, Holman House. Courtesy Doug Magedanz Collection.

page 193: Isaac Hodgson, Jr., House. *American Architect and Building News*, 17 October 1891.

page 194: Julius Loewenberg House. Courtesy Betty Ledbetter Meier Cronin.

page 195: Entrance hall, Loewenberg House. Courtesy Betty Ledbetter Meier Cronin.

page 196: Dr. Kenneth A. J. Mackenzie House. Photo by William J. Hawkins, III.

page 196: Entrance hall, Mackenzie House. Photo by William J. Hawkins, III.

page 197: Main stairway and fireplace inglenook, Mackenzie House. Photo by William J. Hawkins, III.

page 197: Main stairway, Mackenzie House. Photo by William J. Hawkins, III.

page 198: Dining room fireplace, Mackenzie House. Photo by William J. Hawkins, III.

page 198: Library, Mackenzie House. Photo by William J. Hawkins, III.

page 198: Original dining room buffet, Mackenzie House. Photo by William J. Hawkins, III.

page 200: George F. Heusner House. Photo by William J. Hawkins, III.

page 201: Henry J. Hefty House. *Oregon Souvenir*, 1892. Courtesy Oregon Historical Society (ORHI#87863).

page 201: Henry J. Corbett House. Courtesy Oregon Historical Society (CN#023195).

page 202: William Honeyman House. Courtesy Oregon Historical Society (ORHI#24618).

page 203: Theodore B. Wilcox House. Photo by William J. Hawkins, III.

page 203: Entrance portal, Wilcox House. Photo by William J. Hawkins, III.

page 204: Entrance hall, Wilcox House. Photo by William J. Hawkins, III.

page 204: Main interior stairway, Wilcox House. Photo by William J. Hawkins, III.

page 205: Dining room, Wilcox House. Photo by William J. Hawkins, III.

page 205: Howard Stratton House. Photo by William J. Hawkins, III.

page 206: Henry Noble House. Photo by William J. Hawkins, III.

page 207: Hardy C. Wortman House. Photo by William J. Hawkins, III.

page 207: Emil Schacht House. *Portland Daily Abstract*, 1906. From the collection of William J. Hawkins, III.

page 208: R. B. Lamson House. Courtesy Oregon Historical Society (CN#021622).

Chapter 9, Colonial Revival—Phase I

page 211: Portland, overlooking Laurelhurst, circa 1930. Courtesy Oregon Historical Society (ORHI#54060).

page 213: Portland, overlooking Portland Heights, circa 1910. Courtesy Oregon Historical Society (ORHI#55817).

page 214: Shingleside, Swampscott, Massachusetts. *Building News*, 28 April 1882.

page 214: Interiors, Shingleside. *Building News*, 28 April 1882.

page 214: Interiors, Shingleside. *Building News*, 28 April 1882.

page 215: The Appleton House, Lenox, Massachusetts. From George W. Sheldon, *Artistic Country Seats*, vol. I, New York, 1886.

page 215: George D. Howe House, Manchester-by-the-Sea, Massachusetts. From George W. Sheldon, *Artistic Country Seats*, vol. II, New York, 1886.

page 215: H. A. C. Taylor House, Newport, Rhode Island. From George W. Sheldon, *Artistic Country Seats*, vol. II, New York, 1886.

page 216: House at 34 Chestnut Street, Salem, Massachusetts. Photo by William J. Hawkins, III.

page 220: Entrance to house on SW Vista Avenue. Photo by William J. Hawkins, III.

page 221: Lucien W. Wallace House. *Oregon Souvenir*, 1892. Courtesy Oregon Historical Society (ORHI#87869).

page 222: Charles B. Bellinger House. *Oregon Souvenir*, 1892. Courtesy Oregon Historical Society (ORHI#87868).

page 222: Theodore B. Trevitt House. Courtesy Oregon Historical Society (ORHI#10119).

page 223: Winslow B. Ayer House. Photo by William J. Hawkins, III.

page 224: Zera Snow House. Courtesy Oregon Historical Society.

page 225: Judge Wallace McCamant House. Photo by William J. Hawkins, III.

page 226: William E. MacKenzie House. Photo by William J. Hawkins, III.

page 226: Isom White House. Courtesy Oregon Historical Society (ORHI#11484).

page 227: Nahum A. King House. Courtesy Oregon Historical Society (ORHI#3805).

page 228: Dr. Henry Coe House. Courtesy Oregon Historical Society (CN#020238).

page 228: Dining room, Coe House. Courtesy Oregon Historical Society (CN#016217).

page 229: David T. Honeyman House. Courtesy Oregon Historical Society (ORHI#37576).

page 230: Philip Buehner House. Photo by William J. Hawkins, III.

page 231: Abbott Mills House. Photo by William J. Hawkins, III.

page 231: Main interior stairway and entrance hall, Mills House. Photo by William J. Hawkins, III.

page 233: Max H. Hauser House. Photo by William J. Hawkins, III.

page 234: James E. Wheeler House. Photo by William J. Hawkins, III.

page 234: George H. Watson House. Photo by William J. Hawkins, III.

page 235: H. Russell Albee House. Photo by William J. Hawkins, III.

page 235: Rear parkside elevation, Albee House. Photo by William J. Hawkins, III.

page 236: Dr. Ami Nichols House. Courtesy Oregon Historical Society (CN#021706).

page 237: J. W. Creath House. Photo by William J. Hawkins, III.

page 238: Riverview Cemetery Caretaker's House. Photo by William J. Hawkins, III.

page 239: James G. Gault House. Photo by William J. Hawkins, III.

page 239: Samuel Rosenblatt House. Photo by William J. Hawkins, III.

page 240: Osmond B. Stubbs House. Photo by William J. Hawkins, III.

page 240: Harold T. Prince House. Photo by William J. Hawkins, III.

page 241: Dr. Lawrence Selling House. Photo by William J. Hawkins, III.

page 242: Iva L. McFarlan House. Photo by William J. Hawkins, III.

Chapter 10, Colonial Revival—Phase II

page 245: Colonial Revival houses on Portland Heights. Photo by William J. Hawkins, III.

page 246: Entrance porch of the James Semple House, Williamsburg, Virginia. Reproduced from Samuel Chamberlain, *New England Doorways*, Hastings House, New York, 1939.

page 246: House in Close, Salisbury, England. Courtesy British Architectural Library, RIBA, London. Reproduced from Fletcher 1996.

page 247: Bristol House entrance porch, New Haven, Connecticut. Courtesy British Architectural Library, RIBA, London. Reproduced from Fletcher 1996.

page 247: Typical New England Colonial Revival house, Greenfield Hill, Connecticut. Reproduced from Samuel Chamberlain, *New England Doorways*, Hastings House, New York, 1939.

page 248: Craigie House, Cambridge, Massachusetts. Courtesy British Architectural Library, RIBA, London. Reproduced from Fletcher 1996.

page 248: Alfred A. Pope House, Farmington, Connecticut. Drawing by Madelaine Thatcher. Reproduced from Mary Mix Foley, *The American House*, Harper & Row, New York, 1980.

page 252: Entrance to the Lewis H. Mills House. Photo by William J. Hawkins, III.

page 253: Lewis H. Mills House. Courtesy Oregon Historical Society (CN#021069).

page 254: Raymond Wilcox House. Photo by William J. Hawkins, III.

page 254: Leslie M. Scott House. Photo by William J. Hawkins, III.

page 255: Theodore B. Wilcox House and estate. Courtesy Oregon Historical Society (CN#014689).

page 256: Front elevation, Wilcox House. Courtesy Oregon Historical Society (CN#014528).

page 256: Rear elevation and formal gardens, Wilcox House. Photo by William J. Hawkins, III.

page 256: Main entrance, Wilcox House. Photo by William J. Hawkins, III.

page 257: Entrance door interior, Wilcox House. Photo by William J. Hawkins, III.

page 257: Main interior stairway, Wilcox House. Photo by William J. Hawkins, III.

page 258: Milton Markewitz House. Photo by William J. Hawkins, III.

page 259: Paul C. Carey House. Photo by William J. Hawkins, III.

page 260: J. C. Braly House. Photo by William J. Hawkins, III.

page 260: Edward D. Kingsley House. Photo by William J. Hawkins, III.

page 262: William P. Hawley House. Photo by William J. Hawkins, III.

page 262: William T. Waerner House. Photo by William J. Hawkins, III.

page 263: Dr. D. C. Burkes House. Courtesy Oregon Historical Society (CN#019803).

page 263: Garden elevations, Burkes House. Courtesy Oregon Historical Society (CN#019802).

page 264: William Haseltine House. Photo by William J. Hawkins, III.

page 265: Dr. John P. Cleland House. Photo by William J. Hawkins, III.

page 265: Donald McGraw House. Courtesy Oregon Historical Society (ORHI#63551).

page 266: Ernest Haycox House. Photo by William J. Hawkins, III.

page 267: Theodore B. Wilcox House. Courtesy Oregon Historical Society (CN#006527).

page 267: Garden elevation, Wilcox House. Photo by William J. Hawkins, III.

page 267: Entrance hall and stairway, Wilcox House. Photo by William J. Hawkins, III.

page 268: Dining room door and wallpaper, Wilcox House. Photo by William J. Hawkins, III.

Chapter 11, Tudor

page 269: The William Gadsby House, on NW Twenty-fifth Avenue. Courtesy Oregon Historical Society (CN#022674).

page 270: Ockwells Manor House, Berkshire, England. Courtesy British Architectural Library, RIBA, London. Reproduced from Fletcher 1996.

page 270: Leycester's Hospital, Warwick, England. Reproduced from Fletcher 1996.

page 270: Leycester's Hospital courtyard. Reproduced from Fletcher 1996.

page 271: British executive commissioner and delegates' residences and staff office, Centennial International Exhibition, Philadelphia. *American Builder*, April 1876.

page 274: Entrance to the D. R. Munroe House. Photo by William J. Hawkins, III.

page 275: Frank E. Hart House. Photo by William J. Hawkins, III.

page 276: William Gadsby House. Photo by William J. Hawkins, III.

page 276: Blaine R. Smith House. Courtesy Oregon Historical Society (CN#023224).

page 277: Reverend Charles Scadding House. Photo by William J. Hawkins, III.

page 278: Henry Miller House. Courtesy Special Collections, Knight Library, University of Oregon, CN 984.

page 278: D. R. Munroe House. Photo by William J. Hawkins, III.

page 279: Cameron Squires House. Courtesy Special Collections, Knight Library, University of Oregon, CN 1115.

page 280: Stanley C. E. Smith House. Courtesy Special Collections, Knight Library, University of Oregon, CN 962.

page 280: Architect Herman Brookman's sketch for the M. Lloyd Frank House. Courtesy the Archives, Lewis and Clark College Library.

page 281: Garden-side elevation, Frank House. Courtesy the Archives, Lewis and Clark College Library.

page 282: Brookman's sketch of the Frank estate and gardens. Courtesy the Archives, Lewis and Clark College Library.

page 283: Aerial photo of the Frank estate and gardens. Courtesy Oregon Historical Society (ORHI#80339).

page 283: Interior wood-paneled walls and door, Frank House. Photo by William J. Hawkins, III.

page 284: Interior stairway, Frank House. Courtesy the Archives, Lewis and Clark College Library.

page 284: Dining room, Frank House. Courtesy the Archives, Lewis and Clark College Library.

page 285: Dr. Zimmerman House. Photo by William J. Hawkins, III.

page 286: Thomas J. Autzen House. Photo by William J. Hawkins, III.

page 287: Carl C. Jantzen House. Courtesy Heritage Investment.

page 288: J. L. Easson House. Photo by William J. Hawkins, III.

page 288: Roy Hunt House. Courtesy Oregon Historical Society (CN#020302).

page 289: Roy Gangware House. Photo by William J. Hawkins, III.

page 290: Dr. James J. Rosenberg House. Photo by William J. Hawkins, III.

page 290: Paul F. Murphy House. Photo by William J. Hawkins, III.

page 291: Dean B. Webster House. Photo by William J. Hawkins, III.

page 292: Wesley P. Steinmetz House. Photo by William J. Hawkins, III.

Chapter 12, Jacobethan

page 293: "Hillside Vista Point," from *The Greater Portland Plan* by Edward H. Bennett, 1912. From the collection of William J. Hawkins, III.

page 294: Hatfield House, Hertfordshire, England. Reproduced from Fletcher 1996.

page 294: Holland House, Kensington, England. Courtesy British Architectural Library, RIBA, London. Reproduced from Fletcher 1996.

page 294: Lytes Cary Manor House, Somerset, England. Reproduced from Christopher Hussey, *English Country Houses Open to the Public*, Charles Scribners' Sons, New York, 1951.

page 294: Great Chalfield, Wiltshire, England. Courtesy British Architectural Library, RIBA, London. Reproduced from Fletcher 1996.

page 295: Compton Wynyates, Warwickshire, England. Courtesy British Architectural Library, RIBA, London. Reproduced from Fletcher 1996.

page 295: Stuart Duncan House, Newport, Rhode Island. Drawing by Madelaine Thatcher. Reproduced from Mary Mix Foley, *The American House*, Harper & Row, New York, 1980.

page 296: Typical Tudor style entrance hall. Courtesy Oregon Historical Society.

page 296: Typical Tudor style dining room. Courtesy Oregon Historical Society.

page 300: Entrance to the Frank J. Cobb House. Photo by William J. Hawkins, III.

page 301: Allen L. Lewis House. Photo by William J. Hawkins, III.

page 301: Entrance, Lewis House. Photo by William J. Hawkins, III.

page 302: Winslow B. Ayer House. Courtesy Oregon Historical Society (ORHI#67013).

page 303: Cicero Hunt Lewis House. Courtesy Oregon Historical Society (CN#020716).

page 303: Daniel Kern House. Courtesy Oregon Historical Society (CN#020401).

page 304: Frank J. Cobb House. *Architect and Engineer*, 1918.

page 304: Rear garden elevation, Cobb House. *Architect and Engineer*, 1918.

page 305: Windows of the main stairway, Cobb House. Photo by Dan Shallou.

page 305: Main stairway, Cobb House. Photo by Dan Shallou.

page 306: Dining room, Cobb House. Photo by Dan Shallou.

page 306: Living room, Cobb House. Photo by William J. Hawkins, III.

page 307: Breakfast room, Cobb House. Photo by William J. Hawkins, III.

page 308: Leon Hirsch House. Photo by William J. Hawkins, III.

page 309: Aaron Holtz House. Courtesy Oregon Historical Society (CN#021406).

page 309: William Scott House. Photo by William J. Hawkins, III.

page 309: Living room, Scott House. Photo by William J. Hawkins, III.

page 310: Wall paneling and fireplace details, Scott House. Photo by William J. Hawkins, III.

page 310: Stairway, Scott House. Photo by William J. Hawkins, III.

Chapter 13, French Renaissance

page 311: Drawing of original proposed landscape for the Henry L. Pittock Mansion, by Thomas Hawkes, landscape architect. Courtesy the Pittock Mansion Society.

page 312: Chateau de Fontainbleu, Paris. Photo by William J. Hawkins, III.

page 312: George W. Vanderbilt Estate (Biltmore), Asheville, North Carolina. Reprinted with the permission of The Free Press, a division of Simon and Schuster from *Architecture, Ambition and Americans: A Social History of American Architecture*, Revised Edition by Wayne Andrews. Copyright © 1978 by The Free Press.

page 312: Louis XII Wing, Chateau de Blois, France, 1498–1504. Reproduced from Nigel Nicolson, *Great Houses of the Western World*, G. P. Putnam's Sons, New York, 1968.

page 313: Montgeoffroy, Maine-et-Loire, France. Reproduced from Nigel Nicolson, *Great Houses of the Western World*, G. P. Putnam's Sons, New York, 1968.

page 313: Azey Le Rideau, Indre-et-Loire, France. Reproduced from Nigel Nicolson, *Great Houses of the Western World*, G. P. Putnam's Sons, New York, 1968.

page 313: Interior stairway, Chateau d'Anet, Eure-et-Loire, France. Reproduced from Nigel Nicolson, *Great Houses of the Western World*, G. P. Putnam's Sons, New York, 1968.

page 313: Hotel, Rue du Cherche-Midi, Paris. Courtesy British Architectural Library, RIBA, London. Reproduced from Fletcher 1996.

page 316: Entrance to the A. J. Lewthwaite House. Photo by William J. Hawkins, III.

page 317: Henry L. Pittock Mansion. Courtesy Doug Magedanz Collection.

page 318: Terrace and drawing room bay, Pittock Mansion. Photo by William J. Hawkins, III.

page 319: Entrance, Pittock Mansion. Photo by William J. Hawkins, III.

page 319: Gatekeeper's lodge, Pittock Mansion. Photo by William J. Hawkins, III.

page 320: Central stairway, Pittock Mansion. Photo by Kim Reynal.

page 320: Drawing room, Pittock Mansion. Photo by Kim Reynal.

page 320: Library, Pittock Mansion. Photo by Kim Reynal.

page 320: Dining room, Pittock Mansion. Photo by Kim Reynal.

page 322: A. J. Lewthwaite House. Photo by William J. Hawkins, III.

page 323: Philip L. Jackson House. Courtesy Oregon Historical Society (ORHI#51721).

page 323: Burt Brown Barker House. Photo by William J. Hawkins, III.

page 324: Gordon Barde House. Courtesy Oregon Historical Society (CN#019786).

Chapter 14, Mediterranean

page 325: Proposed residence on Council Crest. *Portland Architectural Club Catalogue*, 1909.

page 326: Villa Medici, Rome. From *Roma Vetus et Nuova* by J. Laurus, 1614.

page 326: Courtyard of the Palazzo Ricardi, Florence, Italy. *John L. Stoddard's Lectures*, "Italy," Balch Brothers, Boston, 1898.

page 326: Villa Ambra, Poggio a Caiano, Italy. Reproduced from James S. Ackerman, *The Villa: Form and Ideology of Country Houses*, Princeton University Press, 1990.

page 327: Villa Bombicci, Florence, Italy. Reproduced from Georgina Masson, *Italian Villas and Palaces*, Harry N. Abrams, New York, 1966.

page 330: Entrance to the O. L. Price House. Photo by William J. Hawkins, III.

page 331: Robert F. Lytle House. Courtesy Oregon Historical Society (CN#021628).

page 331: David A. E. Rocky House. Photo by William J. Hawkins, III.

page 332: Front terrace and entrance canopy, Rocky House. Photo by William J. Hawkins, III.

page 332: Small open court on the river-oriented elevation, Rocky House. Photo by William J. Hawkins, III.

page 333: Dorothy H. Jacobson House. Courtesy Mrs. William C. Lawrence, III.

page 333: Main entrance and arrival court, Jacobson House. Photo by William J. Hawkins, III.

page 333: Entrance door, Jacobson House. Photo by William J. Hawkins, III.

page 334: Original two-story living room, Jacobson House. Courtesy Mrs. William C. Lawrence, III.

page 334: Library, Jacobson House. Courtesy Mrs. William C. Lawrence, III.

page 335: Cornwell and Perry Building Co. House. Photo by William J. Hawkins, III.

page 336: Joseph R. Bowles House. Photo by William J. Hawkins, III.

page 336: Mediterranean style loggia, Bowles House. Photo by William J. Hawkins, III.

page 337: Ward R. Bowles House. Photo by William J. Hawkins, III.

page 337: Jacob N. Barde House. Photo by William J. Hawkins, III.

page 338: Clarissa Inman House. Courtesy Mr. and Mrs. David and Patricia Miller.

page 339: Entrance portico, Inman House. Photo by William J. Hawkins, III.

page 339: Music room, Inman House. Courtesy Mr. and Mrs. David and Patricia Miller.

page 339: Master bedroom, Inman House. Courtesy Mr. and Mrs. David and Patricia Miller.

page 340: Barbara Price House. Photo by William J. Hawkins, III.

page 340: Dr. H. W. Howard House. *The Oregonian*, 28 August 1927. Photo courtesy Sam Moment.

page 341: Carved panel of the entrance door, Howard House. Photo by William J. Hawkins, III.

page 341: Massive fireplace, Howard House. Photo by William J. Hawkins, III.

page 342: Frank A. McGuire House. Photo by William J. Hawkins, III.

page 342: Living room, McGuire House. Photo by William J. Hawkins, III.

page 343: Otho Pool House. Photo by William J. Hawkins, III.

page 343: Harry A. Green House. Photo by William J. Hawkins, III.

page 344: Wrought-iron entrance gate, Green House. Courtesy Oregon Historical Society (ORHI#084338).

page 344: Rear facade and parterre, Green House. Photo by William J. Hawkins, III.

page 345: French doors leading to the parterre, Green House. Photo by William J. Hawkins, III.

page 345: Interior stairway, Green House. Courtesy Oregon Historical Society (ORHI#084337).

page 346: Major Watson Eastman House. Courtesy Oregon Historical Society (ORHI#73301).

page 346: Garden facade, Eastman House. Courtesy Oregon Historical Society (ORHI#73300).

page 347: Entrance hall, Eastman House. Photo by Michael Mathers.

page 347: Living room, Eastman House. Courtesy Oregon Historical Society (ORHI#73298).

page 347: Dining room, Eastman House. Courtesy Oregon Historical Society (ORHI#73299).

page 348: Thomas Christianson House. Photo by William J. Hawkins, III.

page 349: O. L. Price House. Photo by William J. Hawkins, III.

Chapter 15, English Cottage

page 351: Eastmoreland District, Portland, circa 1911. Courtesy Reed College Archives.

page 352: "Rose-Covered Cottage," England. *John L. Stoddard's Lectures,* "England," Balch Brothers, Boston, 1898.

page 352: Anne Hathaway's cottage, England. *John L. Stoddard's Lectures,* "England," Balch Brothers, Boston, 1898.

page 352: "An English Inn." *John L. Stoddard's Lectures,* "England," Balch Brothers, Boston, 1898.

page 353: Cottage at Lustleigh, Devon, England. Reproduced from Fletcher 1996.

page 353: Group of six cottages, Ashby St. Ledgers, England. Reproduced from Weaver 1925.

page 356: Entrance to the Bert C. Ball House. Photo by William J. Hawkins, III.

page 357: Edward Ehrman House. From the collection of William J. Hawkins, III.

page 357: View-side elevation, Ehrman House. From the collection of William J. Hawkins, III.

page 358: Stonework at the chimney and bay window, Ehrman House. From the collection of William J. Hawkins, III.

page 358: Living room, Ehrman House. Photo by William J. Hawkins, III.

page 359: Plans for the Ehrman House and grounds. From the collection of William J. Hawkins, III.

page 359: Paul F. Murphy House. Photo by William J. Hawkins, III.

page 360: Bert C. Ball House. Photo by William J. Hawkins, III.

page 360: Garden elevation, Ball House. Courtesy Oregon Historical Society (CN#019902).

page 360: Main stairway, Ball House. Photo by William J. Hawkins, III.

page 362: Dr. James Rosenfeld House. Photo by William J. Hawkins, III.

page 363: Max S. Hirsch House. Photo by William J. Hawkins, III.

page 363: Coleman Wheeler House. Photo by William J. Hawkins, III.

page 364: C. H. Farrington House. Photo by William J. Hawkins, III.

page 365: Frank Boutain House. Photo by William J. Hawkins, III.

page 365: J. O. Frye House. Photo by William J. Hawkins, III.

page 366: Frank B. Upshaw House. Photo by William J. Hawkins, III.

Chapter 16, Prairie

page 369: Portland, overlooking Ladd's Addition, circa 1915. Courtesy Oregon Historical Society (ORHI#39917).

page 370: William H. Winslow House, River Forest, Illinois. From Frank Lloyd Wright, *A Testament,* Horizon Press, New York, 1957.

page 370: Joseph W. Husser House, Chicago, Illinois. Reproduced from Henry-Russell Hitchcock, *In the Nature of Materials: The Buildings of Frank Lloyd Wright, 1887–1941,* Duell, Sloan and Pearce, New York, 1942.

page 371: Frank W. Thomas House, Chicago, Illinois. Photo by William F. Willingham.

page 371: W. W. Willits House, Highland Park, Illinois. Reproduced from Edgar Kaufman and Ben Raeburn, *Frank Lloyd Wright: Writings and Buildings,* Meridan Books, Inc., New York, 1960.

page 371: Willits House plan. Reproduced from Edgar Kaufman and Ben Raeburn, *Frank Lloyd Wright: Writings and Buildings,* Meridan Books, Inc., New York, 1960.

page 372: Harold C. Bradley House, Woods Hole, Massachusetts. Photo by Frank R. Sweet. Reproduced from H. Allen Brooks, *The Prairie School Architecture,* University of Toronto Press, Toronto, 1975.

page 376: Entrance to the Thomas Mostyn House. Photo by William J. Hawkins, III.

page 377: Walter F. Burrell House. Courtesy Mrs. Howard Holman.

page 378: Marcus J. Delahunt House. Photo by William J. Hawkins, III.

page 378: John Virginius Bennes House. Photo by William J. Hawkins, III.

page 379: Carl M. Little House. Photo by William J. Hawkins, III.

page 380: Robert McBride House. Photo by William J. Hawkins, III.

page 380: Emma McCauley House. Photo by William J. Hawkins, III.

page 381: Aaron H. Maegley House. Photo by William J. Hawkins, III.

page 382: Porte-cochere detail, Maegley House. Courtesy Oregon Historical Society (ORHI#57049).

page 382: Living room, Maegley House. Courtesy Oregon Historical Society (ORHI#56559).

page 382: Interior stair detail, Maegley House. Courtesy Oregon Historical Society (ORHI#56555).

page 383: Bedroom, Maegley House. Courtesy Oregon Historical Society (ORHI#56558).

page 384: Lilian K. Pollock House. Photo by William J. Hawkins, III.

page 385: C. Spies House. Photo by William J. Hawkins, III.

page 385: Thomas Mostyn House. Courtesy Oregon Historical Society (CN#019939).

Chapter 17, Bungalow

page 387: Laurelhurst District, Portland, circa 1916. Courtesy Oregon Historical Society (ORHI#63786).

page 388: A "Bangla" house, or "A Bungalow in Ceylon." *John L. Stoddard's Lectures*, "India," Norwood Press, Norwood, Massachusetts, 1897.

page 389: "A European's Residence, Colombo." *John L. Stoddard's Lectures*, "India," Norwood Press, Norwood, Massachusetts, 1897.

page 389: Edhofer House, Brünig, Switzerland. Reproduced from Hans Jurgen Hansen, editor, *Architecture in Wood*, Faber and Faber, London, 1971.

page 390: "Cottage Design XI," from *Village and Farm Cottages* by Henry W. Cleaveland, William Backus, and Samuel D. Backus, 1856.

page 391: D. B. Gamble House, Pasadena, California. Photograph by Maynard Parker. Reproduced from James Marston Fitch, *American Building: The Historical Forces that Shaped It*, Charles Scribner's Sons, New York, 1947.

page 394: Garden gate of the Frederick Alva Jacobs House. Photo by William J. Hawkins, III.

page 395: Fred A. Shogren House. Photo by William J. Hawkins, III.

page 396: G. W. Sherk House. Photo by William J. Hawkins, III.

page 396: Gertrude Smith House. Photo by William J. Hawkins, III.

page 396: Main interior stairway, Smith House. Photo by William J. Hawkins, III.

page 397: Dining room and buffet, Smith House. Photo by William J. Hawkins, III.

page 397: Woods Hutchinson House. Photo by William J. Hawkins, III.

page 398: Emma M. Austin House. Photo by William J. Hawkins, III.

page 399: Catherine H. Percival House. Photo by William J. Hawkins, III.

page 399: Lewis T. Gilliand House. Photo by William J. Hawkins, III.

page 400: Drawing of a house published in *The Craftsman*, April 1907.

page 400: M. C. White House. Photo by William J. Hawkins, III.

page 401: H. P. Palmer House. Photo by William J. Hawkins, III.

page 401: Side elevation, Palmer House. Photo by William J. Hawkins, III.

page 402: Decorative lantern at the entrance of the Palmer House. Photo by William J. Hawkins, III.

page 402: Belle Ainsworth Jenkins House. Photo by William J. Hawkins, III.

page 403: George A. Eastman House. Courtesy Oregon Historical Society (ORHI#46521).

page 404: Frederick Alva Jacobs House. *Portland Architectural Club Exhibit Catalogue*, 1913.

page 404: South elevation, Jacobs House. *Portland Architectural Club Exhibit Catalogue*, 1913.

page 405: Living room, Jacobs House. Photo by William J. Hawkins, III.

page 405: Dining room, Jacobs House. Photo by William J. Hawkins, III.

page 405: Main interior stairway, Jacobs House. Photo by William J. Hawkins, III.

page 407: Wilbur Reid House. Photo by William J. Hawkins, III.

page 407: E. J. Ellison House. Photo by William J. Hawkins, III.

page 408: C. S. Jackson House. Courtesy Oregon Historical Society (ORHI#R6-17).

page 409: William H. Hossack House. Photo by William J. Hawkins, III.

page 409: Bungalow "A" House. Photo by William J. Hawkins, III.

page 410: H. E. Schegel House. Photo by William J. Hawkins, III.

Chapter 18, Craftsman

page 411: Portland, overlooking Portland Heights, circa 1910. Photo by Wesley Andrews. Courtesy Oregon Historical Society (ORHI#24396).

page 412: William J. Hawkins House, Portland. Postcard from the collection of William J. Hawkins, III.

page 413: Japanese tea-house. *John L. Stoddard's Lectures*, "Japan," Norwood Press, Norwood, Massachusetts, 1897.

page 413: Hall of the Butchers' Guild, Hereford, England. Courtesy British Architectural Library, RIBA, London. Reproduced from Fletcher 1996.

page 413: Bernese middle-land farmhouse, Emmental, Switzerland. Reproduced from Hans Jurgen Hansen, editor, *Architecture in Wood*, Faber and Faber, London, 1971.

page 414: "House with court, pergolas, outdoor living rooms and sleeping balconies," from *The Craftsman*, January 1909.

page 416: Entrance to the Sarah Rosenblatt House, 1915. Photo by William J. Hawkins, III.

page 417: C. A. Landenberger House. Courtesy Oregon Historical Society (ORHI#79148).

page 417: Parlor, Landenberger House. Courtesy Oregon Historical Society (ORHI#79160).

page 417: Dining room, Landenberger House. Courtesy Oregon Historical Society (ORHI#79159).

page 418: Henry Hahn House. *Residential Portland*, 1911.

page 419: Gustav Freiwald House. Photo by William J. Hawkins, III.

page 419: J. S. Bradley House. Photo by William J. Hawkins, III.

page 420: Belle and Maude Ainsworth House. Courtesy Oregon Historical Society (ORHI#75005).

page 421: Charles J. Schnabel House. Courtesy Oregon Historical Society (ORHI#77345).

page 421: John E. Wheeler House. Photo by William J. Hawkins, III.

page 422: Frank H. Ransom House. Photo by William J. Hawkins, III.

page 422: Living room, Ransom House. *Portland Architectural Club Catalogue*, 1908.

page 423: W. F. Donahae House. Photo by William J. Hawkins, III.

page 424: Amedee M. Smith House. *Portland Architectural Club Catalogue*, 1909.

page 424: William Biddle Wells House. *Residential Portland*, 1911.

page 426: Dwight Edwards House. Courtesy Oregon Historical Society (CN#010235).

page 427: Dr. A. M. Stolte House. Photo by William J. Hawkins, III.

page 427: George H. Howell House. Courtesy Oregon Historical Society (CN#010162).

page 428: Emerson L. Mills House. Courtesy Oregon Historical Society (CN#023189).

Chapter 19, Craftsman/Colonial

page 429: "Proposed $125,000 Improvement of Vista Avenue on Portland Heights, Prepared by Olmstead Brothers." *The Evening Telegram*, 30 May 1908.

page 430: Street facade of the Newport Casino, Newport, Rhode Island. Historic American Building Survey.

page 430: W. Chandler House, Tuxedo Park, New York. *Architecture and Building*, 18 September 1886.

page 430: Frank Lloyd Wright House, Oak Park, Illinois. Photo by William F. Willingham.

page 430: Cyrus McCormick House, Richfield Springs, New York. From Scully 1955.

page 431: John Calvin Stevens House, Portland, Maine. From John Calvin Stevens and Albert W. Cobb, *Examples of American Domestic Architecture*, New York, 1889.

page 431: F. W. Sprague House, Kennebunkport, Maine. *American Architect and Building News*, 1882.

page 434: Entrance to the Edward L. Harmon House. Photo by William J. Hawkins, III.

page 435: Edward C. Hochapfel House. Photo by William J. Hawkins, III.

page 435: Architect's original drawing, front elevation, Hochapfel House. From the collection of William J. Hawkins, III.

page 435: Architect's original drawing, side elevation, Hochapfel House. From the collection of William J. Hawkins, III.

page 436: Edward L. Harmon House. Courtesy Oregon Historical Society (CN#021498).

page 437: Christine Becker House. *Northwest Architect*, September 1910. Courtesy Special Collections, Knight Library, University of Oregon, CN 1334.

page 437: Entrance hall, Becker House. *Northwest Architect*, September 1910. Courtesy Special Collections, Knight Library, University of Oregon, CN 1335.

page 437: Living room, Becker House. *Northwest Architect*, September 1910. Courtesy Special Collections, Knight Library, University of Oregon, CN 1336.

page 439: John A. Veness House. Photo by William J. Hawkins, III.

page 439: F. E. Bowman House. Photo by William J. Hawkins, III.

page 440: John L. Bowman House. Courtesy Special Collections, Knight Library, University of Oregon, CN 1116.

Chapter 20, Arts and Crafts

page 441: Ida Catlin and Edwin T. Burke Houses on SW Hawthorne Terrace, Portland Heights. Photo by William J. Hawkins, III.

page 442: Red House, Kent, England. Photo by Jack Scheerboom. Reproduced from Lloyd et al.

page 442: Julian Sturgis House, Surrey, England. Photo courtesy British Architectural Library, RIBA, London. Reproduced from Hitchcock 1958.

page 443: Glen Andred, Sussex, England. Photo courtesy of F. Goodwin. Reproduced from Hitchcock 1958.

page 443: Broadleys, Lake Windermere, England. Photo by J. Brandon-Jones. Reproduced from Hitchcock 1958.

page 443: The Deanery, Sonning, England. Reproduced from Weaver 1925.

page 444: Homewood, Knebworth, England. Reproduced from Weaver 1925.

page 444: Folly Farm, Berkshire, England. Reproduced from Weaver 1925.

page 444: Papillon Hall, near Market Harborough, England. Reproduced from Weaver 1925.

page 448: Entrance to the Theodore F. Brown House. Photo by William J. Hawkins, III.

page 449: Ellis F. Lawrence House. Courtesy Doug Magedanz Collection.

page 449: Garden elevation, Lawrence House. Courtesy Doug Magedanz Collection.

page 450: Dining room, Lawrence House. *Portland Architectural Club Catalogue*.

page 450: Living room, Lawrence House. Courtesy Doug Magedanz Collection.

page 450: Josef Jacobberger House. Courtesy Oregon Historical Society (CN#023222).

page 451: George W. Collins House. Courtesy Oregon Historical Society (CN#020235).

page 452: Michael F. Brady House. Photo by William J. Hawkins, III.

page 452: Arts and Crafts "A" House. Photo by William J. Hawkins, III.

page 453: Living room, Arts and Crafts "A" House. Photo by William J. Hawkins, III.

page 453: John M. Pipes House. Courtesy Oregon Historical Society (ORHI#39038).

page 454: Alfred T. Smith House. Photo by William J. Hawkins, III.

page 455: Dr. Andrew J. Geisy House. Courtesy Oregon Historical Society (ORHI#76337).

page 455: Entrance stair hall, Geisy House. Courtesy Oregon Historical Society (CN#020479).

page 455: Dining room, Geisy House. Courtesy Oregon Historical Society (CN#020477).

page 456: Michael J. Walsh House. Photo by William J. Hawkins, III.

page 457: T. H. Sherrard House. Courtesy Oregon Historical Society (CN#020256).

page 457: William Grey Purcell House. Photo by William J. Hawkins, III.

page 458: C. P. Osborne House. Photo by William J. Hawkins, III.

page 459: Woerner Lewis House. Photo by William J. Hawkins, III.

page 459: Purcell House. Photo by William J. Hawkins, III.

page 460: George Pipes House. Courtesy Oregon Historical Society (CN#021241).

page 461: Theodore F. Brown House. Photo by William J. Hawkins, III.

page 461: Rear elevation, Brown House. Photo by William J. Hawkins, III.

page 461: Gatekeeper's Lodge, M. Lloyd Frank Estate. Photo by William J. Hawkins, III.

page 462: An early photograph of the Frank Estate Gatekeeper's Lodge. Courtesy the Archives, Lewis and Clark College Library.

page 462: John G. Edwards House. Courtesy Ackroyd Photography Inc., #10072-1.

page 463: John A. Laing House. Photo by William J. Hawkins, III.

page 463: Charles T. Ladd House. Courtesy Oregon Historical Society (ORHI#28771A).

page 464: Frank Robertson House. Photo by William J. Hawkins, III.

page 465: Caroline and Louise Flanders House. Photo by William J. Hawkins, III.

page 465: Charles Green House. Photo by William J. Hawkins, III.

page 466: Ida Catlin House. Photo by William J. Hawkins, III.

page 467: Edwin T. Burke House. Photo by William J. Hawkins, III.

page 467: Joseph R. Gerber House. Photo by William J. Hawkins, III.

page 468: James Leland House. Photo by William J. Hawkins, III.

page 469: George Black House. Photo by William J. Hawkins, III.

page 469: Original entrance doors, Black House. Photo by William J. Hawkins, III.

page 469: Living room, Black House. Photo by William J. Hawkins, III.

page 469: Dining room, Black House. Photo by William J. Hawkins, III.

page 470: Mary E. Parker House. Photo by William J. Hawkins, III.

page 471: George P. Berky House. Courtesy Oregon Historical Society (CN#019784).

page 471: Charles Barker House. Photo by William J. Hawkins, III.

page 472: Dr. Frank Kistner House. Photo by William J. Hawkins, III.

page 472: Garden elevation, Kistner House. Photo by William J. Hawkins, III.

page 474: Walter S. Zimmerman House. Courtesy Heritage Investment.

page 474: Garden elevation, Zimmerman House. Courtesy Heritage Investment.

page 474: Interior stairway, Zimmerman House. Courtesy Oregon Historical Society (CN#023027).

page 476: E. S. Beach House. Courtesy Oregon Historical Society (ORHI#70439).

page 477: E. T. Samuelson House. Photo by William J. Hawkins, III.

page 477: Richard Sundeleaf House. Photo by William J. Hawkins, III.

page 478: Properties Unlimited House. Photo by William J. Hawkins, III.

Chapter 21, Stripped Traditional/Transitional

page 481: Original view of the Portland Hotel, circa 1881. Courtesy Oregon Historical Society (ORHI#23406-b).

page 481: Destruction of the Portland Hotel, 1951. Photo by Allan J. De Lay. Courtesy Courtesy Oregon Historical Society (CN#024215).

page 483: Original perspective drawing of the Lee S. Elliot House by Herman Brookman. Courtesy Special Collections, Knight Library, University of Oregon.

page 484: Masonic Temple, Portland. Photo by William J. Hawkins, III.

page 484: Fruit and Flower Nursery, Portland. Photo by Walter Boychuk. Courtesy Oregon Historical Society (ORHI#42134).

page 485: Temple Beth Israel, Portland. Photo by William J. Hawkins, III.

page 485: U.S. Federal Courthouse, Portland. Photo by Walter Boychuk. Courtesy Oregon Historical Society (CN#015553).

page 486: Sixth Church of Christ Scientist, Portland. Photo by William J. Hawkins, III.

page 486: Charles F. Berg Building, Portland. Photo by William J. Hawkins, III.

page 490: Entrance to the Lee S. Elliot House. Photo by William J. Hawkins, III.

page 491: Julius Meier House. Photo by William J. Hawkins, III.

page 491: Living room, Meier House. Courtesy Oregon Historical Society (ORHI#39350).

page 492: Elizabeth Clarke House. Photo by William J. Hawkins, III.

page 493: Herman Brookman House. Photo by William J. Hawkins, III.

page 493: Studio entrance, Brookman House. Photo by William J. Hawkins, III.

page 494: Leon Savaria House. Photo by William J. Hawkins, III.

page 495: Lee S. Elliot House. Photo by William J. Hawkins, III.

page 495: Interior stairway, Elliot House. Photo by William J. Hawkins, III.

page 496: Living room ceiling detail, Elliot House. Photo by William J. Hawkins, III.

page 497: Kenneth Eckert House. Photo by William J. Hawkins, III.

page 497: Living room, Eckert House. Reproduced with permission of the Herman Brookman Collection, Ph. 114, Special Collections, University of Oregon Library. Photo courtesy Jane Turville.

page 498: Johns-Manville House. Photo by William J. Hawkins, III.

page 499: Leon H. Baruh House. Courtesy Oregon Historical Society (CN#021893).

page 499: Donald M. Drake House. Photo by William J. Hawkins, III.

page 500: Adrienne Arnsberg House. Photo by William J. Hawkins, III.

page 500: Entrance door, Arnsberg House. Photo by William J. Hawkins, III.

page 501: Original perspective sketch by Herman Brookman, Arnsberg House. Courtesy Adrienne Arnsberg.

Chapter 22, Modernistic/International

page 503: Promotional advertisement for the Westover Terraces development in Northwest Portland. From the collection of William J. Hawkins, III.

page 504: Philip Lovell House, Los Angeles, California. J. Lentz, delineator, for the Historic American Building Survey.

page 505: Walter Dodge House, Los Angeles, California. Reproduced from Hitchcock 1958.

page 505: Villa Savoie, Poissy, France. Reproduced from Boesiger and Girsberger, *Le Corbusier 1910–60*, George Wittenborn, New York, 1960.

page 508: Entrance to the George J. Turner House. Photo by William J. Hawkins, III.

page 509: George J. Turner House. Photo by William J. Hawkins, III.

page 509: Harvey S. Hudson House. Photo by William J. Hawkins, III.

page 510: Thaddeus B. Bruno House. Courtesy Gregg Nelson.

page 510: Original sketch of street elevation by Van Evera Bailey, Bruno House. Courtesy Gregg Nelson.

page 511: Original sketch of the garden elevation by Van Evera Bailey, Bruno House. Courtesy Gregg Nelson.

page 511: Living room, Bruno House. Courtesy Gregg Nelson.

page 511: Curved porch, Bruno House. Courtesy Gregg Nelson.

page 512: Jan De Graaff House. Courtesy Gregg Nelson.

page 512: Side view, Jan De Graaff House. Courtesy Oregon Historical Society (ORHI#39956).

page 512: Living room, Jan De Graaff House. Courtesy Gregg Nelson.

page 513: William H. De Graaff House. Courtesy Oregon Historical Society (ORHI#70452).

page 514: R. J. O'Donnell House. Photo by William J. Hawkins, III.

page 514: Keith Gilbert Powers House. Courtesy Lucia E. Powers.

page 515: Side view, Powers House. Courtesy Lucia E. Powers.

page 515: Porch and balcony, Powers House. Photo by Jane Turville.

page 516: Living room, Powers House. Courtesy Lucia E. Powers.

page 516: Kitchen, Powers House. Courtesy Lucia E. Powers.

page 517: Dr. D. C. Burkes House. Courtesy Pietro and Marjorie Belluschi.

page 517: Living room, Burkes House. Courtesy Oregon Historical Society (ORHI#46688).

Chapter 23, Northwest Style

page 519: Barn, Aurora, Oregon. Photo by William J. Hawkins, III.

page 521: Harry Wentz Cottage, Neahkahnie, Oregon. Photo by William J. Hawkins, III.

page 521: Cloud Cap Inn, Mount Hood, Oregon. Photo by William J. Hawkins, III.

page 522: Ise Shrine, Naiku, Japan. Photo by William J. Hawkins, III.

page 522: Katsura Imperial Villa, Katsura, Kyoto Prefecture, Japan. Photo by William J. Hawkins, III.

page 526: Entrance courtyard to the Aubrey R. Watzek House. Courtesy Oregon Historical Society (ORHI#37151).

page 527: Pietro Belluschi House. Courtesy Pietro and Marjorie Belluschi.

page 528: Garden elevation, Belluschi House. Courtesy Pietro and Marjorie Belluschi.

page 528: Living/dining room, Belluschi House. Courtesy Pietro and Marjorie Belluschi.

page 529: Aubrey R. Watzek House, garden facade. Courtesy Oregon Historical Society (ORHI#87874).

page 529: Entrance facade, Watzek House. Courtesy Oregon Historical Society (ORHI#37147).

page 530: Stone wall and steps, Watzek House. Courtesy Oregon Historical Society (ORHI#37155).

page 531: Living room, Watzek House. Courtesy John Yeon Estate.

page 531: Dining room, Watzek House. Courtesy John Yeon Estate.

page 532: Jennings R. Sutor House. Courtesy Pietro and Marjorie Belluschi.

page 533: Living room, Sutor House. Photo by Walter Boychuk. Courtesy Pietro and Marjorie Belluschi.

page 533: Dining room, Sutor House. Photo by Walter Boychuk. Courtesy Pietro and Marjorie Belluschi.

page 534: Victor Jorgensen House. Courtesy John Yeon Estate.

page 534: Living room, Jorgensen House. Courtesy John Yeon Estate.

page 535: Covered entrance walkway, Jorgensen House. Courtesy John Yeon Estate.

page 535: John W. S. Platt House. Photo by William J. Hawkins, III.

page 536: Living room, Platt House. Photo by William J. Hawkins, III.

page 536: Dining room, Platt House. Photo by William J. Hawkins, III.

page 536: Garden terrace, Platt House. Courtesy Oregon Historical Society (ORHI#46691).

page 538: W. R. Scott House. Photo by William J. Hawkins, III.

page 538: Ben Freedman House. Photo by William J. Hawkins, III.

page 539: Lee Hawley Hoffman House. Courtesy Oregon Historical Society (ORHI#39953).

page 540: David Eyre House. Courtesy Oregon Historical Society (ORHI#39954).

page 540: Dr. Merle Moore House. Photo by William J. Hawkins, III.

page 541: William W. Wessinger House. Courtesy Oregon Historical Society (ORHI#46749).

page 542: E. W. Van Buren House. Photo by William J. Hawkins, III.

page 542: Garden elevation, Van Buren House. Courtesy Oregon Historical Society (ORHI#37186).

page 542: Living/dining room, Van Buren House. Courtesy John Yeon Estate.

page 543: Dr. Kenneth C. Swan House. Courtesy Oregon Historical Society (ORHI#37208).

page 543: Living room, Swan House. Courtesy Oregon Historical Society (ORHI#37211).

page 544: Dr. James Rosenfeld House. Photo by William J. Hawkins, III.

page 544: Allen Meier House, garden elevation. Courtesy Walter and Margaret Gordon.

page 545: George Cottrell House. Courtesy Oregon Historical Society (ORHI#37196).

page 545: P. L. Menefee House. Courtesy Pietro and Marjorie Belluschi.

page 546: Lawrence Shaw House. Courtesy John Yeon Estate.

page 546: Front elevation, Shaw House. Courtesy John Yeon Estate.

page 547: Living room, Shaw House. Courtesy John Yeon Estate.

Additional thanks are offered to those who granted permission for use of materials but who are not named individually in this list of credits. While every reasonable effort has been made to contact copyright holders and secure permission for all materials reproduced in this work, we offer apologies for any instances in which this was not possible and for any inadvertent omissions.